Women, Crime, and Justice

Women, Crime, and Justice

Edited by
SUSAN K. DATESMAN
FRANK R. SCARPITTI

New York   Oxford
OXFORD UNIVERSITY PRESS
1980

To our parents,
Richard and Kathryn Datesman
Frank and Geneva Scarpitti

Copyright © 1980 by Oxford University Press, Inc.

Library of Congress Cataloging in Publication Data
Main entry under title:

Women, crime, and justice.

  Bibliography: p.
  1. Female offenders—Addresses, essays, lectures.
2. Female offenders—United States—Addresses, essays,
lectures. 3. Delinquent girls—Addresses, essays,
lectures. 4. Women prisoners—Addresses, essays,
lectures. I. Datesman, Susan K. II. Scarpitti,
Frank R.
HV6046.W65   364.3'74   79-18791.
ISBN 0-19-502676-4

This reprint, 1981

Printed in the United States of America

Preface

The topic of crime in general has long aroused considerable interest. It was not until the 1970s, however, that the topic of female crime began to attract much attention, largely because of a broader interest in the topic of women fostered by the emergence of the women's movement in the late sixties. During the seventies, a considerable amount of information on women, crime, and justice was accumulated and provided much needed documentation in areas such as the disparate treatment of the sexes by the criminal justice system. At the same time, there has been substantial disagreement on such issues as the actual involvement of women in crime and the relation between women's crime and the women's movement. This book, therefore, brings together, in our estimation, some of the best and most interesting work in this rapidly growing area of criminological and criminal justice study so that the reader can better understand the relations among women, crime, and justice.

The book is divided into five parts. In Part I, we discuss the extent and nature of female crime, including trends in female crime over the past two decades, drawing upon official statistics and self-report data. Part II deals with the etiology of female crime, Part III examines some patterns of female criminal behavior, and Part IV focuses on the treatment of women in the criminal justice system. In Part V, we tackle the controversial issue of the relation between women's crime and the women's movement. Since a number of the selections speak to this issue, but do not necessarily agree, it is appropriate that the evidence be reviewed and that some conclusions be drawn at this point.

In selecting the readings for Parts II, III, and IV, we drew upon the contributions of various scholars and writers, including those who have published important comments and findings in sources to which most students do not have access. Sociology, criminology, and criminal justice sources are represented along with law and political science sources. Two of the selections were prepared especially for this book. The other selections have all been published since 1973 with one exception. It should also be noted that selections are included on both juvenile and adult female offenders.

It is our belief that this book will have applicability in a variety of criminology, delinquency, and criminal justice courses as well as courses in sex roles and women's studies. The book should also be of interest to anyone who is interested in the problems of crime, injustice, and inequality between the sexes. We hope that the readings, along with the original material, will be informative and will stimulate further interest and research in these areas.

We would like to thank those authors and publishers who permitted their work to appear in this book. We also wish to thank Nancy Amy of Oxford University Press for her editorial help and Mary Tucker for her secretarial help. We owe special thanks to our families and to John Pfuhl for their help and encouragement.

Contents

I   THE EXTENT AND NATURE OF
FEMALE CRIME   3

II   THE ETIOLOGY OF FEMALE CRIME   65

The Etiology of Female Crime: A Review of the
Literature **Dorie Klein**   70

Female Deviance and the Female Sex Role: A Preliminary
Investigation **Karen E. Rosenblum**   106

Female Delinquency and Broken Homes: A Reassessment
Susan K. Datesman and **Frank R. Scarpitti**   129

The Interaction Between Women's Emancipation and
Female Criminality: A Cross-Cultural Perspective
Freda Adler   150

III   PATTERNS OF FEMALE CRIME   167

Crimes of Violence by Women **David A. Ward,
Maurice Jackson,** and **Reneé E. Ward**   171

Searching for Women in Organized Crime **Alan Block**   192

Women, Heroin, and Property Crime   **James A. Inciardi**   214

The Economics of Prostitution   **Gail Sheehy**   223

The Molls   **Walter B. Miller**   238

IV   WOMEN IN THE CRIMINAL JUSTICE
    SYSTEM   249

Discriminatory Sentencing of Women Offenders: The
    Argument for ERA in a Nutshell
    Carolyn Engel Temin   255

Chivalry and Paternalism: Disparities of Treatment in
    the Criminal Justice System   **Elizabeth F. Moulds**   277

Unequal Protection for Males and Females in the Juvenile
    Court   **Susan K. Datesman** and **Frank R. Scarpitti**   300

Women in Prison: Discriminatory Practices and Some
    Legal Solutions   **Marilyn G. Haft**   320

Mothers Behind Bars: A Look at the Parental Rights of
    Incarcerated Women   **Kathleen Haley**   339

V   WOMEN'S CRIME AND WOMEN'S
    EMANCIPATION   355

Women, Crime, and Justice

The Extent and Nature of Female Crime

For about two decades Americans have expressed increasing concern about the problems of crime and juvenile delinquency. Presidential commissions have studied the problems, the media have devoted many of their resources to examining them, politicians have deplored their increase and vowed to combat them, and academicians have contributed volumes dealing with the causes and control of crime and delinquency. Although both public and professional concern has been acute, certain areas of the overall crime situation have been virtually ignored. Until recently, this has been the case with female criminality and delinquency.

The crime and delinquency committed by women and girls in American society has commanded little interest from those institutions and agencies that have traditionally devoted a great deal of attention to male criminality. Until recently, few stories were written about female criminals, they seldom appeared in television dramas, and their even being mentioned in popular discussions of crime was considered extraordinary. The few women who did enter into crime were usually depicted in sex-stereotyped ways as "acting like women":

falling in love (with a deviant man), being a little too out of control of their emotions (becoming mentally ill), using their sexuality exploitatively but not that differently from other women (becoming a prostitute), or exhibiting some other neurotic weakness or impulsiveness common to women (as becoming a shoplifter).[1]

Social and behavioral science research has not taken us much further, however. Sociologists, psychologists, and criminologists have, by and large, concentrated their professional attention on the male criminal to the exclusion of the female. Although these disciplines abound with theories of crime and delinquency causation, identity, and career development, little more than a casual examination is necessary to show that they were developed to fit male models. Females are either excluded from all consideration or are assumed to fit the general pattern. Unfortunately, general patterns of criminal behavior are usually based upon male role sets and are seldom applicable to females. Anthony Harris, for example, has recently argued that the inclusion of the sex variable in supposedly general theories of criminal deviance has dire consequences for most theories.[2] He suggests that the failure to start with the sex variable in theories of criminal deviance "has been the major failure of deviance theorizing in this century."[3]

NEGLECT OF FEMALE CRIME

Why hasn't female criminality and delinquency been subject to the same concern that has characterized male criminality and delinquency for many years? Perhaps the most obvious reason is the negligible involvement of females in legal misconduct as reported by official crime statistics. According to official statistics, females commit only a small fraction of all crimes. This presents the researcher with a very practical problem in the sense that small numbers of cases complicate the analysis and make generalizing from the findings risky. Researchers are thus more likely to study male offenders simply because they are more numerous and more available as research subjects.

In addition, female criminals and delinquents have not commanded much attention because of the nature of their offenses. Most discussions of female crime and delinquency have emphasized its individualistic, less serious nature when compared with male law violation. Many observers seem to view male violations as "real" crime, dangerous, serious, often organized and injurious to the social order. Males also present a more persistent recidivist problem than females; a recent study found that over 90 percent of those with four or more previous arrests were male.[4] Female crimes, on the other hand, are often seen as victimless, most harmful to the offender, and having minimal impact on the social order. In the case of delinquency, emphasis is often placed on its predominantly sexual nature. Aspects of female delinquency other than sexual delinquencies have been largely overlooked. For example, the discussion of female delinquency in *The Delinquent Girl* published in 1970 is limited to the runaway girl, the incorrigible girl, the sex delinquent girl, the probation violator girl, and the truant girl.[5] The authors state that: "Approximately 75 to 85 percent of the offenses leading to commitment of delinquent girls are found in the 'big five' grouping. The underlying vein of many of these offenses is sexual misconduct by the girl delinquent."[6]

The focus on the illicit sexual and related activities of females partially explicates the status of female delinquency as a minor problem. First, sexual delinquency connotes personal harm rather than aggressive behavior directed toward injuring other persons or toward the violation of property rights as is generally the case with male delinquency. Further, sexual offenses or euphemistic charges, for example, "running away," "incorrigibility," and "truancy," constitute criminal acts only when committed by a juvenile.[7] Such acts of misbehavior are commonly termed juvenile status offenses, since only juveniles can commit them. According to the President's Commission on Law Enforcement and Administration of Justice, more than half of the girls coming to the attention of the juvenile courts were referred for conduct that would not be considered crimes if committed by adults; only one-fifth of the boys were referred for such conduct.[8] A survey of Connecticut institutions indicated that juvenile status offenses accounted for 80 percent of the delinquencies for which girls were institutionalized but only 18 percent of the delinquencies for which boys were institutionalized.[9] Similarly, over 80 percent of the girls in a state correctional institution in New Jersey were accused of such offenses as running away from home, being incorrigible, ungovernable and beyond the control of parents, being truant, engaging in sexual relations, and becoming pregnant.[10] Since such offenses are not considered crimes when committed by an adult, they are "corrected" by the simple expedient of attaining adult status. Thus, female delinquency is assumed to be less negativistic in its societal impact than male delinquency both in terms of its seriousness and its duration.

In summary, then, at least two fairly straightforward reasons may be advanced to account for the lack of social science study of the female offender: Female criminals and delinquents are simply less numerous than their male counterparts; and female crime and delinquency is assumed to be less serious than male criminality. Thus, attempts to study female criminality may be thwarted by the difficulty of obtaining a sample of women and girls that is sufficiently large to allow any meaningful statistical analysis. Furthermore, female offenses are commonly assumed to be less serious, often sexual, individualistic crimes that are less damaging to the social order than male offenses.

These are not the only reasons, however. Social scientists usually study and write about what interests them as that interest in defined on either intrinsic or pragmatic grounds, such as the availability of research funds. Since most social scientists are male, it is not surprising that they have usually studied other males. Women in general have not been considered worthwhile research topics. In part, then, the lack of data about female offenders reflects a lack of interest on the part of predominately male social scientists, and perhaps an inability to empathize. Moreover, what little work has been done suffers from bias and stereotypes about women.[11]

Perhaps, too, female criminality and delinquency have not attracted much research attention because, unlike male criminality and delinquency, they have not been defined as significant social problems. The definition of certain social phenomena and not others as problems affects the availability and distribution of research funds. Research funds, in turn, tend to define to a great extent areas of sociological interest. Frances Heidensohn has made an interesting observation on this relationship:

> One need not go so far as to argue that high rates of sociological interest in a problem area produce appropriately high "problem situation" responses; but one might well be forgiven for wondering whether the deviance of women is a nonproblem both to the social scientist and to society in general, because so little effort has been devoted to studying it.[12]

Within the past decade, both public and professional interest in female criminality and delinquency have greatly increased along with interest in the general topic of women. Coverage of female crime in the mass media has fostered the belief that female crime rates are increasing at a rapid rate and that women are committing more violent crimes.[13] Female criminals have been in the headlines as murderers, bank robbers, kidnappers, highjackers, and revolutionaries. The activities of women active in radical revolutionary groups such as the Weather Underground and the Symbionese Liberation Army were well-publicized in the media. Also in the headlines were three women in the cult "family" of Charles Manson who were convicted of participating in wanton murders at his direction, as well as the attempted assassinations of President Gerald Ford by Lynette Fromme and Sara Jane Moore. These women have been taken as indicative of a new breed of female criminal, more violent than the traditional female lawbreaker. This belief has been buttressed by such criminologists as Freda Adler who states:

> Females . . . are now being found not only robbing banks
> singlehandedly, but also committing assorted armed robberies,
> muggings, loan-sharking operations, extortion, murders, and a
> wide variety of other aggressive, violence-oriented crimes which
> previously involved only men.[14]

To evaluate this belief and to understand more precisely the
current magnitude and nature of female criminality, it is now
necessary to examine the available data in some detail.

OFFICIAL DATA ON FEMALE CRIME

As with male crime, just about all the official data on female
crime and delinquency comes from the Federal Bureau of Investigation's *Uniform Crime Reports* (UCR). Crime reports are
collected from contributing law enforcement agencies and com-
piled, analyzed, and published annually by the FBI to give us our
only national data on both adult and juvenile crime and ar-
restees. In 1977, nearly 15,000 law enforcement agencies covering 98 percent of the United States population voluntarily
submitted monthly and annual reports to the FBI.[15] Law enforcement agencies report, among other things, the number of
crimes that become known to them in seven major crime categories, designated as a Crime Index. Index crimes, which are
composed of murder and nonnegligent manslaughter, forcible
rape, aggravated assault, robbery, burglary, larceny-theft, and
auto theft, are serious or frequently occurring crimes thought
to have more chance of being reported to the police than other
offenses.[16] These reports also contain information on arrests
and include the age, sex, and race of each person arrested.
Arrests are reported for twenty-two nonindex crimes in addition to the seven index crimes.

Many students of crime have pointed to the faults of official
criminal statistics such as the UCR.[17] Among other things, such
statistics reflect only crimes that become known to the police
and cannot take into acount what most observers believe to be

large amounts of unreported crime. Thus, crimes known to the police are only a sample of the crimes that have taken place and are related to actual crimes in some unknown way. A recent study has shown, however, that the UCR "crimes known" data, while not on a one-to-one basis with actual crime, are at least moderately correlated with victimization survey results.[18] In any case, crimes known to the police are a better measure of actual crimes than other official criminal statistics, for as one criminologist has pointed out, "the value of criminal statistics as a basis for measurement of criminality in geographic areas decreases as the procedures take us further away from the offense itself."[19] Thus, crimes known to the police are a more reliable indicator of actual crimes than arrest statistics, arrest statistics are more reliable than court statistics, and court statistics are more reliable than prison statistics.

Unfortunately, the UCR does not report crimes known to the police separately for males and females. Therefore, we will have to rely on arrest statistics to give us some indication of the extent and nature of female criminality. Arrest statistics are obviously biased by the relative efficiency of police agencies and by the exercise of discretion by police officers. Since the police are seldom capable of responding to all known crimes with equal investigative skill and commitment, the arrest rate for some offenses is higher than it is for others. In 1977, for example, police who reported crimes to the FBI cleared by arrest 75 percent of the murder offenses, 51 percent of the forcible rapes, 62 percent of the aggravated assaults, 27 percent of the robberies, 16 percent of the burglaries, 20 percent of the larceny-thefts, and 15 percent of the auto thefts.[20]

Likewise, police discretion often permits law enforcement officers to respond to known crime in ways that do not result in someone's arrest. The decision to arrest may be affected by extralegal factors such as the sex of the offender. It is commonly believed that law enforcement agents are usually reluctant to arrest females. Mary Owen Cameron, for example, studied factors related to decisions to prosecute shoplifters apprehended in a large Chicago department store and found that men were referred to the police for prosecution in 35 percent of the cases as compared with 10 percent of the women.[21] Michael Hindelang, on the other hand, found that the percentages of male and female shoplifters referred to the police were about the same (26 percent and 25 percent, respectively) in his study of shoplifters apprehended by large chains of grocery and drug stores.[22] Lawrence Cohen and Rodney Stark also found that the sex of the shoplifter was unrelated to the decision to release or prosecute in a large metropolitan department store located in California.[23]

Another piece of evidence on differential arrest practices comes from Jerome Skolnick's study.[24] In *Justice Without Trial,* Skolnick reports that the traffic warrant policemen he observed were inclined to give special consideration to women. He states:

> It is degrading for a man to exert coercion upon a woman, especially in public view. A woman who resists arrest by shouting or screaming is inevitably an embarrassment to a police officer, and the problem of controlling her through physical force could become awkward.[25]

Traffic warrant policemen were especially reluctant to make an arrest in case of women who had children. As one officer put it: "It's not only a helluva lot of trouble to put away a whole family, but you feel like hell locking up a bunch of kids because their mother couldn't post twenty-two dollars bail."[26]

Arrest statistics, then, are influenced by these and other factors for both men and women, and should not be viewed as a definitive statement of the amount of criminality. If women, as some authorities claim, do commit many unreported crimes, if these are crimes that generally have a low police clearance rate (property crimes, for example), and if the community and law enforcement agents usually try to protect the female from arrest, we may conclude that our official statistics grossly underrepresent the amount of female criminality. Despite these warnings, we shall examine some of the official data on female criminality, focusing mostly on the UCR. Although these data may suffer from a number of faults, they are the only major data source currently available, and if not taken too seriously, can be instructive.

Arrests for total crimes and index crimes by sex for each year from 1960 through 1977 are shown in Table 1. It is important to note that these statistics may not be based on the same reporting units or procedures each year and therefore are not necessarily comparable from year to year. However, while care should be exercised in any direct year-to-year comparisons, long-term trends may be noted. Table 1 shows that female arrests have gradually increased from 10.7 percent of total arrests in 1960 to 16 percent in 1977, an increase of about 5 percent. Table 1 also shows that the female percent of arrests for index crimes nearly doubled during this period, increasing from 10.1 percent to 20.1 percent. Thus, while the female percent of arrests for all crimes increased between 1960 and 1977, the female percent of arrests for index crimes increased even more rapidly.

Index crimes may be grouped into violent crimes and property crimes as shown in Table 2. In Table 2 we see that the increase in the female percent of arrests for index crimes during the period 1960–1977 was due to the increase in the female percent of arrests for property crimes among index offenses. Female arrests for property crimes steadily increased from 10 percent of the persons arrested for property crimes in 1960 to 22.4 percent in 1977, an increase of over 12 percent. On the other hand, the female percent of arrests for violent crimes during this period remained around 10 percent, fluctuating only about half a percent in either direction. That is, females accounted for approximately the same share of the arrests for violent crimes in 1977 as they did in 1960 and in all intervening years.

A closer examination of the FBI's index offenses reveals that between 1960 and 1977, female involvement in murder and nonnegligent manslaughter ranged from a high of 18.8 percent in 1962 to a low of 14.5 percent in 1977. Overall, females appear to account for a slightly smaller percent of arrests in this category

TABLE 1. Arrests for Total Crimes and Index Crimes by Sex, 1960–1977[a]

	Arrests Male Total Crimes	Arrests Female Total Crimes	% Arrests Female	Arrests Male Index Crimes	Arrests Female Index Crimes	% Arrests Female Index Crimes
1960[b]	3,639,322	438,274	10.7	484,674	54,525	10.1
1961	3,875,245	475,695	10.9	546,684	64,094	10.5
1962	3,897,426	492,743	11.2	540,680	71,400	11.7
1963[c]	3,996,984	513,851	11.4	611,408	81,089	11.7
1964	4,138,099	546,981	11.7	679,897	97,919	12.6
1965	4,431,625	599,768	11.9	719,778	111,703	13.4
1966	4,406,639	609,768	12.2	748,531	120,523	13.9
1967	4,829,918	688,502	12.5	853,675	140,103	14.1
1968	4,891,343	725,496	12.9	895,336	148,740	14.2
1969	5,058,200	804,046	13.7	934,724	173,753	15.7
1970	5,623,576	946,897	14.4	1,055,472	215,291	16.9
1971	5,923,052	1,043,770	15.0	1,153,905	240,631	17.3
1972	5,955,783	1,057,411	15.1	1,159,275	254,854	18.0
1973	5,502,284	997,580	15.3	1,112,485	256,739	18.8
1974	5,185,110	994,296	16.1	1,192,666	279,535	19.0
1975	6,751,545	1,262,100	15.7	1,528,401	370,369	19.5
1976	6,671,909	1,240,439	15.7	1,429,982	354,474	19.9
1977	7,581,262	1,448,073	16.0	1,584,813	398,297	20.1

a. Based upon data reported in the FBI *Uniform Crime Reports*, 1960–1977.
b. 1960–1962 figures were tabulated from city and rural arrests.
c. 1963–1977 figures were tabulated from total arrests.

TABLE 2. Arrests for Violent Crimes and Property Crimes Among Index Offenses by Sex, 1960–1977[a]

	Arrests Male Violent Crimes	Arrests Female Violent Crimes	% Arrests Female Violent Crimes	Arrests Male Property Crimes	Arrests Female Property Crimes	% Arrests Female Property Crimes
1960[b]	94,297	11,101	10.5	390,377	43,424	10.0
1961	104,875	12,073	10.3	441,809	52,021	10.5
1962	102,228	11,895	10.4	438,452	59,505	11.9
1963[c]	109,508	12,588	10.3	501,900	68,501	12.0
1964	120,798	14,093	10.4	559,099	83,826	13.0
1965	133,238	15,127	10.2	586,540	96,576	14.1
1966	148,257	16,615	10.1	600,274	103,908	14.8
1967	170,341	18,444	9.8	683,334	121,659	15.1
1968	179,904	18,765	9.4	715,432	129,975	15.4
1969	195,350	20,844	9.6	739,374	152,909	17.1
1970	218,665	23,240	9.6	836,807	192,051	18.7
1971	245,788	27,421	10.0	908,117	213,210	19.0
1972	269,268	29,953	10.0	890,007	224,901	20.2
1973	260,800	29,582	10.2	851,685	227,157	21.1
1974	264,481	30,136	10.2	928,185	249,399	21.2
1975	332,133	38,320	10.3	1,196,268	332,049	21.7
1976	303,433	35,416	10.5	1,126,549	319,058	22.1
1977	346,510	40,296	10.4	1,238,303	358,001	22.4

a. Based upon data reported in the FBI *Uniform Crime Reports*, 1960-1977.
b. 1960-1962 figures were tabulated from city and rural arrests.
c. 1963-1977 figures were tabulated from total arrests.

in recent years. A similar pattern may be observed in the case of aggravated assault arrests with the percent female ranging from a high of 14.5 percent in 1960 to a low of 12.4 percent in 1968 to 12.8 percent in 1977. The female percent of robbery arrests, on the other hand, has shown a small but steady increase during this period from 4.6 percent to 7.4 percent. However, females still account for a smaller percent of the arrests for robbery than they do for either murder or aggravated assault. In 1977, murder and nonnegligent manslaughter comprised 0.2 percent of all female arrests, robbery made up 0.6 percent, and aggravated assault contributed 2 percent.

Analysis of the arrests by sex for individual property crimes among index offenses demonstrates that the female percent of arrests for both burglary and auto theft has shown a small but steady increase during the period 1960–1977. The female percent of burglary arrests ranged from a low of 2.9 percent in 1960 to a high of 6 percent in 1977. Similarly, the female percent of arrests for auto theft increased from a low of 3.6 percent in 1960 to a high of 8.1 percent in 1977. However, increases in the female percent of arrests among property crimes were most evident in the case of larceny-theft. Females were involved in 15.8 percent of larceny arrests in 1960 increasing to a high of 31.8 percent in 1977, an increase of 16 percent.

Thus, it appears that larceny arrests were primarily responsible for the increase in the female percent of arrests for index crimes between 1960 and 1977. While the female percent of arrests also increased for robbery, burglary, and auto theft, the increases were small. Further, it should be noted that larceny accounted for 22.1 percent of all female arrests in 1977 compared with only 0.6 percent for robbery, 1.9 percent for burglary, and 0.8 percent for auto theft.

Larceny-theft is defined in the UCR as "the unlawful taking, carrying, leading, or riding away of property from the possession or constructive possession of another. Thefts of bicycles, automobile accessories, shoplifting, pocket-picking, or any stealing of property or article which is not taken by force and violence or by fraud. Excludes embezzlement, 'con' games, forgery, worthless checks, etc."[27] In 1977, thefts of auto parts and accessories and other thefts from automobiles accounted for 37 percent of larceny-thefts known to the police. Thefts from buildings contributed 16 percent, and thefts of bicycles and shoplifting each made up 11 percent, with the remainder distributed among pocket-picking (1 percent), purse-snatching (1 percent), thefts from coin-operated machines (1 percent), and miscellaneous types of larceny-thefts (20 percent).[28] Unfortunately, the UCR does not provide data on the sex of arrested persons for specific types of larcenies. Moreover, the category of larceny-theft includes both petty (under $50) and grand ($50 and over) larceny, but does not distinguish between them or give any information on the sex distribution.[29]

Some information, however, is available from other sources. Cameron, in her study of shoplifting, estimated that 80 percent of the women charged with petty larceny were shoplifters.[30] She also found that most shoplifters were not professional thieves ("boosters") stealing for sale. In the department store sample, less than 1 percent of the women shoplifters had been arrested before compared with 12 percent of the men. Similarly, only 10 to 15 percent of the women but 66 percent of the men tried for shoplifting in court had prior arrest records. Further, adult females shoplifted items of lesser value than adult males. The average value of items recovered was $16.40 for women, $8.06 for girls, $28.36 for men, and $7.14 for boys. In a more recent study, Cohen and Stark also found that males were more likely than females to take more expensive merchandise.[31] In 1977, the UCR reports that the average value of items stolen by shoplifters was $42, although there is no breakdown by sex.[32]

It is probable that a large part of the increase in the larceny-theft category is due to increases in the arrests of females for shoplifting. Some evidence on this point comes from Silverman et al. who compared female crime in Tampa, Florida for the years 1962 and 1972.[33] An analysis of police arrest data for females age 17 and over indicated that property crimes showed the most significant increase over this period and that shop-lifting was responsible for over 95 percent of this increase. Further, they found that shoplifting accounted for over half of the total increase in female crime between 1962 and 1972. However, small increases in female involvement for larcenies other than shoplifting may also be occurring. Hindelang, for example, examined data from the National Crime Survey, a national survey of victims, for the years 1972 to 1976.[34] The larceny category included personal larceny (such as pocket-picking and purse-snatching), household larceny (larceny that happens to the entire household), and larcenies of unattended property (such as bicycles or a purse from a desk). Shoplifting, however, was not included. Nonetheless, the NCS data showed a slight rise in female involvement for larceny.

In the case of nonindex crimes, the largest increases in the female percent of arrests during the period 1960–1977 were for fraud, forgery and counterfeiting, embezzlement, and runaway. Fraud and embezzlement were treated as a single category in the UCR until 1964. In 1960, females accounted for 15 percent of the arrests in the combined fraud and embezzlement category. In 1964, females were involved in 19 percent of the arrests for fraud and 17.3 percent of those for embezzlement. The female percent of the fraud arrests increased to a high of 36.6 percent in 1976 and constituted 35.6 percent in 1977. The female percent of the embezzlement arrests reached a high of about 31 percent in 1975 and 1976, dropping to 22.7 percent in 1977. In the case of forgery and counterfeiting, female involvement rose from a low of 15.6 percent of all arrests in 1960 to a high of 29.6 percent in 1976 to 29.1 percent in 1977. Since 1964, when juvenile runaway was first included in the UCR, the female percent of arrests in this category has increased from 44.1 percent to 57.6 percent in 1977.

The female percent of arrests also increased slightly for other assaults, from a low of 9.7 percent in 1960 to a high of 14 per-cent in 1976 to 13.8 percent in 1977, an increase of about 4 percent. The female percent of arson, which was a new UCR category in 1964, decreased from 8.7 percent to 6.9 percent in 1967 but has since increased to just over 11 percent in the 1975–1977 period. Females have also increased their share of vagrancy arrests, although a pattern is difficult to discern and to interpret, possibly because vagrancy laws are particularly subject to varying interpretations by law enforcement officers. Vagrancy statutes, for example, are widely used to control undesirables and criminals in the community and have sometimes been used to control the movement of migratory workers.[35] In the case of women, vagrancy laws are often used to control prostitution whether or not the statute makes explicit reference to prostitutes.[36] In 1960, females made up 7.7 percent of all vagrancy arrests, gradually increasing to 21.9 percent in 1971, then to over 34 percent in 1972 and 1973, dropping to 12.5 percent in 1974 and 10.5 percent in 1975, and increasing again to 22 percent in 1976 and 34.6 percent in 1977. Other nonindex crimes that show more or less even patterns of fairly small increases are stolen property, vandalism, weapons, offenses against the family, driving under the influence, disorderly conduct, suspicion, and curfew violations. In 1977, vandalism, weapons, and driving under the influence each involved females in about 8 percent of the cases, as did 10.3 percent of the offenses against the family, 10.8 percent of the stolen property offenses, 14.3 percent of the suspicion cases, 17.2 percent of the disorderly conduct offenses, and 21.9 percent of the curfew violations.

The female percent of arrests remained relatively stable for narcotic drug law violations, gambling, liquor law violations, drunkenness, and all other offenses. In 1977, females comprised 13.9 percent of the persons arrested for narcotic drug law offenses, 8.9 percent of the gambling arrests, 14.8 percent of liquor law arrests, 7.2 percent of the drunkenness arrests, and 15.4 percent of 'all other arrests. It is interesting to note that the female percent of arrests for sex offenses actually decreased by half from 18 percent in 1960 to 8.9 percent in 1977. In the case of prostitution and commercialized vice, the female percent of arrests increased during the 1960s but has declined in the 1970s.

It is apparent from an examination of nonindex crime data that prostitution and commercialized vice and running away are the only offense categories reported by the FBI where females account for a higher percent of the total arrests than males. In 1977, females accounted for 70.7 percent of the prostitution arrests and 57.6 percent of those for runaways. In some jurisdictions, prostitution statutes specifically include woman or female in their definition of prostitution, thereby excluding their male counterparts from the possibility of arrest.[37] Even when prostitution statutes are neutrally phrased, however, they are usually enforced only against female prostitutes. Further, the activities of male clients are usually not criminalized or are criminalized to a lesser degree than those of the female prostitute. Again, even when male clients are liable to arrest under the law, this rarely occurs. In fact, one authority has pointed out that arrests of male clients are usually made with no expectation that criminal prosecution will be carried through but rather to induce the male to cooperate in convicting the woman.[38] Since both the language and enforcement of prostitution laws are biased against females, it is hardly surprising that females constitute the bulk of arrests in this category. Running away is applicable only to juveniles and will be discussed at greater length in the following section of this chapter.

Thus, our examination of nonindex crimes shows a pattern similar to that among index crimes with the only major increases occurring for property crimes—fraud, forgery and counterfeiting and embezzlement—and for running away from home. Of the three property crimes, fraud accounts for the largest percent of total arrests of females, 5.3 percent in 1977, compared with only 1.4 percent for forgery and counterfeiting and 0.1 percent for embezzlement. Fraud and embezzlement are frequently considered white-collar crimes, defined by Edwin Sutherland as "a crime committed by a person of respectability and high status in the course of his occupation."[39] However, the little evidence there is suggests that this may not be the case for females. Fraud, for example, is defined in the UCR as "fraudulent conversion and obtaining money or property by false pretenses. Includes bad checks except forgeries and counterfeiting. Also includes larceny by bailee."[40] Dale Hoffman-Bustamante suggests that most women arrested for fraud are involved in con games, welfare fraud, or possibly as accessories in fraudulent business practices.[41]

Embezzlement, according to the UCR, is "misappropriation or misapplication of money or property entrusted to one's care, custody, or control."[42] Alice Franklin's account of employee theft provides some information on this kind of crime.[43] She studied 447 "known" dishonest employees in a large retail organization who were involved in theft of cash and/or other merchandise or misuse of organizational equipment between 1973 and 1975. Although males made up 40 percent of the work force, they were responsible for 56 percent of the thefts. Over 80 percent of the females who committed theft were employed in sales as compared with 55 percent of the males. All of the persons in managerial positions who committed theft were male, as were 87 percent of those in stock and three-quarters of those in "others," including maintenance, technicians, and garage operators. Females accounted for 53 percent of employee thefts in sales and 64 percent in clerical positions. Female employees also committed smaller thefts than males. Male violators committed about half of the thefts between $1 and $150 but 70 percent of those over $1,000. Eighty-one percent of the thefts committed by females were between $1 and $150. Embezzlement, which accounted for the greatest loss and involves skills in accounting and financial manipulation, was most closely associated with higher level positions occupied by males. Franklin concludes that the petty nature of female employee theft reflects differences in the opportunities as well as the skills of men and women. Thus, it appears that most women arrested for fraud and embezzlement at the present time do not occupy positions of "high social status" and cannot be considered white-collar criminals, at least as Sutherland used that term.[44]

The UCR defines forgery and counterfeiting as "making, uttering or possessing, with intent to defraud, anything false which is made to appear true. Includes attempts."[45] As in the case of fraud and embezzlement, the forgeries committed by women tend to involve relatively small amounts of money. One study of women imprisoned for "paperhanging," including forgery, uttering, false pretenses, and fraud, found that about 60 percent had been involved in offenses where the amount was less than $500.[46] Another study placed this figure at 45 percent, and in 27 percent of the cases, the amount was less than $50.[47]

Table 3 shows the offenses for which males and females were arrested in 1960 and 1975 rank ordered by the percent of total arrests in their respective sex cohorts.[48] It should be noted that, unlike the annual, noncomparable UCR arrest statistics used in Tables 1 and 2, the data used in this table are comparable since only those units were used that had the same data reporting system for the years under consideration. Both in 1960 and 1975, the four categories of offenses for which females were most frequently arrested were drunkenness, the miscellaneous category of all other offenses, disorderly conduct, and larceny. Drunkenness and larceny, however, have changed places. Drunkenness was the most common offense for which females were arrested in 1960, accounting for over one-quarter of all female arrests. By 1975, drunkenness ranked fourth but involved only 6.5 percent of all female arrests. Larceny, ranked fourth in 1960 and accounting for 8.8 percent of all female arrests, was the most common female offense in 1975 and comprised nearly one-quarter of the total arrests for females. Prostitution ranked fifth in 1960 and seventh in 1975, accounting for 4.9 percent and 4.2 percent, respectively, of all female arrests.

Several other interesting shifts in rank order can be seen from 1960 to 1975. During that time, for example, the frequency of sex offense violations dropped from a tie for eleventh in 1960 to twenty-first in 1975. A similar drop was experienced by vagrancy, ranked eighth in 1960 and eighteenth in 1975, and by gambling, ranked ninth in 1960 and nineteenth in 1975. On the other hand, several offenses ranked low in 1960 have risen. Narcotic drug law violations, for example, rose from a tie for fourteenth in 1960 to fifth in 1975. Robbery and buying and receiving stolen property tie for fourteenth in 1975 moving from twentieth and a tie for twenty-first, respectively, in 1960. Driving under the influence, fraud and weapons offenses also moved up in rank. It should be noted, however, that robbery, buying and receiving stolen property, and weapons offenses each still account for less than 1 percent of total female arrests.

Table 3 also allows a comparison of male and female arrest patterns in 1960 and 1975. In some ways, the pattern of female arrests is quite similar to that of males. In other ways, there are striking differences. For example, drunkenness, all other offenses, disorderly conduct, and larceny were the four most common offenses for both males and females in 1960. However, drunkenness, ranked first in 1960 for both males and females, accounted for 38.8 percent of the total arrests for males but only 27.7 percent of the total arrests for females. In 1975, drunkenness, ranked second for males and fourth for females, constituted only 17.1 percent of all male arrests and 6.5 percent of all female arrests. This decline may have had less to do with changes in actual behavior than with changes in public attitudes and police arrest practices regarding this offense. The percentage of total male and female arrests accounted for by disorderly conduct also declined, although much less dramatically than for drunkenness, while larceny increased markedly for females and less so for males. These four offenses accounted for 67.3 percent of all males and 68.9 percent of all females arrested in 1960. In 1975, the respective percentages were 52.4 percent and 64.3 percent.

Narcotic drug law violations, ranked relatively low for both sexes in 1960, moved into a tie for sixth for males and fifth for females in 1975, accounting for 6.6 percent and 5.5 percent, respectively, of the total arrests for males and females. A num-

TABLE 3. Rank Order of Male and Female Arrests Based on the Percent of Total Arrests 1960 and 1075[a]

	Females				Males			
	1960		1975		1960		1975	
	%	Rank	%	Rank	%	Rank	%	Rank
Drunkenness	27.7	1.0	6.5	4.0	38.8	1.0	17.1	2.0
All other offenses (except traffic)	17.9	2.0	22.3	2.0	12.2	2.0	18.0	1.0
Disorderly conduct	14.5	3.0	10.9	3.0	10.8	3.0	7.0	5.0
Larceny—theft	8.8	4.0	24.6	1.0	5.5	4.0	10.3	3.0
Prostitution & commercialized vice	4.9	5.0	4.2	7.0	0.2	21.5	0.3	22.0
Other assaults	3.5	6.0	4.1	8.0	3.8	7.0	4.9	8.0
Liquor laws	3.4	7.0	2.5	10.0	2.5	10.0	2.9	9.0
Vagrancy	2.9	8.0	0.6	18.0	3.9	6.0	0.5	20.0
Gambling	2.7	9.0	0.5	19.0	3.3	9.0	1.0	16.0
Driving under the influence	2.4	10.0	4.6	6.0	4.7	5.0	10.1	4.0
Aggravated assault	2.1	11.5	2.3	11.0	1.5	12.0	2.8	10.0
Sex offenses (except forcible rape and prostitution)	2.1	11.5	0.3	21.0	1.2	14.0	0.8	17.0
Fraud	1.4	13.0	4.0	9.0	1.0	15.5	1.5	14.5

Burglary	1.0	14.5	1.9	12.0	3.7	8.0	6.6	6.5
Forgery and counterfeiting	1.0	14.5	1.4	13.0	0.6	19.0	0.7	18.5
Narcotic drug laws	1.0	14.5	5.5	5.0	0.7	18.0	6.6	6.5
Offenses against family and children	0.9	17.0	0.4	20.0	1.3	13.0	0.7	18.5
Auto theft	0.5	18.5	0.7	17.0	1.7	11.0	1.9	13.0
Weapons	0.5	18.5	0.9	14.5	1.0	15.5	2.1	12.0
Robbery	0.4	20.0	0.9	14.5	0.9	17.0	2.4	11.0
Murder and nonnegligent manslaughter	0.2	21.5	0.2	22.0	0.1	23.5	0.2	23.0
Stolen property	0.2	21.5	0.9	14.5	0.3	20.0	1.5	14.5
Manslaughter by negligence	*	23.5	*	23.5	0.1	23.5	*	24.0
Forcible rape	*	23.5	*	23.5	0.2	21.5	0.4	21.0

a. Based upon data reported in the FBI *Uniform Crime Reports*, 1975.
* Less than one-tenth of one percent.

ber of other crimes appear to occur with the same relative frequency for females, compared to the total, as for males. Thus, in 1975 murder constituted 0.2 percent of the total arrests for each sex, aggravated assault 2.8 percent for males and 2.3 percent for females, other assaults 4.9 percent for males and 4.1 percent for females, liquor law violations 2.9 percent for males and 2.5 percent for females, vagrancy 0.5 percent for males and 0.6 percent for females, and so on for several other offenses that show very little difference. On the other hand, some crimes appear to occur with greater or lesser frequency for females, compared to the total, than for males. In 1975, for example, larceny arrests made up 24.6 percent of total female arrests but only 10.3 percent of total male arrests. Female rates in 1975 were also greater for fraud, prostitution and commercialized vice, and disorderly conduct. Male rates in 1975 were greater for drunkenness, driving under the influence, and burglary.

Up to this point, we have been examining arrest rates for all females without regard to age group. When arrest rates are examined separately for adult and juvenile females, some interesting differences emerge. Statistics have been tabulated to show the increase in arrests for each sex and age group over time. However, a note of caution must be introduced. The rate of increase can be misleading if viewed out of context. It is important to remember that a high percentage increase can be obtained when the base figure is very small. For example:

Juvenile Arrests for Murder[a]

	1960	1975	Difference in Absolute Numbers	Percent Increase
Female	28	105	77	275.0
Male	331	1,012	681	205.7

a. Based on data reported in the FBI *Uniform Crime Reports*, 1975.

As can be seen, the rate of increase was higher for juvenile females because of the small base figure in 1960, even though the difference in absolute numbers was greater for juvenile males. In addition to the rate of increase, therefore, the percent of arrests accounted for by females in a particular crime category must also be considered to provide a more balanced view of changes in the magnitude and nature of female criminal arrests.

Arrest trends of adult females between 1960 and 1975, shown in Table 4, reveal the same general pattern as arrests for all females. During this period, arrests for all offenses increased 66.2 percent for adult females but only 6.9 percent for their male counterparts. In 1960, adult females were involved in 10.2 percent of all arrests as compared with 15.1 percent in 1975, a 4.9 percent increase. When only the index crimes are considered, arrests for adult females and males increased by 346.4 percent and 121.7 percent, respectively. This constituted an increase of 9.4 percent for female index arrests as a percent of all arrests for index crimes. It appears that this increase was due to the 441.8 percent growth in the rate of arrests of women for property crimes among index offenses. The female percent of arrests for property crimes increased by 13.2 percent during this period.

In the case of violent index crimes, the rate of increase was somewhat greater for adult males than females and the female percent of arrests for this crime category actually declined by 0.8 percent. Among violent index crimes, the rate of increase of adult females was greater than that of adult males only for robbery;[49] robbery arrests for women rose by 293.4 percent compared with a 166.5 percent rise for men. Even so, women were responsible for only 2.1 percent more of the arrests for robbery over this time period.

Arrest rates for adult females increased much faster than those of adult males for all crimes of property. Arrests for burglary among adult females increased by 258 percent, about two and one-half times the increase among adult males. Auto theft showed an increase of 204.1 percent for adult females, almost three and one-half times that for adult males. This constituted an increase of 2.4 percent and 2.8 percent, respectively, for arrests of adult females for burglary and auto theft as a percent of all

TABLE 4. Arrest Trends by Sex for Adults, 1960–1975[a]

	Arrests 1960	Arrests 1975	% Increase 1960–1975	% Arrests Female 1960	% Arrests Female 1975	% Change 1960–1975
Total Crimes						
Female	304,165	505,673	66.2	10.2	15.1	4.9
Male	2,665,044	2,847,612	6.9			
Index Crimes						
Female	31,076	138,725	346.4	11.6	21.0	9.4
Male	236,281	523,893	121.7			
Violent Crimes						
Female	9,074	19,510	115.0	11.4	10.6	−0.8
Male	70,635	163,872	132.0			
Property Crimes						
Female	22,002	119,215	441.8	11.7	24.9	13.2
Male	165,646	360,021	117.3			
Murder						
Female	802	1,602	99.8	18.2	16.1	−2.1
Male	3,605	8,364	132.0			

Robbery						
Female	1,084	4,264	293.4	4.8	6.9	2.1
Male	21,593	57,537	166.5			
Aggravated assault						
Female	7,176	13,546	88.8	15.3	13.5	−1.8
Male	39,690	86,612	118.2			
Burglary						
Female	2,011	7,200	258.0	3.3	5.7	2.4
Male	59,317	120,192	102.6			
Larceny						
Female	19,281	109,856	469.8	18.3	34.7	16.4
Male	85,889	206,982	141.0			
Auto theft						
Female	710	2,159	204.1	3.4	6.2	2.8
Male	20,440	32,847	60.7			

a. Based upon data reported in the FBI *Uniform Crime Reports*, 1975.

arrests in these crime categories. However, the greatest gain is seen for larceny where female arrests increased almost 470 percent whereas male arrests increased only 141 percent. This represents more than a 16 percent increase in the percent of larceny arrests involving women. No other index offense exhibited such an increase over that time period.

A comparison of Tables 4 and 5 indicates that there were some interesting differences in arrest trends for adult and juvenile females. The arrest rates for both juvenile females and males increased at a much faster rate than their adult counterparts. The total arrests of juvenile females increased by 253.9 percent compared with a 125.3 percent increase for juvenile males during the period 1960–1975. Female juveniles made up 21.2 percent of all arrests in 1975, a 6.6 percent increase over 1960. The total increase for index crimes was over 425 percent, more than three and one-half times the increase for juvenile males. Unlike adult women, however, a greater increase was evidenced in violent crimes than in property crimes. Among juvenile females, arrests for violent crimes increased by 503.5 percent while arrests for property crimes increased by 420.4 percent. The juvenile female percent of violent crimes, however, increased by only 3.7 percent whereas their percent of property crimes increased by 11 percent.

Table 5 further indicates that the rate of increase for juvenile females was greater than that for juvenile males for all the violent index offenses. Unlike adult women, murder and aggravated assault showed a greater increase for juvenile females than juvenile males. Murder and nonnegligent manslaughter evidenced a 275 percent increase for juvenile females compared with a 205.7 percent increase for juvenile males. Similarly, arrests for aggravated assault increased 438 percent and 217.1 percent, respectively, for juvenile females and males. This constituted an increase of 1.6 percent and 6.1 percent, respectively, for arrests of juvenile females for murder and aggravated assault as a percent of all arrests in these crime categories. The most dramatic increases in index arrests for juveniles of both sexes took place for robbery; arrests of juvenile females for robbery increased 646.8 percent while arrests of males in the same age category increased 361.3 percent. However, the juvenile female percent of robbery arrests only increased by 2.8 percent over the same period.

Like adult females, the rate of increase was greater for juvenile females than males for all crimes of property. Burglary evidenced a 327.5 percent increase among juvenile females compared with an increase of 132 percent among juvenile males, accounting for 2.2 percent more of all arrests for burglary over this period. The female percent of arrests for auto theft increased by 3.6 percent, representing a 140.3 percent increase among juvenile females compared with a 19.5 percent increase among juvenile males. Again like adult females, the greatest increases for juvenile females in the property crime category took place for larceny. There was a 457.3 percent increase in larceny arrests among juvenile females compared with 111.7 percent increase for juvenile males. Juvenile females made up 15.6 percent more of total larceny arrests in 1975 than in 1960.

Turning now to nonindex crimes, we find that the adult female percent of arrests between 1960 and 1975 increased in all categories except sex offenses, liquor laws, drunkenness, narcotic drug laws, and gambling. For the most part, however, increases were small. The largest increases were for fraud, forgery and counterfeiting, disorderly conduct, and vagrancy. Over this period, the adult female percent of arrests increased 20.3 percent for fraud, 14.2 percent for forgery and counterfeiting, 11.2 percent for disorderly conduct, and 10.2 percent for vagrancy. In the case of juvenile females, the percent of arrests increased for all nonindex crimes except sex offenses. Again, most of the increases were relatively small. However, juvenile females did make up 8.5 percent more of the arrests for fraud, 8.2 percent more for offenses against the family, 7.6 percent more for liquor laws, 7.5 percent more for other assaults, and 7.2 percent more for forgery and counterfeiting. While the female percent of arrests for fraud and forgery and counter-

TABLE 5. Arrest Trends by Sex for Juveniles, 1960–1975[a]

	Arrests 1960	Arrests 1975	Increase 1960–1975	% Arrests Female 1960	% Arrests Female 1975	% Change 1960–1975
Total Crimes						
Female	70,925	251,008	253.9	14.6	21.2	6.6
Male	414,082	933,097	125.3			
Index Crimes						
Female	17,589	92,421	425.4	8.7	18.7	10.0
Male	184,942	402,111	117.4			
Violent Crimes						
Female	1,065	6,427	503.5	6.9	10.6	3.6
Male	14,277	53,925	277.7			
Property Crimes						
Female	16,524	85,994	420.4	8.8	19.8	11.0
Male	170,665	348,186	104.0			
Murder						
Female	28	105	275.0	7.8	9.4	1.6
Male	331	1,012	205.7			

Robbery						
Female	355	2,651	646.8	4.8	7.6	2.8
Male	7,034	32,448	361.3			
Aggravated assault						
Female	676	3,637	438.0	10.7	16.8	6.1
Male	5,671	17,980	217.1			
Burglary						
Female	1,595	6,819	327.5	2.8	5.0	2.2
Male	55,780	129,423	132.0			
Larceny						
Female	13,661	76,128	457.3	14.1	29.7	15.6
Male	82,949	180,589	117.7			
Auto theft						
Female	1,268	3,047	140.3	3.8	7.4	3.6
Male	31,936	38,174	19.5			

a. Based upon data reported in the FBI *Uniform Crime Reports*, 1975.

feiting increased for both adult and juvenile females, increases were greater for adult women.

In general, the arrest trends for adult females from 1968–1977 and from 1973–1977 are similar to those observed for the period 1960–1975. Over the ten-year period, the female percent of arrests increased 4.6 percent for all crimes and 6.8 percent for index crimes. The increase in the female percent of index crimes was again due to the greater involvement of adult women in property crimes among index offenses (8.4 percent), particularly larceny (7.1 percent). Among nonindex crimes, the adult female percent of arrests increased in all categories except prostitution and suspicion of committing a crime, with largest increases occurring for fraud (13.4 percent), vagrancy (13.4 percent), forgery and counterfeiting (9 percent), and disorderly conduct (5.4 percent). Over the five-year period, adult females accounted for 2.6 percent more of the arrests for all crimes, 2.9 percent more of the arrests for index crimes, and 3.2 percent more of the arrests for property crimes among index offenses. The female percent of arrests increased 2.3 percent and 1.9 percent, respectively, for larceny and auto theft. Adult women were more involved in all nonindex crimes except prostitution and suspicion, particularly vagrancy (10.2 percent), fraud (6.6 percent), disorderly conduct (4.4 percent), sex offenses (4 percent), and forgery and counterfeiting (3.6 percent).

The pattern of arrests for juvenile females for the 1968–1977 period is also similar to that for the period 1960–1975. Over this period, the juvenile female percent of arrests increased 3.3 percent for all crimes, 6 percent for index crimes, 3.5 percent for violent index crimes, and 6.5 percent for property crimes among index offenses. Juvenile females were responsible for 4.8 percent more of the arrests for aggravated assault and 7.7 percent more of those for larceny. They were more involved in all nonindex crimes except sex offenses and narcotic drug laws, with the juvenile female percent of arrests increasing most for offenses against the family (12 percent), forgery and counterfeiting (9.8 percent), running away (8.7 percent), fraud (7 percent), liquor laws (6.6 percent), and vagrancy (5.9 percent). Over the five-year period, however, the juvenile female percent of arrests stayed about the same for total crimes and for all index crimes except auto theft, where juvenile females made up 2.8 percent more of the arrests. For nonindex crimes, the juvenile female percent of arrests decreased in seven categories (prostitution, sex offenses, suspicion, narcotic drug laws, gambling, all other offenses, and vagrancy) and increased only slightly in the other categories. The largest increase in the juvenile female percent of arrests occurred for fraud (9.7 percent).

According to UCR statistics, over one-quarter of the juvenile females arrested in 1977 were taken into custody for running away from home or for curfew violations, as compared with less than one-tenth of their male counterparts. Traditionally, juvenile females have been arrested for these and other offenses such as incorrigibility and truancy commonly believed to constitute euphemisms for sexual offenses. Several older studies that used police records found much the same picture of female delinquency. In 1952, William Wattenberg and Frank Saunders analyzed data on juvenile girls from the files of the Detroit Police Department's Juvenile Bureau.[50] They found that of the total complaints on record for that year, 3,451 were boys and 1,082 were girls. By and large, girls became known to the police for incorrigibility, sexual delinquency, or truancy, while boys were apprehended for burglary, assault, or malicious mischief. It is interesting to note that the nature of girl delinquency seemed to change at about the age of thirteen. Before that age, girls in this Detroit study were principally involved in the property offense of shoplifting, being similar in this regard to boys who were involved in property crime in all age categories. A 1957 California study indicated that sexual misconduct among adolescent girls aroused great societal reaction and resulted in girls being arrested more often than boys on that or related charges.[51] Another study in New York State during the late 1950s concluded that female delinquents were almost exclusively involved in sexual misbehavior of one type or another, and were most frequently arrested by the police directly for that or on euphemistic charges.[52]

Although the UCR presents arrest data by sex and by race, the data cannot be cross-tabulated by these two variables. Therefore, we will have to turn elsewhere for these data. A recent study by Susan Katzenelson provides some information on crime patterns analyzed by sex, race, and age.[53] The data for this study cover all known adult offenses resulting in arrest in Washington, D.C., during 1973, except federal and traffic offenses, drunkenness, disorderly conduct, and municipal violations. Females were responsible for 16.4 percent of all arrests, 11.6 percent of those for violent crimes, 15.2 percent of those for property crimes, and 22.8 percent of those for victimless crimes. Victimless crimes accounted for 43 percent of all female arrests, property crimes for 32 percent, violent crimes for 23 percent, and all other offenses for 2 percent. This compared to a distribution of all male arrests as 28 percent victimless crimes, 35 percent property crimes, 35 percent violent crimes, and 2 percent all other offenses.

However, offense patterns showed considerable variation by age. Overall, female crime peaked at age 23 compared with age 19 for males. Among females, victimless crimes peaked first (21–25), followed by property crimes (31–35), and violent crimes (41–45). Among males, property crimes peaked first (16–20) followed by violent and victimless crimes (46 and over). Victimless crimes were more frequent for females than males between the ages of 16 and 30, property crimes between the ages of 31 and 40, and violent crimes between the ages of 36 and 45.

When offense patterns were analyzed by sex and race, there were some interesting differences. Blacks comprised 79 percent of the female arrests and 88 percent of the male arrests. Females were involved in 25 percent of white arrests and 15 percent of black arrests. In general, the offense patterns of males and females were more similar for blacks than whites. Among blacks, property crimes accounted for 35.7 percent of all male arrests compared with 32.4 percent for their female counterparts, giving a difference of just over 3 percent. Among whites, property crimes made up 33.9 percent of all male arrests but only 24.1 percent of all female arrests, giving a difference of almost 10 percent. Similarly, victimless crimes made up 27 percent of black male arrests and 40 percent of black female arrests compared with 44.5 percent and 64.3 percent, respectively, of white male and female arrests. The percentage differences between males and females for violent crimes were about the same for both blacks (9.8 percent) and whites (10.7 percent). Among females, violent crimes and property crimes made up a much higher proportion of total arrests for blacks than whites while the opposite obtained for victimless crimes.

In sum, UCR arrest statistics tell us the following about the nature and extent of female involvement in criminality and delinquency: Females are involved mostly in nonviolent and property crimes. Only in the categories of larceny, forgery and counterfeiting, fraud, embezzlement, prostitution and commercialized vice, disorderly conduct, vagrancy, curfew violations, and running away from home did the percent of arrests accounted for by females in 1977 exceed their overall arrest rate of 16 percent. Larceny was the most frequent female crime in 1977 and constituted 22.1 percent of all female arrests. Runaway and disorderly conduct each contributed 7.4 percent to total female arrests, followed by driving under the influence, drunkenness, drug abuse violations, and fraud, each contributing about 5 or 6 percent. Runaway and curfew violations accounted for over one-quarter of the total arrests of juvenile females.

Female crime is increasing and females are accounting for a larger share of total arrests. It is important to note, however, that females still are responsible for only a fraction of all crime; in 1977, females were involved in 1,448,073 arrests out of 9,029,335 or 16 percent of the total. Moreover, the percent of arrests accounted for by females during the period 1960–1975 increased by only 5 percent, hardly a dramatic rise. Among adult women, the female percent of arrests for violent index crimes remained constant over all time periods examined. Juvenile women, on the other hand, accounted for a greater percentage of arrests for violent index crimes owing to increases in aggravated assault. When only the past five years are considered, however, the juvenile female percent of arrests for aggravated assault has stayed the same. Moreover, the pattern for the nonindex crime of simple assault is similar, with the juvenile female percent of arrests increasing but remaining relatively stable in recent years.

Among both adult and juvenile women, the female percent of arrests has increased most dramatically for larceny and fraud and to a lesser extent for forgery and counterfeiting and embezzlement, although the latter two offenses constitute only a small percentage of total female arrests. Among adult women, the female percent of arrests also increased for vagrancy although the pattern of arrests for this offense has been somewhat erratic over the years. Juvenile females also made up more of the arrests for liquor laws and running away. For the most part, these are offenses that traditionally have been considered "women's crimes" in that they require behavior that is consistent with traditional female roles. For example, larceny and forgery and counterfeiting "fit well into the everyday round of activities in which women engage, especially their role of buying most family necessities and paying the family bills."[54]

As indicated above, however, the female percent of arrests has not increased significantly for those offenses that require stereotyped male behavior such as robbery and burglary. This is illustrated more parsimoniously in a recent paper by Darrell Steffensmeier who defined as masculine those "crimes involving physical strength and daring, elements of coercion and confrontation with the victim, and/or specialized skills."[55] Crimes categorized as masculine included murder, aggravated assault, robbery, other assaults, weapons, burglary, auto theft, vandalism, and arson. Using UCR data, Steffensmeier found that the female percent of arrests for masculine crimes was 8.2 percent in 1965 and 9.5 percent in 1976. Moreover, these crimes constituted only 9.7 percent of total female arrests in 1965 and 11.2

percent in 1976. Arrest gains for females, therefore, have occurred not for those categories of crime considered more compatible with expected male roles but rather for those considered more compatible with expected female roles.

Finally, it should be noted that we cannot be certain that this increase is solely the result of increased criminality on the part of women. The possibility should be considered that at least part of this increase may be due to the fact that law enforcement officers are simply more willing to arrest the female offender. At this point, however, it is difficult to assess the relative contribution of each of these factors to the rise in the female crime rate.

SELF-REPORTED DATA ON FEMALE CRIME

The deficiencies of official arrest statistics mentioned earlier make it necessary for us to look elsewhere for supplementary information on the extent of female criminality. One important source of such information is the self-report studies of crime and delinquency that have been appearing in the criminological literature with some frequency. Self-report studies, guaranteeing anonymity to the respondent, simply ask the persons to admit to those law violations they have committed. Studies of this sort would appear to reflect more accurately the actual incidence of criminality among the sexes, provided, of course, the respondents are candid and truthful. Evidence seems to indicate that people generally are honest in situations of this sort and self-reports have a high degree of validity.[56]

It should be kept in mind, however, that males and females may differ in their willingness to admit to criminal acts. Ruth Morris, for example, found that delinquent girls felt more shame about their delinquencies than did delinquent boys and were more reluctant to admit to their police contacts.[57] Delinquent boys, on the other hand, showed a greater willingness to admit to such contacts and were more likely than girls to boast about their delinquencies. In another study, Gold found that 72 percent of his validity sample reported their offenses accurately while 17 percent concealed offenses and the rest were questionable.[58] Boys most often concealed acts of breaking and entering, property destruction, and carrying concealed weapons. Girls most often concealed acts of breaking and entering, property destruction, unauthorized driving away of an auto, gang fighting, miscellaneous theft, and sexual offenses. With these considerations in mind, we turn now to a review of self-report studies.

Self-report studies of adult criminality are few. One such study was conducted by James Wallerstein and Clement Wyle who administered a questionnaire to some 1,698 adults, asking them which of 49 offenses they had committed.[59] All of the offenses were serious enough to draw a maximum sentence of not less than one year. Among 678 women who responded to the questionnaire, 83 percent admitted to having committed at least one grand larceny as an adult, 81 percent to malicious mischief, 76 percent to disorderly conduct, and 74 percent to indecency. Other offenses ranged below these and included admissions of assault, auto theft, burglary, fraud, and even robbery. The mean number of offenses committed by women in their adult lives ranged from a low of 9.8 for laborers to a high of 14.4 for those in military and government work. The average number for all women was 11, compared to an overall average of 18 for men. Whereas men admitted to an average of 3.2 juvenile offenses, women admitted to half that number.

In the 1950s, a study of unrecorded delinquency was conducted in a western state by James Short and F. Ivan Nye, who compared high school students with youths in training schools.[60] Among high school students they found variations in male and female delinquency rates similar to variations in official arrest figures. The somewhat higher official sex ratio was taken as indicative of the bias of formal and informal control agencies in underreporting female delinquency. Comparisons between high school and training school girls showed a large number of high school girls admitted to the relatively minor offenses of skipping school, defying their parents, or stealing items of small value. Among the training school girls, however, even larger numbers admitted to these behaviors, while many said they had been involved in more serious offenses as well. For the training school girls, the commitment of serious offenses was coupled with repetitive involvement. Although few of the high school students admitted having engaged in even the petty misbehaviors more that once or twice, girls in the training school revealed committing both minor and serious offenses repeatedly. Some 81.5 percent of the incarcerated girls admitted to frequent acts of sexual intercourse, 80.5 percent said they drank frequently, and 32.1 percent acknowledged repeated acts of property damage.

In her attempt to discover the respective delinquency involvement of males and females, Shirley Merritt Clark analyzed information from 200 institutionalized delinquent girls and from 426 boys in a state training school.[61] The two groups were reasonably similar in that 16 was the average age for each, while 69 percent of the girls were white compared to 67 percent of the boys. Clark found that the girls in her study were very much like the boys in terms of their self-reported misconduct, as well as the age of first reported delinquency. Although the extensiveness of unreported offenses was slightly higher for boys, the difference was not great. The prevalence of undetected law violating behavior by the girls in this study caused Clark to conclude that female involvement is much greater than ordinarily expected.

Differences between official and unofficial delinquencies are dramatically highlighted by Clark's analysis of the offenses that brought the girls into court the first time, as well as into the institution. Seventy-four percent of the girls became officially known to the juvenile court the first time for "wayward" behavior: truancy, incorrigibility, and sexual misconduct. Only 23 percent of the boys, on the other hand, had their initial contact with the court for such misbehavior. The particular behavior leading to the girls' commitment to the institution fell even more frequently into this "wayward" category. In fact, 88.5 percent of the offenses leading to commitment were of this nature, compared with only 22 percent for boys. It is interesting to note that these officially delinquent girls became labeled as delinquent and were incarcerated largely because of behavior that would not be considered criminal in an adult, while more typically criminal behavior to which they admitted was ignored and overlooked by the social control agents of society.

Another study of self-reported delinquency was conducted by Martin Gold and was based on interviews with a representative sample of 522 teenagers in Flint, Michigan. [62] Overall, girls were much less delinquent than boys. Girls committed none of the armed robberies or thefts of car parts or gas, only 10 percent of the concealed weapons offenses, 15 percent of the assaults, gang fighting, extortion, and property destruction, and 20 percent of thefts, fornication, false ID, and unlawful driving away of an automobile. Further, they accounted for only 25 percent of the threatened assaults, shoplifting, and trespassing, 35 percent of the truancies and illegal entries, and 40 percent of the drinking incidents. Girls were also responsible for 45 percent of the runaways and half of the reported acts of striking parents. One surprising finding of this study was that running away, incorrigibility, and fornication accounted for only 8 percent of the total acts reported by girls and 6 percent of those reported by boys. Gold suggests that "a more accurate picture of girls' delinquency shows it to be quite similar to boys,' only smaller."[63]

Two studies of self-reported male and female delinquency are available from the mid-1960s. Nancy Wise investigated unreported delinquency among 589 middle-class youths in a Connecticut high school.[64] She found that the reported delinquencies of middle-class boys and girls were essentially similar and generally of a noncoercive, nonviolent nature, with both sexes participating about equally in sex and alcohol delinquencies. However, middle-class girls reported a much less frequent involvement in other offenses, accounting for only 39.3 percent of the driving offenses, 36.2 percent of the ungovernability offenses, 34.9 percent of the thefts, 28.9 percent of the vandalism offenses, and 21.4 percent of the assaults. Over half of the girls had bought or consumed alcohol, about two-fifths had skipped school, over one-third admitted taking things of small value, and about one-third had participated in a sex offense. The pattern of involvement in more serious behaviors was far less pronounced, though. About 21 percent admitted to fistfighting, while fewer than that confessed to vandalism, and none indicated a prior use of drugs.

Jensen and Eve's study presents self-report delinquency data by both sex and race. [65] The data were gathered during the 1964–1965 school year from over 4,000 junior and senior high school students in Western Contra Costa County, California. Although girls reported less delinquent involvement than boys for all six delinquency items, the pattern of female delinquency was similar to that of males. The most common offenses for both sexes were theft under $2 and fighting, while the least common offenses were theft over $50 and taking a car without the owner's permission. The ratio of male to female rates by race was about the same for grand theft. However, for fighting and vandalism there was a greater difference in the ratios for white males and females than for blacks, whereas for petty theft and taking a car without the owner's permission the ratios of male to female rates were greater for blacks than for whites. Racial differences in self-reporting delinquency were slight for both sexes, although a larger percentage of black than white girls admitted to having beaten up someone on purpose (29 percent v. 15 percent).

Information on the self-reported delinquent involvement of middle- to lower-middle-class male and female adolescents is presented by Michael Hindelang. [66] In his study of 763 students in a Catholic high school in Oakland, California, Hindelang found that the percent of males who reported engaging in an act at least once exceeded the percent of females for 24 delinquent activities; the mean sex ratio was 2.56, which is substantially smaller than official data suggest. Moreover, the mean frequency of delinquent involvement was significantly greater for males than females for all activities except hit-and-run accidents and nonmarijuana drug use. The pattern of delinquent involvement, however, was very similar for males and females; the most and least frequent activities for both sexes were nearly identical. Among females, the most frequent activities were drinking (19.52 percent) and cheating on school exams (14.91 percent); the least frequent activities were gang fighting with weapons (0.69 percent), shaking down others for money (0.80 percent), gang fistfighting (0.82 percent), and using heroin (0.80 percent). Among males, drinking (13.73 percent), minor theft (9.03 percent), and cheating on school exams (8.93 percent) were the most frequent activities, while using heroin (0.36 percent), being involved in hit-and-run accidents (0.53 percent), gang weapon fighting (0.68 percent), shaking down others for money (0.73 percent), and gang fistfighting (0.79 percent) were the least frequent activities. It is interesting to note that engaging in promiscuous sexual behavior contributed only 4.24 percent to the total delinquencies reported by girls and 8.19 percent to those reported by boys. Hindelang also found that the delinquent behavior of his sample tended to be more general than specialized and, further, the delinquent activities of girls were more general than those of boys.

Additional evidence is contained in Kratcoski and Kratcoski's self-report survey of 248 eleventh and twelfth grade students in three public high schools.[67] A much higher percentage of boys than girls reported fist fighting (90 percent v. 38 percent), gambling (79 percent v. 31 percent), and destroying property (53 percent v. 15 percent). A number of offenses were reported by about the same percentages of boys and girls, however, including buying or drinking alcohol, defying parental authority, using drugs, skipping school, and running away from home. This study also found little difference in the mean number of offenses committed by upper-and middle-class boys and girls when compared with their counterparts in the working and lower class.

A recent study by Joseph Weis had findings similar to the studies reported above.[68] Weis investigated the self-reported delinquent involvement of 555 eighth and eleventh grade girls and boys in an upper-middle-class suburb in the San Francisco Bay area. Consistent with previous research, the percent of males within each grade who admitted to an act at least once exceeded the percent of females for most of 34 delinquent activities; however, more eleventh grade girls reported cheating in school and cutting classes than their male counterparts, while more eighth grade girls admitted to cheating in school and defacing walls than boys in the same grade. The mean sex ratio across all 34 activities was 1.95 for eighth grade students and 3.15 for eleventh grade students. Further, the mean frequency of delinquent involvement was greater for males than females with these exceptions: eleventh grade girls engaged more often than eleventh grade boys in cutting classes, cheating in school, shoplifting, and stealing money; eighth grade girls engaged more often than eighth grade boys in cutting classes, cheating in school, shoplifting, curfew violation, and defacing walls. Weis also found that the pattern of involvement was very similar for both sexes. The girls, however, were almost completely non-violent and there seemed to be a small group of boys doing most of the fighting.

A more comprehensive study of self-reported delinquency was conducted by the Illinois Institute for Juvenile Research.[69] Between October, 1971, and April, 1972, a self-administered questionnaire was given to 3,112 fourteen- to eighteen-year-olds in the state of Illinois. Among other things, these youth were asked to respond to a checklist of delinquent behaviors including impropriety, alcohol use, drug use, automobile violations, theft, and violence. Improper behaviors included cheating at school, making anonymous phone calls, truancy, and running away. Within racial groups, there were no major differences between males and females in reporting these behaviors. Only about 15 percent had ever run away from home and less than 4 percent had done so repeatedly. Almost half (46 percent) reported that they had ever been truant and about one-quarter reported that they had been truant more than once or twice.

About equal percentages of white males and females reported drinking but older white males more often reported ever being drunk and purchasing alcohol. Younger nonwhite females were less likely to report drinking or being drunk than younger nonwhite males and nonwhite females of all ages less often purchased alcohol. However, older nonwhite females purchased alcohol more often than older white females, although there was little difference between white and nonwhite females in the proportion reporting serious involvement in alcohol violations. Drug use was similarly distributed among males and females, whites and nonwhites, although heroin was somewhat more likely to be used by nonwhites. About 22 percent reported ever using marijuana. For automobile violations, males were more likely than females to report driving without a license and white males were more likely than white females to report ever driving recklessly. Automobile violations were more often reported by white than nonwhite females.

Theft included petty theft under $2, shoplifting, keeping and using stolen goods, property damage, larceny $20 and over, and breaking and entering. In general, white males reported engaging in theft more often than white females, although sex differences were somewhat smaller among the 14–15-year-olds than the 16–18-year-olds. Also, there were few substantial differences between white males and females who reported engaging in theft more than once or twice. About equal percentages of nonwhite males and females reported ever committing theft, although 14–15-year-old nonwhite females less often reported petty theft and keeping and using stolen goods. There were also few substantial differences between nonwhite males and females who admitted theft more than once or twice. Within racial groups, there were no sex differences for serious theft, except that older white females were less involved than older white males. Older nonwhite females were also more likely than older white females to report serious involvement in theft. Further, lower-class nonwhite females were more often serious theft offenders than white females in that class, although it is probable that more of the nonwhite females lived in conditions of extreme poverty.

The categories of violence surveyed in this study included fistfighting, carrying weapons, gang fighting, using weapons, and strong-arm theft. Within racial groups, males were more involved in violence than females. In general, sex differences were larger for whites than nonwhites in the percentages reporting that they had never been involved in each of the violent acts. For example, 35 percent of white males compared with 79 percent of white females never participated in a fistfight, a difference of 44 percent. The corresponding percentages for nonwhite males and females were 27 percent and 42 percent, respectively, a difference of 15 percent. More males than females also reported engaging in each of the violent acts a few times or often, although sex differences within racial groups were about the same. For example, 7 percent of white females reported engaging in fistfights a few times or often whereas 28 percent of white males had done so. The respective percentages for nonwhite females and males were 23 percent and 44 percent, a difference of 21 percent in both cases.

White females were the least involved in violent acts, with three-quarters reporting none of the violent acts. About equal percentages of nonwhite females and white males, 33 percent and 31 percent, respectively, reported no violent involvement. Nonwhite males were the most likely to engage in violence, with only 22 percent reporting no violent acts. Nonwhite males were also the most likely to report serious levels of involvement (27 percent), followed by nonwhite females (23 percent), white males (16 percent), and white females (5 percent). Nonwhite females were more involved in all forms of violence than white females. For example, 79 percent of white females had never participated in a fistfight compared with 42 percent of nonwhite females, while 93 percent and 68 percent, respectively, had never carried weapons.

The self-reported studies discussed thus far span the period from the mid-1950s to the early 1970s. A comparison across studies of the percentages of girls and boys reporting various delinquent acts shows that delinquency has generally increased somewhat for both sexes.[70] The largest increases occurred for drinking alcohol and drug use, particularly marijuana. We also attempted to determine whether sex differences in delinquency have narrowed by comparing the ratio of the percentage of males who reported engaging in a delinquent act to the percentage of females across all studies. The only clearly discernable narrowing occured for theft under $2. The other offenses either showed no difference in the sex ratio over time or a clear pattern could not be discerned. However, a number of factors make these studies difficult to compare. Among other things, there were differences in sample size, selection, and composition, in the number of kinds of delinquent acts surveyed, in the precise wording of the delinquency items, and in the research techniques.

Therefore, we will turn to recent work by Martin Gold and his colleagues whose studies of self-reported delinquency over time are more amenable to comparison and trend analysis. In 1967, Gold and Williams conducted the first National Survey of Youth intended to determine the seriousness, frequency, and nature of delinquency in the United States.[71] They surveyed 847 teenagers chosen to be representative of all Americans between the ages of 13 and 16. As shown in Table 6, the respondents admitted to a wide range of delinquencies.

These findings tend to confirm official records that suggest boys are more delinquent than girls. In this national survey, that conclusion was especially evident for the more serious property offenses and aggressive behaviors. Little difference was seen, however, for drug use, running away, and hitting parents. As Gold and Haney point out, when striking a parent and running away from home are combined with fornication, they account for only 11 percent of the girls' delinquencies.[72] They contend that, "This demonstrates that the assumption that running away, incorrigibility, and fornication are typical of 'female-style' delinquency is wrong. Boys do their share of these offenses, and

TABLE 6. Percent of Respondents Who Committed Each Offense at Least Once in the Three Years Prior to the Interview[a]

	National Sample	
Offense	Boys	Girls
Trespass	54	24
Drinking	43	29
Theft	54	31
Threatened assault	49	31
Truancy	43	34
Property destruction	48	25
Entering	42	33
Assault	39	15
False I.D.	31	27
Gang fight	34	14
Fraud	23	15
Concealed weapon	12	1
Hitting parents	9	11
UDAA[a]	7	3
Runaway	6	5
Drugs	2	2
Arson	1	0
Extortion	1	0
Armed robbery	0	0

a. Adapted from table appearing in Bill Haney and Martin Gold, "The Juvenile Deliquent Nobody Knows," *Psychology Today,* (September 1973), p. 50.

b. Unauthorized driving away of an automobile.

the girls do their share of stealing, truancy, and other delinquencies."[73] This study also showed that girl delinquency increases steadily with age; older teenage girls not only commit more delinquencies than younger girls, but also engage in more serious law violations.

A second National Survey of Youth conducted in 1972 by Gold and Reimer allows comparisons to be made over time using comparable and representative samples of boys and girls.[74]

Overall, boys in 1972 reported less delinquent behavior than their counterparts in 1967, whereas girls in 1972 reported more delinquent behavior. Further, a seriousness index declined by almost 14 percent for boys, but stayed about the same for girls. Boys in 1972 reported more drug use—mostly marijuana—but less larceny, threatened assault, trespassing, forcible and non-forcible entry, and gang fighting. Girls in 1972 also admitted using drugs—mostly marijuana but also alcohol—more often, while reporting less larceny, property destruction, and breaking and entering. When drinking and marijuana and drug use were excluded, boys showed a 20 percent decline in the number of offenses per capita from 1967 to 1972 while girls showed no change.

Comparisons are also reported for various subgroups of boys and girls differentiated on the basis of race, age, socioeconomic status (SES), and area of residence. The frequency of delinquent behavior declined about the same for white and black males, but only whites showed a decline in seriousness, partly because of a decline in reporting assault and threat behavior among white boys. The increase in frequency was greater among white than blacks girls, largely because of a sharper rise in drinking and in marijuana and drug use among white girls, but seriousness stayed about the same for both groups. Compared with their counterparts in 1967, white girls in 1972 reported more fraud to obtain alcohol, shoplifting, trespassing, drinking, and marijuana and drug use, but less larceny, assault, threat, and breaking and entering. Black girls in 1972 had a higher incidence of carrying a concealed weapon, drinking, and using marijuana and drugs, but a lower incidence of property destruction and gang fighting. In 1967, the most common offense for white girls was truancy, followed by drinking, illegal entry, trespassing, and theft. In 1972, drinking was the most common offense among white girls, followed by truancy, marijuana and drug use, trespassing, and theft. Black girls in 1967 admitted to gang fighting most often, followed by truancy, property destruction, illegal entry, and larceny. In 1972, the most common offense among black girls was truancy, then drinking, shoplifting, fraud, and illegal entry.

Increases in delinquent behavior between 1967 and 1972 were most marked among 15- and 16-year-old girls, largely because of their greater increase in the use of alcohol and marijuana drugs. Fifteen-year-old boys constitute an exception to the overall pattern among boys in that they became slightly more delinquent over time. When drinking and marijuana and drug use were excluded, this increase disappeared but the decline for 13-, 14-, and 16-year-old boys was more striking. For both boys and girls, increases in the use of alcohol and marijuana and drugs were more pronounced at ages 15 and 16. The decline in delinquent behavior among boys tended to be greatest in the lowest SES stratum and smallest in the highest SES stratum. Among boys, the increase in marijuana and drug use was largest in the middle SES stratum while among girls, the rise in marijuana and drug use was fairly uniform across strata. Another exception to the overall pattern among boys occurred in towns. Among this group of boys, the level of delinquent behavior appears to have remained constant, even when drinking and marijuana use were excluded. In rural areas, the level of marijuana and drug use did not change among boys while the increase among rural girls was smaller than in any other area of residence.

Although practically all of the self-report studies available in the literature deal with juveniles, they contribute to our understanding of the picture being painted by official statistics. Self-report studies have indicated for three decades that a great deal of "hidden" female criminality exists. However, while male and female crime rates are closer together than revealed by official statistics, males are still much more involved in criminal activities than females. The individual self-report studies show that delinquency increased among both sexes over the period covered by the studies. Also, the sex ratio decreased for theft under $2 although no other clear patterns could be discerned. The self-report study of comparable and representative samples of girls and boys in 1967 and 1972 showed that delinquency declined among boys but increased among girls due to their greater use of alcohol and marijuana. Self-report studies also show that the pattern of delinquent involvement is very similar for both sexes. In general, girls seem to be involved in the same delinquencies as boys although at a reduced rate. In particular, they suggest that official statistics greatly exaggerate the sexual nature of female delinquency.

How can we explain why official statistics show female delinquency to be largely sexual in nature? It is important to note that officially recorded delinquency is actually officially recognized delinquency, that is, behavior which has been reacted to as delinquent by society's control agents. Along this line, Clayton Hartjen suggests that official criminal statistics measure "the amount of social labeling taking place in any society."[75] From this perspective, official statistics tell us less about the actual incidence and distribution of delinquent behavior than about the labeling activities of officials. In this view, the higher official female rate for sexual misconduct would indicate that girls are more likely than boys to have their sexual behavior labeled as delinquent by others. In other words, it is not that girls are proportionately more involved in sexual offenses than boys, but rather that girls who are sexually active have a much greater probability of being officially handled as delinquent than their male counterparts.

The large number of female arrests for sexual offenses or related charges, such as running away, curfew violations, and incorrigibility, is related to the female sex role. Parents protect their female children to a greater extent than their male children, and are also more anxious about the sexual activity of their female children. It is probable that a parental request for official intervention will more likely occur in the case of a daughter who stays out late, runs away from home, or behaves in other ways that suggest the possibility of sexual activity.[76] It is also probable that police arrest practices are similarly influenced by this double standard. Hoffman-Bustamante suggests, for example, that the police are more likely to stop girls than boys who are out late at night, and may use curfew arrests to control underage prostitution or girls parking with older males.[77]

Some evidence is available concerning arrest practices with male and female juveniles. Thomas Monahan, for example, investigated cases of juvenile offenders who had contact with the police in Philadelphia.[78] Police contact records are kept whether or not an arrest is made. Monahan found that two-thirds of the boys contacted by the police but only one-third of the girls were arrested for major offenses as a whole. Girls were arrested disproportionately less frequently than boys for robbery, burglary, larceny, and auto theft. However, when girls and boys were apprehended by the police for minor offenses, they were arrested in about the same proportions. Within the minor offense category, the police evidenced less willingness to arrest girls than boys who came to their attention for minor assault, disorderly conduct, and vandalism; however, girls who got into the hands of the police for sex offenses were more likely to be arrested than were their male counterparts.

Similar findings are reported by Patricia Miller using the self-report data from the Illinois study.[79] Comparing self-report and arrest data, she found that girls, particularly whites, were "under-arrested" most often for violent and property crimes and least often for "victimless" offenses such as sexual misconduct and drunkenness. She suggests that, "given an apparent reluctance to enforce the law where the offender is female (or, alternatively, a remarkable ability to avoid detection), that reluctance is lowest where the offense is consistent with existing stereotypes about delinquent girls."[80] She also found that black girls compared with whites were arrested in greater approximation to their self-reported delinquent involvement in theft and strong-arm robbery and to a lesser extent in fistfighting and using or carrying a weapon.

Another study by Kathie Teilman and Pierre Landry, Jr., used data from California and Arizona to determine whether girls were overarrested for runaway and incorrigible behaviors.[81] Using the California data, they found that girls made up 45.5

percent of the self-reported runaways but constituted 61.5 percent of those arrested for these offenses, indicating a tendency for girls to be overarrested for runaway compared with boys. In the case of incorrigible, however, the opposite was found, with girls accounting for 29.8 percent of the self-reported cases but only half as many of the arrests. Using the Arizona data, they found that girls were overarrested for runaway and particularly for incorrigible behavior. Girls made up only 47.2 percent of the self-reported incidents of incorrigible behavior but represented 78.1 percent of the self-reported arrests for this offense, a difference of about 31 percent. The authors suggest that the Arizona data should be given more weight since the sample is larger and more representative. They conclude that "the difference in percentages of almost 31% is one that must be taken seriously. Indeed girls seem to be disproportionately arrested for incorrigible behaviors."[82]

It appears that the harsher treatment of girl sexual delinquents continues after arrest. Research indicates that girls are more often detained pending juvenile court proceedings than are boys and for longer periods of time,[83] and that girls referred for juvenile status offenses are more often held in pretrial detention than are girls referred for criminal offenses.[84] Also, it has been found that the juvenile court makes less severe dispositions against girls than boys when they are involved in a criminal offense, but more severe dispositions against girls than boys when they are involved in a juvenile status offense.[85]

Meda Chesney-Lind has further suggested that the juvenile court actively sexualizes offenses committed by girls.[86] She examined the records of the Honolulu Juvenile Court for the years 1929 to 1955 and discovered that about 70 to 80 percent of the girls processed through the court were given gynecological examinations. She comments that:

> The court's specific interest in these examinations was made explicit by the doctor's comments on the forms with regard to the condition of the hymen. Notations such as "hymen ruptured," "hymen torn—admits intercourse," and "hymen intact"

were routine despite the fact that the condition of the hymen is usually irrelevant to health or illness. Further, gynecological examinations were administered even when the female was referred for offenses which did not involve sexuality such as larceny or burglary.[87]

On the basis of this information, specific legal violations were sometimes recast into the broader categories of incorrigibility, running away, or sex delinquency. Thus, a girl originally apprehended for shoplifting may subsequently have appeared in official statistics as a sexual delinquent.

In sum, it appears that researchers have been asking the wrong question about female sexual delinquency. Along this line, Gold has suggested that the question that should guide our theorizing about female delinquency is not "Why do girls rather than boys run away from home, commit sexual offenses, and seriously misbehave at home?" but "Why do girls commit less delinquency of all kinds compared to boys, with the exception of running away from home and striking their parents?"[88]

SEX DIFFERENCES IN CRIME

In 1950, Otto Pollak, recognizing that "the criminality of women is a neglected field of research," published a book, *The Criminality of Women,* which became the major work on the subject for the next quarter of a century.[89] Pollak offers a dissenting opinion concerning the differential involvement of the sexes in criminality. He asserts that official criminal statistics convey a biased account of the illegal behavior of women by reflecting and perpetuating the myth that the incidence of criminal behavior is very much greater among men than among women. He postulates that the discrepancy between male and female crime rates is a statistical artifact that can be attributed to the masked character of female criminality incidental to their culturally defined roles. He argues that women's social roles as homemaker, rearer of children, nurse of the sick, and domestic helper furnish them many opportunities to commit a variety of offenses that may go undetected. For example, he points out that women who kill use poison more than any other means since it can be easily obtained and administered in connection with the homemaker role. Since poison is not easily detectable, the murders committed by women, according to Pollak, are masked more often than those committed by men. He further argues that the cultural distribution of the sex roles affects the nature of women's criminality by channeling her criminal behavior into the types of crimes (shoplifting, thefts by prostitutes, domestic thefts, abortions, perjury, and disturbance of the peace) that are rarely reported to or prosecuted by law enforcement agencies.

It is important to note, however, that this is also the case for many more serious crimes, such as white-collar crimes. Sutherland and Cressey have pointed out that white-collar crimes are extremely widespread and far more dangerous to society than other crimes in their effects on private property and social institutions.[90] However, prosecution is often avoided because the parties concerned are politically or financially important, because the crimes are apparently trivial, because evidence sufficient for prosecution is difficult to secure, particularly when corporations are involved, and because methods other than criminal prosecution may be used. They contend that fraud is the most prevalent crime in America but that many occupations have developed expert techniques of concealment. Hoffman-Bustamante suggests that the bulk of fraud, false advertising, product defects, and occupationally oriented frauds that are not likely to be detected or prosecuted are more often committed by men who are owners or managers of large corporations.[91] Conversely, she suggests that the high arrest rate of women for fraud is due to the fact that women commit the types of fraud that are more easily detected and ones that the police are more likely to investigate such as con games or welfare frauds. Likewise, she suggests that women who embezzle are more likely to be caught than men who embezzle since women generally have lower-status positions, less training and experience in financial manipulations, and less ability to offer restitution.

Pollak also contends that the attributes associated with femaleness, such as passiveness and inactivity, force women in many cases to play the role of instigator rather than performer of the overt criminal act, consequently removing them from apparent connection with the illegal act. No data are offered to support this contention. Walter Reckless buttresses this argument by pointing out that the criminal law is almost exclusively "doer-centered," thus screening women who instigate crimes from contact with official control agencies.[92] In fact, Ward et al., using data from the California Institution for Women, found that women who committed crimes of violence usually acted alone and seldom as instigators, although it could, of course, be argued that women who do act as instigators are unlikely to be caught.[93] Thus, it is difficult to find evidence to either support or refute Pollak's contention.

In summary, Pollak states that:

> If we then further visualize the amount of undetected female homicides, or undetected female accomplices of apprehended male criminals, the unprosecuted crimes of prostitutes because of the noncooperation of the victims with the police, the opportunities for blackmail resulting from the sex mores of our culture, the complete disregard of female homosexuality and of the sex offenses of women committed on children under the cover of child care, their undiscovered wrong accusations against men which land the victims in jail and let the women offenders go free, we have little choice but to accept the conclusion that the numerical sex differential in crime as visualized in the past is a myth.[94]

Most commentators agree that Pollak's argument is overstated. Pollack is probably correct that a large amount of female crime is "hidden." It is also probably correct that a large amount of male crime is "hidden." For example, Pollak contends that women, in their role as childrearer, may commit crimes against children, who are ill equipped to resist and unlikely to report such crimes to the authorities. He overlooks the fact that men may also commit crimes against children as well as against wives. Until recently, wife beating has been a hidden problem; only within the past few years has it been recognized as a problem of substantial proportions. In fact, according to some law enforcement officials, wife beating is the single most underreported crime in the country.[95]

Pollak also discusses false accusations committed by women who allege rape: "The offenders are said to be usually young girls still in the state of pubescence, or women suffering from hysteria."[96] He adds that "the allegation of a sex attack establishes immediate sympathy with the accuser and prejudice against her victim"[97] However, the FBI states that rape is "one of the most underreported crimes . . . due primarily to the victims' fear of their assailants and their sense of embarrassment over the incident."[98] Moreover, a study conducted for the *Washington Post* found that rape was the charge most often dismissed by judges or dropped by prosecutors primarily because corroborative evidence was insufficient; rape cases also took the longest time from arrest to disposition, apparently because of special inherent witness and evidence requirements.[99] An article in the *American Criminal Law Review* has this to say:

> Many commentators still are obsessed by the fear that innocent men are often convicted of rape due to the malice of "sick" women, who either fabricate stories of forcible rape or "trap" men in situations from which they can reasonably infer consent. These fears are largely groundless. It is more likely that guilty assailants escape due to the reluctance of victims to report the crime, police and district attorneys to prosecute, and jurors to convict. Due to the traumatic experience which a victim must go through in order to attempt to secure the attacker's successful prosecution, it is amazing that any rape cases ever come to trial.[100]

Examples of this sort suggest that a great deal of hidden criminality exists for both males and females. It appears that both sexes engage in some kinds of crime that have a low probability of being detected or reported. Thus, while male and female crime rates are closer together than official data indicate, it is highly improbable that they are anywhere near equal.

It appears that a great deal of the difference between male and female involvement in crime lies in what is expected of men and women and in the different social roles they are taught to enact. Because of different socialization and social expectations, being a male in our society has traditionally meant being more active and aggressive, taking greater risks and experiencing more freedom and independence, while the female role has meant the opposite. The customs of our society have dictated that women be inactive and passive, restrained in their activity, and generally excluded from participation in many forms of aggressive behavior. In the United States males have, therefore, been involved in crime more prominently than females because of their social position, a position that has included greater freedom and less supervision than that afforded females. The different social positions of men and women determine how much criminal opportunity they will be exposed to, as well as the intensity of crime producing motivations. Sutherland and Cressey have put it this way:

> Probably the most important difference is that the girls are supervised more carefully and behave in accordance with anti-criminal behavior patterns taught to them with greater care and consistency than in the case of boys. From infancy, girls are taught that they must be nice, while boys are taught that they must be rough and tough; a boy who approaches the behavior of girls is regarded as a "sissy." This difference in care and super-vision presumably rested originally on the fact that the female sex is the one which becomes pregnant. The importance of avoiding the personal and familial consequences of illicit preg-nancy led to special protection of the girl, not only in respect to sex behavior but also in respect to social codes in general.[101]

They point out that the female crime rate is lowest in countries in which females are closely supervised and highest in countries in which females have the greatest freedom and equality with males.

CONCLUSION

In this section we have examined the magnitude and nature of female criminality and delinquency. Examination of arrest and self-report data disclose that females are generally much less involved in criminal activities than males, although self-report data show smaller sex differences than arrest data. Female crime is increasing and females are accounting for a greater share of total arrests, although not dramatically so. The female percent of arrests for violent index crimes has stayed about the same for adult women. While there is some evidence in the UCR that the juvenile female percent of arrests has increased for aggravated and other assault, this appears to have been stabilized in recent years. Moreover, self-report studies of delinquency do not show a decrease in the sex ratio for such violent acts as fist-fighting, gang fighting, and strong-arm theft. The female percent of arrests has increased most dramatically for larceny and fraud and to a lesser extent for forgery and counterfeiting and embezzlement. Among adult women, the female percent of vagrancy arrests has increased while juvenile females are more often involved in running away and liquor law violations.

Both the popular press and some criminologists have suggested that increases in the rates of female crime have been at least influenced if not caused by the women's liberation movement.[102] Others have contended that both increases in female crime rates and the women's movement are consequences of changing economic and social conditions.[103] Both sides have marshalled evidence to support their contentions and the debate has become quite heated at times. In the concluding section, we shall consider the arguments advanced by both sides, review the available empirical work, and come to our own conclusions.

Whatever the "causes" of increasing crime rates among females, it is clear that we have been sensitized to the existence of female criminality and delinquency as social and as sociological problems. Perhaps it is now time for social scientists to direct their attention to the broader range of female criminality, becoming especially concerned with understanding the phenomenon in a context devoid of sexual stereotypes and biases. We have attempted to do that in this book.

NOTES

1. Marcia Millman, "She Did It All for Love: A Feminist View of the Sociology of Deviance," in Marcia Millman and Rosabeth Moss Kanter (eds.), *Another Voice: Feminist Perspectives on Social Life and Social Science* (Garden City, New York: Anchor Books, 1975), p. 253.

2. Anthony Harris, "Sex and Theories of Deviance: Toward a Functional Theory of Deviant Type-Scripts," *American Sociological Review,* 42 (February 1977), pp. 3–16.

3. Ibid., p. 14.

4. Susan Katzenelson, "The Female Offender in Washington, D.C.," unpublished paper, Institute for Law and Social Research (September 1975), p. 8.

5. Clyde B. Vedder and Dora B. Somerville, *The Delinquent Girl* (Springfield, Illinois: Charles C Thomas, 1970).

6. Ibid., p. 147.

7. The predominant opinion in the literature on female delinquency seems to be that charges such as "running away," "incorrigibility," "truancy," and "ungovernability" constitute euphemisms for sexual offenses. For example, Albert J. Reiss states in "Sex Offenses: The Marginal Status of the Adolescent," *Law and Contemporary Problems,* 25 (Spring 1960), p. 311:

> The omnibus provision for "immoral conduct or behavior" can be construed to cover all deviations from sexual conduct norms. The body of legal opinion and decision for delinquent acts similarly reflects considerable ambiguity as to what sexual conduct is to be defined as a violation and what is permitted sexual behavior for adolescents. Juveniles who are held to be guilty of a sex offense often are not charged with a specific sex conduct violation. The categories of "ungovernability," "loitering," "immoral or indecent conduct," "runaway," and similar designations are the preferred charges, particularly if the court has a policy to avoid stigmatizing an individual with a sex offense. The term "sex offense" and "sex offender" are not clearly defined, then, for adolescents in legal codes or in the adjudication of cases involving the violation of sexual conduct norms.

8. President's Commission on Law Enforcement and Administration of Justice, *The Challenge of Crime in a Free Society* (Washington, D.C.: U.S. Government Printing Office, 1967), p. 56.

9. Kristine Olson Rogers, " 'For Her Own Protection . . . ': Conditions of Incarceration for Female Juvenile Offenders in the State of Connecticut," *Law and Society Review,* 7 (Winter 1972), p. 225.

10. Paul Lerman, "Child Convicts," *Trans-Action,* 8 (July/August 1971), p. 35.

11. In the past few years, a number of critical reviews of the literature on female offenders have appeared. See, for example, Dorie Klein, "The Etiology of Female Crime: A Review of the Literature," *Issues in Criminology,* 8 (Fall 1973), pp. 3–30. Reprinted in Part II of this volume; Christine E. Rasche, "The Female Offender as an Object of Criminological Research," *Criminal Justice and Behavior,* 1 (December 1974), pp. 301–320; Nanci Koser Wilson and Constance M. Rigsby, "Is Crime a Man's World? Issues in the Exploration of Criminality," *Journal of Criminal Justice,* 3 (1975), pp. 131–139; Carol Smart, *Women, Crime and Criminology* (London: Routledge and Kegan Paul, 1976); Carol Smart, "Criminological Theory: Its Ideology and Implications Concerning Women," *British Journal of Sociology,* 28 (March 1977), pp. 89–100.

12. Frances Heidensohn, "The Deviance of Women: A Critique and an Enquiry," *British Journal of Sociology,* 19 (June 1968), p. 162.

13. See, for example, Lester David, "'The Gentle Sex? I'd Rather Meet a Cougar!'" *Today's Health* (July 1972), pp. 47ff.; "Women Catching Up with Men in One More Field: Crime," *U.S. News and World Report* (September 23, 1974), pp. 45–48; "The Woman's Touch," *Newsweek* (January 6, 1975), p. 35.

14. Freda Adler, *Sisters in Crime* (New York: McGraw-Hill, 1975), p. 14.

15. Federal Bureau of Investigation, U.S. Department of Justice, *Uniform Crime Reports–1977* (Washington, D.C.: U.S. Government Printing Office, 1978), p. 1ff.

16. Prior to January, 1973, the offenses known to the police definition of larceny-theft was limited to larceny of $50 and over. Since that time, the category has included all larcenies, both over and under $50. The arrest data has always included all larcenies. See Darrell Steffensmeier, "A review and Assessment of Trends in Female Crime, 1965–76," unpublished paper (1978), p. 38, n. 6.

17. See, for example, Marvin E. Wolfgang, "Uniform Crime Reporting: A Critical Appraisal," *University of Pennsylvania Law Review,* III (April 1963), pp. 708–738; Sophia M. Robinson, "A Critical View of the Uniform Crime Reports," *Michigan Law Review,* 64 (April 1966), pp. 1031–1054; James A. Inciardi, "The Uniform Crime Reports: Some Considerations on Their Short-comings and Utility," *Public Data Use,* 6 (November 1978), pp. 3–16.

18. Wesley G. Skogan, "The Validity of Official Crime Statistics: An Empirical Investigation," *Social Science Quarterly,* 55 (June 1974), pp. 25–38.

19. Thorsten Sellin, "The Significance of Records of Crime," in Edwin H. Sutherland and Donald R. Cressey, *Criminology* (Philadelphia: J. B. Lippincott, 1974), pp. 25–26.

20. *Uniform Crime Reports–1977,* op. cit., p. 160.

21. Mary Owen Cameron, *The Booster and the Snitch* (Glencoe, Illinois: The Free Press, 1964), p. 123.

22. Michael J. Hindelang, "Decisions of Shoplifting Victims to Invoke the Criminal Justice Process," *Social Problems,* 21 (April 1974), pp. 580–593.

23. Lawrence E. Cohen and Rodney Stark, "Discriminatory Labeling and the

Five-Finger Discount—An Empirical Analysis of Differential Shoplifting Dispositions," *Journal of Research in Crime and Delinquency*, 11 (January 1974), pp. 25-39.

24. Jerome Skolnick, *Justice Without Trial* (New York: John Wiley, 1966).
25. Ibid., p. 85.
26. Ibid., p. 86.
27. *Uniform Crime Reports—1977*, p. 304.
28. Ibid., p. 30.
29. See note 17.
30. Mary Owen Cameron, op. cit., pp. 56, 71-72, 106, 115, 119.
31. Lawrence E. Cohen and Rodney Stark, op. cit.
32. *Uniform Crime Reports—1977*, p. 28.
33. Ira. J. Silverman, Manual Vega, and A. Leo Gray, "Female Criminality in a Southern City: A Comparison Over the Decade 1962-1972," paper presented at the annual meeting of the American Society of Criminology, Tucson, Arizona (1976).
34. Michael J. Hindelang, "Sex Differences in Criminal Activity," personal communication (1978).
35. Wiliam J. Chambliss, "The Law of Vagrancy," in William J. Chambliss (ed.), *Crime and the Legal Process* (New York: McGraw-Hill, 1969), pp. 51-63.
36. Charles Rosenbleet and Barbara Pariente, "The Prostitution of the Criminal Law," *The American Criminal Law Review*, 11 (Winter 1973), pp. 377-378; 422-427.
37. Ibid., pp. 373-427.
38. B. J. George, Jr., "Legal, Medical and Psychiatric Considerations in the Control of Prostitution," in Leo Kanowitz, *Women and the Law* (Albuquerque: University of New Mexico Press, 1969), p. 17.
39. Edwin H. Sutherland, *White Collar Crime* (New York: The Dryden Press, 1949), p. 9.
40. *Uniform Crime Reports—1977*, p. 304.
41. Dale Hoffman-Bustamante, op. cit., p. 127.
42. *Uniform Crime Reports—1977*, p. 304.
43. Alice Franklin in Freda Adler and Rita James Simon (eds.), *The Criminology of Deviant Women* (Boston: Houghton Mifflin, 1979), pp. 167-170.
44. Embezzlement does, however, meet the definition of white-collar crime proposed by Richard Quinney, "The Study of White Collar Crime: Toward a Reorientation in Theory and Research," *Journal of Criminal Law, Criminology and Police Science*, 55 (June 1964), pp. 208-214. Quinney has suggested that all violations that occur in the course of any occupational activity be included, regardless of the social status of the offender.
45. *Uniform Crime Reports—1977*, p. 304.
46. Rudi G. Denys, "Lady Paperhangers," *The Canadian Journal of Corrections*, 11 (1969), p. 180.
47. R. J. McCaldon, "Lady Paperhangers," *The Canadian Journal of Corrections*, 9 (1967), p. 245.

48. The following offenses are excluded since data was not collected in 1960: arson, vandalism, curfew, and runaways. Embezzlement was included with fraud until 1964.

49. Forcible rape has not been included in Tables 4 and 5 since females account for only about 1 percent of arrests for rape at the present time.

50. William Wattenberg and Frank Saunders, "Sex Differences Among Juvenile Offenders," *Sociology and Social Research*, XXXIX (September-October 1954), pp. 24–31.

51. Charlotte D. Elmott, Jane Criner, and Gertrude Hengerer, *Girls and Young Women in Conflict With the Law in California* (Sacramento, California Committee on the Older Girl and the Law, 1958).

52. Ruth S. Cavan, *Juvenile Delinquency* (Philadelphia: J. B. Lippincott, 1969), pp. 162–163.

53. Katzenelson, op. cit.

54. Dale Hoffman-Bustamante, op. cit., p. 126.

55. Darrell Steffensmeier, op. cit., p. 13.

56. See, for example, the study reported by John P. Clark and Larry L. Tifft, "Polygraph and Interview Validation of Self-Reported Deviant Behavior," *American Sociological Review*, 31 (August 1966), pp. 516–523. See also H. B. Gibson, Sylvia Morrison, and D. J. West, "The Confession of Known Offenses in Response to a Self-Reported Delinquency Schedule," *British Journal of Criminology*, 10 (1970), pp. 277–280.

57. Ruth R. Morris, "Attitudes Toward Delinquency by Delinquents, Non-Delinquents and Their Friends," *British Journal of Criminology*, 5 (July 1965), pp. 249–265.

58. Martin Gold, *Delinquent Behavior in an American City* (Belmont, California: Brooks/Cole, 1970), pp. 19–24.

59. James S. Wallerstein and Clement J. Wyle, "Our Law-abiding Lawbreakers," *National Probation* (March-April 1947), pp. 107–112.

60. James F. Short, Jr., and F. Ivan Nye, "Extent of Unrecorded Delinquency: Tentative Conclusions," *Journal of Criminal Law, Criminology, and Police Science*, 49 (November-December 1958), pp. 296–302.

61. Shirley Merritt Clark, "Systematic Comparison of Female and Male Delinquency," in Walter C. Reckless, *The Crime Problem* (New York: Appleton-Century-Crofts, 1967), pp. 161–164.

62. Martin Gold, op. cit., pp. 61–66.

63. Ibid., p. 118.

64. Nancy B. Wise, "Juvenile Delinquency Among Middle-Class Girls," in Edmund W. Vaz (ed.), *Middle-Class Juvenile Delinquency* (New York: Harper and Row, 1967), pp. 179–188.

65. Gary J. Jensen and Raymond Eve, "Sex Differences in Delinquency: An Examination of Popular Sociological Explanations," *Criminology*, 13 (February 1976), pp. 179–188.

66. Michael J. Hindelang, "Age, Sex, and the Versatility of Delinquent Involvements," *Social Problems*, 18 (Spring 1971), pp. 522–535.

67. Peter C. Kratcoski and John E. Kratcoski, "Changing Patterns in the

Delinquent Activities of Boys and Girls: A Self-reported Delinquency Analysis," paper presented at the annual meeting of the American Sociological Association, New York (1973).

68. Joseph G. Weis, "Middle Class Female Delinquency," paper presented at the annual meeting of the American Society of Criminology, Toronto, Canada (October 1975).

69. Gary Schwartz and Joseph E. Puntil, *Summary and Policy Implications of the Youth and Society in Illinois Reports,* unpublished report, Institute for Juvenile Research (no date).

70. Delinquent acts examined were fist-fighting, strong-arm theft, gang fighting, theft under $2, theft $2–$50, theft $50 and over, drinking alcohol, property damage, truancy, runaway, joyriding, and drug use.

71. Jay R. Williams and Martin Gold, "From Delinquent Behavior to Official Delinquency," *Social Problems,* 20 (Fall 1972), pp. 209–229.

72. Bill Haney and Martin Gold, "The Juvenile Delinquent Nobody Knows," *Psychology Today* (September 1973), pp. 49–55.

73. Ibid., p. 50.

74. Martin Gold and David J. Reimer, "Changing Patterns of Delinquent Behavior among Americans 13 through 16 Years Old: 1967–1972," *Crime and Delinquency Literature* (December 1975), pp. 483–517.

75. Clayton A. Hartjen, *Crime and Criminalization* (New York: Praeger, 1974), p. 160.

76. R. Hale Andrews, Jr., and Andrew H. Cohn, "Ungovernability: The Unjustifiable Jurisdiction," *Yale Law Journal,* 83 (1974), p. 1395, n. 83, 88; p. 1397, n. 95.

77. Dale Hoffman-Bustamante, op. cit., pp. 130–131.

78. Thomas P. Monahan, "Police Dispositions of Juvenile Offenders: The Problem of Measurement and A Study of Philadelphia Data," *Phylon,* XXI (Summer 1970), pp. 138–139.

79. Patricia Y. Miller, "Delinquency and Gender," unpublished paper, Institute for Juvenile Research (no date).

80. Ibid., p. 42.

81. Kathie S. Teilman and Pierre H. Landry, Jr., "Gender Bias in Juvenile Justice," unpublished paper (1978).

82. Ibid., p. 22.

83. See, for example, Meda Chesney-Lind, "Judicial Enforcement of the Female Sex Role: The Family Court and the Female Delinquent," *Issue in Criminology,* 8 (Fall 1973), pp. 56–57; 62–63.

84. Margery L. Velimesis, *Report on the Survey of 41 Pennsylvania County Court and Correctional Services for Women and Girl Offenders,* Section Three, Girls and the Juvenile Court, Pennsylvania Division of the American Association of University Women (April 1969), pp. 26–27.

85. Susan K. Datesman and Frank R. Scarpitti, "Unequal Protection for Males and Females in the Juvenile Court," pp. 59–77 in Theodore N. Ferdinand (ed.), *Juvenile Delinquency: Little Brother Grows Up* (Sage, 1977). Reprinted in Part IV of this volume.

86. Chesney-Lind, op. cit., pp. 51–69.

87. Ibid., p. 56.

88. Gold, op. cit., p. 64.

89. Otto Pollak, *The Criminality of Women* (New York: A. S. Barnes & Company, Inc., 1961). Originally published in 1950.

90. Sutherland and Cressey, op. cit., p. 40–44.

91. Dale Hoffman-Bustamante, op. cit., pp. 127-128.

92. Walter C. Reckless, "Female Criminality," *National Probation and Parole Association Journal*, 3 (January 1957), pp. 1–5.

93. David A. Ward, Maurice Jackson and Renee E. Ward, "Crimes of Violence by Women," in Donald J. Mulvihill, Melvin M. Tumin, and Lynn A. Curtis (eds.), *Crimes of Violence*, 13, A Staff Report Submitted to the National Commission on the Causes and Prevention of Violence (Washington, D.C.: U.S. Government Printing Office, 1969), p. 867. Expected in Part III of this volume.

94. Pollak, op. cit., p. 56.

95. Nancy Loving and Lynn Olson, Proceedings: *National Conference on Women & Crime*, February 26-27, 1976, Washington, D.C., National League of Cities and U.S. Conference of Mayors (1976), p. 61.

96. Otto Pollak, op. cit., p. 25.

97. Ibid.

98. *Uniform Crime Reports—1977*, p. 14.

99. Eugene L. Meyer, "Plea Bargaining is Found to be Rare in Rape Cases," *The Washington Post* (June 11, 1975).

100. Pamela Lakes Wood, "Note, The Victim in a Forcible Rape Case: A Feminist View," *The American Criminal Law Review*, 11 (Winter 1973), p. 335.

101. Sutherland and Cressey, op. cit., p. 130.

102. See, for example, "Serious Crimes by Women Rise 80 Percent, Liberation Movement Blamed," Globe and Mail, Toronto (March 1, 1973) in Ellen Rosenblatt and Cyril Greenland, "Female Crimes of Violence," *Canadian Journal of Criminology and Corrections*, 16 (April 1974), p. 8, n. 4; Adler, op. cit.

103. See, for example, Joseph G. Weis, "Liberation and Crime: The Invention of the New Female Criminal," *Crime and Social Justice* (Fall-Winter 1976), pp. 17–27 and Laurel L. Rans, "Women's Crime: Much Ado About. . . ?" *Federal Probation*, XXXXII (March 1978), pp. 45–49.

The Etiology of Female Crime

According to a report submitted to the National Commission on the Causes and Prevention of Violence, "Our knowledge of the causes and correction of female criminality is at the same stage of development that characterized our knowledge of male criminiality some thirty or more years ago."[1] While there has been an evolution in theories of male criminality from Lombrosian positivism to the newer conflict and critical theories, this evolution has been largely absent in theories of female criminality. Most theorists have emphasized the biological and psychological aspects of female criminality. There has also been a tendency to regard male criminality as a much more complex phenomenon than female criminality. Further, as Dorie Klein points out, most theorists have made assumptions about the inherent nature of women and have touched only tangentially, if at all, on the larger social, economic, and political forces affecting female criminality. In "The Etiology of Female Crime: A Review of the Literature," Klein critically examines classical studies of female criminality, including Lombroso, W.I. Thomas, Freud, Kingsley Davis, and Otto Pollak, and emphasizes the continuity between these works and contemporary works. She suggests that future

research on the etiology of female criminality break with traditional assumptions and employ a feminist perspective.

A biological factor that continues to be linked to female
criminality is the menstrual cycle. In the late nineteenth century,
Lombroso and Ferrero found that 71 out of 80 women were
menstruating when they were arrested for resistance against
public officials.[2] Similarly, a study conducted over three-quarters
of a century later at the North Carolina Correctional Center for
Women found that the frequency of aggressive acts by inmates
increased during the premenstrual and early menstrual phases
of the cycle.[3] The authors state that:

> In the case of the woman who kills or maims her husband, lover,
> child or other relative or who is killed or maimed, this study
> suggests that it is important to ask the question: What was her
> menstrual condition at the time of the event?[4]

The study was among those cited in a 1971 article appearing in
the *UCLA Law Review* to demonstrate the relationship between
the premenstrual syndrome and female criminal behavior.[5] The
authors of this article argue that female criminal defendants
suffering from the premenstrual syndrome could raise defenses
founded upon insanity, diminished capacity, and unconscious-
ness, or use the premenstrual syndrome as a means to mitigate
punishment. In a recent review of the literature on the link
between menstruation and crime, Julie Horney contends that
methodological problems make the interpretation of this research questionable.[6] For example, there are problems with
whether women can accurately recall menstrual cycle data from
memory and with the representativeness of the results. In
addition, she suggests that antisocial and criminal behavior may
produce the hormonal changes associated with the menstrual
cycle rather than the converse. For example:

> If a woman were quickly arrested and jailed after committing a
> crime and that trauma brought on early menstruation, a later
> calculation would indicate that the woman had been in the
> premenstrual phase of her cycle at the time of the criminal
> behavior.[7]

Horney therefore concludes that an insanity defense based on the premenstrual syndrome is inappropriate.

Role theory represents an attempt to explain female criminality in other than biological or psychological terms. In "Female Deviance and the Female Sex Role: A Preliminary Investigation," Karen Rosenblum analyzes the relationship of the female sex role to the call girl form of prostitution, utilizing Edwin Lemert's concepts of primary and secondary deviance. Primary deviance is an act of sheer rule-violation while secondary deviance arises from the societal reaction to primary deviance. "The secondary deviant . . . is a person whose life and identity are organized around the facts of deviance."[8] Rosenblum contends that elements of primary deviance are contained within the female sex role in that women are socialized to employ their sexuality for gain in nonsexual interaction. It is suggested that the transition from primary to secondary deviance within prostitution requires only an exaggeration of this situation.

In "Female Delinquency and Broken Homes: A Reassessment," Susan Datesman and Frank Scarpitti reexamine the relationship between the broken home and female delinquency. The relationship between delinquency and broken homes has been investigated throughout this century. In her review of these studies, Karen Wilkinson states that, "Although the research on the broken home and male delinquency has yielded somewhat inconsistent results, the relationship between the broken home and female delinquency has been consistently supported."[9] The study by Datesman and Scarpitti is one of the few studies to have examined the relationship between female delinquency and broken homes by type of offense. They found that the higher incidence of broken homes among female delinquents when type of offense is not controlled represents their greater involvement in public policy offenses such as ungovernability, running away, and promiscuity. Since this study uses official data, it is likely that the relationship between delinquency and broken homes is confounded by the referral decision. For example, a much higher proportion of juvenile females than males charged with ungovernability and running away were referred to court by parents or relatives. A family that is in some way "broken" may be more likely to refer their female children to court, on the assumption that they need greater supervision than one parent can provide. Further examination of this relationship using various measures of broken homes and self-report delinquency data is necessary before more firm conclusions can be drawn.

It has been argued by some that recent increases in female criminality can be linked with the emancipation of women. Freda Adler discusses this relationship in "The Interaction Between Women's Emancipation and Female Criminality: A Cross-cultural Perspective." Adler contends that American women have become involved in all categories of crime as they have moved into male positions. She further contends that cross-national data show that decreases in the social and economic disparities between the sexes are correlated with increases in female criminality. Not all of her data, however, support this thesis. For example, females have accounted for approximately 5 percent of all persons prosecuted in Finland since 1950 and increases have been about the same for both males (53 percent) and females (55 percent). Also, the female percent of total convictions in Poland increased between 1932 and 1951 but decreased between 1951 and 1972. Adler reasons that traditional normative controls may have continued to operate to limit female criminality in Poland. In any case, these data suggest that the relationship between women's emancipation and female criminality is not a simple one. This relationship will be examined at length in Part V of this volume.

NOTES

1. David A. Ward, Maurice Jackson, and Renee E. Ward, "Crimes of Violence by Women," in Donald J. Mulvihill, Melvin M. Tumin, and Lynn A. Curtis

(eds.), *Crimes of Violence,* 13, A Staff Report Submitted to the National Commission on the Causes and Prevention of Violence (Washington, D.C.: U.S. Government Printing Office, 1969), p. 847.

2. Julie Horney, "Menstrual Cycles and Criminal Responsibility," paper presented at the annual meeting of the American Society of Criminology, Dallas, Texas (November 1978), pp. 5–6.

3. Desmond P. Ellis and Penelope Austin, "Menstruation and Aggressive Behavior in a Correctional Center for Women," *Journal of Criminal Law, Criminology and Police Science,* 62 (1971), pp. 388–395.

4. Ibid., p. 395.

5. Aleta Wallach and Larry Rubin, "The Premenstrual Syndrome and Criminal Responsibility," *UCLA Law Review,* 19 (1971), pp. 209–312.

6. Julie Horney, op. cit.

7. Ibid., p. 19.

8. Edwin M. Lemert, *Human Deviance, Social Problems, and Social Control* (Englewood Cliffs, New Jersey: Prentice-Hall, Inc., 1967), pp. 40–41.

9. Karen Wilkinson, "The Broken Family and Juvenile Delinquency: Scientific Explanation or Ideology?" *Social Problems,* 21 (June 1974), pp. 736–737.

The Etiology of Female Crime:
A Review of the Literature

Dorie Klein

INTRODUCTION

The criminality of women has long been a neglected subject area of criminology. Many explanations have been advanced for this, such as women's low official rate of crime and delinquency and the preponderance of male theorists in the field. Female criminality has often ended up as a footnote to works on men that purport to be works on criminality in general.

There has been, however, a small group of writings specifically concerned with women and crime. This paper will explore those works concerned with the etiology of female crime and delinquency, beginning with the turn-of-the-century writing of Lombroso and extending to the present. Writers selected to be included have been chosen either for their influence on the field, such as Lombroso, Thomas, Freud, Davis, and Pollak, or because they are representative of the kinds of work being published, such as Konopka, Vedder and Somerville, and Cowie, Cowie and

Dorie Klein, "The Etiology of Female Crime: A Review of the Literature," *Issues in Criminology*, Vol. 8, No. 2, (Fall 1973), pp. 3–30. © Crime and Social Justice, P.O. Box 4373, Berkeley, CA., 94704. Reprinted by permission.

I wish to acknowledge the major contributions made by the Women's Caucus of the School of Criminology, University of California, Berkeley.

Slater. The emphasis is on the continuity between these works, because it is clear that, despite recognizable differences in analytical approaches and specific theories, the authors represent a tradition to a great extent. It is important to understand, therefore, the shared assumptions made by the writers that are used in laying the groundwork for their theories.

The writers see criminality as the result of *individual* characteristics that are only peripherally affected by economic, social and political forces. These characteristics are of a *physiological* or *psychological* nature and are uniformly based on implicit or explicit assumptions about the *inherent nature of women.* This nature is *universal,* rather than existing within a specific historical framework.

Since criminality is seen as an individual activity, rather than as a condition built into existing structures, the focus is on biological, psychological, and social factors that would turn a woman toward criminal activity. To do this, the writers create two distinct classes of women: good women who are "normal" noncriminals, and bad women who are criminals, thus taking a moral position that often masquerades as a scientific distinction. The writers, although they may be biological or social determinists to varying degrees, assume that individuals have *choices* between criminal and noncriminal activity. They see persons as atomistically moving about in a social and political vacuum; many writers use marketplace models for human interaction.

Although the theorists may differ on specific remedies for individual criminality, ranging from sterilization to psychoanalysis (but always stopping far short of social change), the basic thrust is toward *individual adjustment,* whether it be physical or mental, and the frequent model is rehabilitative therapy. Widespread environmental alterations are usually included as casual footnotes to specific plans for individual therapy. Most of the writers are concerned with *social harmony* and the welfare of the existing social structure rather than with the women involved or with women's position in general. None of the writers come from anything near a "feminist" or "radical" perspective.

In *The Female Offender,* originally published in 1903, Lombroso described female criminality as an inherent tendency produced in individuals that could be regarded as biological atavisms, similar to cranial and facial features, and one could expect a withering away of crime if the atavistic people were prohibited from breeding. At this time criminality was widely regarded as a physical ailment, like epilepsy. Today, Cowie, Cowie and Slater (1968) have identified physical traits in girls who have been classified as delinquent, and have concluded that certain traits, such as bigness, may lead to aggressiveness. This theme of physiological characteristics has been developed by a good number of writers in the last seventy years, such as the Gluecks (1934). One sees at the present time a new surge of "biological" theories of criminality; for example, a study involving "violence-prone" women and menstrual cycles has recently been proposed at UCLA.[1]

Thomas, to a certain degree, and Freud extend the physiological explanation of criminality to propose a psychological theory. However, it is critical to understand that these psychological notions are based on assumptions of universal *physiological* traits of women, such as their reproductive instinct and passivity, that are seen as invariably producing certain psychological reactions. Women may be viewed as turning to crime as a *perversion of* or *rebellion against* their *natural feminine roles.* Whether their problems are biological, psychological, or social-environmental, the point is always to return them to their roles. Thomas (1907; 1923), for example, points out that poverty might prevent a woman from marrying, whereby she would turn to prostitution as an alternative to carry on her feminine service role. In fact, Davis (1961) discusses prostitution as a parallel illegal institution to marriage. Pollak (1950) discusses how women extend their service roles into criminal activity due to inherent tendencies such as deceitfulness. Freud (1933; Jones, 1961) sees any kind of rebellion as the result of a failure to develop healthy feminine attitudes, such as narcissism, and

Konopka (1966) and Vedder and Somerville (1970) apply Freudian thought to the problem of female delinquency.

The specific characteristics ascribed to women's nature and those critical to theories of female criminality are uniformly *sexual* in their nature. Sexuality is seen as the root of female behavior and the problem of crime. Women are defined as sexual beings, as sexual capital in many cases, physiologically, psychologically and socially. This definition *reflects* and *reinforces* the economic position of women as reproductive and domestic workers. It is mirrored in the laws themselves and in their enforcement, which penalize sexual deviations for women and may be more lenient with economic offenses committed by them, in contrast to the treatment given men. The theorists accept the sexual double standard inherent in the law, often noting that "chivalry" protects women, and many of them build notions of the universality of *sex repression* into their explanations of women's position. Women are thus the sexual backbone of civilization.

In setting hegemonic standards of conduct for all women, the theorists define *femininity,* which they equate with healthy femaleness, in classist, racist, and sexist terms, using their assumptions of women's nature, specifically their sexuality, to justify what is often in reality merely a defense of the existing order. Lombroso, Thomas, and Freud consider the upper-class white woman to be the highest expression of femininity, although she is inferior to the upper-class white man. These standards are adopted by later writers in discussing femininity. To most theorists, women are inherently inferior to men at masculine tasks such as thought and production, and therefore it is logical that their sphere should be reproductive.

Specific characteristics are proposed to bolster this sexual ideology, expressed for example by Freud, such as passivity, emotionalism, narcissism, and deceitfulness. In the decisions of criminality, certain theorists, such as Pollak, link female criminality to these traits. Others see criminality as an attempt away from femininity into masculinity, such as Lombroso, although the specifics are often confused. Contradictions can be clearly seen, which are explained by the dual nature of "good" and "bad" women and by the fact that this is a mythology attempting to explain real behavior. Many explanations of what are obviously economically motivated offenses, such as prostitution and shoplifting, are explained in sexual terms, such as prostitution being promiscuity, and shoplifting being "kleptomania" caused by women's inexplicable mental cycles tied to menstruation. Different explanations have to be made for "masculine" crimes, e.g., burglary, and for "feminine" crimes, e.g., shoplifting. Although this distinction crops up consistently, the specifics differ wildly.

The problem is complicated by the lack of knowledge of the epidemiology of female crime, which allows such ideas as "hidden crime," first expressed by Pollak (1950), to take root. The problem must be considered on two levels: women, having been confined to certain tasks and socialized in certain ways, are *in fact* more likely to commit crime related to their lives, which are sexually oriented; yet even nonsexual offenses are *explained* in sexual terms by the theorists. The writers ignore the problems of poor and Third World women, concentrating on affluent white standards of femininity. The experiences of these overlooked women, who *in fact* constitute a good percentage of women caught up in the criminal justice system, negate the notions of sexually motivated crime. These women have real economic needs which are not being met, and in many cases engage in illegal activities as a viable economic alternative. Furthermore, chivalry has never been extended to them.

The writers largely ignore the problems of sexism, racism, and class, thus their work is sexist, racist, and classist in its implications. Their concern is adjustment of the woman to society, not social change. Hence, they represent a tradition in criminology and carry along a host of assumptions about women and humanity in general. It is important to explore these assumptions and traditions in depth in order to understand what kinds of myths have been propagated around women and crime. The discussions of each writer or writers will focus on these assumptions and their relevance to criminological theories. These assumptions of universal, biological/psychological characteristics, of individual responsibility for crime, of the necessity for maintaining social harmony, and of the benevolence of the state link different theories along a continuum, transcending political labels and minor divergences. The road from Lombroso to the present is surprisingly straight.

LOMBROSO: "THERE MUST BE SOME ANOMALY. . . ."

Lombroso's work on female criminality (1920) is important to consider today despite the fact that his methodology and conclusions have long been successfully discredited. Later writings on female crime by Thomas, Davis, Pollak, and others use more sophisticated methodologies and may proffer more palatable liberal theories. However, to varying degrees they rely on those sexual ideologies based on *implicit* assumptions about the physiological and psychological nature of women that are *explicit* in Lombroso's work. Reading the work helps to achieve a better understanding of what kinds of myths have been developed for women in general and for female crime and deviance in particular.

One specific notion of women offered by Lombroso is women's physiological immobility and psychological passivity, later elaborated by Thomas, Freud, and other writers. Another ascribed characteristic is the Lombrosian notion of women's adaptability to surroundings and their capacity for survival as being superior to that of men. A third idea discussed by Lombroso is women's amorality: they are cold and calculating. This is developed by Thomas (1923), who describes women's manipulation of the male sex urge for ulterior pruposes; by Freud (1933), who sees women as avenging their lack of a penis on men; and by Pollak (1950), who depicts women as inherently deceitful.

When one looks at these specific traits, one sees contradictions. The myth of compassionate women clashes with their reputed coldness; their frailness belies their capacity to survive. One possible explanation for these contradictions is the duality of sexual ideology with regard to "good" and "bad" women.[2] Bad women are whores, driven by lust for money or for men, often essentially *"masculine"* in their orientation, and perhaps afflicted with a touch of penis envy. Good women are chaste, "feminine," and usually not prone to criminal activity. But when they are, they commit crime in a most *ladylike* way such as poisoning. In more sophisticated theory, all women are seen as having a bit of both tendencies in them. Therefore, women can be compassionate *and* cold, frail *and* sturdy, pious *and* amoral, depending on which path they choose to follow. They are seen as rational (although they are irrational, too!), atomistic individuals making choices in a vacuum, prompted only by personal, physiological/psychological factors. These choices relate only to the *sexual* sphere. Women have no place in any other sphere. Men, on the other hand, are not held sexually accountable, although, as Thomas notes (1907), they are held responsible in *economic* matters. Men's sexual freedom is justified by the myth of masculine, irresistible sex urges. This myth, still worshipped today, is frequently offered as a rationalization for the existence of prostitution and the double standard. As Davis maintains, this necessitates the parallel existence of classes of "good" and "bad" women.

These dual moralities for the sexes are outgrowths of the economic, political, and social *realities* for men and woman. Women are primarily workers within the family, a critical institution of reproduction and socialization that services such basic needs as food and shelter. Laws and codes of behavior for women thus attempt to maintain the smooth functioning of women in that role, which requires that women act as a conservative force in the continuation of the nuclear family. Women's main tasks are sexual, and the law embodies sexual limitations for women, which do not exist for men, such as the prohibition of promiscuity for girls. This explains why theorists of female criminality are not only concerned with sexual violations by female offenders, but attempt to account for even *nonsexual* offenses, such as prostitution, in sexual terms, e.g., women enter prostitution for sex rather than for money. Such women are not only economic offenders but are sexual deviants, falling neatly into the category of "bad" women.

The works of Lombroso, particularly *The Female Offender* (1920), are a foremost example of the biological explanation of crime. Lombroso deals with crime as an atavism, or survival of "primitive" traits in individuals, particularly those of the female and nonwhite races. He theorizes that individuals develop differentially within sexual and racial limitations which differ hierarchically from the most highly developed, the white men, to the most primitive, the nonwhite women. Beginning with the assumption that criminals must be atavistic, he spends a good deal of time comparing the crania, moles, heights, etc., of convicted criminals and prostitutes with those of normal women. Any trait that he finds to be more common in the "criminal" group is pronounced an atavistic trait, such as moles, dark hair, etc., and women with a number of these telltale traits could be regarded as potentially criminal, since they are of the atavistic type. He specifically rejects the idea that some of these traits, for example obesity in prostitutes, could be the *result* of their activities rather than an indicator of their propensity to them. Many of the traits depicted as "anomalies," such as darkness and shortness, are characteristic of certain racial groups, such as the Sicilians, who undoubtedly comprise an oppressed group within Italy and form a large part of the imprisoned population.

Lombroso traces an overall pattern of evolution in the human species that accounts for the uneven development of groups: the white and nonwhite races, males and females, adults and children. Women, children, and nonwhites share many traits in common. There are fewer variations in their mental capacities: "Even the female criminal is monotonous and uniform compared with her male companion, just as in general woman is inferior to man" (Ibid.:122), due to her being "atavistically nearer to her origin than the male" (Ibid.:107). The notion of women's mediocrity, or limited range of mental possibilities, is a recurrent one in the writings of the twentieth century. Thomas and others note that women comprise "fewer geniuses, fewer lunatics, and fewer morons" (Thomas, 1907:45); lacking the imagination to be at either end of the spectrum, they are conformist and dull . . . not due to social, political, or economic constraints on their activities, but because of their innate physiological limitations as a sex. Lombroso attributes the lower female rate of criminality to their having fewer anomalies, which is one aspect of their closeness to the lower forms of less differentiated life.

Related characteristics of women are their passivity and conservatism. Lombroso admits that women's traditional sex roles in the family bind them to a more sedentary life. However, he insists that women's passivity can be directly traced to the "immobility of the ovule compared with the zoosperm" (1920: 109), falling back on the sexual act in an interesting anticipation of Freud.

Women, like the lower races, have greater powers of endurance and resistance to mental and physical pain than men. Lombroso states: "Denizens of female prisoners . . . have reached the age of 90, having lived within those walls since they were 29 without any grave injury to health" (Ibid.:125). Denying the humanity of women by denying their capability for suffering justifies exploitation of women's energies by arguing for their suitability to hardship. Lombroso remarks that "a duchess can adapt herself to new surroundings and become a washerwoman much more easily than a man can transform himself under analogous conditions" (Ibid.:272). The theme of women's adaptability to physical and social surroundings, which are male initiated, male controlled, and often expressed by saying that women are actually the "stronger" sex, is a persistent thread in writings on women.

Lombroso explains that because women are unable to feel pain, they are insensitive to the pain of others and lack moral refinement. His blunt denial of the age-old myth of women's compassion and sensitivity is modified, however, to take into account women's low crime rate:

> Women have many traits in common with children; that their moral sense is deficient; that they are revengeful, jealous. . . . In ordinary cases these defects are neutralized by piety, maternity, want of passion, sexual coldness, weakness and an undeveloped intelligence. (Ibid.:151)

Although women lack the higher sensibilities of men, they are thus restrained from criminal activity in most cases by lack of intelligence and passion, qualities which *criminal* women possess as well as all *men*. Within this framework of biological limits of women's nature, the female offender is characterized as *masculine* whereas the normal woman is *feminine*. The anomalies of skull, physiognomy, and brain capacity of female criminals, according to Lombroso, more closely approximate that of man, normal or criminal, than they do those of the normal woman; the female offender often has a "virile cranium" and considerable body hair. Masculinity in women is an anomaly itself, rather than a sign of development, however. A related notion is developed by Thomas, who notes that in "civilized" nations the sexes are more physically different.

> What we look for most in the female is femininity, and when we find the opposite in her, we must conclude as a rule that there must be some anomaly. . . . Virility was one of the special features of the savage woman. . . . In the portraits of Red Indian and Negro beauties, whom it is difficult to recognize for women, so huge are their jaws and cheek bones, so hard and coarse their features, and the same is often the case in their crania and brains. (Ibid.:112)

The more highly developed races would therefore have the most feminized women with the requisite passivity, lack of passion, etc. This is a *racist* and *classist* definition of femininity—just as are almost all theories of *femininity* and as, indeed, is the thing itself. The ideal of the lady can only exist in a society built on the exploitation of labor to maintain the woman of leisure who can *be* that ideal lady.

Finally, Lombroso notes women's lack of *property sense,* which contributes to their criminality.

> In their eyes theft is . . . an audacity for which account compensation is due to the owner . . . as an individual rather than a social crime, just as it was regarded in the primitive periods of human evolution and is still regarded by many uncivilized nations. (Ibid.:217)

One may question this statement on several levels. Can it be assumed to have any validity at all, or is it false that women have a different sense of property than men? If it is valid to a degree, is it related to women's lack of property ownership and nonparticipation in the accumulation of capitalist wealth? Indeed, as Thomas (1907) points out, women are considered property themselves. At any rate, it is an interesting point in Lombroso's book that has only been touched on by later writers, and always in a manner supportive of the institution of private property.

THOMAS: "THE STIMULATION SHE CRAVES"

The works of W. I. Thomas are critical in that they mark a transition from purely physiological explanations such as Lombroso's to more sophisticated theories that embrace physiological, psychological, and social-structural factors. However, even the most sophisticated explanations of female crime rely on implicit assumptions about the *biological* nature of women. In Thomas' *Sex and Society* (1907) and *The Unadjusted Girl*

(1923), there are important contradictions in the two approaches that are representative of the movements during that period between publication dates: a departure from biological Social-Darwinian theories to complex analyses of the interaction between society and the individual, i.e., societal repression and manipulation of the "natural" wishes of persons.

In *Sex and Society* (1907), Thomas poses basic biological differences between the sexes as his starting point. Maleness is "katabolic," the animal force which is destructive of energy and allows men the possibility of creative work through this outward flow. Femaleness is "anabolic," analogous to a plant which stores energy, and is motionless and conservative. Here Thomas is offering his own version of the age-old male/female dichotomy expressed by Lombroso and elaborated on in Freud's paradigm, in the structural-functionalist "instrumental-expressive" duality, and in other analyses of the status quo. According to Thomas, the dichotomy is most highly developed in the more civilized races, due to the greater differentiation of sex roles. This statement ignores the hard physical work done by poor *white* women at home and in the factories and offices in "civilized" countries, and accepts a *ruling-class* definition of femininity.

The cause of women's relative decline in stature in more "civilized" countries is a subject on which Thomas is ambivalent. At one point he attributes it to the lack of "a superior fitness on the motor side" in women (Ibid.:94); at another point, he regards her loss of *sexual freedom* as critical, with the coming of monogamy and her confinement to sexual tasks such as wifehood and motherhood. He perceptively notes:

> Women were still further degraded by the development of property and its control by man, together with the habit of treating her as a piece of property, whose value was enhanced if its purity was assured. (Ibid.:297)

However, Thomas' underlying assumptions in his explanations of the inferior status of women are *physiological* ones. He attributes to men high amounts of sexual energy, which lead them to pursue women for their sex, and he attributes to women maternal feelings devoid of sexuality, which lead *them* to exchange sex for domesticity. Thus monogamy, with chastity for women, is the *accommodation* of these basic urges, and women are domesticated while men assume leadership, in a true market exchange.

Why, then, does Thomas see problems in the position of women? It is because modern women are plagued by "irregularity, pettiness, ill health, and inserviceableness" (Ibid.:245). Change is required to maintain *social harmony*, apart from considerations of women's needs, and women must be educated to make them better wives, a theme reiterated throughout this century by "liberals" on the subject. Correctly anticipating a threat, Thomas urges that change be made to stabilize the family, and warns that "no civilization can remain the highest if another civilization adds to the intelligence of its men the intelligence of its women" (Ibid.:314). Thomas is motivated by considerations of social integration. Of course, one might question how women are to be able to contribute much if they are indeed anabolic. However, due to the transitional nature of Thomas' work, there are immense contradictions in his writing.

Many of Thomas' specific assertions about the nature of women are indistinguishable from Lombroso's; they both delineate a biological hierarchy along race and sex lines.

> Man has, in short, become more somatically specialized an animal than women, and feels more keenly any disturbance of normal conditions with which he has not the same physiological surplus as woman with which to meet the disturbance. . . . It is a logical fact, however, that the lower human races, the lower classes of society, women, and children show something of the same quality in their superior tolerance of surgical disease. (Ibid:36).

Like Lombroso, Thomas is crediting women with superior capabilities of survival because they are further down the scale in terms of evolution. It is significant that Thomas includes the lower classes in his observation; is he implying that the lower classes are in their position *because* of their natural unfitness, or perhaps that their *situation* renders them less sensitive to pain? At different times, Thomas implies both. Furthermore, he agrees with Lombroso that women are more nearly uniform than men, and says that they have a smaller percentage of "genius, insanity, and idiocy" (Ibid.: 45) than men, as well as fewer creative outbursts of energy.

Dealing with female criminality in *Sex and Society* (1907), Thomas begins to address the issue of morality, which he closely links to legality from a standpoint of maintaining social order. He discriminates between male and female morality:

> Morality as applied to men has a larger element of the contractual, representing the adjustment of his activities to those of society at large, or more particularly to the activities of the male members of society; while the morality which we think of in connection with women shows less of the contractual and more of the personal, representing her adjustment to men, more particularly the adjustment of her person to men. (Ibid.:172)

Whereas Lombroso barely observes women's lack of participation in the institution of private property, Thomas' perception is more profound. He points out that women *are* property of men and that their conduct is subject to different codes.

> Morality, in the most general sense, represents the code under which activities are best carried on and is worked out in the school of experience. It is preeminently an adult and male system, and men are intelligent enough to realize that neither women nor children have passed through this school. It is on this account that man is merciless to woman from the standpoint of personal behavior, yet he exempts her from anything in the way of contractual morality, or views her defections in this regard with allowance and even with amusement.(Ibid.:234)

Disregarding his remarks about intelligence, one confronts the critical point about women with respect to the law: because they occupy a *marginal* position in the productive sphere of exchange commodities outside the home, they in turn occupy a marginal position in regard to "contractual" law which regulates relations of property and production. The argument of differential treatment of men and women by the law is developed in later works by Pollak and others, who attribute it to the "chivalry" of the system which is lenient to women committing offenses. As Thomas notes, however, women are simply not a serious *threat* to property, and are treated more "leniently" because of this. Certain women do become threats by transcending (or by being denied) their traditional role, particularly many Third World women and political rebels, and they are *not* afforded chivalrous treatment! In fact, chivalry is reserved for the women who are least likely to ever come in contact with the criminal justice system: the ladies, or white middle-class women. In matters of *sexual* conduct, however, which embody the double standard, women are rigorously prosecuted by the law. As Thomas understands, this is the sphere in which women's functions *are* critical. Thus it is not a matter of "chivalry" how one is handled, but of different forms and thrusts of social control applied to men and women. Men are engaged in productive tasks and their activities in this area *are* strictly curtailed.

In *The Unadjusted Girl* (1923), Thomas deals with female delinquency as a "normal" response under certain social conditions, using assumptions about the nature of women which he leaves unarticulated in this work. Driven by basic "wishes," an individual is controlled by society in her activities through institutional transmission of codes and mores. Depending on how they are manipulated, wishes can be made to serve social or antisocial ends. Thomas stresses the institutions that socialize, such as the family, giving people certain "definitions of the situation." He confidently—and defiantly—asserts:

> There is no individual energy, no unrest, no type of wish, which cannot be sublimated and made socially useful. From this standpoint, the problem is not the right of society to protect itself from the disorderly and antisocial person, but the right of the disorderly and antisocial person to be made orderly and socially valuable. . . . The problem of society is to produce the right attitudes in its members. (Ibid.:232-233)

This is an important shift in perspective, from the traditional libertarian view of protecting society by punishing transgressors, to the *rehabilitative* and *preventive* perspective of crime control that seeks to control *minds* through socialization rather than to merely control behavior through punishment. The autonomy of the individual to choose is seen as the product of his environment which the state can alter. This is an important refutation of the Lombrosian biological perspective, which maintains that there are crime-prone individuals who must be locked up, sterilized, or otherwise incapacitated. Today, one can see an amalgamation of the two perspectives in new theories of "behavior control" that use tactics such as conditioning and brain surgery, combining biological and environmental viewpoints.[3]

Thomas proposes the manipulation of individuals through institutions to prevent antisocial attitudes, and maintains that there is no such person as the "crime prone" individual. A hegemonic system of belief can be imposed by sublimating natural urges and by correcting the poor socialization of slum families. In this perspective, the *definition* of the situation rather than the situation *itself* is what should be changed; a situation is what someone *thinks* it is. The response to a criminal woman who is dissatisfied with her conventional sexual roles is to change not the roles, which would mean widespread social transformations, but to change her attitudes. This concept of civilization as repressive and the need to adjust is later refined by Freud.

Middle-class women, according to Thomas, commit little crime because they are socialized to sublimate their natural desires and to behave well, treasuring their chastity as an investment. The poor woman, however, "is not immoral, because this implies a loss of morality, but amoral" (Ibid.:98). Poor women are not objectively driven to crime; they long for it. Delinquent girls are motivated by the desire for excitement or "new experience," and forget the repressive urge of "security." However, these desires are well within Thomas' conception of *femininity:* delinquents are not rebelling against womanhood, as Lombroso suggests, but merely acting it out illegally. Davis and Pollak agree with this notion that delinquent women are not "different" from nondelinquent women.

Thomas maintains that it is not sexual desire that motivates delinquent girls, for they are no more passionate than other women, but they are *manipulating* male desires for sex to achieve their own ulterior ends.

> The beginning of delinquency in girls is usually an impulse to get amusement, adventure, pretty clothes, favorable notice, distinction, freedom in the larger world. . . . The girls have usually become "wild" before the development of sexual desire, and their casual sex relations do not usually awaken sex feeling. Their sex is used as a condition of the realization of other wishes. It is their capital. (Ibid.:109)

Here Thomas is expanding on the myth of the manipulative woman, who is cold and scheming and vain. To him, good female sexual behavior is a protective measure—"instinctive, of course" (1907:241), whereas male behavior is uncontrollable as men are caught by helpless desires. This is the common Victorian notion of the women as seductress which in turn perpetuates the myth of a lack of real sexuality to justify her responsibility for upholding sexual mores. Thomas uses a market analogy to female virtue: good women *keep* their bodies as capital to sell in matrimony for marriage and security, whereas bad women *trade* their bodies for excitement. One notes, of course, the familiar dichotomy. It is difficult, in this framework, to see how Thomas can make *any* moral distinctions, since morality seems to be merely good business sense. In fact, Thomas' yardstick is social harmony, necessitating *control*.

Thomas shows an insensitivity to real human relationships and needs. He also shows ignorance of economic hardships in his denial of economic factors in delinquency.

> An unattached woman has a tendency to become an adventuress not so much on economic as on psychological grounds. Life is

rarely so hard that a young woman cannot earn her bread; but she cannot always live and have the stimulation she craves. (Ibid.:241)

This is an amazing statement in an era of mass starvation and illness! He rejects economic causes as a possibility at all, denying its importance in criminal activity with as much certainty as Lombroso, Freud, Davis, Pollak and most other writers.

FREUD: "BEAUTY, CHARM AND SWEETNESS"

The Freudian theory of the position of women is grounded in explicit biological assumptions about their nature, expressed by the famous "Anatomy is Destiny." Built upon this foundation is a construction incorporating psychological and social-structural factors.

Freud himself sees women as anatomically inferior; they are destined to be wives and mothers, and this is admittedly an inferior destiny as befits the inferior sex. The root of this inferiority is that women's *sex organs* are inferior to those of men, a fact *universally* recognized by children in the Freudian scheme. The girl assumes that she has lost a penis as punishment, is traumatized, and grows up envious and revengeful. The boy also sees the girl as having lost a penis, fears a similar punishment himself, and dreads the girl's envy and vengeance. Feminine traits can be traced to the inferior genitals themselves, or to women's inferiority complex arising from their response to them: women are exhibitionistic, narcissistic, and attempt to compensate for their lack of a penis by being well dressed and physically beautiful. Women become mothers trying to replace the lost penis with a baby. Women are also masochistic, as Lombroso and Thomas have noted, because their *sexual* role is one of receptor, and their sexual pleasure consists of pain. This woman, Freud notes, is the *healty* woman. In the familiar dichotomy, the men are aggressive and pain inflicting. Freud comments:

> The male pursues the female for the purposes of sexual union, seizes hold of her, and penetrates into her . . . by this you have precisely reduced the characteristic of masculinity to the factor of aggressiveness. (Millett, 1970:189)

Freud, like Lombroso and Thomas, takes the notion of men's activity and women's inactivity and *reduces* it to the sexual level, seeing the sexual union itself through Victorian eyes: ladies don't move.

Women are also inferior in the sense that they are concerned with personal matters and have little social sense. Freud sees civilization as based on repression of the sex drive, where it is the duty of men to repress their strong instincts in order to get on with the worldly business of civilization. Women, on the other hand,

> have little sense of justice, and this is no doubt connected with the preponderance of envy in their mental life; for the demands of justice are a modification of envy; they lay down the conditions under which one is willing to part with it. We also say of women that their social interests are weaker that those of men and that their capacity for the sublimation of their instincts is less. (1933:183)

Men are capable of sublimating their individual needs because they rationally perceive the Hobbesian conflict between those urges and social needs. Women are emotional and incapable of such an adjustment because of their innate inability to make such rational judgments. It is only fair then that they should have a marginal relation to production and property.

In this framework, the deviant woman is one who is attempting to be a *man*. She is aggressively rebellious, and her drive to accomplishment is the expression of her longing for a penis; this is a hopeless pursuit, of course, and she will only end up "neurotic." Thus the deviant woman should be treated and helped to *adjust* to her sex role. Here again, as in Thomas' writing, is the notion of individual accommodation that repudiates the possibility of social change.

In a Victorian fashion, Freud rationalizes women's oppression by glorifying their duties as wives and mothers:

> It is really a stillborn thought to send women into the struggle for existence exactly the same as men. If, for instance, I imagined my sweet gentle girl as a competitor, it would only end in my telling her, as I did seventeen months ago, that I am fond of her, and I implore her to withdraw from the strife into the calm, uncompetitive activity of my home. . . . Nature has determined woman's destiny through beauty, charm and sweetness . . . in youth an adored darling, in mature years a loved wife. (Jones, 1961:117–118)

In speaking of femininity, Freud, like his forebearers, is speaking along racist and classist lines. Only upper- and middle-class women could possibly enjoy lives as sheltered darlings. Freud sets hegemonic standards of femininity for poor and Third World women.

It is important to understand Freudianism because it reduces categories of sexual ideology to explicit sexuality and makes these categories *scientific*. For the last fifty years, Freudianism has been a mainstay of sexist social theory. Kate Millett notes that Freud himself saw his work as stemming the tide of feminist revolution, which he constantly ridiculed:

> Coming as it did, at the peak of the sexual revolution, Freud's doctrine of penis envy is in fact a superbly timed accusation, enabling masculine sentiment to take the offensive again as it had not since the disappearance of overt misogyny when the pose of chivalry became fashionable. (Millett, 1970:189)

Freudian notions of the repression of sexual instincts, the sexual passivity of women, and the sanctity of the nuclear family are conservative not only in their contemporary context, but in the context of their own time. Hitler writes:

> For her [woman's] world is her husband, her family, her children, and her home. . . . The man upholds the nation as the woman upholds the family. The equal rights of women consist in the fact that in the realm of life determined for her by nature, she

> experience the high esteem that is her due. Woman and man represent quite different types of being. Reason is dominant in man. . . . Feeling, in contrast, is much more stable than reason, and woman is the feeling, and therefore the stable, element. (Ibid.:170)

One can mark the decline in the position of women after the 1920's through the use of various indices: by noting the progressively earlier age of marriage of women in the United States and the steady rise in the number of children born to them, culminating in the birth explosion of the late forties and fifties; by looking at the relative decline in the number of women scholars; and by seeing the failure to liberate women in the Soviet Union and the rise of fascist sexual ideology. Freudianism has had an unparalleled influence in the United States (and came at a key point to help swing the tide against the women's movement) to facilitate the return of women during the depression and postwar years to the home, out of an economy which had no room for them. Freud affected such writers on female deviance as Davis, Pollak, and Konopka, who turn to concepts of sexual maladjustment and neurosis to explain women's criminality. Healthy women would now be seen as masochistic, passive, and sexually indifferent. Criminal women would be seen as *sexual* misfits. Most importantly, *psychological* factors would be used to explain criminal activity, and social, economic, and political factors would be ignored. Explanations would seek to be *universal,* and historical possibilities of change would be refuted.

DAVIS: "THE MOST CONVENIENT SEXUAL OUTLET FOR ARMIES . . ."

Kingsley Davis' work on prostitution (1961) is still considered a classical analysis on the subject with a structural-functionalist perspective. It employs assumptions about "the organic nature of man" and woman, many of which can be traced to ideas proffered by Thomas and Freud.

Davis sees prostitution as a structural necessity whose roots lie in the *sexual* nature of men and women; for example, female humans, unlike primates, are sexually available year-round. He asserts that prostitution is *universal* in time and place, eliminating the possibilities of historical change and ignoring critical differences in the quality and quantity of prostitution in different societies. He maintains that there will always be a class of women who will be prostitutes, the familiar class of "bad" women. The reason for the universality of prostitution is that sexual *repression,* a concept stressed by Thomas and Freud, is essential to the functioning of society. Once again there is the notion of sublimating "natural" sex urges to the overall needs of society, namely social order. Davis notes that in our society sexuality is permitted only within the structure of the nuclear family, which is an institution of stability. He does not, however, analyze in depth the economic and social functions of the family, other than to say it is a bulwark of morality.

> The norms of every society tend to harness and control the sexual appetite, and one of the ways of doing this is to link the sexual act to some stable or potentially stable social relationship. . . . Men dominate women in economic, sexual and familial relationships and consider them to some extent as sexual property, to be prohibited to other males. They therefore find promiscuity on the part of women repugnant. (Ibid.:264)

Davis is linking the concept of prostitution to promiscuity, defining it as a *sexual* crime, and calling prostitutes sexual transgressors. Its origins, he claims, lie not in economic hardship, but in the marital restraints on sexuality. As long as men seek women, prostitutes will be in demand. One wonders why sex-seeking women have not created a class of male prostitutes.

Davis sees the only possibility of eliminating prostitution in the liberalization of sexual mores, although he is pessimistic about the likelihood of total elimination. In light of the contemporary American "sexual revolution" of commercial sex, which has surely created more prostitutes and semi-prostitutes rather than eliminating the phenomenon, and in considering the revolution in China where, despite a "puritanical" outlook on sexuality, prostitution has largely been eliminated through major economic and social change, the superficiality of Davis' approach becomes evident. Without dealing with root economic, social, and political factors, one cannot analyze prostitution.

Davis shows Freudian pessimism about the nature of sexual repression:

> We can imagine a social system in which the motive for prostitution would be completely absent, but we cannot imagine that the system will ever come to pass. It would be a regime of absolute sexual freedom with intercourse practiced solely for pleasure by both parties. There would be no institutional control of sexual expression . . . All sexual desire would have to be mutually complementary . . . Since the basic causes of prostitution—the institutional control of sex, the unequal scale of attractiveness, and the presence of economic and social inequalities between classes and between males and females—are not likely to disappear, prostitution is not likely to disappear either. (Ibid.: 286)

By talking about "complementary desire," Davis is using a marketplace notion of sex: two attractive or unattractive people are drawn to each other and exchange sexual favors; people are placed on a scale of attractiveness and may be rejected by people above them on the scale; hence they (*men*) become frustrated and demand prostitutes. Women who become prostitutes do so for good pay *and* sexual pleasure. Thus one has a neat little system in which everyone benefits.

> Enabling a small number of women to take care of the needs of a large number of men, it is the most convenient sexual outlet for armies, for the legions of strangers, perverts and physically repulsive in out midst. (Ibid.:288)

Prostitution "functions," therefore it must be good. Davis, like Thomas, is motivated by concerns of social order rather than by concerns of what the needs and desires of the women involved might be. He denies that the women involved are economically oppressed; they are on the streets through autonomous, *individual* choice.

> Some women physically enjoy the intercourse they sell. From a purely economic point of view, prostitution comes near the situation of getting something for nothing. . . . Women's wages could scarcely be raised significantly without also raising men's. Men would then have more to spend on prostitution. (Ibid.:277)

It is important to understand that, given a *sexual* interpretation of what is an *economic* crime, and given a refusal to consider widespread change (even equalization of wages, hardly a revolutionary act), Davis' conclusion is the logical technocratic solution.

In this framework, the deviant women are merely adjusting to their feminine role in an illegitimate fashion, as Thomas has theorized. They are *not* attempting to be rebels or to be "men," as Lombroso's and Freud's postitions suggest. Although Davis sees the main difference between wives and prostitutes in a macrosocial sense as the difference merely between legal and illegal roles, in a personal sense he sees the women who *choose* prostitution as maladjusted and neurotic. However, given the universal necessity for prostitution, this analysis implies the necessity of having a perpetually ill and maladjusted class of women. Thus oppression is *built into* the system, and a healthy *system* makes for a sick *individual*. Here Davis is integrating Thomas' notions of social integration with Freudian perspectives on neurosis and maladjustment.

POLLAK: "A DIFFERENT ATTITUDE TOWARD VERACITY"

Otto Pollak's *The Criminality of Women* (1950) has had an outstanding influence on the field of women and crime, being the major work on the subject in the postwar years. Pollak advances the theory of "hidden" female crime to account for what he considers unreasonably low official rates for women.

A major reason for the existence of hidden crime, as he sees it, lies in the *nature* of women themselves. They are instigators rather than perpetrators of criminal activity. While Pollak admits that this role is partly a socially enforced one, he insists that women are inherently deceitful for *physiological* reasons.

> Man must achieve an erection in order to perform the sex act and will not be able to hide his failure. His lack of positive emotion in the sexual sphere must become overt to the partner, and pretense of sexual response is impossible for him, if it is lacking. Woman's body, however, permits such pretense to a certain degree and lack of orgasm does not prevent her ability to participate in the sex act. (Ibid.:10)

Pollak *reduces* women's nature to the *sex act*, as Freud has done, and finds women inherently more capable of manipulation, accustomed to being sly, passive, and passionless. As Thomas suggests, women can use sex for ulterior purposes. Furthermore, Pollak suggests that women are innately deceitful on yet another level:

> Our sex mores force women to conceal every four weeks the period of menstruation. . . . They thus make concealment and misrepresentation in the eyes of women socially required and must condition them to a different attitude toward veracity than men. (Ibid.:11)

Women's abilities at concealment thus allow them to successfully commit crimes in stealth.

Women are also vengeful. Menstruation, in the classic Freudian sense, seals their doomed hopes to become men and arouses women's desire for vengeance, especially during that time of the month. Thus Pollak offers new rationalizations to bolster old myths.

A second factor in hidden crime is the roles played by women which furnish them with opportunities as domestics, nurses, teachers, and housewives to commit undetectable crimes. The *kinds* of crimes women commit reflect their nature: false accusation, for example, is an outgrowth of women's treachery, spite, or fear, and is a sign of neurosis; shoplifting can be traced in many cases to a special mental disease—kleptomania. Economic factors play a minor role; *sexual-psychological* factors account for female criminality. Crime in women is *personalized* and often accounted for by mental illness.

Pollak notes:

> Robbery and burglary . . . are considered specifically male offenses since they represent the pursuit of monetary gain by overt action. . . . Those cases of female robbery which seem to express a tendency toward masculinization comes from . . . [areas] where social conditions have favored the assumptions of male pursuits by women. . . . The female offenders usually retain some trace of femininity, however, and even so glaring an example of masculinization as the "Michigan Babes," an all woman gang of robbers in Chicago, shows a typically feminine trait in the modus operandi. (Ibid.:29)

Pollak is defining crimes with economic motives that employ overt action as *masculine,* and defining as *feminine* those crimes for *sexual* activity, such as luring men as baits. Thus he is using circular reasoning by saying that feminine crime is feminine. To fit women into the scheme and justify the statistics, he must invent the notion of hidden crime.

It is important to recognize that, to some extent, women *do* adapt to their enforced sexual roles and may be more likely to instigate, to use sexual traps, and to conform to all the other feminine role expectations. However, it is not accidental that theorists label women as conforming even when they are *not;* for example, by inventing sexual motives for what are clearly crimes of economic necessity, or by invoking "mental illness" such as kleptomania for shoplifting. It is difficult to separate the *theory* from the *reality,* since the reality of female crime is largely unknown. But it is not difficult to see that Pollak is using sexist terms and making sexist assumptions to advance theories of hidden female crime.

Pollak, then, sees criminal women as extending their sexual role, like Davis and Thomas, by using sexuality for ulterior purposes. He suggests that the condemnation of extramarital sex has "delivered men who engage in such conduct as practically helpless victims"(Ibid.:152) into the hands of women blackmailers, overlooking completely the possibility of men blackmailing women, which would seem more likely, given the greater taboo on sex for women and their greater risks of being punished.

The final factor that Pollak advances as a root cause of hidden crime is that of "chivalry" in the criminal justice system. Pollak uses Thomas' observation that women are differentially treated by the law, and carries it to a sweeping conclusion based on *cultural* analyses of men's feelings toward women.

> One of the outstanding concomitants of the existing inequality . . . is chivalry, and the general protective attitude of man toward woman. . . . Men hate to accuse women and thus indirectly to send them to their punishment, police officers dislike to arrest them, district attorneys to prosecute them, judges and juries to find them guilty, and so on. (Ibid. :151)

Pollak rejects the possibility of an actual discrepancy between crime rates for men and women; therefore, he must look for factors to expand the scope of female crime. He assumes that there is chivalry in the criminal justice system that is extended to the women who come in contact with it. Yet the women involved are likely to be poor and Third World women or white middle-class women who have stepped *outside* the definitions of femininity to become hippies or political rebels, and chivalry is *not* likely to be extended to them. Chivalry is a racist and classist concept founded on the notion of women as "ladies" which applies only to wealthy white women and ignores the double sexual standard. These "ladies," however, are the least likely women to ever come in contact with the criminal justice system in the first place.[4]

THE LEGACY OF SEXISM

A major purpose in tracing the development and interaction of ideas pertaining to sexual ideology based on implicit assumptions of the inherent nature of women thoughout the works of

Lombroso, Thomas, Freud, Davis, and Pollak is to clarify their positions in relation to writers in the field today. One can see the influence their ideas still have by looking at a number of contemporary theorists on female criminality. Illuminating examples can be found in Gisela Konopka's *Adolescent Girl in Conflict* (1966), Vedder and Somerville's *The Delinquent Girl* (1970), and Cowie, Cowie, and Slater's *Delinquency in Girls* (1968). The ideas in these minor works have direct roots in those already traced in this paper.

Konopka justifies her decision to study delinquency in girls rather than in boys by noting girls' *influence* on boys in gang fights and on future generations as mothers. This is the notion of women as instigators of men and influencers of children.

Konopka's main point is that delinquency in girls can be traced to a specific emotional response: loneliness.

> What I found in the girl in conflict was . . . loneliness accompanied by despair. Adolescent boys too often feel lonely and search for understanding and friends. Yet in general this does not seem to be the central core of their problems, not their most outspoken ache. While these girls also strive for independence, their need for dependence is unusually great. (1966:40)

In this perspective, girls are driven to delinquency by an emotional problem—loneliness and dependency. There are *inherent* emotional differences between the sexes.

> Almost invariably her [the girl's] problems are deeply personalized. Whatever her offense—whether shoplifting, truancy or running away from home—it is usually accompanied by some disturbance or unfavorable behavior in the sexual area. (Ibid.:4)

Here is the familiar resurrection of female personalism, emotionalism, and above all, *sexuality*—characteristics already described by Lombroso, Thomas and Freud. Konopka maintains:

> The delinquent girl suffers, like many boys, from lack of success, lack of opportunity. But her drive to success is never separated from her need for people, for interpersonal involvement. (Ibid.: 41)

Boys are "instrumental" and become delinquent if they are deprived of the chance for creative success. However, girls are "expressive" and happiest dealing with people as wives, mothers, teachers, nurses, or psychologists. This perspective is drawn from the theory of delinquency as a result of blocked opportunity and from the instrumental/expressive sexual dualism developed by structural-functionalists. Thus female delinquency must be dealt with on this *psychological* level, using therapy geared to their needs as future wives and mothers. They should be *adjusted* and given *opportunities* to be pretty, sociable women.

The important point is to understand how Konopka analyzes the roots of girls' feelings. It is very possible that, given women's position, girls may be in fact more concerned with dependence and sociability. One's understanding of this, however, is based on an understanding of the historical position of women and the nature of their oppression. Konopka says:

> What are the reasons for this essential loneliness in girls? Some will be found in the nature of being an adolescent girl, in her biological make-up and her particular position in her culture and time. (Ibid.)

Coming from a Freudian perspective, Konopka's emphasis on female emotions as cause for delinquency, which ignores economic and social factors, is questionable. She employs assumptions about the *physiological* and *psychological* nature of women that very well may have led her to see only those feelings in the first place. For example, she cites menstruation as a significant event in a girl's development. Thus Konopka is rooted firmly in the tradition of Freud and, apart from sympathy, contributes little that is new to the field.[5]

Vedder and Somerville (1970) account for female delinquency in a manner similar to that of Konopka. They also feel the need to justify their attention to girls by remarking that (while female delinquency may not pose as much of a problem as that of boys) because women raise families and are critical agents of socialization, it is worth taking the time to study and control them. Vedder and Somerville also stress the dependence of girls on boys and the instigatory role girls play in boys' activities.

Like Freud and Konopka, the authors view delinquency as blocked access of maladjustment to the normal feminine role. In a blatant statement that ignores the economic and social factors that result from racism and poverty, they attribute the high rates of delinquency among black girls to their lack of "healthy" feminine narcissism, *reducing* racism to a psychological problem in totally sexist and racist terms.

> The black girl is, in fact, the antithesis of the American beauty. However loved she may be by her mother, family and community, she has no real basis of female attractiveness on which to build a sound feminine narcissism. . . . Perhaps the "black is beautiful" movement will help the Negro girl to increase her femininity and personal satisfaction as a black woman. (Ibid.: 159-160)

Again the focus is on a lack of *sexual* opportunities for women, i.e., the Black woman is not Miss America. *Economic* offenses such as shoplifting are explained as outlets for *sexual* frustration. Since healthy women conform, the individual delinquents should be helped to adjust; the emphasis is on the "definition of the situation" rather than on the situation.

The answer lies in *therapy*, and racism and sexism become merely psychological problems.

> Special attention should be given to girls, taking into consideration their constitutional biological and psychological differences, and their social position in our male dominated culture. The female offender's goal, as any woman's, is a happy and successful marriage; therefore her self-image is dependent on the establishment of satisfactory relationships with the opposite sex. The double standard for sexual behavior on the part of the male and female must be recognized. (Ibid.:153)

Like Konopka, and to some extent drawing on Thomas, the authors see female delinquents as extending femininity in an illegitimate fashion rather than rebelling against it. The assumptions made about women's goals and needs, including *biological* assumptions, lock women into a system from which there is no escape, whereby any behavior will be sexually interpreted and dealt with.

The resurgence of biological or physiological explanations of criminality in general has been noteworthy in the last several years, exemplified by the XYY chromosome controversy and the interest in brain waves in "violent" individuals.[6] In the case of women, biological explanations have *always* been prevalent; every writer has made assumptions about anatomy as destiny. Women are prey, in the literature, to cycles of reproduction, including menstruation, pregnancy, maternity, and menopause; they experience emotional responses to these cycles that make them inclined to irrationality and potentially violent activity.

Cowie, Cowie, and Slater (1968) propose a *chromosomal* explanation of female delinquency that hearkens back to the works of Lombroso and others such as Healy (1926), Edith Spaulding (1923), and the Gluecks (1934). They write:

> The chromosomal difference between the sexes starts the individual on a divergent path, leading either in a masculine or feminine direction. . . . It is possible that the methods of upbringing, differing somewhat for the two sexes, may play some part in increasing the angle of this divergence. (Ibid.:171)

This is the healthy, normal divergence for the sexes. The authors equate *masculinity* and *femininity* with *maleness* and *femaleness,* although contemporary feminists point out that the first categories are *social* and the latter ones *physical*.[7] What relationship exists between the two—how femaleness determines femininity—is dependent on the larger social structure. There is no question that a wide range of possibilities exist historically, and in a non-sexist society it is possible that "masculinity" and "femininity" would disappear, and that the sexes would differ only biologically, specifically by their sex organs. The authors, however, lack this understanding and assume an ahistorical sexist view of women, stressing the *universality* of femininity in the Freudian tradition, and of women's inferior role in the nuclear family.[8]

In this perspective, the female offender is *different* physiologically and psychologically from the "normal" girl.

The authors conclude, in the tradition of Lombroso, that female delinquents are *masculine*. Examining girls for physical characteristics, they note:

> Markedly masculine traits in girl delinquents have been commented on . . . [as well as] the frequency of homosexual tendencies. . . . Energy, aggressiveness, enterprise and the rebelliousness that drives the individual to break through conformist habits are thought of as being masculine. . . . We can be sure that they have some physical basis. (Ibid.:172)

The authors see crime as a *rebellion* against sex roles rather than as a maladjusted expression of them. By defining rebellion as *masculine,* they are ascribing characteristics of masculinity to any female rebel. Like Lombroso, they spend time measuring heights, weights, and other *biological* features of female delinquents with other girls.

Crime defined as masculine seems to mean violent, overt crime, whereas "ladylike" crime usually refers to sexual violations and shoplifting. Women are neatly categorized no matter *which* kind of crime they commit: if they are violent, they are "masculine" and suffering from chromosomal deficiencies, penis envy, or atavisms. If they conform, they are manipulative, sexually maladjusted, and promiscuous. The *economic* and *social* realities of crime—the fact that poor women commit crimes, and that most crimes for women are property offenses—are overlooked. Women's behavior must be *sexually* defined before it will be considered, for women count only in the sexual sphere. The theme of sexuality is a unifying thread in the various, often contradictory theories.

CONCLUSION

A good deal of the writing on women and crime being done at the present time is squarely in the tradition of the writers that have been discussed. The basic assumptions and technocratic concerns of these writers have produced work that is sexist, racist, and classist; assumptions that have served to maintain a repressive ideology with its extensive apparatus of control. To do a new kind of reasearch on women and crime—one that has feminist roots and a radical orientation—it is necessary to understand the assumptions made by the traditional writers and to break away from them. Work that focuses on human needs, rather than those of the state, will require new definitions of criminality, women, the individual and her/his relation to the state. It is beyond the scope of this paper to develop possible areas of study, but it is nonetheless imperative that this work be made a priority by women *and* men in the future.

NOTES

1. Quoted from the 1973 proposal for the Center for the Study and Reduction of Violence prepared by Dr. Louis J. West, Director, Neuropsychiatric Institute, UCLA: "The question of violence in females will be examined from the point of view that females are more likely to commit acts of violence during the premenstrual and menstrual periods"(1973:43).

2. I am indebted to Marion Goldman for introducing me to the notion of the dual morality based on assumptions of different sexuality for men and women.

3. For a discussion of the possibilities of psychosurgery in behavior modification for "violence-prone" individuals, see Frank Ervin and Vernon Mark, *Violence and the Brain* (1970). For an eclectic view of this perspective on crime, see the proposal for the Center for the Study and Reduction of Violence (note #1).

4. The concept of hidden crime is reiterated in Reckless and Kay's report to the President's Commission on Law Enforcement and the Administration of Justice. They note:

> A large part of the infrequent officially acted upon involvement of women in crime can be traced to the masking effect of women's roles, effective practice on the part of women of deceit and indirection, their instigation of men to commit

their crimes (the Lady Macbeth factor), and the unwillingness on the part of the public and law enforcement officials to hold women accountable for their deeds (the chivalry factor) (1967:13).

5. Bertha Payak in "Understanding the Female Offender" (1963) stresses that women offenders have poor self-concepts, feelings of insecurity and dependency, are emotionally selfish, and prey to irrationality during menstruation, pregnancy, and menopause (a good deal of their life!).

6. See Theodore R. Sarbin and Jeffrey E. Miller, "Demonism Revisited: The XYY Chromosomal Anomaly," *Issues in Criminology* 5(2)(Summer 1970).

7. Kate Millett (1970) notes that "sex is biological, gender psychological and therefore cultural . . . if the proper terms for sex are male and female, the corresponding terms for gender are masculine and feminine; these latter may be quite independent of biological sex" (Ibid.:30).

8. Zelditch (1960), a structural-functionalist, writes that the nuclear family is an inevitability and that within it, women, the "expressive" sex, will inevitably be the domestics.

REFERENCES

Bishop, Cecil
    1931   Women and Crime, London: Chatto and Windus.

Cowie, John, Valerie Cowie, and Eliot Slater
    1968   Delinquency in Girls, London: Heinemann.

Davis, Kingsley
    1961   "Prostitution." Contemporary Social Problems. Edited by Robert K. Merton and Robert A. Nisbet. New York: Harcourt Brace Jovanovich. Originally published as "The Sociology of Prostitution." American Sociological Review 2(5)(October 1937).

Ervin, Frank and Vernon Mark
    1970   Violence and the Brain. New York: Harper and Row.

Fernald, Mabel, Mary Hayes, and Almena Dawley
    1920   A Study of Women Delinquents in New York State. New York: Century Company.

Freud, Sigmund
    1933   New Introductory Lectures on Psychoanalysis. New York: W. W. Norton.

Glueck, Eleanor and Sheldon
    1934   Four Hundred Delinquent Women. New York: Alfred A. Knopf.

Healy, William and Augusta Bronner
    1926   Delinquents and Criminals: Their Making and Unmaking. New York: Macmillan.

Hemming, James
  1960   Problems of Adolescent Girls. London: Heinemann.

Jones, Ernest
  1961   The Life and Works of Sigmund Freud. New York: Basic Books.

Konopka, Gisela
  1966   The Adolescent Girl in Conflict. Englewood Cliffs, New Jersey: Prentice-Hall.

Lombroso, Cesare
  1920   The Female Offender (translation). New York: Appleton. Originally published in 1903.

Millet, Kate
  1970   Sexual Politics. New York: Doubleday.

Monahan, Florence
  1941   Women in Crime. New York: I. Washburn.

Parsons, Talcott
  1942   "Age and Sex in the Social Structure." American Sociological Review 7 (October).

Parsons, Talcott and Renée Fox
  1960   "Illness, Therapy and the Modern 'Urban' American Family." The Family. Edited by Norman Bell and Ezra Vogel. Glencoe, Illinois: The Free Press.

Payak, Bertha
  1963   "Understanding the Female Offender." Federal Probation XXVII.

Pollak, Otto
  1950   The Criminality of Women. Philadelphia: University of Pennsylvania Press.

Reckless, Walter and Barbara Kay
  1967   The Female Offender. Report to the President's Commission on Law Enforcement and the Adminstration of Justice. Washington, D.C.: U.S. Government Printing Office.

Sarbin, Theodore R. and Jeffrey E. Miller
  1970   "Demonism Revisited: The XYY Chromosomal Anomaly." Issues in Criminology 5(2)(Summer).

Schwendinger, Herman and Julia.
  1973   "The Founding Fathers: Sexists to a Man." Sociologists of the Chair. New York: Basic Books.

Spaulding, Edith
  1923   An Experimental Study of Psychopathic Delinquent Women. New York: Rand McNally.

Thomas, W. I.
  1907   Sex and Society. Boston: Little, Brown.
  1923   The Unadjusted Girl. New York: Harper and Row.

Vedder, Clyde and Dora Somerville
    1970   The Delinquent Girl. Springfield, Illinois: Charles C Thomas.

West, Dr. Louis J.
    1973   Proposal for the Center for the Study and Reduction of Violence. Neuropsychiatric Institute, UCLA (April 10).

Zelditch, Morris, Jr.
    1960   "Role Differentiation in the Nuclear Family: A Comparative Study." The Family. Edited by Norman Bell and Ezra Vogel. Glencoe, Illinois: The Free Press.

Female Deviance and the Female Sex Role: A Preliminary Investigation

Karen E. Rosenblum

The primary questions toward which this paper is directed lie within that area Frances Heidensohn aptly described as "obscure and largely ignored,"[1] that is, deviance in women. The intent here is to delineate certain of the parallels between the attributes of the female sex role and the characteristics of female deviance. Given that the participation of women in deviant roles is found primarily within the area of prostitution, and given that prostitutes are almost exclusively female, any understanding of female deviance and therefore of prostitution can best be achieved through an understanding of the female sex role. The specific questions toward which this investigation is directed are the following: What characteristics of the female sex role are conducive to the entrance of some women into the area of prostitution and why is prostitution a uniquely female form of deviance? Working from the interactionist approach to deviance as

Karen E. Rosenblum, "Female Deviance and the Female Sex Role: A Preliminary Investigation," *British Journal of Sociology*, 26 (1975), pp. 169–185. Reprinted by permission of Routledge & Kegan Paul.

I would like to thank Joyce M. Nielsen for her helpful comments on an earlier draft of this paper.

formulated by Edwin Lemert,[2] this analysis will (a) delineate the complexities of prostitution and specifically distinguish the call girl form of prostitution, (b) point out past inadequacies in the analysis of prostitution, and (c) utilize the call girl pattern to illuminate the characteristics of the female sex role. It will be argued that prostitution utilizes the same attributes characteristic of the female sex role, and uses those attributes toward the same ends; that the transition from non-deviance to deviance within prostitution requires only an exaggeration of the situation experienced as a non-deviant woman; and that given Lemert's definition of primary deviance, all women, to the degree to which they reflect the contemporary female sex role, are primary deviants.

For a period of nine months I spent most of my leisure time with a group of five "outlaw" call girls,[3] i.e., call girls operating without pimps. While I will frequently use my experience with this group to provide examples of specific points, the discussions and conclusions are based primarily on the published literature.

The research on prostitution falls within two broad categories; firstly, those accounts concerned solely with prostitution, generally written within an historical or psychological framework.[4] Secondly, those works which examine prostitution as an illustration of a particular theoretical position on the nature of deviance.[5] Generally, the research in both of these areas has been of good quality. There appears to be well-founded agreement on the nature and extent of prostitution. There are no great errors in observation or interpretation in response to which one could claim the discovery of a new perspective. However, I do contend that rather than some grand misinterpretation of prostitution, there has accrued a collection of small mistakes, the accumulation of which has not led to faulty analysis but more typically to incomplete analysis. Theorists have not generally reasoned incorrectly; they have simply omitted certain factors that would have made prostitution a much more revealing topic in that they have consistently failed to deal with prostitution as *female* deviance.

There should be little argument with the contention that prostitutes are, almost exclusively, female. Those relatively rare instances of male prostitution tend to be limited to homosexual rather than heterosexual relations. There seems to be no male counterpart, in type or quantity, to female prostitution.[6]

DISTINGUISHING PATTERNS OF CALL GIRLS

Most research (including the work considered at a later point in this discussion) alludes to the various forms in which commercial prostitution can occur, and then proceeds to analyze prostitution as a unified whole. This approach is not completely groundless. Most basically, all forms of prostitution can be reduced to "sexual intercourse characterized by barter, promiscuity, and emotional indifference."[7] However, this treatment is something akin to discussing all forms of theft simultaneously. The analysis must be reduced to the most common denominator with the result that conclusions are misleadingly simplified. As with any other form of deviance, in prostitution there are distinct patterns of participation in which the variance in income, method, and social status is considerable. It is precisely because the forms of prostitution are so diverse, that attempts at generalization must proceed cautiously. Rather than examine all forms of prostitution, this discussion will focus on call girls and the commentary they provide on non-deviant, generally "middle-class" women.

Benjamin and Masters[8] divide full-time prostitutes into several categories, the most common of which are call girl, street-walker, bar prostitute, and flea bag.[9] The streetwalker approaches men as she walks her "beat," the bar prostitute operates out of a "workingman's bar" (considered to be a little above the skid row level), and the flea bag, through a variety of methods, services skid row. Though there can be some overlap between categories in method, the distinctions noted above generally hold true.

Call girls can initially be differentiated on the basis of income. While fees vary by individual and region, Greenwald (1970) estimated that a call girl grossed about $30,000 a year, charging from $50 to $100 per client.[10] Winick and Kinsie (1971) estimated that the average prostitute grossed about $9,300 a year, charging about $10 a client.[11] The group of call girls with whom I was familiar (1971-72) charged upwards of $50 per climax per client, the variance in price depending upon the nature of the client's desires. "Straight" sex was $50, anything unusual was at least $100. If two women were involved with one client the fee was a minimum of $100 per call girl. If anything other than sex was requested (e.g., a dinner or theater date) the fee increased considerably, with the explicit intention of discouraging such requests by clients. The most established woman in this group earned about $48,000 a year, the least established $15,000.[12] Although they spent a great deal of their earnings, a proportion was very thoughtfully invested. The most established member of the group subleased three apartments (two of them to other call girls in the group) at about 100 percent profit per apartment. She also owned two homes in other states and had, at various times, profitably invested in stocks.

The second major distinction between call girls and other prostitutes may be determined by examining each group's general method of operation. Flea bags, streetwalkers, and bar prostitutes operate in public and either approach customers themselves or through a pimp. The call girl rarely solicits in public. Winick mentions that occasionally a call girl may go to an upper class bar to approach males. The more usual procedure in this group and among call girls generally is to obtain clients through the recommendation of other call girls or pimps and, when financially pressed, solicit past clients over the telephone.[13] The call girl either entertains those clients in her own home or goes to their residence, while other prostitutes usually take customers to a hotel room which does not double as the woman's home. Additionally, call girls neither barter with nor steal from clients, while all other forms of prostitution are typified by these characteristics.[14]

The nature of the occupation demands that the call girl spend the greatest portion of her time at home. In order to develop and maintain a clientele she must be easily accessible. Although the call girl may have an answering service or a telephone tape recorder, there is a reluctance to use them unless she is already occupied with a client. A client who calls only to discover a tape recording, or a switchboard operator, may not be in the mood later or may take his business elsewhere.

The upper- and upper-middle class nature of the call girl's clients requires that she maintain herself in an appropriate style. This generally entails a lavish apartment and an equally lavish wardrobe. The novice call girl in this group was earning about $15,000 a year, yet paying $600 a month in rent and spending a considerable sum on clothing and beauty aids.

The final distinction between call girls and other prostitutes is one of clientele. To afford a call girl on a regular basis (the call girls I knew had several regularly scheduled clients), one must be either upper- or upper-middle class. The exception to this characterization are those middle-class males who occasionally "splurge" on a call girl. In contrast, other prostitutes see a more varied group of men on a one-time basis and do not develop the steady, homogeneous clientele characteristic of call girls.

The analysis of clientele most forcefully points to the middle-class origin of call girls, a conclusion supported by Greenwald.[15] Most necessary for the call girl's development of a stable, monied clientele is the ability to provide not just sex for a price but sex couched in a style comparable to that of the buyer. While some of those accoutrements can certainly be purchased, the importance of unselfconscious speech patterns, topics of discussion, and surroundings cannot be underestimated. The prostitute who is to successfully meet the demands of the more wealthy segments of society must be in a position to understand and fulfill even the most subtle of expectations.

Any hypothesizing about the origin and nature of prostitution must carefully distinguish between these women who are, and those women who are not, financially compelled to become prostitutes. Given the middle-class origin of most call girls, financial need for them certainly cannot count as a motivating factor comparable to that experienced by those lower- and lower-middle-class women who become streetwalkers, bar girls, or flea bags. While the monetary returns of call girls are much greater than what those women could earn in non-deviant occupations, the non-deviant occupations available to them are unquestionably more numerous than those available to lower-class women. The women who become call girls are not forced to do so in order to survive; hence the conclusion that the call girl form of prostitution is fundamentally a commentary on the status of "middle-class" women.

PAST INACCURACIES IN ANALYSIS

Lemert's work provides key insights into the current sociological attitude towards prostitution in that it represents the prevalent views on the composition, patterns of participation, and societal reaction to prostitution. The whole of Lemert's theoretical approach is based on the continuing interaction between society, that is, the relevant community, and the individual. Lemert presents the identification of deviance as a "progressive reciprocal relationship"[16] which Heidensohn succinctly defines as the "process of definitions of deviance and the labelling of deviants by means of a complex of feedbacks and reinforcements through societal reaction."[17] A community does not arbitrarily or automatically label an individual as deviant. Nor does an individual necessarily see himself as deviant upon the commission of a deviant act. Instead, what Lemert describes is a constant, possibly escalating, interaction, the culmination of which may lead to the labelling of deviance by the society and the parallel self-labelling by the individual.

Yet in his analysis of prostitution, Lemert disregards his own theoretical framework on two counts. First, "although his stated aim in this study [on prostitution] is to examine the way in which primary deviance becomes reinforced into secondary deviance through societal reactions and personal definitions, in fact, when dealing with prostitution he concentrates on structural aspects of prostitution: the socio-economic background of prostitutes, occupations associated with prostitution, ecological factors and red light districts."[18] Second, and most important for this discussion, Lemert unhesitatingly classifies prostitution as *sexual* deviance.[19]

The chapter entitled "Prostitution and the Prostitute" in *Social Pathology* is introduced with something of a disclaimer. Were it not for the "disproportionate significance"[20] attached to prostitution and the number of inadequate analyses of the topic, Lemert indicates that homosexuality could as easily have been used as an illustration of sexual deviance. He argues that apart from obvious distinctions, homosexuality, "psychopathic" sexual behavior, and prostitution can all be classified as various forms of sexual deviance in that they represent violations of the norms regarding sexual relations. However, there are important complexities in this classification of prostitution that Lemert fails to consider.

Homosexuality can be characterized as a specific, socially censured form of sexual desire. The same applies to "psychopathic" sexual deviation (exhibitionism, sexual sadism, etc.). Both society and the stigmatized individual agree on what is being labelled deviant—specific sexual desires as manifested in behavior. However, except in a few cases, prostitution is clearly not the result of unusual or excessive sexual desire. In fact, by Lemert's own definition prostitution is characterized as emotionally indifferent promiscuity.[21] The prostitute's most basic motivation is monetary gain. The homosexual and sexual psychopath also participate in unsanctioned sexual acts, but as a result of unsanctioned sexual desire, not as an illegitimate occupation. The homosexual prostitute is condemned on two counts; one for his sexual urges, and the second for his deviant occupation. Though both forms are encompassed in a single sexual act, they are in fact two distinct forms of deviance. By accepting as a given the classification of prostitution as sexual deviation, Lemert has assumed congruence between the action performed and the norms violated and thus in part disregarded his commitment to the interactionist approach. More seriously, the classification of prostitution as sexual deviance means, at least implicitly, that deviance is not being discussed on its own terms, but rather from the perspective of the societal reaction to it. Though Lemert concedes that this is his method of classification, in this instance the unequivocal classification of prostitution as sexual deviance seems primarily a reaction to and reinforcement of the dominance of sexuality in the female sex role—an issue to be expanded upon at a later point.

PRIMARY AND SECONDARY DEVIANCE WITHIN PROSTITUTION

The previous discussion examined a situation in which the specific analysis did not meet the requirements of the theory it was used to illustrate. For the remainder of the discussion, effort will be directed at broadening the scope of what is fundamentally sound theoretical work so that it can productively encompass the area of prostitution, i.e., so that it can yield an understanding of "female deviance as an aspect of the female sex role and its relationship with the social structure." [22]

Lemert argues that the social reaction to behavior contravening expectations is first to attempt to normalize that behavior or situation, i.e., alter expectations, remind the subject of the norms, or ignore the incident. If the behavior is persistent, of high visibility, or viewed as particularly disruptive—in general, resistant to normalization—a situation may develop in which the behavior is labelled as deviant. Implicit in the interaction prior to labelling is a process Lemert calls valuation, i.e., that process preceding action in which values (most basically, "factors which affect choice") are compared to costs ("other values which must be sacrificed in order to satisfy any given value").[23] Thus, the response to unusual behavior will depend both on the values which have been violated and on the values which must be sacrificed in order to exact obedience. "From the point of view of valuational choice, normalization will persist so long as the value satisfactions contingent on the interactional bond are of a higher order than those sacrificed by continued normalization."[24] The identification of behavior as deviant, however, does not necessarily mean that measures of social control will be instituted. The development of such measures is dependent upon later interactions and whether or not accomodation can be achieved.

Valuation also describes the process undergone by all actors confronted with conflicting roles. The individual experiencing role or value conflict may attempt to resolve that conflict through an action that might be defined as deviant depending upon how the situation progresses (Lemert's risk-taking action). Resolutions involving risk are not at all unusual. The term primary deviation encompasses the numerous actions resulting from risk-taking action which come to public attention, are seen as undesirable, but can be normalized. Primary deviations are socially excused—they do not result in a change of "status and psychic structure of the person concerned".[25]

In contrast, secondary deviation is that point at which either real or potential

> stigmatization, punishments, segregation, and social control . . . become central facts of existence for those experiencing them, altering psychic structure, producing specialized organization of social roles and self-regarding attitudes. . . . *The secondary deviant . . . is a person whose life and identity are organized around the facts of deviance.*[26]

It is most important to note that primary deviation need not necessarily lead to secondary deviation.

In order to understand why some women become prostitutes, and to understand the relation of the female sex role to prostitution, it is perhaps easiest to work backwards, i.e., to first identify the characteristics of secondary deviation within prostitution, then examine the transition from primary to secondary deviance, and finally grapple with the concept of primary deviance.

RECOGNIZING SECONDARY DEVIANCE

The reorganization of "life and identity" around the "facts of deviance" characteristic of that stage called secondary deviation can be gauged by several indicators. In the following, Lemert points to the most dramatic instance of the "specialized organization of social roles" within prostitution:

> The sex act is bereft of ambiguous feelings; male-female relationships undergo a rigid structuring to prevent the energy-exhausting interaction of an informal date or courtship event and the frustration following brief "love" affairs. The girl becomes "hardened" in manner and speech and betrays the cues of professionalization.[27]

While the altered male-female relationship is the most obvious indicator of secondary deviance, it is certainly not the only facet of existence that becomes reorganized around deviance. For all prostitutes, and particularly call girls, the most mundane routines of living become rigidly restructured. As previously noted, the call girl must spend the largest portion of her time at home—waiting for telephone calls. Even the shortest of trips outside her home (e.g., groceries, hairdresser) must be scheduled around the possible call. In the group with which I was familiar, a decision to go out for dinner with other call girls was always prefaced by a lengthy discussion about what business each of them might miss. One woman in the group was always on the brink of financial disaster because she periodically took vacations to visit her family. In the course of those vacations, she lost both income and previously steady customers.

Additionally, the occupation has a marked effect on the type and quality of relationships available to the call girl. Through various lines of communication, a woman with the desire of entering the business makes contact with an established call girl, and is taken on as an apprentice, a relationship advantageous to both parties.[28] An established call girl can only maintain her clientele if she can provide a bored client with a new girl; recommend another woman on those occasions when she is busy; and be able to call on another call girl when more than one woman is needed for a client. From the novice, the professional collects a percentage—usually 50 percent—of the fee from the woman's initial contact with the client. Out of this relationship, there develops a group of about four or five call girls who maintain a constant emotionally and financially reciprocal relationship.

Because call girls outside one's own group are not trusted, and because the contact within the group is so frequent, what begins as a working relationship becomes an emotional attachment—though not necessarily a sexual attachment. The women, because of the stigma attached to prostitution, have very few non-prostitute or non-deviant friends in whom to confide. The exchange of clients becomes a means of aiding financially troubled friends. All social life and all decisions come to be oriented around the group, in part because their schedules coincide, but also because there are few other people around whom the women can relax.

Perhaps the most revealing measure of the "altered psychic structure and self-regarding attitudes" characteristic of secondary deviance can be inferred from the work of James H. Bryan on "outlaw" call girls. Most noteworthy was Bryan's finding (from a rating scale administered to 28 active call girls) that "customers were evaluated by the call girl as being as worthwhile as herself, and as significantly better than her colleagues".[29] Bryan perceives a weak and exploitive relationship among the members of the call girl group and therefore is not particularly surprised by his findings. However, my own experience and the knowledge that "outlaw" call girls in particular have few non-call girl relationships around which to focus activities and emotions, leads me to believe that the dependence on the group is much greater than Bryan suggests. At the same time it seems that his conclusions regarding the call girl's perception of group members is accurate. Thus, Bryan's research might well be interpreted as indicating ambivalence about one's own worth ("self-regarding attitudes") and about the merits of the occupation in which one is involved.

THE TRANSITION FROM PRIMARY TO SECONDARY DEVIANCE

The indicators of the presence of secondary deviance are, in the call girl form of prostitution, fairly obvious. Given the definition of secondary deviance, this would naturally be the case. However, determining why primary deviance occasionally evolves into secondary deviance is decidedly more difficult. Some tentative answers have come out of the recent women's movement literature. Many of these answers are not particularly novel. In a more general form they have been a long-standing part of the sociological study of prostitution, yet rarely have these hypotheses been subjected to systematic inquiry.

The shift from primary to secondary deviance must not be taken for granted. Lemert goes to great lengths to stress that primary deviance need not necessarily lead to secondary deviance. If that shift should in fact occur, it can be made intelligible through an examination of (i) specific precipitating factors and (ii) aspects of the female sex role conducive to a commitment to prostitution.

(i) In the examination of call girls, specific precipitating factors seem to be both few in number and small in impact. They can be identified simply as independence and money.

> The difference between being a prostitute and being a wife is the security a wife's got. But it's also the difference in having a lot of men versus having just one. If you have a lot of men—like if you have ten a day—then you're not dependent on any one of them. They can always be replaced. . . . But you can't do that if you're married and you can't do that if you're being kept. Of course, you can't depend on any john either. . . . But that's the thing I wanted—never to be dependent. I spent the night with a john only once, and I wouldn't even go out to dinner.[30]

For the call girl, the idea of being independent of men is a most important, but extremely confused, issue. Even in their most depressed moments, the women I knew would claim that at least they didn't need men. Three of them had in the past been deserted by husbands or boyfriends for whom they cared a great deal. They often cited that experience as their reason for entering prostitution. However, their emotions seemed to fluctuate between appreciation of the independence from men they had achieved "in the business" and complaints about how lonely they were—how much they would like to find a man and get out of "the life." While they occasionally had male lovers, the more typical pattern was either to have no affectionate relationship at all, or to develop a homosexual relationship—though not necessarily with a member of the group. On the surface, then, it would appear that call girls actually achieve the independence they so covet.

However, the claims to independence must be tempered by an awareness that the call girl's income depends solely on her ability to please the client. The use of the word "trick" to refer to the client implies that the call girl has gotten something for nothing—that she has been paid for the temporary use of "only" her body. Determining who is the real butt of this "trick" is more complicated than that, however, for the basic nature of prostitution is that the male for a limited time buys power over the female.

> But what they're buying, in a way, is power. You're supposed to please them. They can tell you what to do and you're supposed to please them, follow orders. Even in the case of masochists, who like to follow orders themselves, you're still following *his* order to give him orders.[31]

There are some very real questions, then, about who controls (or has power over) whom. Ultimately whatever independence the call girl achieves is based on her willingness to systematically place herself in a dependent, i.e., powerless, situation. Thus the claim to independence from men is rather tenuous, though the desire for independence does stand as a motivating factor for entrance into prostitution.

> I don't think you can ever eliminate the economic factor motivating women to prostitution. Even a call girl could never make as much in a straight job as she could at prostitution. All prostitutes are in it for the money. *With most uptown call girls, the choice is not between starvation and life, but it is a choice between $5,000 and $25,000 or between $10,000 and $50,000. That's a pretty big choice: a pretty big difference.*[32]

Money, far in excess of anything she can earn in a non-deviant occupation, is the second significant factor in the decision to become a call girl.[33] This was the moving force among the call girls with whom I had experience. In the past, all of them had held legitimate jobs but those jobs simply could not compare with the financial rewards they saw their call girl friends obtain. Once they became call girls, there was absolutely no limit to the amount of money they wanted to acquire. All of them expressed a desire to get out of the business, but only when they had accumulated enough money to last apparently forever. All time was spent either working or waiting to go to work, so that just "X" more dollars could be earned.

While the difference between $10,000 and $50,000 is considerable, it would seem that the risks one takes for that difference (in the form of arrest and/or public stigmatization) are also considerable. In fact, however, risk is minimal for the call girl. Most of the call girl's illegal actions are arranged over the telephone, after previous recommendation of the client by another trusted call girl. The recommending call girl will describe the appearance and interests of the client and indicate when a call from him should be expected. When a call is received, the client is questioned to confirm that he has been recommended. If the client does not fit the description or cannot indicate who recommended him, no date is made. Through this method police are generally weeded out of the call girl's customers. Since the call girl does not publicly solicit and typically entertains clients in her own home, the possibility of arrest is further reduced.

Thus, it is my contention that some women become call girls in part because that occupation provides them a degree of immunity from the law comparable to what they experienced as members of the non-deviant middle class.[34] That degree of immunity, which a woman considering the call girl form of prostitution would recognize in the small number of arrests among her call girl friends,[35] makes prostitution in that particular form a much less "risky" operation—a not insignificant factor for the middle-class woman.

However, this is not to argue that the factors of independence and money alone provide a sufficient explanation of the transition from primary to secondary deviance. They are precipitating factors, the impact of which greatly depends on the number and quality of contacts with women already "in the business." The discussion presupposes that the potential call girl knows or has access to call girls and finds the occupation worthy of consideration.

(ii) Though I noted financial gain and a desire for independence as precipitating factors within the call girl form of prostitution, compared to the financial plight of the potential streetwalker or of the pressures on her by a lover/pimp, these factors appear to be more in the realm of rationalization than necessity. What would seem to be operating in the case of call girls is a decision not particularly a product of external social constraint. Because for many call girls the decision to enter the profession was reached independent of *overt* external pressures towards prostitution, the call girl form of prostitution can more readily be seen as a consequence and extension of fundamental aspects of the female sex role. While all prostitutes have, to varying degrees, been subjected to and utilized the characteristics of that sex role, it is the call girl form of prostitution that stands as the clearest extension of the female sex role simply because it is uncomplicated by various forms of compulsion. The following remarks, though specifically directed at call girls, are applicable to all prostitutes.

Certainly the most significant parallel between the female sex role and prostitution is in the area of female sexuality:

> The final mythic outsidedness of woman is that ultimately she is beyond sex. Steeped in sex, drugged on sex, defined by sex, *but never actually realized through sex.* . . . Woman has been defined primarily in her society as a sexual object—either one of lust or one of chastity . . . there isn't a woman alive who is not obsessed with her sexual desirability. Not her sexual *desire.* Her sexual *desirability.*[36]

The socialized passivity of women in both sexual and non-sexual interaction, and a culture that "normally disposes woman to utilize sex for many purposes outside of the marriage relationship"[37] are two factors long noted by sociologists. The important linkage between these two factors is the following: a woman not socialized to expect sexual gratification routinely, but encouraged to employ her sexuality in non-sexual interaction, knows the value of desirability but has relatively limited expectations regarding sexual fulfilment.[38] While men are also concerned with their sexual desirability, their opinion of themselves is not founded primarily on that desirability, for occupational achievement provides an important alternative to a self-identity based on sexual desirability. The alternatives available to females are fewer and generally carry lower social esteem, resulting in an inordinately high value being placed on sexual desirability.

Desirability for both the call girl and the non-deviant woman is most basically measured by physical appearance and the ability to make a man feel "masculine." Neither the call girl nor the non-deviant woman have high expectations about receiving sexual gratification (though to differing degrees), and both expect some type of "pay off" for their desirability (though the prostitute's payment is generally more tangible). The difference between the utilization of and the expectations regarding sexuality is only one of degree. The decision to become a call girl simply requires an exaggeration of one aspect of the situation experienced as a non-deviant woman.

The significance I attach to the parallel between the place of sexuality in the female sex role and its functioning within the occupation of prostitution is particularly warranted in view of the information about the disproportionately small number of women engaged in other deviant occupations.

> Fairly reliable data tell us that there are fewer female criminals, hobos, radicals, and gamblers. While this can be explained partly as being due to internal limits which make certain roles unattractive to women, it is also a partial measure of the unwillingness of others to accept women in certain sociopathic roles. A young woman without a physical handicap is seldom a professional beggar chiefly because most men who encountered her in such a role would treat her as a prostitute, as would the police.
>
> The criteria for membership in organized sociopathic groups may be just as rigid and exclusive [as it is for non-deviant groups] . . . *any person aspiring to a given role, whether it is organized around approved or disapproved behaviour will be restricted by the social definition of his pre-existing social status.*[39]

In short, the social reaction to women participating in deviant activities is to assume that they are also, or perhaps only, prostitutes. The very fact that these women are perceived as prostitutes, illuminates first, the paramount importance of sexuality in the *non*-deviant female sex role ("any person aspiring to a given role . . . will be restricted by the social definition of his [or her] pre-existing status") and second, the general conceptions about what that sexuality in *non*-deviant female behavior entails—i.e., "the employment of sex for non-sexual ends."[40] The assumption that deviant women are prostitutes reveals that non-deviant women are perceived as and expected to be pre-eminently sexual beings who utilize that sexuality not for sexual fulfilment but to achieve some other, ulterior purpose.

But what is the nature of those other goals? Again, call girls make explicit those factors operating more covertly in the non-deviant world. Kingsley Davis several years ago alluded to the relationship between the nature of the female sex role and the social status of women by implying that for a woman, sex could well be a means of obtaining advantages "to which [she] is not entitled by [her] position in the scale of dominance."[41] Much of the recent women's movement literature has noted the use of "back door power," in this instance the utilization of sex and/or sexuality for the attainment of ulterior goals as a part of the contemporary female sex role. In effect, call girls expand upon and make explicit the "back door power" they utilized as members of the non-deviant female community. For the call girl, the situation is a cut-and-dried version of her non-deviant role—"For 'X' dollars I will perform the following sexual acts." It might even be argued that the call girl has more power ("back door" or otherwise) than does the non-deviant woman in that the call girl is able to use the payment for her sexuality in any way she wishes. For the non-deviant woman that pay off is less tangible and tied to the number of demands the male will allow her to make of him.

But perhaps a recognition of the parallels between the female sex role and prostitution raises as many questions as it answers—one of which was succinctly formulated by Kingsley Davis. If the factors of financial gain, desire for independence, or access to prostitutes—either singly or in combination—provide sufficient impetus for becoming a prostitute "the question is not why so many women become prostitutes, but why so few of them do."[42] It was noted earlier that specific precipitating factors do not in themselves provide a sufficient explanation of the entrance of women into the occupation of call girl. Those factors must be seen in conjunction with fundamental aspects of the non-deviant female sex role that make the transition from primary to secondary deviance acceptable to some women. Yet if the parallels between the female sex role and prostitution are so great, the question of why so few women become prostitutes is made even more difficult to explain. At this point the only hypothesis that can be put forward is that access to prostitutes and perhaps specific incidents in the life of the individual provide the initiative to act upon the potential for prostitution inherent in the female sex role. What is most important for our purposes is the recognition of that potential.

PRIMARY DEVIANCE

It could be argued that the primary deviant within prostitution is that woman who once, or even occasionally, exchanges sexual favors for pay. There may be a variety of reasons behind this occasional prostitution, e.g., the woman may have an immediate need for money and/or she may know of a man willing to pay to have sexual intercourse with her, or she may be encouraged by a lover/pimp or prostitute friend to experiment. In any event, she neither sees herself as a prostitute, nor reorganizes her life around prostitution.

But using the above definition of primary deviance within prostitution immediately raises problems concerning the definition of the terms "sexual favors" and "pay." Should sexual favors refer only to sexual intercourse or can it be a good-night kiss, coy behavior, or merely "the pleasure of my company"? In a like manner, how is one to recognize payment—as a finite amount of cash or the indefinite financial support guaranteed by marriage? Given that women generally have lower social status than men, and given that sexuality would be the main tool through which women would obtain "advantages to which [they are] not entitled by [their] position in the scale of dominance,"[43] the exploitation of sexuality would provide the most obvious resolution for a multitude of situations. All of the above behaviors can generally be classified as primary deviance in that they represent (1) the exchange of sexual favors for pay and thus on an absolute level contradict normative expectations regarding the functions of sex and sexuality; and (2) risk-taking solutions on the part of women, in that sexuality is utilized to achieve those personal ambitions not generally fulfilled by the roles and overall social status one holds through behavior that could potentially be labelled deviant. Primary deviance within prostitution is difficult to identify not because of any inadequacies built into the concept, but because for women, primary deviance in the form of prostitution is indistinguishable from that behavior encompassed by the non-deviant female sex role, i. e., the dominance of sexuality within the female sex role. Non-deviant male and female expectations concerning how women use that sexuality, and the exploitation of sexuality to achieve gain otherwise unavailable all add up to a routine exchange of sexual favors for pay. While the resulting behavior may be fairly commonplace, it is nonetheless an instance of primary deviance *built into* the female sex role.

Is this to say that all women are prostitutes—an argument many self-proclaimed prostitutes vehemently put forward? The distinction between prostitution and the mundane characteristics of the female sex role simply are not as distinct as one might hope, a conclusion exemplified by the lengths to which Kingsley Davis had to go in order to distinguish prostitutes from non-deviant women.[44] However, the consequences of living life as a prostitute as opposed to functioning as a non-deviant woman are too distinct to be overlooked. The non-deviant woman, regardless of the degree of prostitution implicit in her role, does not undergo the emotional and physical suffering experienced by prostitutes. The desire to get out of "the business" repeatedly expressed by women in "the business" is perhaps the best proof that the claim that all women are prostitutes is exaggerated and misleading. The attributes of prostitution implicit in the non-deviant female sex role neither mean that those attributes must of necessity be utilized by individual women, nor that the women who do in fact utilize those attributes are, therefore, prostitutes. This, however, does not mitigate the difficulties and unpleasantness of routinely participating in the primary deviance of prostitution simply as a function of one's sex.

In sum, prostitution is a uniquely female form of deviance because of the attributes built into the female sex role and the proximity of those attributes to the requirements of the occupation of prostitution. In those cases in which secondary deviance within prostitution develops out of that very shady area called primary deviance, certainly one must look to specific precipitating factors and previous contact with prostitutes. However, the sociologist cannot afford to neglect those aspects of the female sex role that allow those precipitating factors to carry the weight that they occasionally do.

NOTES

1. Frances Heidensohn, "The Deviance of Women: A Critique and an Enquiry," *Brit. J. Sociol.*, vol. 19 (June 1968), p. 160.
2. Edwin Lemert, *Social Pathology*, New York, McGraw-Hill, 1951; and E. Lemert, *Human Deviance, Social Problems, and Social Control*, Englewood Cliffs, N.J., Prentice-Hall, 1972.
3. My contact with the group (in 1971 and 1972) stemmed from my being related to one of the women.
4. For example, Charles Winick and Paul Kinsie, *The Lively Commerce*, Chicago, Quadrangle Books, 1971; and Harold Greenwald, *The Elegant Prostitute: A Social and Psychoanalytic Study*, New York, Walker and Co., 1970.
5. For example, Kingsley Davis, "The Sociology of Prostitution," *Amer. Sociol. Rev.*, vol. 2 (October 1937), pp. 744–55; Edwin Lemert (1951), op. cit.; Alexander Liazos, "The Poverty of the Sociology of Deviance: Nuts, Sluts, and Perverts," *Social Problems*, vol. 20 (Summer 1972), pp. 103–20.
6. One can anticipate and respond to the following objections to this claim: (1) Male heterosexual prostitutes can be found, and in numbers great enough to merit consideration. There appears to be no research that substantiates either of these arguments. (This conclusion is supported by Winick and Kinsie, op. cit., p. 184.) (2) Gigolos, i.e., "kept" men, can be found and seen as the male counterpart to female prostitution. Regardless of the many questions concerning the extent of gigolo activity, being "kept" does not qualify as prostitution in that it is not strictly characterized by "barter and promiscuity." Neither the standard research about prostitution, nor prostitutes themselves,

classify the "kept" woman as a prostitute and the same rationale would apply to gigolos. (3) Men, because of biological restrictions, cannot function as heterosexual prostitutes and therefore the predominance of females in prostitution is simply a consequence of the female biology. The male's inability to indiscriminately achieve an erection would present some problems to his participation in prostitution but it would not prevent him from offering other forms of sexual activity. Male homosexual prostitutes vary their fees and the types of sexual activities in which they will participate according to the desirability of the customer. Thus, the difficulties of male heterosexual prostitution could certainly be overcome by offering sexual activities commensurate with the desires, and hence the ability, of the male prostitute.

7. E. Lemert (1951), op. cit., p. 238.

8. Harry Benjamin and R. E. L. Masters, *Prostitution and Morality*, London, Souvenir Press, 1965.

9. The most complete listing of the types of female prostitutes, including overlaps and those types of questionable existence in the contemporary United States, would include the following: call girl, streetwalker, bar girl, flea bag, dance hall girl, adolescent, camp follower, brothel prostitute, interracial prostitute, elderly prostitute, child prostitute, and "beat" prostitute. One might also mention those prostitutes who deal only with specific sexual desires, e.g., fetishism and sadomasochism.

10. H. Greenwald, op. cit., p. 10.

11. C. Winick and P. Kinsie, op. cit., pp. 4–5.

12. Call girls must be at least nominally involved in some legitimate occupation in order to explain their means of support both to their families and to the Internal Revenue Service. This requires an occasional interior decorating, modelling, or acting job and an accountant knowledgeable in fraudulent income tax returns.

13. James H. Bryan, "Apprenticeships in Prostitution," *Social Problems*, vol. 12 (Winter 1965), pp. 292–94; and C. Winick and P. Kinsie, op. cit., p. 177.

14. C. Winick and P. Kinsie, op. cit., p. 176.

15. H. Greenwald, op. cit., p. 163 and 202–3.

16. E. Lemert (1951), op. cit., p. 76.

17. F. Heidensohn, op. cit., p. 168.

18. F. Heidensohn, op. cit., pp. 168–9.

19. Ibid.

20. E. Lemert (1951), op. cit., p. 237.

21. E. Lemert (1951), op. cit., p. 238.

22. F. Heidensohn op. cit., p. 170.

23. E. Lemert (1972), op. cit., p. 31.

24. E. Lemert (1972), op. cit., p. 51.

25. E. Lemert (1972), op. cit., p. 62.

26. E. Lemert (1972), op. cit., p. 63. Emphasis added.

27. E. Lemert (1951), op. cit., p. 270.

28. For a detailed explanation, see J. Bryan (1965), op. cit.

29. James H. Bryan, "Occupational Ideologies and Individual Attitudes of Call Girls," *Social Problems*, vol. 13 (Spring 1966), p. 447.

30. Kate Millett, "Prostitution: A Quartet for Female Voices" in V. Gornick and B. Moran (eds.), *Woman in Sexist Society*, New York, Basic Books, 1971, p. 40.

31. K. Millett, op. cit., p. 46. Emphasis in the original.

32. K. Millett, op. cit., p. 50. Emphasis added.

33. The median annual earnings of full-time, year-round female civilian workers in 1972 was $5,903. U.S. Bureau of the Census, *Statistical Abstract of the United States: 1974*, Washington, D.C., 1974.

34. This argument derives from Chapman's discussion of the class-based distribution of immunity from legal processes in the form of differential policing patterns, treatment in the courts and, most relevant to call girls, the differential distribution of privacy, i.e., "amount of time spent in private places." Dennis Chapman, *Sociology and The Stereotype of the Criminal*, London, Tavistock Publications, 1968.

35. There were five women in the group with whom I was familiar. Their experience as call girls ranged from 7 years to 3 months. To my knowledge there had been only two arrests in their cumulative histories.

36. Vivian Gornick, "Woman as Outsider" in V. Gornick and B. Moran, op. cit., p. 80.

37. E. Lemert (1951), op. cit., p. 246.

38. One might also wonder whether the emphasis on sexual desirability redirects attention that might be paid to sexual fulfilment.

39. E. Lemert (1951), op. cit., p. 82 and 81. Emphasis added.

40. K. Davis, op. cit., p. 746.

41. K. Davis, op. cit., p. 745. I have, I think justifiably, substituted the word "she" for "he" in the last line of the following remarks: "For example, if a weaker animal secures food and a stronger one comes to take it away from him, the weaker animal immediately presents himself sexually, no matter whether his sex be the same or different. If he thus diverts the dominant animal's attention, he can swallow his food. In such cases it is by means of his sex reactions that a monkey obtains advantages to which he is not entitled by his position in the scale of dominance."

42. K. Davis, op. cit., p. 750.

43. K. Davis, op. cit., p. 745.

44. The distinction Davis arrives at revolves around the functional position of each within the social order, rather than a distinction between the nature of prostitution and the nature of the female sex role.

Female Delinquency and
Broken Homes: A Reassessment

Susan K. Datesman
Frank R. Scarpitti

> *But the most common observation about the differential effect of*
> *the broken home has been that delinquent girls come from broken*
> *homes more often than delinquent boys. [Rodman and Grams,*
> *1967: 196]*

The above statement contained in the Task Force Report on
Juvenile Delinquency and Youth Crime has been well documented by empirical data. For the most part, inquiries into the
motivational factors in female delinquency have the family as a
common focus. Several decades of research have produced evidence suggesting that female delinquency is largely attributable
to deficient family relationships which require that the girl seek
compensatory affectional responses outside the home. For example, Monahan found that both male and female delinquents
are less likely to come from intact family backgrounds than their
nondelinquent counterparts, but that "among the females the
proportions from incomplete families are so high that there can
hardly be any doubt as to the importance of parental deprivation
to them" (1957: 258). Similar observations may be found in more
recent studies (Trese, 1962; Morris, 1964; Cockburn and Maclay,
1965; Cowie et al., 1968; Adamek and Dager, 1969; Cloninger and
Guze, 1970; and Reige, 1972).

"Female Delinquency and Broken Homes: A Reassessment." by Susan K.
Datesman and Frank R. Scarpitti is reprinted from *Criminology*, 13 (May 1975),
pp. 33–55 by permission of the Publisher, Sage Publications, Inc. (Beverly
Hills/London).

It is argued that the effects of family disorganization are more acute for females than for males because of existing patterns of sex-appropriate behavior. Toby (1957) accounts for the differential impact of broken homes on males and females by postulating that the institutionalized pattern of family control is much greater for females than for males. Family disorganization thus does not operate to divert males into delinquency since firm supervision is not as large a normative component of the male role as it is of the female role. Toby posits that the less discrepant sex ratio among black than among white delinquents is related to the fact that family instability is more common among blacks. That is, the ratio of male to female arrests for blacks will be closer because black females must contend more often than white females with the detrimental effects of family disorganization.

Morris (1964) suggests that broken homes may constitute a predisposing factor in delinquent conduct for females to a greater extent than for males, since the focal concerns of females are more intimately linked to the family situation. She hypothesizes that obstacles to economic-power status are most likely to lead to delinquency in boys, while obstacles to maintaining positive affective relationships are most likely to lead to delinquency in girls. The socially defined importance of relational goals for females is thus reflected by the higher incidence of broken homes among female delinquents since broken homes may be seen as an obstacle to fulfilling relational goals.

However, none of the above studies has taken into account the nature of the delinquent acts for which males and females are commonly apprehended. In a 1940 study, Weeks found that the differential effects of broken homes on the sexes disappeared when type of offense was controlled. He hypothesized that the sex difference in the incidence of broken homes indicated by official criminal statistics was an artifact associated with the type of delinquency for which males and females are commonly apprehended and the source of referral to the court. According to Weeks, family disorganization is likely to be a causative factor in offenses against the family, e.g., truancy, ungovernability, and running away, which constitute the largest proportion of delinquencies committed by females. Because of the nature of their offenses, females are likely to be referred to court by their parents, in which case family disorganization becomes a salient factor in the referral decision. A significant difference in broken home rates by sex failed to appear when the type of offense and the referral agency were held constant. Weeks concluded that the sex differential in broken home rates indicated a qualitative difference in the type of offense committed by males and females rather than the differential effects of a disorganized family situation. However, the number of cases was not sufficiently large to allow comparable statistical analysis of offenses other than ungovernability and running away.

The present study is concerned with pursuing this issue. Primary attention is given to the question, will the more detrimental effects of broken homes on females hold up when type of offense is controlled? In addition, the study examines the relationship between broken homes and sex controlling for the source of referral to court.

DESCRIPTION OF THE SAMPLE

The data presented in this paper were drawn from court records and from questionnaires administered to 1,103 juveniles appearing before the Family Court in New Castle County, Delaware from July 1, 1968, to January 31, 1969, who agreed to participate in the survey. The attained sample included 103 white females, 97 black females, 559 white males, and 344 black males. Although the original research design had anticipated the inclusion of the total population of juveniles processed through the Family Court during this 7-month period, with the exception of traffic violators, 104 juveniles refused to respond to the questionnaire or were missed because of organizational contingencies. A statistical analysis of the participants and nonparticipants in the court survey on the basis of background characteristics obtained from juvenile court statistical cards revealed no significant self-selection bias that would introduce any systematic error into the sampling frame itself.[1]

As operationalized here, a broken home refers to a family situation other than the husband and wife family; that is, a home with at least one of the parents missing due to separation, divorce, or death. An unbroken home is operationally defined as one in which both parents are present in the home. For purposes of the analysis, offenses have been categorized into person, property, and public policy groups. Public policy offenses include juvenile crimes, sex offenses, and violations of public ordinances.[2]

FINDINGS

As may be seen in Table 1, the marital status of parents is weakly related to sex (+.10) when the type of offense is not controlled; female delinquents come from broken homes slightly more often than male delinquents. However, the difference of 12% is hardly striking in view of the emphasis which has been attached to broken homes as an assumed cause of female delinquency. Controlling for type of offense reveals a conditional relationship: the marital status of parents and sex are unrelated for person (+.01) and property (-.02) offenses, but more strongly related for public policy offenses (+.16). That is, females referred to court for public policy offenses are somewhat more likely to come from broken homes than are their male counterparts.

Ungovernability and running away account for approximately two-thirds of the public policy offenses in our sample for which females are charged as compared to slightly more than one-fourth of the public policy arrests for males. The data indicate that males who are charged with ungovernability and running away are about as likely to live in incomplete families (55%) as male offenders against the person (51%) or against property

TABLE 1. Relationship between Marital Status of Parents and Sex by Offense Type

Marital Status of Parents	Total Sample		Person		Property		Public Policy	
	Male	Female	Male	Female	Male	Female	Male	Female
Unbroken Home	54.1% (480)	41.7% (83)	49.4% (41)	48.0% (12)	50.9% (147)	53.7% (22)	56.6% (292)	36.8% (49)
Broken Home	45.9% (408)	58.3% (116)	50.6% (42)	52.0% (13)	49.1% (142)	46.3% (19)	43.4% (224)	63.2% (84)
Total Percent	100% (888)	100% (199)	100% (83)	100% (25)	100% (289)	100% (41)	100% (516)	100% (133)
Kendall's tau b	+.10		+.01		−.02		+.16	
Chi-square	9.44		.01		.03		15.75	
P	<.01		<.95		<.90		<.001	

(49%). In contrast, females referred to juvenile court for ungovernability and running away are more likely to come from broken homes (68%) than are females who commit person (52%) or property (46%) offenses. It appears that the higher incidence of broken homes among female delinquents when type of offense is not controlled represents their greater involvement in these offenses.

The finding that females charged with ungovernability and running away come from broken homes more often than their male counterparts can be interpreted two ways, both of which are probably valid. First, it may be that ungovernability and running away are primarily reactions to a confused home situation. The data are generally consistent with the claim that the effects of family disorganization are more acute for females than for males, who are accustomed to less supervision and management by parents. Moreover, since the focal concerns of females are more intimately linked to the family situation, the position that broken homes predispose females more than males to run away from home and to act in an ungovernable manner seems quite reasonable.

Present-day sex differentiation practices may contribute to the seemingly more deleterious effects of broken homes on females in the case of ungovernability and running away in another manner. The normative definition of sex roles specifies different codes of conduct for males and females, generally with respect to maintaining the dualism of activity and passivity, but more particularly with respect to maintaining the double standard of sexual morality. It is frequently observed that: "In effect, (the double standard) calls for strong condemnation of female sexual transgression, but only mild condemnation, if not tolerance or even encouragement, of male sexual adventure" (Sebald, 1968: 393). The imprecise definitions of the behaviors constituting the categories of "ungovernability" and "running away" and the implied discretionary power allocated formal and informal social control agencies function to sanction legally the double standard of sexual conduct for males and females.[3] The family tends to be more protective and watchful of girls' than of boys' activities and to scrutinize more closely the behavior of girls than that of boys. Most parents use the double standard to define the parameters of acceptable and unacceptable behavior for their children and are therefore more anxious about the sexual misbehavior of their female children. Rarely do parents evidence much alarm when confronted with indications that their sons are sexually active. However, parents fear their daughters' sexual misbehavior and may brand as delinquents girls who exercise the sexual rights that traditionally have been reserved for boys. Thus, a parental request for court intervention is likely to occur in the case of a daughter who engages in overt sexual activity or who behaves in ways which suggest the possibility of sexual delinquency such as failing to keep her parents informed of her whereabouts, often coming home at a late hour, or staying away from home a few nights. Similar behavior on the part of their male children is more likely to be regarded by parents as mere boyish foolery (Gold, 1971: 591).

The above discussion suggests that females charged with ungovernability and running away will be referred to court by parents and relatives more frequently than will males charged with these offenses. This expectation is supported by our data (Table 2). Among ungovernables and runaways, 53% of the females as compared to 24% of the males are reported by parents and relatives. Conversely, law enforcement agencies account for 64% of male referrals and 33% of female referrals in the categories of ungovernability and running away. It may be the case that the difference in referral agencies connotes a difference in the types of behaviors which are labeled as ungovernability and running away for males and females. The fact that the police apprehend proportionately more males than females suggests that ungovernability and running away among males may represent primarily nonsexual, "acting-out" behavior which exceeds the degree of aggression which is permissively legitimate in the role expectations for boys. However, the police are much less likely to refer females, perhaps indicating that

TABLE 2. Relationship between Marital Status of Parents and Sex by Referral Agency for Ungovernables and Runaways

Marital Status of Parents	Law Enforcement Agency		Parents or Relatives		Other[a]	
	Male	Female	Male	Female	Male	Female
Unbroken Home	45.3%	24.1%	46.9%	39.1%	43.8%	25.0%
	(39)	(7)	(15)	(18)	(7)	(3)
Broken Home	54.7%	75.9%	53.1%	60.9%	56.3%	75.0%
	(47)	(22)	(17)	(28)	(9)	(9)
Total Percent	100%	100%	100%	100%	100%	100%
	(86)	(29)	(32)	(46)	(16)	(12)
Kendall's tau b	+.19		+.08		+.19	
Chi-square	3.23		.20		.39	
P	<.10		<.70		<.70	

a. Other sources of court referrals include schools, social agencies, probation officers, private citizens, private police such as store detectives, and complaints from correctional institutions.

female ungovernability and running away is more sexual in nature and thus more likely to be visible to the family and other extra-legal sources.

Our data show the females come from broken homes more often than do males in the case of ungovernability and running away whether the source of referral is the home or the police (Table 2). When parents and relatives are doing the referring, the percentage of broken homes among females is 61% as compared to 53% among males. A family which is in some way "broken" may be more prone to refer a daughter than a son to court for mildly rebellious behavior, on the assumption that females need the "protective" environment of a complete family more often than do males. This difference is even more pronounced when males and females are charged with ungovernability and running away by law enforcement agencies: 76% of the females and 55% of the males come from incomplete homes. Since the police force is made up mostly of men, it is probable that the application of morals statutes reflects and reinforces the focal concerns, values, and interests of men. The police are probably more likely to allow males a latitude of conduct denied to females of the same age status, and to take into greater account the composition of the home in the case of females, with the result that girls from broken homes are more frequently held for court action.

When controls for race are applied, some interesting findings emerge (Tables 3 and 4).[4] With regard to crimes against the person, the absence of a relationship for the total sample of delinquents between the marital status of parents and sex as seen in Table 1 derives from the contingent associations for blacks and whites having opposite signs—negative in the case of blacks ($-.20$), and positive in the case of whites ($+.33$). The results for whites are compatible with the usual research findings concerning the effects of broken homes on females: 71% of the females as compared to 29% of the males arrested for offenses against the person are from incomplete homes.[5] Among blacks, the pattern reverses: 44% of the females as contrasted with

TABLE 3. Relationship between Marital Status of Parents and Sex by Offense Type, Whites

Marital Status of Parents	Total Sample		Person		Property		Public Policy	
	Male	Female	Male	Female	Male	Female	Male	Female
Unbroken Home	65.0%	49.0%	71.4%	28.6%	61.5%	62.5%	66.3%	46.5%
	(357)	(50)	(25)	(2)	(112)	(15)	(220)	(33)
Broken Home	35.0%	51.0%	28.6%	71.4%	38.5%	37.5%	33.7%	53.5%
	(192)	(52)	(10)	(5)	(70)	(9)	(112)	(38)
Total Percent	100%	100%	100%	100%	100%	100%	100%	100%
	(549)	(102)	(35)	(7)	(182)	(24)	(332)	(71)
Kendall's tau b	+.12		+.33		−.01		+.16	
Chi-square	8.74		2.99		.02		8.97	
P	<.01		<.10		<.90		<.01	

TABLE 4. Relationship between Marital Status of Parents and Sex by Offense Types, Blacks

Marital Status of Parents	Total Sample		Person		Property		Public Policy	
	Male	Female	Male	Female	Male	Female	Male	Female
Unbroken Home	36.3%	34.0%	33.3%	55.6%	32.7%	41.2%	39.1%	25.8%
	(123)	(33)	(16)	(10)	(35)	(7)	(72)	(16)
Broken Home	63.7%	66.0%	66.7%	44.4%	67.3%	58.8%	60.9%	74.2%
	(216)	(64)	(32)	(8)	(72)	(10)	(112)	(46)
Total Percent	100%	100%	100%	100%	100%	100%	100%	100%
	(339)	(97)	(48)	(18)	(107)	(17)	(184)	(62)
Kendall's tau b	+.02		−.20		−.06		+.12	
Chi-square	.08		1.86		.17		3.03	
P	<.80		<.20		<.70		<.10	

67% of the males who commit person crimes are from incomplete homes. The noncorrelation also observed in the total sample of delinquent property offenders persists for whites (−.01) while a slight relationship obtains for blacks (−.06). Again, black males come from intact homes slightly less often than do black females (difference = 9%), although the difference is not large enough to be significant.

It is notable that black males who commit person and property offenses come from broken homes more often than do their female counterparts. This finding runs counter to the usual argument that females are more vulnerable to the reduction in supervision which generally accompanies the breakup of the parental home. Thus, it seems necessary to view our findings against black norms and standards with respect to family structure and sex roles since these represent a deviation from white patterns.

The Moynihan report (1965) presents statistics which indicate that family instability and female-headed homes are more prevalent among blacks than among whites. While a husband and a wife present in the home is statistically the most common family structure among both blacks and whites, the percentages of female-headed homes are somewhat higher among blacks (21%) than among whites (9%). Moynihan contends that statistics collected at one point in time tend to underestimate the extent of family instability and estimates that intact family backgrounds are to be found only among a minority of black children by the time they reach the age of eighteen.

Rainwater (1970: 164–166) states that lower-class black families are matrifocal in type and center around feminine authority, feminine equality, and male marginality whether the husband is absent or present in the family unit.[6] *Matrifocal* means that "the continuing existence of the family is focused around the mother, that the father is regarded (to a greater or lesser degree) as marginal to the continuing family unit composed of mother and children"(Rainwater, 1970: 164). Moreover, extended familism has been shown to be a distinctive characteristic of the black family (White, 1970; Hays and Mindel, 1973), regardless of whether the family unit is intact or broken (Mercer, 1967). Kin attachments prevailing among blacks are generally a matri-central form (Rainwater, 1970: 114–117) and tend to be "surprisingly stable, at least on the female side" (Gans, 1967: 451).

The matrifocal emphasis in family and kinship systems reflects the fact that many black females have been forced to assume control of the economic function in the family because of structural impediments which lessen the economic viability of black males. Since black males are likely to be denied access to the usual avenues of achievement, they may encounter difficulties in acting out the cultural prescription for male dominance, at least with respect to educational and occupational success. Liebow (1967: 29–71) discusses the predicament of black males who are confronted with menial, dead-end jobs which do not provide an income sufficient to maintain a household; he points out that no one seems surprised when the black male is unable to fulfill his male function as "provider" and as "head of household" (1967: 210–212).

Consequently, included in the socialization of black females is an attempt to prepare them for the contingency that the black male will fail in his role as "breadwinner." Thus Rainwater (1966: 199) points out that:

> The female role models available to girls emphasize an exaggerated self-sufficiency (from the point of view of the middle class) and the danger of allowing oneself to be dependent on men for anything that is crucial.

And Ladner observes that: "In sum, women were expected to be *strong* and parents socialized their daughters with this intention because they never knew what the odds were for them having to utilize this resourcefulness in later life" (1971: 131). It appears that the traditional division of labor, which defines the proper milieu of females as the home, e.g., expressive as opposed to task functions, is less tenable among blacks than among whites. The passivity and dependency aspects of the female role are deemphasized in the socialization of black females since these traits would prove dysfunctional for enabling them to cope with the exigencies of marriage. Thus Axelson (1970: 459) found a greater acceptance of working wives among black males than among white males and suggests that "the dominating white culture, more than the Negro subculture, has a well defined set of normative sanctions supporting the role of wife and mother."

It is probable that "growing up" occurs at an earlier age among black females than among white females. For example, adolescent black females are charged with the responsibility of caring for and disciplining younger siblings and with managing a larger part of the household duties (Schulz, 1969: 21-58). Further, release from parental controls for black females is generally concomitant with the birth of their first child. Zelnick and Kantner (Time, 1972: 69-70) report that 41% of the blacks in their sample of teenage girls as compared to 10% of the whites had been or were pregnant. Pregnancy for black females, according to Rainwater (1966: 187), is regarded as "the real measure of maturity, the dividing line between adolescence and womanhood." Childbearing confers on black females the status and privileges of womanhood, even in the case where the child is incorporated into the family unit and the mother continues to live in the parents' home (Ladner, 1971: 215-220).

In sum, the above discussion indicates that the present organization of the social structure and the black family operates to mitigate the detrimental effects of the broken home on black females. With respect to engaging in crimes against the person or against property, black females react less adversely to a break in the parental home than do black males, which appears to derive from the matricentral focus of the black family and of the extended kinship system, and from the fact that the female role is structured to include aspects of the traditional male role such as resource provision, responsibility, and autonomy. It appears that black females are less acclimatized to supervision than are white females and that family controls in general are somewhat more attenuated among blacks than among whites, with the consequence that black females do not respond to a break in the parental home in as negative a fashion as do white females with respect to engaging in delinquent acts.[7] It may be the case that the more convergent rates of delinquency for black males and females represent the muting of traditional sex roles among blacks rather than the more deleterious effects of broken homes on black females as suggested by Toby (1957).

In the case of public policy offenses, the original relationship between the marital status of parents and sex (+.16) is generally maintained for both blacks (+.12) and whites (+.16), although the relationship is slightly attenuated among blacks. If one considers only the offenses of ungovernability and running away, the results indicate that females who come from broken homes are more liable to be referred to court than their male counterparts; again, the percentage differences between males and females from broken homes are less pronounced in the case of blacks (9%) than in the case of whites (17%).

The data show that parents and relatives refer 63% of the white females and 35% of the white males charged with ungovernability and running away. The corresponding figures for police referrals are 24% for females and 48% for males. It is probable that somewhat more stringent behavioral boundaries are placed around whites, especially females, by the home so that mere "misbehavior" is more likely to be noticed and reported by white parents and relatives than is the case for blacks. Consistent with the findings for the total sample, the proportion of broken homes is higher among white females than among white males regardless of the referral agency. Sixty-nine percent of white females as compared to 39% of white males referred to court by parents and relatives come from broken homes; when a law agency initiates the referral, 60% of the white females and 53% of the white males come from broken homes.

It is surprising that black females, who come from broken homes less frequently than black males arrested for person and property crimes, would be responding to the influence of broken homes more often in the case of ungovernability and running away. The data show black females who are ungovernable or who run away from home are referred to court with approximately equal frequency by the home (43%) and the police (41%).[8]

. . . The larger proportion of broken homes among black females results from those cases referred by the police and other law enforcement officers (84%) rather than from those cases referred by the home (50%). In contrast, the lower broken-home rate for black males comes from the high percentage of cases referred by law enforcement agencies: 79% of black male ungovernables and runaways are brought to court by the police while only 13% are referred by the home. The broken home rate is 56% when police do the referring as compared to 89% when cases are reported by parents and relatives. It may be that a break in the parental home is not that salient a factor in the decision of parents and relatives to refer black females to court because of the structure of the black family and the arrangement of sex roles discussed above. It seems likely that the higher broken home rate among black females apprehended for ungovernability and running away reflects a differential selection by police who are more reluctant to return black females than black males to a home which has experienced a parental break.

SUMMARY

In summary, the findings indicate that the relationship between broken homes and sex varies depending on the type of offense involved. Among whites, a greater percentage of females than of males come from broken homes in the case of person crimes. However, it is not apparent that a break in the parental home harms white females to any greater extent than white males with respect to committing property offenses. The potentially most important finding to emerge in this study is that black males who engage in offenses against the person and property come from broken homes more often than do black females. The discussion indicated that the explanations offered for the more deleterious effects of broken homes on females have tended to reflect a normative model of white family structure and sex-typing which is inapplicable to blacks.

We found that the incidence of broken homes is higher among females than among males apprehended for ungovernability and running away from home for both blacks and whites. However, the differences for blacks were not significant and appeared to derive from the larger proportion of broken homes among black females referred to court by the police. It was argued that charges such as ungovernability and running away are characterized by ambiguous criteria which permit the implementation of different codes of conduct and discriminatory legal treatment for the sexes, particularly with regard to the desirability of premarital sexual relations for males and females.

If female sexual delinquency represents primarily a moralistic evaluation by male legislators and law enforcement agents of the "proper" role of females, we might expect a decrease in rates of female sexual delinquency as sex roles become less differentiated. Further, the larger number of extra-legal sources initiating court referrals for females than for males may be expected to decline as cultural prescriptions regarding sex-restrictive behavior become less binding since the sexual activity of females will be less likely to elicit a delinquent label. Conversely, empirical evidence exists which indicates that whenever females are allowed more role freedom, e.g., in pre-adolescence or during periods of war, male and female crime rates and criminal behavior patterns tend to converge. Increases in the rates of female delinquency in the areas usually associated with males should thus parallel decreases in the rates of female sexual delinquency. Perhaps, then, we should direct more research attention to the nonsexual aspects of female delinquency.

In conclusion, this study raises some questions about the

differential impact of broken homes on males and females when delinquent acts are not treated as unidimensional. It appears that the larger proportion of broken homes among female delinquents reported by most previous studies represents their greater involvement in "morals" offenses. Quite clearly, a re-examination of the relationship between broken homes and sex is needed which takes into account the nature of the offense for which delinquents are brought into court.

NOTES

1. An important question concerns potential generalizations of these findings. The court sample obviously does not constitute a randomly selected sample so that the results cannot legitimately be generalized to any larger population with the use of significance tests. The uncritical use of significance tests with nonprobability samples has generated much controversy in recent years about their functions and their usefulness. Significance testing tends both to subsume and to obscure the question of the strength of a relationship. Gold (1957, 1969) has reported on the proclivity of sociologists to equate implicitly statistical significance with substantive importance while neglecting to compute measures of the degree of association among variables. Also, when the female sample is subdivided by race and offense type, the small size of the subsamples minimizes finding statistically significant differences. For these reasons, the analysis will be based on an examination of multivariate contingency tables and Kendall's tau b-coefficients rather than on significance tests of questionable legitimacy. However, the chi-square test will be reported for the reader's information. Our study must therefore be considered as exploratory and our findings as tenative. It is hoped that our findings may stimulate further inquiry along these lines.

2. More specifically, public policy offenses include: weapons, sex offenses, drugs, drunkenness, disorderly conduct, riot, breach of peace, concealed weapon, common nuisance, conspiracy, contempt of court, contributing to the delinquency of a minor, accessory after the fact, running away, truancy, curfew, ungovernability, possessing and drinking liquor, false complaint, glue sniffing, hold for authorities, indecent exposure, loitering, nonsupport of wife, night prowling, possessing firearms, review commitment, tampering with an automobile, trespassing, resisting arrest, suspicion of crime, and gambling.

3. Reiss voices the predominant opinion in the literature when he states that: "Juveniles who are held to be guilty of a sex offense often are not charged with a specific sex conduct violation. The categories of 'ungovernability,'

'loitering,' 'immoral or indecent conduct,' 'runaway,' and similar designations are the preferred charges, particularly if the court has a policy to avoid stigmatizing an individual with a sex offense" (1960: 311).

4. The data indicate that race-sex-family status interaction for person/property crimes seems to be present. The log-linear unsaturated model which contains only the 2-factor interactions yields a chi-square of 22.18 with 5 degrees of freedom. Considering the model with the 2-factor interactions and race-sex-family status interaction, we obtain a chi-square of 10.43 with 4 degrees of freedom. The difference between the chi-square values is 11.75 with one degree of freedom and a p-value less than .001.

5. It should be recognized that the small subsamples produced by utilizing simultaneous controls for race and offense type reduce the confidence with which we may view our findings.

6. It was not possible to utilize socioeconomic status as a variable in the present study since blacks were overwhelmingly concentrated in the lower half of the income distribution for the total sample.

7. Rainwater (1970: 230–232) indicates that black children have available to them potentially discrediting information about their parents, e.g., knowledge of drinking and sexual deviations, which they may employ as a means to negate their parents' right to discipline them. Parents may accede a certain degree of autonomy to their children to avoid precipitating confrontations where their respectability may be challenged. Rainwater writes: "(Parents) feel vulnerable in their efforts to exercise authority, vulnerable to being shamed by their children, and this situation allows the children to arrogate to themselves quite early the right to set their own standards" (1970: 231). Parental authority in general thus appears to be somewhat more tenuous in the case of blacks than in the case of whites.

8. The fact that police referrals account for 41% of the referrals of black females as compared to 24% of the referrals of white females charged with ungovernability and running away may indicate that these charges are less sexual in nature for black females. Reiss contends that proscribed sexual behavior has a higher potential for being defined as delinquent among white females than among black females since: "Upper- and particularly middle-status persons in American society are regarded as the guardians of morality; women are so regarded more than men. . . . Proscribed sexual relations between parties who have low social status, such as Negroes, criminals, or 'low-class,' are more readily accepted than proscribed sexual acts between whites, conformers, or middle-class persons" (1960: 319). Ladner, among others, points out that blacks do not endorse the moral codes subscribed to by white middle-class society: "premarital sex is not regarded by the majority of low-income Black people as an immoral act. It is viewed as one of those human functions that one engages in because of its natural functions" (1971: 201). Premarital sexual relations particularly within a stable relationship may be regarded as evidence of maturity for black females so that black parents may be much less likely to intervene in the sexual activities of a daughter than would be the case for whites.

REFERENCES

Adamek, R.J. and E.Z. Dager (1969) "Familial experience, identification, and female delinquency." Soc. Focus 2 (Spring): 37–62.

Axelson, L.J. (1970) "The working wife: Differences in perception among negro and white males." J. of Marriage and the Family 32 (August): 457–464.

Cloninger, C.R. and S.B. Guze (1970) "Female criminals: Their personal, familial, and social backgrounds." Archives of General Psychiatry 23 (December): 554–558.

Cockburn, J.J. and I. Maclay (1965) "Sex differentials in juvenile delinquency." British J. of Criminology 5 (July): 289–308.

Cowie, J., V. Cowie, and E. Slater (1968) Delinquency in Girls. London: Heineman.

Gans, H.J. (1967) "The negro family: Reflections on the Moynihan report," pp. 445–457 in L. Rainwater and W.L. Yancey (eds.) The Moynihan Report and the Politics of Controversy. Cambridge: MIT Press.

Gold, D. (1969) "Statistical tests and substantive significance." Amer. Sociologist 4 (February): 42–46.

——— (1957) "A Note on Statistical Analysis in the American Sociological Review." American Sociological Review 22 (June): 332–333.

Gold, S. (1971) "Equal protection for juvenile girls in need of supervision in New York State." New York Law Forum 17: 570–598.

Hays, W.C. and C.H. Mindel (1973) "Extended kinship relations in black and white families." J. of Marriage and the Family 35 (February): 51–57.

Ladner, J. (1971) Tomorrow's Tomorrow. Garden City, N.Y.: Doubleday.

Liebow, E. (1967) Tally's Corner: A Study of Negro Streetcorner Men. Boston: Little, Brown.

Mercer, C.V. (1967) "Interrelations among family stability, family composition, residence, and race." J. of Marriage and the Family 29 (August): 456–460.

Monahan, T.P. (1957) "Family status and the delinquent child: A reappraisal and some new findings." Social Forces 35 (March): 250–258.

Morris, R. (1964) "Female delinquency and relational problems." Social Forces 43 (October): 82–89.

Moynihan, D.P. (1965) The Negro Family. Washington, D.C.: Department of Labor.

Rainwater, L. (1970) Behind Ghetto Walls. Chicago: Aldine.

——— (1966) "Crucible of identity: The negro lower-class family." Daedalus 95 (Winter): 172–216.

Reige, M.G. (1972) "Parental affection and juvenile delinquency in girls." British J. of Criminology 12 (January): 55–73.

Reiss, A.J. (1960) "Sex offenses: The marginal status of the adolescent." Law and Contemporary Problems 25 (Spring): 309–333.

Rodman, H. and P. Grams (1967) "Juvenile delinquency and the family: A review and discussion." President's Commission on Law Enforcement and Administration of Justice, Task Force Report: Juvenile Delinquency and Youth Crime.

Schulz, D.A. (1969) Coming Up Black: Patterns of Ghetto Socialization. Englewood Cliffs, N.J.: Prentice-Hall.

Sebald, H. (1968) Adolescence: A Sociological Anaylsis. New York: Meredith Corporation.

Time (1972) "Outmoded virginity." (May 22): 69–70.

Toby, J. (1957) "The differential impact of family disorganization." Amer. Soc. Rev. 22 (October): 505–512.

Trese, L.J. (1962) 101 Delinquent Girls. Notre Dame, Ind.: Fides.

Weeks, H.A. (1940) "Male and female broken home rates by types of delinquency." Amer. Soc. Rev. 5 (August): 601–609.

White, J. (1970) "Toward a black psychology." Ebony 25 (September): 44–52.

The Interaction Between Women's Emancipation and Female Criminality: A Cross-cultural Perspective

> *Keep strict watch over a headstrong daughter, lest, when she finds liberty, she use it to her hurt.*
>
> ECCLESIASTICUS, XXVI, 10

Traditionally, the perpetration of crime has been regarded as a male prerogative. Consistent with their restricted social roles, women had been relegated to the status of second-class criminals whose presence in the crime statistics was tolerated only in the categories of prostitution, shoplifting, and an occasional husband-poisoning. But the "second sex" has risen. The rise was accompanied by a fall in the double standard. Women have entered all categories of the crime statistics. It took a general social movement sweeping the world with egalitarian forces to provide women with the opportunity for a more equal footing in the criminal hierarchy. And it appears that women have used this opportunity.

Throughout history men have attempted to solve the mystery of the female, dealing with her as if she were a foreign species which did not have like needs for security and status. The real mystery would seem to revolve more appropriately around the issues of why and how this unawareness of basic motivations

Freda Adler, "The Interaction Between Women's Emancipation and Female Criminality: A Cross-cultural Perspective," *International Journal of Criminology and Penology*, 5 (1977), pp. 101–112. Reprinted by permission.

has persisted and why men have chosen to exaggerate the natural differences and to perpetuate century old myths. By post hoc-propter hoc reasoning dissimilar observed behaviors led to the untested conclusion that women must have inherently different motivations and goals. This reasoning forms mental sets which are difficult to extirpate because it safeguards the dominant structure of the male hierarchy, it shapes a perceptual-conceptual framework which tends to impose boundaries on observations and conjecture to premolded ideas, and, in addition, it serves as a security mechanism for those in the disadvantaged group. These ancient notions may have elevated the status of men but they were injurious to the women who accepted them for the most part without question.

But changes are taking place. Economic, political, medical, and technological advances have released women from unwanted pregnancies, unfettered them from kitchens and baby carriages, equipped them with male occupational skills, and equalized their strength with weapons. Women are now found amongst the ranks of admirals and sea-going sailors, heads of state and stevedores; there are female sky marshals and detectives; they can be seen driving tractor-trailor trucks and flying commercial airplanes; they have campaigned for and won powerful political positions all over the world, and they have even begun to enter the ranks of scholars and philosophers who create and test theories about women.

Indeed, these transitions are merely harbingers of what may become a massive worldwide movement. Indicators of change are already identifiable in countries with widely divergent cultures and ideologies. In Brazil, for instance, the world's largest Roman Catholic country, where in August 1974, the requests for separation almost equaled the number of marriages, women are mounting pressures against divorce laws. In Cairo women are beginning to use baby-sitters and are even considering males for this traditionally female role.[1] In 1967 the press reported that, "although only a little over four years ago, Afghan women rarely set foot inside a mosque because, as many men said, 'their presence would interfere with sober prayer' . . . today . . . that is all changed."[2] Korean farmers are replacing dowries with college education for their daughters, in Japan women have traded in their place three steps behind the male for a place beside him, and in Saudi Arabia veiled female university students are now permitted to work with their male instructors (albeit, as yet, via closed circuit tv). In Papua, New Guinea, where married women risk prison sentences for having affairs while men escape penalties, there are plans to reform adultery laws. In an Arab country an old male chauvinist folk tale with a new feminist twist became a popular opener of the 1975 theater season.[3]

There is a darker side, however, to this movement for equality. Just as women are clamoring for and attaining opportunities in the legitimate fields, some among them are prying their way into the arena of major crime by succeeding at illegitimate endeavors which traditionally have been "for men only." When we consider that the barriers which once protected male prerogatives are breaking down and socially defined gender roles are looking increasingly alike, it should come as no surprise that once women are armed with male opportunities they would endeavor to gain status, criminal as well as civil. The fact that woman is advancing so aptly into male positions strongly suggests that the old order rested much more on male cultural domination than on female genetic destiny. While historically it has been, in fact, a man's world, it does not follow that modern man is biologically more dominant than the modern female. Since culture is the final determinant of which characteristics are labelled dominant, it can certainly be argued that the universal dominance of the male may well have grown more from the institutionalization of man's superior physical strength than from innate feminine submissiveness.

Of those parameters that do distinguish the sexes some have been linked with the overrepresentation of men in the criminal justice system: size, strength, aggression, and dominance. While the first two are biological givens, the latter are primarily learned. However, even in non-technological societies, where size and strength were often the final arbiter of social interaction, modern advances, especially the wide distribution of machines, electronic devices, and firearms, reduced the significance of these attributes. But machinery and technology are not the only equalizers. As women gain entrance into the professional, occupational, and social world, with all of its liabilities and assets, they are also subjected to the same temptations, stresses, and frustrations to which men have fallen prey historically. That the social and emotional concomitants of emersion into the heretofore male world are just as powerful as the technological equalizers is dramatically evidenced by the steadily changing criminal behaviors of women throughout the world.

Newspapers in many countries are increasingly informing the public about a changing breed of feminine offender. Although universally, males continue to commit the greater number of offenses, women are beginning to emulate their patterns in both forms and dimensions of criminality, and world wide statistics are indicative of these trends. In the United States, for example, the total arrest rate among females has been rising nearly four times faster than that of males.[4] During the time span between 1960 to 1975, the number of women arrested for robbery rose by 380% while the male figures rose 214%. Similar differences are found in fraud (up 488% for women, 91% for men), larceny (up 465% for women, 130% for men), and burglary (up 298% for women, 117% for men). There has not yet been a comparatively accelerated increase in female arrests for murder and aggravated assualts. This may indicate that female offenders, like their male counterparts, are primarily concerned with bettering their financial positions. On the other hand, the fact that there has been a dramatic increase in female arrest rates for possession of deadly weapons does not auger well for the future numbers of women involved in violent offenses.

Data from other nations concur with the American experience that as the social and economic disparity between the sexes decreases, there is a correlative increase in female criminality.[5] In Western Europe and Australia, for instance, where women enjoy a high degree of equality with men, there has been a rise in the female crime rate. Conversely, the male-female crime rate disparities are most pronounced in countries such as Fiji and Malawi where the social gap between the sexes as yet remains greater.[6] It would, thus, appear that the closer the social standing of sexes vis-a-vis each other, the more similar is their crime rate.[7] Although at this point little cross-cultural data are available to confirm the size of the worldwide female criminality trend, most of the scant statistical evidence demonstrates that the increasing crime rate is a universal phenomenon. Japan's White Paper on Crime, for instance, presents data showing that during the period between 1962 and 1972, the number of female non-traffic Penal Code offenders investigated by the police has increased 1.13 times, contrasted to a decrease 0.78 times for males.[8] Consequently, the percentage of females in the total number of offenders has increased from 9.8% in 1962 to 13.6% in 1972. During this period female arrests for gambling have risen 2.08 times, followed robbery 1.40 times, larceny 1.30 times, indecency 1.28 times, homicide 1.20 times, extortion 1.10 times, and arson 1.08 times. The rates of increase of female arrests for robbery, larceny, homicide, and extortion are even more dramatic when compared with decreased figures for men. Table 1 shows the percentage of females in the total number of nontraffic Penal Code offenders investigated by the police. The consistency of the increase is quite apparent.

Similarly, in England and Wales, the number of women convicted in all courts of indictable offenses excluding dangerous driving causing bodily injury or death has increased 1.87 times between 1961 and 1971 compared with 1.71 times for males.[9] Consequently, the percentage of females in the total number of persons convicted has risen from 13.5% in 1961 to 14.5% in 1971. Rates of increase during this time period show that convictions for indecency have increased 6.0 times, followed by arson 4.56 times, robbery 2.88 times, extortion 2.86 times, stolen property 2.82 times, fraud 2.65 times, and homicide 1.53 times.

TABLE 1. Percentage of females in the total number of offenders in Japan

Year	Percentage of total
1962	9.8
1968	11.6
1969	11.9
1970	12.5
1971	13.3
1972	13.6

In the Federal Republic of Germany, the number of female Penal Code offenders investigated by the police (including both felony and misdemeanor, but excluding traffic offenses and the violation of the National Defense Act) has risen 1.33 times between 1963 and 1970, compared with 1.18 times for males.[10] The percentage of females in the total number of offenders has increased from 15.4% in 1963 to 17.1% in 1970. During that time the number of investigated females charged with robbery and robbery-like extortion increased 2.85 times, followed by larceny 2.08 times, arson 1.75 times, murder and homicide 1.42 times, and aggravated injury 1.05 times. The rates of increase in robbery and robbery-like extortion, larceny, and arson were greater than for males. It is quite apparent that although absolute numbers remain relatively small, slow, steady increases are occuring and, what is even more dramatic, these trends are greatest in property offenses such as larceny, serious offenses against the person such as homicide, and property/personal offenses, such as robbery and extortion, offenses historically considered "masculine."

Canadian statistics point to similar trends. They show that in 1969 women constituted 14% of the total number of persons charged with indictable offenses. In that same year, 6% of all violent crimes against the person were committed by women.[11] However, in 1960 7% of the persons charged with indictable offenses were women and 5% of the violent offenses were

TABLE 2

Year	Total charges	Charges per 100,000 females
1937	2800	358
1938	3000	379
1939	3000	374
1940	2600	319
1941	2500	303
1942	3300	394
1943	2900	343
1944	3200	373
1945	2900	334
1946	2700	306
1947	2400	267
1948	2800	306
1949	2900	311
1950	2900	305
1951	3000	309
1952	3700	373
1953	4600	452
1954	3800	365
1955	4300	405
1956	5300	488
1957	5700	514
1958	6800	599
1959	6600	569
1960	7700	651
1961	8900	737
1962	9900	800
1963	11000	869
1964	14000	1083
1965	14500	1101

committed by them.[12] Except for a small peak during the war years, followed by a decrease after the war, the female crime rate in New Zealand (see Table 2) remained relatively low and constant between 1937 and 1953. After 1953, the rate increased steadily. Total charges preferred against females in the Magistrates' Courts during the period 1937 to 1965 indicate this rise.[13]

In 1971 more than 7000 persons were punished for crime (excluding misdemeanors) in Norway.[14] Approximately 700 were women. A contemporary diagram of female crime in that country would reflect the fact that women today participate in all areas of life and not just those directly connected with their family, kinship, or neighborhood as in the past. Dating back to the initial Norwegian statistics of 1860, and until 1958, never had females accounted for more than 4% of the criminal population. But at that time an upward trend began. Presently, women account for about 10% of the total crime census. Interestingly, during the entire period, theft and other crimes for material gains represented the majority of female crime.

Brazilian data show that although females have consistently accounted for 4 or 5% of the total arrests between 1957 and 1971, in terms of absolute numbers of offenses, among females there has been an 89% increase (from 1310 to 2479), whereas among males the percentage increase was 43% (from 32,139 and 46,268).[15] For women perpetrators, offenses against the person remain low, morals offenses (e.g. prostitution) remain high, abortion, drug addiction and terrorism are increasing, and other crimes, including organized crime, continue to have a low incidence.[16] In many other countries, the increases also are not as pronounced, but nevertheless are observable in the statistics. In Finland, for example, where females have accounted for approximately 5% of all prosecuted persons every year since 1950, in terms of absolute numbers, female prosecutions have increased 55%, males 53%.[17]

Developing countries are not immune to the phenomenon of rising female crime. According to the 1973 statistics from the Central Bureau of Correctional Services of the Government of

India there was a 1.2% increase in the male compared to a 46% increase in the female convict population between 1961 and 1965 (see Table 3).[18] A trend analysis suggests the consistency of the rise (see Table 4).[19] In like fashion, other developing countries are just beginning to feel the effects of female emancipation. In the East African nations, for instance, where women had been traditionally relegated to low status positions, changing conditions are opening new opportunities, new challenges, and new problems. It is in the urban areas where women are finding growing advantages in politics, freedom of choice in marriage, legal rights, education, and employment. These females are experiencing a twofold problem. They are undergoing difficult adaptation: (a) from rural life with its subsistence economy, home education and extended family group to urban existence where the swift pace leaves many behind; and (b) from the security inherent in traditional female roles to the lifestyle of a newly liberated woman. For many who find the compounded stress too arduous, an easy way up or a quick way out is sought and either route leads to deviant behavior. Recent reports from this sector are already indicating that the "drop-out" rate of East African girls is becoming a very serious problem.[20]

The long range Polish data do not appear to support our hypothesis. However, if we consider that Polish women entered the labor force *en masse* a quarter century earlier than Western European or American women, it becomes clear that the Polish experience is consonant with the theory of this paper. The Polish female crime rate increased significantly during the

TABLE 3. Sex-wise classification of convicts and undertrials in India

| Year | Male | | Female | |
	Convicts	Undertrials	Convicts	Undertrials
1961	354,584	484,328	11,000	12,158
1965	359,106	526,922	16,010	17,625
Percentage increase over 1961	1.2	9.0	46	45

TABLE 4. Indian prison population:
percentage increase over 1961

	Convicts		Undertrials	
Year	Male	Female	Male	Female
1962	0.0	6.3	0.1	2.1
1963	4.1	3.6	1.9	4.6
1964	10.1	21.4	11.6	31.8
1965	1.2	46.0	8.9	45.0

years—following World War II—when Polish women were first fully integrated into the socio-economic maelstrom of Polish life (see Table 5). Interestingly enough, the subsequent decrease of the female crime rate may give rise to the hypothesis that normative controls (e.g. church and state) may have continued to operate, for within a decade, Polish female criminality had dropped to below pre-World War II levels. Could it be that emancipation transcended the traditional normative controls only temporarily? Could it be that there is a major difference between vocational liberation and psychological liberation? These questions as yet remain unanswered.

Up to this point we have been discussing adult female criminality. By definition the adult arrest rate is indicative of the present state of crime. But it is the statistics for juveniles under eighteen which give us an indication of future trends in rates of adult criminality. Historically, the female delinquency rate has

TABLE 5. Percent of total convictions in Poland

Year	Male	Female
1932	83.3	16.7
1951	74.1	25.9
1960	79.6	20.4
1962	81.7	18.3
1966	85.2	14.3
1968	87.1	12.9
1972	88.6	11.4

trailed far behind the male rate. Since the end of World War II
this has changed radically for many countries. Unprecedented
social forces must have been at work to produce this development. The Uniform Crime Reports of the United States show
that not only does the female delinquency rate outstrip the
male delinquency rate by far but, in most categories, it outstrips
even the adult female crime rate.[21] This amounts to saying that
we will have more crime among tomorrow's female adults than
we have among today's and that the gap between male and
female adult crime rates will narrow even further (Table 6).

A recent German study indicates similar trends in that country.[22] Hidden delinquency research conducted in 1969 and rep-
licated in 1974 shows that in the former year there were 9.1
offenses per boy and 5.4 per girl while in the latter year this
changed to 14.3 per boy and 8.1 per girl. In terms of percentage
increase, there was an increase for boys of 74%, and for girls, of
80%. The offenses showing the greatest increase for girls are
drinking alcohol in public, disorderly behavior, auto theft, and
shoplifting.

Comparable statistics for England and Wales point out that
between 1960 and 1970, the rate of girls 17 to 20 found guilty in
the courts doubled, while the rate for boys increased by less than

TABLE 6. Arrest percentage change (1960–75)*

	Male		Female	
Crime	Under 18	Over 18	Under 18	Over 18
Criminal homicide:				
(a) murder and nonnegli-gent manslaughter	205.7	138.2	275.0	105.7
(b) manslaughter by negli-gence	30.2	−20.2	333.3	−4.8
Aggravated assault	217.1	130.6	438.0	118.8
Robbery	361.3	214.3	646.8	380.5
Burglary	132.0	116.9	327.5	288.8
Larceny-theft	117.7	129.6	457.3	464.6
Auto theft	19.5	35.6	140.3	163.2

*Data from Uniform Crime Reports, 1975.

half (Table 7).[23] It is no longer uncommon for these youngsters to participate in burglaries, auto theft, and even extortion rings which prey upon schoolmates. What is more, they are even beginning to challenge the all-male domain of gang activity. Either as equal participants with males or as rivals in their own all-girl gangs, they are beginning to terrorize the streets as boys have done for generations. In London, for instance, Scotland Yard is expressing alarm over these new female gangs, presently numbering in the dozens, who rove the streets at night attacking old ladies with switchblades and razors.

Of the hundreds of studies of the various aspects of juvenile delinquency,[24] the deviancy of girls has been the subject of only a few. Those who have focused on female delinquency have generally emphasized the demographic and behavioral aspects of sexual proclivities.[25] In other words, more concentration has been placed on transgressions from the female sex role expectation that from the criminal code. Hidden delinquency studies among high school students, however, reveal a considerable amount of female delinquency of the kind that is ordinarily expected from boys,[26] and it appears to be correlated with unisexual role expectations. Since delinquent activity is patterned after non-delinquent behavior, there is reason to anticipate that as the latter sex roles merge, so will the former.[27]

Because juvenile delinquency was, until recently, almost exclusively a male activity to which girls made an unimportant contribution, major theorists have sought explanations for delinquency in the study of male psychology. However, because social forces play a more decisive role in shaping behavior than biological forces,[28] the factors advanced to explain male delin-

TABLE 7. Persons found guilty

	1960	Girls 1970	% Increase	1960	Boys 1970	% Increase
Number	6,767	15,623		138,728	235,262	
Rate per 100000	589	1,666	98	12,116	17,235	42

quency should apply equally well to females. The greater freedom enjoyed by males in every social stratum provided them
with easier access to peer groups, while girls were usually
limited to the family circle. Interestingly, many of the factors
which theorists[29] have advanced as causative of male delinquency—confusing early models, a sharp role shift at puberty,
and peer reinforcement of aggression—apply as well to the
modern girl. She is increasingly disaffected by restraints inherent in her mother's homemaking role; she is prodded into
entering fields formerly barred to females, and changing social
mores grant her access to increasingly aggressive peer groups.
Furthermore, they are observing patterns of sex role conver-
gence in their parents which provide undifferentiated models of
behavior. Both in the way parents act and in their expectations
of their adolescent boys and girls there is a pressure toward
gender uniformity in attitudes, values and practices.[30] This as-
similation of sex roles often amounts to an obscuring of boundaries which have traditionally subdued and safeguarded girls.

One of the most frequently cited cultural influences upon
delinquency is economic. The relationship between growing
affluence and delinquency rates has been the subject of reports
from many countries, including Japan, Argentina, Sweden, the
Netherlands, England and U.S.S.R.[31] There are, however, existing societies which have no concept of delinquency.[32] This is so
because they have no traditional period of adolescence, no period
of uncertainty of future, aimlessness, boredom, or lack of parental control. In folk communities, like the traditional Eskimo
village, certain tribes of India, and some barrios of Mexico, the
minimal problems of bad boys and contrary girls are handled
informally at the family level. For other villages, those in the
transitory period between folk and urban standards, contact
with developed cultures has disseminated new notions to some
of the youngsters, control by the elders is no longer acceptable,
and a new phase in the life cycle—social adolescence—that time
of rebellious and impulsive behavior, is spawned. In several
ways, that period of social adolescence is most traumatic for the

teenage girls reared in developing countries. For them it is a transition within a transition. Not only must they learn to become women in an urbanized structure, but they must also cope with the uncertainties of the female's position in that structure. Adolescence becomes a span of psychological limbo fraught with attempts to use role models who themselves are in a tenuous position. With technological advances reducing the number of unskilled jobs and cultural changes redefining a woman's place, never before have so many young females had so much incentive to desert traditional roles and so few opportunities to find new ones. A rise in delinquency under such turbulent conditions is predictable.

The activities of another group of young women, the politicized females, are likewise increasing and becoming more violent Recently, there was a fervor created throughout the United States when kidnapped newspaper heiress, Patricia Hearst, became an enthusiastic member of a political clique which called itself the Symbionese Liberation Army. What was remarkable about this episode was not so much the revolutionary activities—since the sixties Americans had watched student strikes, riots, and urban guerilla warfare—but the fact that women had organized and staged it. No longer satisfied with their traditional limitation to the typewriter, the mimeograph machine, and the coffee-maker, they are increasingly taking a more active role in the turbulent confrontations. So aggressive did their activities become that on 28 December 1968 the females of the United States reached a criminal landmark when the first one of them was admitted to the infamous Federal Bureau of Investigation "Ten Most Wanted" list.[33] Since that time the inclusion of women for murder, robbery, kidnapping, and violent revolutionary acts has become quite common. West Germany, too, has had world-wide newspaper coverage of its new breed of urban guerrilla—the female terrorist. Ten of the sixteen persons accused of being leading figures in the Baader-Meinholf gang and twenty-two of the 52 alleged terrorists who have been captured are female.[34]

In other parts of the globe women took active roles in the Entebbe highjacking incident, the bombing of a Stockholm embassy, and the Vienna kidnapping of ministers from the Organization of Petroleum Exporting Countries. In sum, there was a time when inhuman hurricanes had female names. Today the human storms include Ulrike Meinholf, Emily Harris, and Leila Khaled.

SUMMARY

What I have depicted is a slow, but increasing social revolution in which females are lessening the distance, legitimate and illegitimate, which has separated them from men. As the gap narrows, the more similar they look and behave. To be sure, there are inherent differences between men and women, but changing behavioral patterns demonstrate that women are first human, then female. Their needs and abilities are similar to those of men. Their opportunities have been different. Women's needs have not changed, but their opportunities are increasing,[35] producing new forms and dimensions of behavior whose full richness and variety have not yet been realized and whose final configuration will have universal effects.[36] Now that they have tapped into the springs of socio-political life, we are finding out that females are not as adverse as men tried to make them believe they were to taking undue advantage of their new positions.

NOTES AND REFERENCES

1. Ralph Slovenko, Are Women More Law Abiding Than Men?, *Police* 1964 (July–August).

2. *Washington Post*, 31 March 1967.

3. *New York Times* 7 October 1975.

4. Crime in the United States, *Uniform Crime Reports*, U.S. Department of Justice, Washington, D.C.: U.S. Government Printing Office, 1975, p. 183.

5. E.H. Sutherland & D.R. Cressey, *Principles of Criminology*. Philadelphia, J.B. Lippincott Co., 1966 (originally published 1924), p.139.

6. International Criminal Police Organization (INTERPOL) Statistics, 1970.

7. See H. vonHentig, *The Criminality of the Colored Woman*. University of Colorado Studies, Series C.I. No. 3, 1942.

8. Summary of the White Paper on Crime, the Research and Training Institute of the Ministry of Justice, Government of Japan, 1973.

9. Home Office, Criminal Statistics, England and Wales, 1961, 1971.

10. Polizeiliche Kriminalstatistik, Deutsche Bundesrepublik, 1963, 1970.

11. Statistics Canada, Statistics on Criminal and Other Offenses, 1969 (Catalogue 85–201) Ottawa: Information Canada, 1973, Table 2. Note: figures do not include Alberta and Quebec.

12. Dominion Bureau Statistics, Statistics of Criminal and Other Offenses, 1960 (Catalogue 85–201) Ottawa: Queen's Printer, 1962, Table 2 and 5.

13. Crime in New Zealand, New Zealand Department of Justice, Wellington, New Zealand, R.E. Owen, 1968.

14. Verbal communication with Dr. Niles Christie.

15. Anúario Estatístico do Brazil, Institute Brasileiro de Estatística, Fundacão Instituto Brasileiro de Geografia and Estatistica, 1954–1973.

16. Written Communication with Dr. Ayush Amar, Member of the Peniteniary Council of the State of Sao Paolo.

17. Statistics, Crimes Known to the Police, Helsinki, Finland, 1970.

18. Neera Kuckreja Sohoni, Women Prisoners, *The Indian Journal of Social Work* 1974 (July) 35, 2 p. 137–148.

19. Ibid.

20. The Status and Role of Women in East Africa, Social Welfare Services in Africa, United Nations, New York, June 1967, p. 10.

21. Uniform Crime Reports, *op. cit.,* p. 183.

22. Gerd Ferdinand Kirchhoff, "Self Reported Delinquency Methodological Notes and Findings of a Replication Study," paper presented at the meeting of the American Society of Criminology in Tucson, Arizona, 1976.

23. Girl Offenders Aged 17 to 20 Years, A Home Office Research Unit Report, London. Her Majesty's Stationery Office, 1972.

24. For an overview of the subject see, David Matza, *Becoming Deviant*. Englewood Cliffs, New Jersey, Prentice-Hall, 1969.

25. See, for example, Clyde B. Vedder and Dora B. Somerville, *The Delinquent Girl*, Springfield, Ill.: Charles C Thomas, 1970.

26. Nancy Barton Wise, "Juvenile Delinquency Among Middle Class Girls," in *Middle-Class Juvenile Delinquency*, Edmund W. Vaz (ed.). New York, Harper and Row, 1967, p. 187.

27. Ibid., p. 188.

28. See Margaret Mead, *Sex and Temperament in Three Primitive Societies*. New York, William Morrow and Co., 1963 (originally published in 1935).

29. T. Parson, Certain Primary Sources and Patterns of Aggression in the Social Structure of the Western World *Psychiatry* 1947 (May), 10, 168–81; Parsons, Age and Sex in the Social Structure of the United States, *American Sociological Review*, 1942 (October) 7, 604–16.

30. Wise, *op. cit.,* p. 181.

31. *Japan*—Jackson Toby, Affluence and Adolescent Crime, In the President's Commission on Law Enforcement and Administration of Justice, Task Force on Juvenile Delinquency: *Task Force Report: Juvenile Delinquency and Youth Crime,* Washington, D.C.: U.S. Government Printing Office, 1967.

Argentina—Lois B. DeFleur, Delinquency in Argentina, Pullman, Washington: Washington State University Press, 1970.

Sweden—Toby, *op. cit.*

Netherlands—J.E. Baur, The Trend of Juvenile Offenses in the Netherlands and the United States, *Journal of Criminal Law, Criminology, and Police Science* 1964 55, 359–369.

U.S.S.R.—Ibid.

32. Ruth S. Cavan & Jordan T. Cavan, *Delinquency and crime: Cross-Cultural Perspective,* Philadelphia, Lippincott Co., 1968.

33. "Ten Most Wanted Fugitives Program," United States Department of Justice, Federal Bureau of Investigation, Washington, D.C., 28 December 1968.

34. Los Angeles Times, 18 November 1976.

35. For an excellent discussion of the relationship between the changing social and economic status of women and its relationship to property offenses see Rita J. Simon, *Women and Crime,* Lexington, Lexington Books, 1975.

36. Freda Adler, *Sisters in Crime,* New York, McGraw Hill, 1975.

III

Patterns of Female Crime

The papers in this part focus on some of the crimes that women commit and on women's roles in these crimes. Women tend to be most involved in crimes that are consistent with the roles they have traditionally played. Even when they commit crimes inconsistent with traditional female roles, their participation tends to reflect those roles, according to the Ward et al. study, "Crimes of Violence by Women." In the part of the study excerpted here, Ward et al. present data on the characteristics of inmates confined in the California Institution for Women. Their examination of women's roles in homicide, assault, robbery, and burglary included whether they acted alone or with others, their choice of victims and victim's condition, whether their crimes were planned, their use of physical strength and weapons, and their motives for committing the crimes. Women's roles in these crimes were found to be closely tied to traditional female roles. For example, women participated in robbery and burglary in secondary, supporting roles to men who played the leading roles.

Many writers on the subject of female criminality, often relying on official data, have suggested that female criminality is primarily promiscuity and prostitution. In Part I of this volume, our review of official and unofficial data revealed that the overemphasis on promiscuity and related status offenses in official delinquency statistics reflects a double standard treatment of male and female juveniles by the police and the courts. In this part, two papers prepared especially for this volume discuss some misconceptions concerning the relationship between female criminality and prostitution. In the first paper, "Searching For Women in Organized Crime," Alan Block contends that contemporary commentators have misrepresented the social world of organized crime as sexually segregated. He further contends that women have been very much involved in organized crime in this century but have been effectively removed because of a belief in conspiracy and because of the Progressive Era imagery of female criminality that still has currency today. Female criminals during the Progressive Era have chiefly been depicted as prostitutes preyed upon by exploitative men. Block's analysis, on the other hand, suggests that female criminals during the Progressive Era and in the decades following engaged in a variety of independent and purposeful criminal activities as a rational adaptation to urban life.

In the second paper, "Women, Heroin, and Property Crime," James Inciardi challenges the traditional monolithic image of the woman addict as a prostitute. Using data on female heroin users in Miami, Florida, he found that women addicts most often reported a property crime as their first criminal offense and that they were involved in a wide variety of criminal activities. Inciardi suggests that prostitution may be less important for drug support than has commonly been assumed.

According to the Uniform Crime Reports, prostitution accounted for only 3.8 percent of all female arrests in 1977 and tied for ninth among female offenses.[1] However, almost 71 percent of those arrested for prostitution were female, in part because of sex bias in the wording and enforcement of prostitution laws.[2] Gail Sheehy takes a closer look at prostitution in "The Economics of Prostitution." Sheehy begins by discussing the profiteers of prostitution, including prostitutes, pimps, street hustlers, hotel operators, pornographers, lawyers, politicians, businessmen, and organized crime. Of these groups, prostitutes are usually the least likely to profit from prostitution. She then describes the various forms in which prostitution can occur, from street hooker to courtesan, and distinguishes among these forms on the basis of income, methods of operation, and social status.

Because the enforcement of prostitution laws is costly and constitutes a burden on the criminal justice system, proposals have been advanced to legalize prostitition.[3] *Legalization* would mean that prostitution would be controlled and regulated by the state which, playing the role of pimp, would profit from prostitution. The preferable alternative would be the *decriminalization* of prostitution, by repealing the laws and, although not ending prostitution, at least reducing the oppression of women prostitutes. According to a recent article supporting decriminalization:

> Decriminalization would not further exploit women, as would legalization. In the first case, prostitutes would not be regulated in any way by the State. The State would neither condone prostitution, act as the pimp, profit from the selling of sex, nor would it make the prostitute solely culpable for prostitution.[4]

The final paper in this part is "The Molls" by Walter Miller. This paper investigates the kinds of delinquent acts engaged in by the Molls, a group of corner-gang girls, their leadership hierarchy, and their associational patterns. The major delinquent acts of the Molls involved truancy, theft, drinking, and vandalism. Miller's research indicates that the Molls did not operate as an autonomous gang but rather depended upon their brother gang for status. He suggests that "the Molls and many of their sisters are either not yet aware of or attracted to the tenets of Women's Liberation." We will return to the relationship between female criminality and women's liberation in Part V of this volume.

Finally, it might be noted that the selection of papers for this part was somewhat easier than for the other parts of this volume. The problem in Part II and particularly in Part IV involved choosing among a number of good papers. However, with the exception of prostitution, there were far fewer papers to choose from in this part. Clearly, there is a need for more good research on female offenders, particularly female property offenders. For example, women constituted almost 36 percent of all persons arrested for fraud in 1977, but we have very little information on the offense behavior or the characteristics of these women. While we can speculate that women are involved mostly in petty fraud or fraud that is not occupationally related, such as welfare fraud or con games, sound research is necessary before such speculations can be confirmed.

NOTES

1. Federal Bureau of Investigation, U.S. Department of Justice, *Uniform Crime Reports—1977* (Washington, D.C.: Government Printing Office, 1978), p. 183.

2. Ibid.

3. Women Endorsing Decriminalization, "Prostitution: A Non-Violent Crime?" *Issues in Criminology* 8 (Fall 1973), pp. 137--162.

4. Ibid., p. 147.

Crimes of Violence by Women

David A. Ward
Maurice Jackson
Reneé E. Ward

This report is an outgrowth of a study of the adjustment that women made to life in prison which was conducted during the early 1960's at the California Institution for Women by Ward and Kassebaum.[1] For that study, basic descriptive data was gathered which pertained to the demographic characteristics, personal histories, and institutional experiences of all inmates housed at CIW between 1962 and 1964 ($N = 832$). In 1968 comparable data was obtained for a 25 percent sample of the inmate population ($N = 200$). Inmates from the earlier study group who were still in the prison were excluded from the sample.

In the analyses that follow, the 1962–63–64 study population (hereinafter referred to as the "1963 group") and the 1968 sample are presented separately. There were no statistically significant differences between the two groups over time, except where noted. (For several items we can present only 1963 or only 1968 data; in one case we mistakenly omitted the item when making up the 1968 coding sheets, in another case the data

Crimes of Violence, Vol. 13, D.J. Mulvihill and M.M. Tumin, eds. (Washington D.C.: U.S. Government Printing Office, 1969), pp. 843–909. Edited and adapted. Reprinted by permission.

pertaining to one study group was rejected because of apparent coding inconsistencies with the other group.)

Information on inmate characteristics was taken from the prison files kept for each inmate confined in the California Institution for Women. Since the validity of some of the file information can be questioned we focused on those items that involved fairly objective issues, such as number of arrests, test scores, age, etc. To keep the abstracting of file information uniform we checked the reliability of decisions made by our coders and had more than one judgment made of ambiguous or difficult items. We recomputed the numerical counts of certain items made by probation officers or institution staff members because there were a sufficient number of mistakes to warrant the effort.

In several cases we established our own guidelines for using or excluding various kinds of file information which dealt with the same item. For psychiatric diagnosis, for example, we coded only reports prepared by psychiatrists or psychologists and not the opinions offered by police officers, prosecutors, judges, and correctional officers. Nor did we use reports made by probation officers or prison case workers because of their highly variable quality.

The most obvious limitation in the use of officially recorded information arises in the area of reports of illegal or illicit behavior. All figures relating to the incidence of sexual promiscuity, prostitution, criminality, delinquency, and homosexuality are only measures of these activities as officially reported and are thus underestimates of true rates.

The specific items gathered for this study do not, of course, represent all the information that would be useful to have on the characteristics and personal histories of female offenders, but they do represent the best information that was consistently reported in the prison records and represent many hours of investigation by various law enforcement, correctional, and social service agencies. Stated simply the inmate files at the California Institution for Women contained the best available supply of basic information on a large sample of female felons we could obtain for an exploratory study. Approximately 10 percent of all women confined in our State and Federal prisons are housed at CIW.

FINDINGS

The discussion and data which follow focus upon women who were committed to prison for crimes against persons: homicide, assault, and robbery. Data on two other groups of female felons are included for comparative purposes: those committed for property crimes (forgery and bad checks, grand theft, burglary), and those committed for violation of narcotics laws. (The latter is more accurately classified as a "crime against morality" than as a crime against a person or property.)

ETHNICITY

It is not easy to determine the most accurate way to present the ethnic and racial composition for different types of offenders. Should it be expressed in terms of the racial distribution of the prison population? The commitment population? Or the population of the State? . . .

The most obvious conclusion to be drawn . . . is that minority group women, given the proportion of the State population they constitute, are substantially overrepresented in terms of their proportion of felony commitments to the California Institution for Women and their proportion of the year-end institution population. Also apparent is the problem of reconciling conclusions based upon the population of women committed to prison on felony charges during a given year with the population of the prison at a given point in time (as reported by the California Department of Corrections and as indicated by our two study groups). Data from 1964 to 1967 show the proportion of Negro women committed to prison has declined and that the proportion of Mexican women has increased. Among the prison population, however, the proportion of women in both minority groups has increased.

One reason for this discrepancy may be due to differences in type of offense committed. Negro and Mexican women are disproportionately represented in the assault commitments and Mexican women also comprise a disproportionate share of narcotics commitments. Since assault and narcotic law violations generally carry longer prison terms than do property offenses, it may be that over time more minority group women "accumulate" in prison.

Whatever the reasons for the differences in ethnic (racial) distributions between prison commitments and prison populations, it seems safe to conclude that, given the proportion of minority group women in the State population, they are overrepresented among offenders convicted of assaultive crimes.

INTELLIGENCE

The IQ scores of women in the 1968 sample tended to be concentrated at the low end of the scale: only one in six scored in the above average range, and two out of six scored below average. The validity of IQ test scores may be questioned, however, when they apply to culturally disadvantaged groups. Since prison populations have large percentages of minority group persons, this issue should be kept in mind in examining IQ distribution for specific groups of offenders. (Among whites in the 1968 sample, 17 percent scored below average and 38 percent scored above average. Contrast this with the percent distribution for women from the minority groups—Mexican and black: 59 percent scored below average and 4 percent scored above average.)

Cross-tabulating offense with IQ we found a significant difference: women serving time for assaultive crimes had significantly lower scores than other offenders.

However, when *race is held constant* (that is, when we cross tabulated offense with IQ for whites and nonwhites *separately*), *differences were no longer significant* . . . for example . . . women committed for assault tended to score below average irrespective of majority-minority status; also, among whites committed for homicide there was an equal number of women in each of the three IQ categories.

CRIMINAL RECORD AND CRIME IN FAMILY OF FEMALE FELONS

Criminal Record

When compared to other offenders, women in both the 1963 prison population and in our 1968 sample committed for homicide were significantly less likely to: (1) have had a criminal record or have been previously confined; (2) have been arrested before age 21; or (3) have been previously committed on a felony charge. Women committed for assault had more extensive criminal records prior to their current commitment than did homicide commitments. Robbery commitments had the most extensive records of the three types of violent offenders.

Noting the differences in the criminal careers of homicide offenders compared to women committed for assault and robbery, if these three groups are combined into the "violent offender" category and then compared to the property offender and narcotics offender categories as a group, violent offenders have less extensive criminal careers. Twenty-one percent of the violent offenders for example had no criminal record reported prior to their commitment to the California Institution for Women but only 6 percent and 3 percent, respectively, of the property and narcotics offenders had no prior record. In terms of prior felony commitments, 63 percent of the violent offenders had no such commitment compared to 39 percent of the property offenders and 38 percent of the narcotic offenders. There were, however, no statistically significant differences between these three groups of offenders in terms of age at first arrest, about one-half of each group was arrested before the age of 21.

Crime in the Offender's Family

In 6 out of 10 homicide cases no member of the family was known to have been arrested—either for a misdemeanor or for a felony. Somewhat fewer families of assault offenders had "clean" records. Looking at the most serious end of this continuum it can be seen that murderers were the least likely to have had a member of the family involved in a felony charge.

Differences between offender categories were significant among the 1963 inmate population essentially because of the large proportion of narcotic offenders whose families had felony arrests or convictions. However, these differences were not significant for the 1968 sample.

PERSONAL, SEXUAL, AND EMOTIONAL TROUBLES

Broken Homes

Are women who commit crimes of violence more likely to come from broken homes than is the case for other offenders? Our data (on the 1968 sample only) reveal that there were no statistically significant differences between offenders committed for crimes against persons, property, or narcotics. On a percentage basis, fewer of the murderers come from homes broken by desertion, separation, divorce, or death than was the case for any other offense group. Inmates in other offense categories were more equally split between those who did and did not come from a broken home.

History of Illegal and Illicit Sexual Behavior

Even though the behavior that individuals keep most private—illegal activities and personal sexual activities—are certainly under-reported in prison records, almost two-thirds of the 1963 population and the 1968 sample were reported to have been promiscuous, to have engaged in prostitution, or both; about one-fifth were reported to have had homosexual involvements or to manifest homosexual traits.

Consistent with their less extensive criminal records, compared to other offenders, the women in our study committed for homicide were least likely to have engaged in prostitution. (Assault commitments, on the other hand, were more likely to have reports of either promiscuity or prostitution or both—at least eighty percent—than any other offense group except narcotics offenders.) In addition, fewer women committed for homicide had reports of homosexual involvements than did other offender groups. The most notable involvement of any offense group in homosexuality was among robbery commitments—a finding we shall refer to later in this paper.

Drinking Problems

Compared to property offenders and narcotics offenders, violent offenders were, to a statistically significant degree, more likely to be labeled as "alcoholics." In 1968, one in three of all inmates serving time for violent offenses was labeled "alcoholic" compared to 1 in 8 and 1 in 16 of the property and narcotics offenders.

. . . For the 1968 sample the percent of alcoholics among the homicide and assault offenders was at least double that of the other offense groups.

Of additional interest is the increase in the percentage of female offenders regarded as alcoholic in the 1968 sample compared with the 1963 population: 18 percent of the sample confined in 1968 had been labeled "alcoholic"—twice the percentage for the earlier study group. The increase among violent offenders was even greater—39 percent of the women confined for murder and 35 percent for assault in the 1968 sample were labeled "alcoholic." In 1963, among these two offender groups, only 14 percent and 13 percent were "alcoholic." We cannot be certain, however, whether these changes represent an actual increase in inmates with an alcoholic history or changes in labeling practices by law enforcement, court, and prison personnel.

Narcotics History

This item of information was gathered on the 1963 population but was omitted in the 1968 record abstract due to an administrative error detected too late in the project to remedy; it is thus possible for us to report on narcotics history among violent offenders for the 1963 group only. In 95 percent of the cases, narcotics "use" referred to the use of heroin or other opiates.

The use of narcotics was distinctly a minority characteristic of the homicide and robbery commitments in the 1963 study population compared to assault commitments, property offenders and, of course, narcotics offenders. The 92-percent figure for narcotics use by persons committed for violation of narcotics laws reflects the fact that a small number of persons sold or were charged with possession of narcotics but did not use drugs themselves.

History of Psychological Disabilities

We gathered data pertaining to psychological disabilities in an effort to answer three questions: (1) How widespread are these disabilities among a population of confined female felons? (2) Has there been an increase in the proportion of inmates who are reported to have these disabilities? (3) Compared to other types of offenders, are women committed for crimes of violence more likely to have these disabilities? We combined the diagnoses of psychiatrists and clinical psychologists into three categories: (1) "No Disability Reported"; (2) "Gross References," which included reports of neuroses, psychopathy, and a number of other psychological conditions which were referred to as disabilities; and (3) "Evidence of Psychosis." When more than one diagnosis was contained in the inmate file, the most serious diagnosis was coded.

It is important to indicate that some of the women in the 1963 CIW population were received at the institution during periods when there was no psychiatrist on the staff. It is the case, however, that violent offenders, particularly homicide commitments, were given diagnostic interviews later in their terms when clinical staff became available. Also most of these offenders had in their files psychiatric reports or testimony which was used at their trials. Similarly, inmates whose behavior in the institution was regarded as bizarre or "disturbed" would have psychiatric interview information added to their files during their terms. In all, 90 of the 832 women in the 1963 group had no psychiatric interview data in their files and rather than classify them "No Disability Reported," we excluded them from this analysis. For the 1968 sample we excluded 10 women for whom this information was not available.

Women in both study groups serving time for assault and homicide were described as psychologically disturbed significantly more often than other offenders.

Some . . . data . . . indicate that female felons have been increasingly diagnosed as suffering from some type of psychological disability. This shift can best be seen among homicide commitments. In 1963, 47 percent were regarded as psychologically disturbed; by 1968 the figure had risen to 81 percent. The percentage of all offenders reported to show evidence of psychosis doubled between 1963 and 1968, but the increase for homicide commitments more than tripled.

The major shift in the diagnoses of assault and robbery offenders was, on the other hand, in the direction of the "Gross reference" category ("Disturbed-but-not-psychotic"). In fact, the proportion of women serving time for these two crimes who showed "Evidence of psychosis" was *lower in 1968* than in 1963.

The increase in reported psychological disability between 1963 and 1968 may reflect a real change in the characteristics of women committed during that period. It may also, however, reflect the fact that more clinical staff members mean more diagnoses and more thorough psychiatric examination, or it may reflect changes in preferences for certain diagnostic categories.[2]

THE ROLES OF WOMEN IN CRIMES OF VIOLENCE

There has been only one really detailed study of the character of criminal homicide in the United States—Marvin E. Wolfgang's *Patterns in Criminal Homicide*.[3] Using police reports of 588 cases of murder which occurred in the city of Philadelphia over a 5-year period, Wolfgang presents data pertaining to the race, age, and sex of persons charged with homicide, the time and place where the homicides occurred, the methods and weapons used to inflict death, and the relationship between victims and offenders. In our effort to focus upon critical elements of the roles played by women in committing violent crimes we used the findings of Wolfgang's study and Pollak's report as the basis for specific lines of inquiry.

After a preliminary search identified those aspects of criminal roles that could be reliably obtained from prison files, we abstracted this information for each inmate confined in the California Institution for Women (in 1963-64 and in 1968) and in the Minnesota Women's Reformatory (1964-66) for the following offenses:

Murder:
   Murder, first
   Murder, second
   Voluntary manslaughter
   Involuntary manslaughter
Assault:
   Assault with/without deadly
     weapon
   Assault with intent to kill; rob
   Attempted murder; assault
   Assault with caustic acid
   Wife, child beating; mayhem

Robbery:
   Robbery first
   Robbery second
   Attempted robbery
   Kidnapping for purpose of
     robbery
   Assault with intent to rob
Burglary:
   Burglalry, first
   Burglary, second
   Attempted burglary

The reasons for including homicide, assault, and robbery cases in a study of crimes of violence are self-evident. We have, however, included burglary which is not in the "crimes against persons" category. We were interested in the involvement of women in this type of crime because it implies behavior that is atypical, given the stereotypical roles of women in our society. Burglary suggests force in terms of breaking and entering and a burglar runs the risk of personal confrontation with victims should he—or she—be discovered in the course of committing the burglary. Crimes such as forgery, bad-check writing, theft, and narcotics use do not involve behavior that are particularly "unladylike." Other crimes important in typologies of male criminals have so little relevance for women that we did not include them for sheer lack of number. The dozen or so women convicted of auto theft, for example, were generally companions to men who actually stole the vehicles. No women were committed to the California or Minnesota prisons for rape and the several "sex offenders" in the CIW population were involved in secondary roles in these crimes. (In one case the woman had obtained money as a "pimp" for a teenage prostitute and in another case the woman had encouraged the statutory rape of her daughter by her new husband.) Data on the cases of women who were convicted of kidnaping, arson, and criminal abortion were gathered, but the small number and the extremely unusual character of most of these crimes did not warrant their being included in our analysis.

The features of crimes of violence and burglary committed by women presented in this paper are by no means all of the items that a criminologist would want to have available if he wished to construct an adequate picture of the situational complex within which a particular form of criminal activity took place. We have mined from police, court, and prison records and from personal statements made by the offenders themselves those data we considered to be the most reliably and accurately reported in prison files. The best source of detailed data on the circumstances under which any crime occurred is where Wolfgang gathered his data—in the records of the homicide detail in a police department. This discussion is thus limited to aspects of criminal homicide which were related to the roles of the participants in the crime drama.

.   .   .

FINDINGS

We present below a summary of the principal conclusions to be drawn from our effort to answer several very basic questions about the nature of violent criminal behavior by women. . . . The aspects of violent crimes examined include: whether the women acted alone or with others, who the victims were, where the crimes took place, whether the crimes were premeditated, what weapons were used, whether physical strength was required, what the condition of the victim was at the time of the assault, and what rationale, justification, or explanation was given by the women for their crimes.

THE CRIMINAL ROLES OF WOMEN

The number of roles women can play in committing crimes of violence and burglary include that of the *conspirator,* who instigates or has knowledge of the crime but who does not participate in committing the criminal act itself; the *accessory,* who plays a secondary role in committing the crime—acting as lookout, driving a getaway car, carrying weapons, tools, or the proceeds of robberies and burglaries; the *partner,* who participates equally in all aspects of the crime; and finally, the woman who acts as the *sole perpetrator* of the crime. Data . . . indicate that most of the women in our study population who committed homicide or assault acted alone, but when they were involved in robberies and burglaries they accompanied someone else. When other persons were involved in homicide and assaults, they were husbands and lovers in about half the cases and friends or acquaintances in the others. In robbery and burglary cases women tended to accompany friends or acquaintances rather than persons intimately related to them.

THE VICTIMS OF FEMALE OFFENDERS

That murder tends to be a family affair has been documented in a number of studies and reports, including the *Uniform Crime Reports:* "The significant fact emerges that most murders are committed by relatives of the victim or persons acquainted with the victim."[4] In 1967 approximately 37 percent of all murders involved a spouse killing a spouse, a parent killing a child, and other family killings, romantic triangles, and lovers' quarrels. Our data on violent crime show that husbands, lovers, or children were the victims in over half of the cases of homicide and in over one-third of the assault cases.

Male adults and female adults were victims of 61 percent and 16 percent, respectively, of the homicide cases; nearly all were friends or acquaintances of the murderer. Assault cases involved strangers and women somewhat more often than in cases of homicide.

. . .

Robbery victims were generally strangers to the offender. Commercial personnel were the victims in about half of these cases; unknown men (i.e., men not victimized in connection with their employment) constituted an additional 28 percent. Few women were victimized.

By definition burglary is not a crime against a person, hence the concept of "victim" was taken more broadly to include a person's property. Women committed to prison for this offense seldom victimized an individual, instead they stole from commercial establishments.

Given the relationship between female offenders and their victims, the finding that 60 percent of the homicides and 50 percent of the assaults took place in the offender's residence is not surprising. (In most of these cases, it was the victim's home also.) Robbery and burglary victims tended to be strangers, since the great majority of these offenses occurred away from the residence and neighborhood of the offender.

PREMEDITATION

We were able to obtain from the prison files of about 70 percent of our study sample some evidence of the degree to which the women consciously and deliberately planned their crimes. Operationalizing the concept of premeditation is no easy task, for the amount of time between the point at which one begins to think about and plan for committing a crime and the time when the criminal act actually occurs, which is necessary to constitute premeditation, is subject to different interpretations by judicial authorities, legal experts, psychiatrists, and sociologists. We have tried to avoid the intricacies of resolving such issues as how long a period can one's behavior be said to be the result of "hot blood" and how much activity is required to constitute a deliberately planned robbery or burglary. To do this we have categorized the crimes of our subjects as premeditated *only* when there was a definite statement about a definite plan of action made by the subject or her crime partners, when the crime was one of a series of similar crimes, or when the crime was first-degree murder. In the latter instance we, in effect, accepted the definition of premeditation used by prosecuting attorneys in determining the degree of murder with which the subject was charged. In the case of other offenses this was not a reliable method of establishing premeditation. File data indicated that in some cases the woman was with someone else who actually planned the crime without her knowledge, but she was charged with the offense in the first degree because once the criminal action began she participated actively; in other cases there was evidence in the file of prior planning but perhaps as the result of "plea bargaining" the subject was actually charged with a lesser degree of the crime. In about one-third of the homicide and assault cases in our sample there was not enough information in the prison files to permit us to designate the crime as premeditated or not. For the remaining cases of homicide 21 percent were classified as premeditated; 40 percent as not premeditated. The classifiable assault cases were evenly divided in terms of whether or not premeditation was evident. Robbery and burglary cases gave greater evidence of planning, as might be expected.

.   .   .

THE USE OF PHYSICAL STRENGTH AND AGILITY BY FEMALE OFFENDERS

Examining this aspect of criminal conduct posed a serious problem for operational definition. Some physical strength is required to engage in any activity and we chose to rely upon a definition that focused upon gross rather than subtle actions. In the cases of murder and assault, we looked for instances of physical combat in which the female fought or attacked the victim with her fists or with a knife or some other weapon. We thus excluded from the "physical-strength-required" category cases where the woman walked up to or came upon the victim and shot him; cases where death was caused by poison or neglect; robbery cases where the female *herself* did not participate in subduing, beating, tying up, or otherwise physically acting against the victim; and burglary cases where the female did not physically force or assist in forcing entry into rooms or buildings. The data . . . indicate the use of some physical strength was required in about 4 of 10 murders and 6 of 10 assaults, but in only a small minority of the robbery and burglary cases. The physical strength aspect of female criminality is meaningful only when it is considered with two other classes of data: the use of weapons, and the "condition" of the victim at the time of the crime.

.   .   .

THE USE OF WEAPONS IN ASSAULTIVE CRIMES

The need for women to use physical strength, particularly in the assault cases, is more understandable in the light of the type of weapons that were at hand at the time of the crime . . . a knife or some household implement (e.g., kitchen utensils, hand tools, lye, gasoline, bottles, closet pole, steam iron, straight razor, garden hose, woman's shoes) was used in almost half of the assaults and about one-third of the murder cases. Guns were less frequently used than knives in the assault cases (it may be that since guns are more likely to produce lethal injuries some assaultive acts become homicides). The use of a gun—the great equalizer—by women in assaults, murder, and in about one-third of the robberies, helps to explain why the use of physical strength is not a necessary feature of these crimes. Since burglaries do not involve physical confrontations with victims, the extremely limited use of weapons in the crimes is not surprising. Our data also indicate that there were very few cases in which women took weapons on burglaries "just in case" someone discovered the crime in progress. Guns were used in some of the robberies or available in some of the burglaries but the women did not personally carry them.[5]

. . .

Although one might assume that an unarmed woman is unable to physically harm a healthy, adult male, in our study population more than half the women's victims were adult males. And, in fact, an examination of the victim's "condition" at the time of assault substantiates this assumption. Victims were incapacitated in some way—either ill, drunk, off-guard, or asleep—in 42 percent of the homicides, 38 percent of the assaults, and 44 percent of the robberies. Furthermore, the female's role in cases of adult male robberies should be viewed in connection with the role played by male partners. Burglaries were not committed against persons in the sense of assaultive crimes and were excluded from analysis for this item.

. . .

OFFENDER'S RATIONALE

Twenty-two percent of the women who committed homicide and 19 percent of those who committed assault claimed self-defense or the defense of others as the rationale for their crimes. Of the homicide cases only 2 percent said the victim "deserved it" and 17 percent said that the crime was accidental compared with 13 percent and 8 percent in these categories for assault offenders. Drunkenness accounted for 5 percent of the rationale in homicide cases and 11 percent in cases of assault. Innocence (i.e., nonguilt) was asserted by 13 percent and by 10 percent of those women who committed homicide and assault. There was not enough information to determine how the offender characterized her action in 21 percent of the homicides and in 13 percent of the assault cases.

. . .

It was even more difficult to determine the rationale of robbery and burglary offenders; 31 percent and 44 percent, respectively, of these cases included no information pertaining to the offender's rationale. Such information as there was suggested that motives for robbery were seldom expressed in terms of personal assault; rather economic and psychological reasons were cited in 28 percent of these cases. Sixteen percent claimed they had been "framed" and 11 percent blamed others for getting them involved in the robberies. Sixteen percent of the burglary offenders indicated that the rationale for their crime was based upon economic factors, while 10 percent claimed drunkenness. These findings should be regarded only as suggestive, due to the large "No-Response" category.

CHANGES IN THE ROLE OF FEMALE VIOLENT OFFENDERS

Were the women in the 1968 sample more aggressive, or did they play a more active role in the commission of their offense than the women in prison at the time of the 1963 phase of the project? Two measures which we felt would shed some light on this question were the use of weapons and the extent of participation in the crime. In both cases a comparison of the two study groups seems to indicate that the women in the 1968 group played more active roles and used guns more often in committing their crimes.

Guns were used in almost half of the murders and robberies committed by the 1968 group, compared to about one-fourth of these crimes committed by the 1963 group. There was, however, no increase in the use of guns in the commission of assaults; in fact a slight decrease was recorded. The use of knives and other houshold implements in assaults also declined, from 61 percent to 39 percent. (The number of assault cases is small, however, and percentage differences can be misleading.)

Slightly more than three-fourths of the women in both study groups who were committed for homicide or assault acted alone; thus the degree of participation for these offender types does not show change over the past 4 or 5 years. The proportion of women acting alone in robbery almost doubled over this period. (Nevertheless, it is still the case that most robberies are committed with other persons.) *But when other persons were* involved in each of the three crimes *there was a tendency for the women in the 1968 group to play more active criminal roles.* This tendency was particularly apparent in the robbery cases. The proportion of women identified as "conspirators" and "accessories" (less active criminal roles) declined, while those who were crime "partners" (a more active criminal role) increased.[6]

SOME GENERAL COMMENTS ON CRIMES OF VIOLENCE BY WOMEN

One of the interesting aspects of crimes of violence and burglary by women is that these actions seem to directly contradict the role women in our society are supposed to play. The notion of the female as an aggressive, fist-swinging, gun-carrying criminal ready to take on any potential victim—healthy, adult males included—is difficult to reconcile with the stereotype of the female as the relatively passive, dependent, physically weaker partner to the male. It was thus our task to examine instances in which women violated not only the criminal law, but also the norms that define behavior appropriate for "ladies." What we found was that the participation of women in robbery and burglary was not consistent with the criminal role males play in these crimes but that their behavior was consistent with their role as women. Our female offenders robbed few healthy, adult males by themselves. In burglaries too they acted as supporting players to men who played the leading criminal role. In short, we found that very few females are arrested for serious crimes, that only a very small portion of the women who were arrested for felonies were involved in robberies and burglaries, and that the women who were involved in these crimes did not, in most cases, act in a very unladylike manner.

In the case of homicides and assaults the salience of the sex role was also apparent. The objects of violent attacks by women were most often persons with whom they had affectional relationships such as husbands, lovers, and children. Unlike male violent offenders, the victims of women rarely included store keepers, service station attendants, or others slain or assaulted in the course of committing robberies and burglaries (some 21 percent of the homicides reported to *Uniform Crime Reports* in 1967 were "felony or suspected felony type" murders). When adult males were the victims of assaults by women, the usual case was not that they were beaten up by women tougher or stronger than they, but that a weapon was used by the woman, that the victim was drunk, asleep, or off-guard, or that the woman had help from other persons.

The most obvious conclusion to be drawn from this study is that female criminality is a separate and distinct order of criminal behavior in which cultural factors relating to sex roles in our society are of critical importance. Those who study the etiology of criminal behavior should be prepared to find that most of the current theories of crime causation are inappropriate when applied to female offenders.

Those persons charged with the responsibility of doing something about the problem of violence in our society will find it difficult to draw policy implications from this study. The problem is based in part perhaps upon the primitive level of knowledge we can provide about female violence, but such data as we have indicate that in order to prevent a major portion of the criminal violence in which women engage, one would have to do something about unhappy marriages and love affairs, drunken brawls, and in some cases, stupidity or bad judgment. Intervention might be possible however in the area of crimes against children, because the assaults occur over time. A major difficulty here is that our data indicate that in many cases other persons did know or have reason to suspect that children were being brutalized but they still did not attempt to intervene or call the situation to the attention of medical, welfare or police agencies. Laws pertaining to protection against libel charges for physicians, the handling of child abuse cases by agencies other than police departments, and more public awareness of the child abuse problem may be helpful in encouraging the reporting of these cases.[7] One other category of violence cases where intervention, that is, prevention of further violence, may be feasible are the cases in which the presence of severe psychological disabilities gives warning of future trouble. The problem here again is in encouraging those most likely to detect the onset of psychological problems, namely family members and friends, to bring cases to the attention of physicians, clergymen, or social agencies which can initiate remedial action. For women overwhelmed by disappointments, crises, and life experiences the availability of community mental health centers would provide valuable orthopsychiatric assistance. Finally we want to remind those who point to the small contribution women make to the overall population of violent offenders that the trend in violence by women is upward, and that the rate may be accelerated as women become emancipated from traditional female role requirements.

REFERENCES

1. David A. Ward and Gene G. Kassebaum, *Women's Prison: Sex and Social Structures*. Chicago: Aldine Publishing Co., 1965.

2. For example, the interest in "brain damage" of one psychiatrist, who joined the CIW staff in 1966, resulted in an increase in the number of inmates who were reported to have this disability.

3. Marvin E. Wolfgang, *Patterns in Criminal Homicide*, op. cit. Brief comments or discussions about crimes of violence by women not cited elsewhere in this report may be found in Evelyn Gibson and S. Klein, *Murder*, Home Office Research Unit Report No: 4, London: Her Majesty's Stationery Office, 1961; John M. Macdonald, *The Murderer and His Victim*, Springfield, Ill.: Charles C Thomas, 1961, pp. 31–32; Nancy Barton Wise, "Juvenile Delinquency Among Middle-Class Girls," in Edmund W. Vaz (ed.), *Middle-Class Juvenile Delinquency*, New York: Harper & Row, 1968, pp. 179–188; James S. Wallerstein and Clement J. Wyle, "Our Law-abiding Law-breakers," *Probation*, 225, Mar.–Apr. 1947, p. 110; Lester Adelson, "Slaughter of the Innocents," *The New England Journal of Medicine*, 264, No. 26, June 1961, pp. 1345–1349. See also the articles by Wolfgang, Mooris, and Blom-Cooper; Verkko; and Bohannan in Marvin Wolfgang, *Studies in Homicide*, New York: Harper & Row, 1967.

4. *Crime in the United States 1967*, Washington, D.C.: U.S. Government Printing Office, p. 8.

5. It should be noted that our "No weapons used" category included those cases in which the subject was an accessory or partner in a crime where a weapon was used by others and those cases where death or injury was the result of beatings, strangulation, or other types of physical attack where the "weapon" was hands, arms, feet, etc.

6. This also applies to women convicted on burglary charges: in 1963, 43 percent of the 42 women serving time for burglary were accessories or conspirators; while among the 38 "burglars" in prison in 1968, 95 percent were either partners (75 percent) or sole participants (20 percent).

7. The problem of child abuse is discussed at length in another report to this Commission by David G. Gil, *Physical Abuse of Children: One Manifestation of Violence in American Society*.

Searching for Women
in Organized Crime

Alan Block

The social world of organized crime* appears to be as persistently male as professional football. Women have no social roles to perform in either arena, it seems, except as commodities such as prostitutes or cheerleaders. Organized criminals, like professional athletes, are increasingly to be understood as members of criminal brotherhoods or male families—fraternal organizations in which young men typically swear some form of allegiance and devotion to other young men while promising to obey older men. One of the latest entries in the growing literature on organized crime, David Chandler's *Brothers in Blood* (1975), is a case in point. The book begins with the statement that "the *men* you will meet . . . will be unknown to you for the most part, yet they have shaped some history. They are the dons, capos, and soldiers of a criminal collective that has evolved over the past five hundred years" (p. 1). In Chandler's view the history of organized crime is solely the story of criminal brotherhoods.

*Organized crime in this essay covers the activities of women and men who were career criminals, as well as those connected to bands, rings, mobs, syndicates, and combinations formed to conduct or aid illegal enterprises.

One of the more remarkable aspects of this monosexual description of organized crime is how different it is from earlier studies. For instance, Herbert Asbury's *Gangs of New York* (1927) presented a sexually integrated underworld in which female criminals played a variety of important roles. Consider his discussion of Fredericka Mandelbaum, "better known as Marm or Mother," who was reportedly "the greatest and most successful fence in the criminal annals of New York." Marm Mandelbaum, according to Asbury, "handled the loot and financed the operations of a majority of the great gangs of bank and store burglars." Asbury went on to note that Mandelbaum was both the patron and friend of such notorious female criminals as Black Lena Kleinschmidt, Ellen Clegg, Big Mary, Queen Liz, Little Annie, Kid Glove Rosey, and Old Mother Hubbard, all pickpockets, sneak thieves, and blackmailers. In this same context was Sophie Lyons, "perhaps the most notorious confidence woman America has ever produced" (pp. 214–218).

The sexually diverse New York underworld of the nineteenth century was similar to other urban underworlds uncovered by Asbury in a series of "informal histories." Among the more interesting female criminals mentioned in his other works are Chicago's Kitty Adams, "who for almost a dozen years was known as the Terror of State Street." During her reign, which began in the mid-1880s, it was estimated by the Chicago police that Adams had taken part in over a hundred robberies and uncounted assaults (Asbury 1940: 96–98). Moving to San Francisco, Asbury recounted the stories of such criminals as the confidence woman, Big Bertha, and madams, Miss Piggott, Pigeon-Toed Sal, the Galloping Cow, and Mother Bronson. The illicit activities of these women were extensive and included procuring, fencing, and "shanghaiing." One final point about female criminality was Asbury's claim that "the membership of the early hoodlum gangs included girls, and several were captioned as maladjusted representatives of the so-called gentler sex." And, he added, these female gang leaders were "invariably more ferocious than their male companions," especially when it came to inventing methods of torture (Asbury 1933: 154, 212- 225).

For the historian of organized crime, the discrepancies between the sexually integrated underworlds of the nineteenth century and the sexually segregated world of organized crime advanced by contemporary scholars raise a number of historical, ideological, and methodological questions. Is it that the women mentioned by Asbury were a tiny minority of "freaks" unrepresentative of the general composition of America's urban underworlds during the last century? Or is it that contemporary commentators have seriously misrepresented the social world of organized crime in the twentieth century for ideological reasons that have barred consideration of female organized criminals? And, could it be that the two opposed descriptions reflect historical changes in organized crime that have caused the exclusion of women from illicit activities?

Confirmation of Asbury's insights can be gained not only from such older work as *Old Bowery Days* (1931) and such primary sources as the Lexow Commission's hearings (1894),[1] but also from modern studies of the London underworld in the nineteenth century, which furnish cross-cultural corroboration. In Kellow Chesney's *The Victorian Underworld* (1970), for example, female criminals play substantial parts. Chesney's discussion of organized thieves shows that women "were among the commonest and most useful accomplices involved in almost every type of robbery." Among street thieves women "most often played a leading part" with one particular variant of street stealing becoming a "feminine specialty." This was the systematic robbing of well-to-do children of their clothes and boots. Actually, there were any number of stealing specialties that were filled by women as they worked in conjunction with the full complement of urban male thieves (pp. 133-137). Another social history of organized crime in nineteenth century England states:

> Women were well represented in the criminal class, and acted as accomplices in a number of ways. . . . They would carry a housebreaker's tools to and from the scene of operations . . .

and would often be entrusted with the stolen property. Prostitutes would sometimes start a riot in a public house to draw the
police away from the scene of an intended burglary, and were
often in league with pickpockets.

The women of the criminal class did not, of course, restrict
their activities to aiding the men; many of them were thieves
themselves. The girls would beg or steal like the boys, with of
course, the additional resort of prostitution when occasion served.
(Tobias, 1967: 92)

Concerning the ferocity of women criminals, this study echoes
Asbury's finding that "though there were proportionately far
fewer women criminals than men, they were said to be worse
than most of the men" (p. 93). Clearly, there seems to be little
reason to believe that organized crime in nineteenth century
America as described by Asbury was either mistaken or unique.

What then of the possibility that today's interpreters have
misread the contemporary social world of organized crime?
Certainly there is a marked disparity in approach between the
social historians of nineteenth century organized crime (including popular writers) and today's scholars. Early writers such as
Asbury, as well as modern historians like Tobias and Chesney,
were interested in describing and analyzing urban underworlds—
real, physical districts that provided a home and market for the
entire range of criminals. Their studies of organized crime are
grounded in the social life of San Francisco's Barbary Coast,
New York's Five Points area and Lower East Side, New Orleans'
Storyville vice section, and London's various criminal districts.
Crucial to this approach is an understanding of the functions of
such urban establishments as saloons, pool parlors, restaurants,
hotels, ethnic market places, transportation terminals, political
clubs, and gambling dens within and around which criminal life
was centered. Organized criminal activities were simply one of
the features of the social life of impoverished districts, and
miscreant females were part of this broad social panorama.
Other historical studies of European cities such as pre-Revo-
lutionary Paris (Kaplow, 1972:148-151), whose purpose is the

social history of the forgotten, rapidly come to the same conclusion.

Contemporary discussion, on the other hand, have little interest in the social context of organized crime. Today's sociology of organized crime is almost totally dominated by the question, "How organized is organized crime"? Geographical considerations of criminal behavior have become, at the same time, the special province of those interested in the sociology of juvenile delinquency.[2] Analyses of modern or indeed historical vice districts and the *urbaneness* of organized criminals play little part in today's sociologies with certain marvelous exceptions (Light, 1974).

But the most pressing question still remains whether or not women have been part of this century's social world of organized crime. The answer is that they have been very much a part of the organized underworlds, but have been effectively removed because of a belief in conspiracy as the engine of organized crime (Smith, 1975), and because of a malign interpretation of female criminality that reached its apotheosis during the Progressive Era (1900–1917) and has remained an intellectual stumbling block ever since.

The only female criminal role discussed during the Progressive period is that of prostitute. And that literature, whether a study of the reformers who moved to eradicate the social evil, or the enterprise itself, depicted women as passive victims of social disequilibrium and the venality and brutality of men. Equally as striking, the image of prostitute, especially as developed by Progressive-Era reformers, was of a lonely, detached, and confused female. Nowhere was it suggested that prostitutes or madams consciously and aggressively chose their activities as a positive adaptation to urban property.[3] Along with this particular view of the "dynamics" of prostitution, Progressive reformers concentrated their energies upon female deviance in the burgeoning immigrant neighborhoods of selected American cities. The controlling metaphor for prostitution during this period was "white slavery," and while there was compassion and concern for the rootless, uneducated, immigrant prostitute, there was only hatred and contempt for the white slavers. It was a Progressive discovery or invention that the slavers were also members of the immigrant communities—in New York, especially, it was claimed that the leaders of supposedly vast vice operations were Russian and Polish Jews. It was undoubtedly of some solace to Progressive moralists that sexual slavery was an alien phenomenon[4] in much the same way that so many contemporary studies keep mistakenly returning to the alien origins of orgnized crime.

Perhaps the classic example of this vision of prostitution was broadcast by *McClure's Magazine* in a famous series of articles published in 1909. One of the essays, written by editor S. S. McClure, began with praise for the "Germanic races" as the architects of Western civilization. In contrast to this achievement, McClure held that the "great masses of primitive peoples from the farms of Europe, transported to this country as laborers, together with a considerable proportion of Negro slaves liberated by the Civil War, have struggled to degrade the standards and guaranties of the civilization of America." For proof, McClure turned to a description of the white slave traffic in New York linking it to Tammany Hall and the East Side immigrant Jews. McClure wrote: "There has grown up, as an adjunct to this herd of female wretchedness, a fraternity of fetid male vermin (nearly all of them being Russian or Polish Jews), who are unmatchable for impudence and beastiality" (pp. 117–118).

Another of the essays was George Kibbe Turner's "The Daughters of the Poor." Turner's interest was the "transfer of a vast empire of prostitution from its European base to the East Side of New York." He noted that around twenty-five years before, during "the third great flush of immigration," which consisted of Hungarian, Austrian and Russian Jews, a very large number of criminals moved to New York. In fact, Turner wrote, it was the Jewish district that "opened the eyes of the minor politician of the slums to the tremendous enterprise, the business of procuring and the traffic in women offered him." It was also stated that the largest number of prostitutes came from immigrant Jewish families and that the East Side Jewish pimp was transferring his activities to other American cities (pp. 47, 49–52.)

Clearly enough, as Arthur A. Goren has pointed out, these writers "played upon the widely shared anxieties of the times: the fear of organized conspiracy by amoral business and political interests," and the degradation of the immigrants who now appeared to control a number of American cities (Goren, 1970: 138–144). More explicitly, Egal Feldman reported in his excellent essay, "Prostitution, the Alien Woman and the Progressive Imagination, 1910–1915" (1967), that there were a couple of distinct campaigns or approaches to the issue of immigrants and crime during those years. First was "a nativistic attack on prostitution with all its ugly xenophobic overtones"; this was "paralleled by an anti-nativist outburst." The nativist simply blamed the immigrant communities for prostitution, while the antinativist not only attempted to uncover the causes and devise cures for prostitution, but also tried "at the same time to disassociate the reputation of the immigrant from commercialized vice" (p. 197). For all its decency of purpose, however, the antinativist position was weak. It was logically unsound since the premise of immigrant innocence precluded discussion of immigrant venality. But more importantly, it subsumed female crime under the single heading of prostitution. And concomitantly it undermined any consideration of female criminality outside the Progressive formula of weak women and brutal, exploitative men.

How wrong, misleading, and chauvinistic this view was and is can be seen by an analysis of one of the finest primary sources for the history of organized crime during this century. The source is the reports of a unique organization known as the Bureau of Social Morals, which was part of a Jewish "self-defense" association called the New York Kehillah.[5] The Kehillah's considerable influence was channeled through its annual

conventions and scientific bureaus, which by the late summer of
1912 included the Bureau of Social Morals formed in the after-
math of the infamous Rosenthal murder. More generally, the
Kehillah and the Bureau were part of the New York Jewish
community's response to accusations of Jewish criminality—that
part of the nativist outburst discussed above. The Kehillah maintained the anticrime Bureau of Social Morals for five years.
Staffed by a number of private investigators, the Bureau focused
on the First Inspection District, the six police precincts of the
Lower East Side. The Bureau's most important communal contribution was the supplying of "detailed information that led to
gambling raids, revocation of licenses, and the arraignment of
individual criminals" (Goren, pp. 159–170).

Unfortunately, there was no summary or final comprehensive
report on organized crime, and there was no particular organizational scheme to the material. The investigators' function was
to document Jewish involvement in crime and then to turn their
evidence over to the law enforcement agencies. But, within the
mass of material there are data concerning ethnicity, criminal
occupations, kinship, past criminal records, the geography of
illegal enterprises, and membership in particular gangs or vice
rings for some of the *311* female criminals identified by the
Bureau.

Analysis of the data indicates that there were five fairly
distinct groups of female criminals: those involved solely in
prostitution; those who achieved a management position usually
in a vice operation or displayed a special business skill such as
fencing stolen goods or corrupt bail bonding; those whose
criminal activities were exclusively some form of stealing, an
exceptionally small group who were both whores and theives;
and those who worked a combination of vice, gambling, and
drug dealing. The 311 women criminals were divided into 149
prostitutes, 18 entrepreneurs, 56 thieves, 4 whore-thieves, and
24 vice, drug, and gambling operatives. Of course, the categories
and numbers alone are telling indications of the varied female
roles in organized crime. And it is sufficient for the purpose of

this essay to point out that a computer analysis of the female criminals clearly shows that the traditional image of the female criminal was and is more representative of male psychology than of female criminality. Let a few examples stand for the extended inquiry.[6]

In contrast to the traditional image of the prostitute, consider the following report filed in August, 1912, by the Bureau's investigators. This extensive investigation was of a whore house owned by the Hertz family located at 7 East First Street on the East Side of Manhattan. The building was known as the Columbia Hotel and was owned by Rosie Hertz, her husband, Jacob Hertz, and Max and David Rosenbach, brothers of Rosie Hertz. Also working there were two of Rosie Hertz's cousins, Hyman and Morris Goldman, the latter of which was the manager. The family were Hungarian Jews and supposedly ran some of the most famous whore houses in New York City. The Bureau noted that Rozie Hertz had made a great deal of money and owned a "few tenement houses on 5th Street, and also the house she occupies in Borough Park, Brooklyn." Concerning her past, the Bureau found out "from an authentic source . . . that Rosie's mother, Gittel, was the first Jewish madam in New York, if not in the entire United States." Rosie's career began when she went "from one coal cellar to another—from one shoe-making basement to another." By living frugally, the Hertz's had succeeded in becoming "bosses in the disorderly house graft"; to protect their interests they "contributed $1,000 every year to both the Democratic and Republican organizations." Other interests that the Hertz family had included the fencing of stolen goods and a small bail bond business: Rosie would "very often sign bonds for gambling houses," although in those cases she reportedly never charged anything. It is absolutely clear from the Bureau's reports that the leader of the Hertz family was Rosie.

Stealing, like prostitution and other criminal activities, was also often a family affair dominated by the women. For example, the Bureau reported on the careers of two brothers, Sam and

Meyer Solomon, and their wives, Tillie and Bessie. Sam, it was claimed, was notorious "for his propensities as a seducer . . . around Hamilton Fish Park from where he graduated a full fledged pickpocket and fagin." Meyer's wife, Bessie, was described as one of the "cleverest boosters–gun molls" in the world. She was supposedly responsible for training a large number of women, including Sam's wife, Tillie, as pickpockets and thieves. When their wives went to work, the brothers retired from active stealing and turned to other pursuits such as gambling, loan sharking, and the fencing of stolen goods. In the fall of 1912, however, the Solomons fell on hard times when the women were arrested.

It is apparent that sexually integrated mobs far removed from the master-slave model of the Progressive imagination abounded among thieves as well as other criminals. Several more examples include Spanish Mary and her husband, Earle Williams, known as the "King of the Panhandlers," who worked ferry boats, elevated trains, and subways. In the same category are Sarah and Jacob Glucksman, May and Joe Hess, and the pickpocket team of Taube and Aaron Goldsbard. One other interesting case is that of Katt Schoenberg, the wife of Joe Feldman, alias Joe English. The Schoenberg family along with the already discussed Hertz and Solomon groups furnishes one of the best examples of the familial dimension of organized crime and the importance of aggressive female participation. The Schoenberg's criminality began in the "old country" when Katt's mother and father started their illegal careers. Following in their parents' footsteps were two sons, one of Katt's brothers-in-law, and her first husband. At the time of the investigation, the Schoenberg-Feldman entourage centered their stealing in the fish markets under the Williamsburg Bridge.

The subject of female involvement in organized crime was dominated by a series of sentimental conceptions dealing especially with prostitution and cast principally by Progressive reformers and their immediate forebears[7] as they grappled with the enormity of urban culture. Once firmly established, these notions left little room for any understanding of female criminality, including prostitution, as a rational method of adaption to urban opportunities and institutions. The sentimentality of the approach fixed concern upon the single question of cause—what could have led girls to so degrade themselves, to ultimately destroy themselves. This view meant that female criminality would really become a part of the general field of juvenile delinquency (in much the same manner as social area analyses), that section of criminology devoted to seeking reasons for the transformation of young people from citizens to criminals.

Adult female criminality had seemingly been settled as a separate topic by that part of the Progressive formula that went inexorably from juvenile female crime to degradation, disease, and death. Under this formulation, mobility in organized crime for females was an explicit, one-way street, leading rapidly downward. As long as this viewpoint prevails, there is little sense in considering adult female criminals as more than the victims of brutal male criminals: used by them until they reach some disgusting level of disease that renders them criminally useless after which they are abandoned. Naturally, within this traditional litany of causes and concerns there is no room for female independence and equality in this century's world of organized crime. Women such as Rosie Hertz, Bessie Solomon, and Katt Schoenberg, therefore, make little sense. Indeed, the female criminal class composed of those women who achieved a management position or displayed special criminal business skills is either a gross misinterpretation or, at best, a historical oddity with no general significance, according to both the Progressive and traditional contemporary views.

The all-male world of organized crime is a product of a special kind of historical insensitivity partially supported by a naive belief in conspiracy and by the remarkable staying power of Progressive imagery. This does not mean that female organized criminals, post-Progressivism, are never mentioned, however. They sometimes are even in the popular works that so resolutely maintain a sexually exclusive underworld. But when female criminals are identified or described, their roles and functions are never analyzed—in a real sense, they are mere scenery. Consider the following examples from three of the more popular works on the history of organized crime.

In the last chapter of informer Vincent Teresa's memoirs, *My Life in the Mafia* (1973), there appear two "rare" women. "Years ago," Teresa states, "there was Butsey Morelli's wife. She was a very, very smart woman, and she helped advise Butsey in the early part of his career as he took over the mob in Rhode Island and the New England area." Teresa adds that "she was well thought of by all the old Mustache Petes and she had plenty of power." Besides Morelli's wife, Teresa remembers "a guy named Rusty—he's big today with the Bonanno mob—who had a wife called Connie." According to Teresa, Connie was a "real tough broad" having been a loanshark and a bookmaker before she married. Connie's attributes were decidedly in the masculine mode as Teresa describes her: "Guys would borrow money from her and figure that because she was just a broad they could make a mark out of her. But Connie fooled the hell out of them. She'd have their legs broken, or she'd go down and shoot them herself." "Even after Rusty and Connie were married," Teresa continues, "she stayed in business and stayed tough." "Once Rusty shot two guys and one of them survived, and he fingered Rusty to be killed." When Rusty went into hiding, "Connie decided to get the guy. . . . She had him set up and gunned down in a cemetery" (pp. 344-345). These rather remarkable women are used by Teresa as a counterpoint to the traditional roles of "mob" wives—silence and the nurturing of children.

Female organized criminals are also mentioned in Paul Sann's biography of Dutch Schultz, *Kill the Dutchman* (1971). In one of the early chapters appears racketeer, Stephanie St. Clair, better known as "Madam Queen of Policy." Sann writes that "this flamboyant figure, sometimes called the Tiger from Marseilles, truly had fought the Dutchman to his death." St. Clair had reportedly "refused to yield her numbers bank to Schultz when he was on his triumphal armed march through the Negro community." Her particular "piece of the policy racket in Harlem" was supposedly worth more than a million dollars a year (pp. 56-57). Also appearing in the Sann book is Polly Adler who was one of New York's most notorious madams during the 1930s. With his eye fixed upon the development of the National Crime Syndicate, Sann has no time or interest in speculating on the femininity of woman or such issues as ethnicity and female criminal specialties.

Let me add, at this point, that a reading of trial documents concerning the Schultz venture into policy in the early 1930s clearly reveals a number of women playing significant roles in numbers gambling. Some banks, in fact, had a preponderance of women at both the collector and controller levels, exceptionally important positions in policy syndicates. When Schultz made his drive to dominate Harlem numbers gambling, his initial success with most independent banks was rapidly short-circuited by what was in effect a strike of collectors and controllers. This job action was undertaken immediately after Schultz cut back the "salaries" of controllers and collectors. The point to consider here is the active role of women first in policy gambling in general, and second in aggressively defending the customary financial arrangements in policy against the usurpations of Schultz (New York State Court of Appeals, The People of the State of New York against James J. Hines).

Because Sann mentions Polly Adler, it also seems appropriate to note that women, not just Polly Adler, were deeply involved in the administration of organized prostitution in New York for at least the first four decades of this century. And remarkable as it may seem for the similarity to policy, madams along with bookers (individuals who rotated the working prostitutes from brothel to brothel in Manhattan on a systematic basis) were subjected to unwanted centralization beginning in 1933 by a crime syndicate headed by Lucky Luciano. In attempting to centralize organized prostitution, Luciano also tampered with customary financial arrangements centering on the madams' margin of profit. This led directly to several covert forms of resistance principally from madams and bookers. In the short run this resistance movement was successfully terrorized by Luciano thugs. However, when Luciano was indicted, tried, and convicted on charges of compulsory prostitution in 1936, women, both working prostitutes and especially madams, were the key witnesses. Following Luciano's removal, organized prostitution reverted back to its traditional structures (New York State Court of Appeals, The People of the State of New York against Charles Luciano et al.).

Even *Murder, Inc.* (1951), the one work that most clearly set the tone and categories for so much of the contemporary misunderstanding of organized crime, contains several passing references to female organized criminals. The most notorious woman mentioned was Virginia Hill who apparently consorted with the following infamous racketeers: the Fischetti brothers of Chicago, Joe Adonis, Lucky Luciano, Frank Costello, Dandy Phil Kastel of New Orleans, Meyer Lansky, and of course, Buggsy Siegel. In addition to being the courtesan of so many racketeers, Hill was suspected of being "the mob's cross-country 'bagman,' or money messenger" (pp. 270-272). Much more interesting than Hill, however, is the "Red Rose of Williamsburg." In a chapter devoted to somewhat sentimental and chauvinistic discussion of the wives and girl friends of various racketeers, the authors, Turkus and Feder, note that "Rose was established as a figure in the Larney gang, a mob of shylocks and killers" (pp. 193-194). What is remarkable about Rose Pantiel and her membership in the Larney gang of gamblers and loansharks is that neither she nor the gang can be fit into the schema of organized crime advanced by Turkus and Feder. This sexually integrated outfit operated independently of the National Crime Syndicate, a fact simply glossed over by Turkus and

Feder.[8] As far as they were concerned, Rose Pantiel's only importance was as the mother of racketeer Chippy Weiner's wife.

There are two other women criminals mentioned by Turkus and Feder: Rose Gold, the owner of a candy store in Brownsville, Brooklyn, that became the "headquarters" of Abe Reles, Martin Goldstein, and Harry Strauss, prominent Brooklyn racketeers and the so-called contract killers employed by the Syndicate; and Lena Frosch, the leader of a family of bail bond racketeers. As might be expected, Turkus and Feder were unable to expand their approach by asking anything interesting about these women or to connect their particular activities to a wider context.

Fortunately, it is not necessary to rely on *Murder, Inc.* for information about Rose Gold and Lena Frosch. Both women were among the subjects of a four-year investigation into official corruption in Brooklyn carried out by Assistant Attorney General John Harlan Amen and summarized in *Report of the Kings County Investigation, 1938–1942.* The *Report* states that on May 4, 1939, Mrs. Rose Gold, "69 years of age, decrepit and unable to read or write English," was charged with seventeen counts of perjury stemming from her attempts to hide her relationship with Reles and his associates. Gold's involvement with the Brooklyn killers was complex, according to Amen. She made frequent court appearances in Brooklyn police stations "to bail out men arrested for disorderly conduct or gambling where the games were operated or protected" by Reles. Gold also provided bail for Reles and the others in several New York courts. After examining Gold's bank account, Amen found "$395,983.70 had been deposited and withdrawn" from November 1937 to December 1938. Among the deposits was a check for $7,236 given to Gold by Louis Capone, a notorious racketeer and associate of Albert Anastasia. Amen established that all the bank transactions were carried out by Gold's daughter, Shirley Herman, whose husband was "an assistant research clerk to Irwin Steingut," the leader of the Democratic minority in the

State Assembly and considered one of Brooklyn's most powerful politicians. Amen also found that part of Rele's loanshark racket was run out of her candy store and was managed by her son known as Sam "The Dapper" Siegel (pp. 73-74).

Amen uncovered the criminal activities of the other woman alluded to by Turkus and Feder, Lena Frosch, while pursuing the links between corrupt bail bonding and Brooklyn racketeers. His major concern was with the current activities of a bail bond conspirator named Abraham Frosch, who when reviewing Frosch's history was compelled to discuss his mother, Lena. Abraham Frosch, whose tesitimony resulted in the "removal or forced retirement of 25 police lieutenants and sergeants," had been in the bonding business since he was fourteen. He started out helping his mother, Lena, a licensed bondswoman, who had sent him after school "either to the courts to check on the disposition of cases on which his mother had gone bond, or to the police stations to get from lieutenants cash deposited by his mother as bail for clients." In 1934 Lena Frosch was convicted of perjury and forgery on bail bonds and her license revoked. But this did not deter her from continuing the business which, by then, consisted of getting her property-owning neighbors to offer their real estate as bail for a percentage of her fee. It became her son's job to shuttle the neighbors to either the courts or police stations, along with helping in the execution of the bonds (pp. 75-76).

One does not have to consider only fleeting references to female criminals in the popular literature or indeed in the *Amen Report,* especially when considering illegal bail bonding. In the mid-1930s, for instance, the revamped New York City Department of Investigation and Accounts undertook a large-scale investigation of municipal government including criminal justice. One of its principal areas of concern was bail bonding, which had been shown to be extraordinarily significant in the social system of organized crime by Samuel Seabury a few years before. What Seabury established in a stunning series of investigations from 1930 to 1932 was the inescapable fact that bonds-people were an integral part of the administration of court business. Bonders played the part, as Seabury puts it, of a general factotum arranging the details and paths through the labyrinth of justice. In numerous cases they acted as a kind of general agent for a defendant, frequently hiring the lawyer, shepherding the witnesses, and taking care of the payoffs necessary to fix the case. While doing so, of course, bail bonders bilked every dollar they could from their clients. For the innocent, bail bonders were the capstone of the justice racket; for the guilty, they managed corruption, acting as a kind of "clearing house between the underworld and the realm of lawfulness." (For Seabury's investigation see New York State Supreme Court, 1932: 103-124.)

Picking up where Seabury's investigation of bonding had ended, the report issued by the Department of Investigation and Accounts (1937) first places bonding within the context of organized crime, and second lists bail-bond racketeers uncovered by the investigators. There are 53 bonders named, twenty-three of whom were women. Female criminals in this important category comprised almost 44 percent of the named racketeers. In addition to the sexual breakdown, the material reveals ethnic identities; about one-half of the women were Jewish, one-third Italian, the remainder either Hispanic or unidentified. Clearly then, throughout the 1930s and presumably in the decades following, women from a variety of ethnic backgrounds were deeply enmeshed within the social system of organized crime (New York City, Department of Investigation and Accounts, 1937: 51-60, 153-160).

Organized crime has been an important part of urban America providing goods and services for a variety of male and female patrons and clients, and potential money and power for male and female criminals. Contrary to many accounts organized crime was not the unique creation of any particular immigrant group such as the Italians, but rather flourished in a variety of ethnic and working-class communities. Criminal enterprises were one way of responding to poverty, and immigrant and native-born males and females realized this. In many cases illegal activities were a familial affair: there were real families of crooked bail bonders, pimps and madams, fences and thieves. Criminal enterprises were staffed by brothers, sisters, cousins, in-laws, mothers, and fathers. Male and female relatives channeled money back and forth from legal to illegal businesses and, when able, conveyed political protection.

Organized crime was frequently an adjunct of the economic, political, and social aspirations of communities such as New York's Lower East Side. Besides the goods and services provided to members of the community, illegal activities run and staffed by men and women pumped money into local real estate and legitimate businesses. Male and female professional criminals were major supporters and sometimes owners of such community enterprises as saloons, candy stores, pool parlors, restaurants, and gambling establishments. Professional criminals also supplied work for the host of male and female intermediaries in the criminal justice system: lawyers, fixers, steerers, and especially bail bonders.

Because organized crime was in so many ways a communal experience, its significance, not to mention its social history, has been lost by many of the contemporary commentators. Their interpretations have been cast in a vacuum, insensitive to the complex communities that nurtured male and female organized criminals. Enamored with proving some gigantic conspiracy hatched by the minds of master criminals (invariably men), writers have narrowed their focus so much that organized crime has been perceived as strictly parasitic, serving no needs and performing no functions apart from enriching criminals.

In not connecting organized crime either to real communities or to concrete criminal justice agencies except for the police, researchers have structured untold members of women outside the social reality of organized crime. In doing so, they have been

supported by, and themselves support, an ideology so contemp-
tuous of women, their roles, power, and actual experiences as to
be profoundly pathological.[9]

NOTES

1. The Lexow Committee, which was the popular name for "The Senate
Committee Appointed to Investigate the Police Department of New York
City," was formed in response to continuing allegations of police corruption
and vice control leveled by the sensational Dr. Charles Parkhurst, pastor of the
Madison Square Presbyterian Church and leader of the Society for the Preven-
tion of Crime. See Logan (1972).

2. For confirmation, see the chapter "Culture Areas" and the footnotes in
Sutherland and Cressey (1974).

3. See Woolston (1969), Seligman (1912), Benjamin and Masters (1964),
Waterman (1932), King (1956), Pivar (1973), Lubove (1963), Feldman (1967),
and, of course, Kneeland (1913).

4. In addition to the works cited above, one should also consult U.S.,
Congress, House, *White Slave Traffic*, H.R. 47, 61st Cong., 2d sess., where it is
noted that "there are few who really understand the true significance of the
term 'white-slave trade' . . . the inmates of many houses of ill fame are made
up largely of women and girls whose original entry into a life of immorality
was brought about by men . . . who by means of force and restraint, compel
their victims to practice prostitution" (p. 10). Much the same view is found in
U.S., Congress, Senate, *Importing Women for Immoral Purposes*, S.D. 196,
61st Cong., 2nd sess.

The reported connections between New York's immigrant Jewish popu-
lation and prostitution moved several residents of New York's Lower East
Side to petition President William H. Taft, protesting communal innocence.
See U.S., Congress, Senate, *Petition of Citizens of Orchard, Rivington, and
East Houston Streets, New York City, Relative to the Reports of Officials and
the Conditions of Immigrants*. S.D. 785, 62nd Cong., 2d sess.

5. Information on the New York Kehillah was obtained from the Judah L.
Magnes Archives, the Central Archives for the History of the Jewish People,
Jerusalem, Israel. I first became acquainted with the material in the Magnes
Archives through Goren (1970). In Goren's note on sources he states that the
Magnes Archives in Jerusalem "contain an outstanding collection of sources for
the study of Jewish life in New York and Jewish communal politics in America
from 1908 to 1922. . . . The largest part of this material consists of the
Kehillah's records which contain a wealth of sources of Jewish education,
religious life, philanthropic organization, industrial conditions, and crime."
Using Goren's citation for the specific material on crime—MA (SP/125–
SP/139)—I wrote to the Central Archives for the History of the Jewish People

and requested a microfilm copy of the almost 2,000 "case histories of Jewish criminals prepared by the Kehillah's chief investigator and based on information supplied by his informers and agents." Ms. Hadassah Assouline of the Central Archives was kind enough to fulfill my request.

The important question of the veracity of the investigators' reports is discussed by Goren who points out a number of instances where legal action followed the filing of reports. In addition, he notes that the Bureau of Social Morals chief investigator was appointed a Deputy Police Commissioner in charge of investigations in the Lower East Side. My own investigation of the geography of organized crime as reported in the Bureau's reports also confirms their accuracy. I checked the reported ownership of various buildings used for illegal activities with the City's official records and found them to be completely accurate.

6. See Block (1977).

7. One of the most interesting discussions of American attitudes concerning sex and degradation that became one of the premises of the Progressive formula can be found in Davis (1957). In a chapter titled, "The Mysterious Power of Sex," Davis remarked that sex had become a "deadly serious issue" by the 1840s and 1850s. He wrote:

> Traditionalists complained about the increasing number of working women, the celibacy of Shakers and Catholic clergy, the mounting number of prostitutes, the alleged immorality of convents, the mistresses of the rich, the spread of birth-control information, the high number of divorces in western states, the rumors of free-love communities, and the polygamy of the Mormons. Social and political issues were dramatized in sexual terms. . . . In 1859 a writer in *The New Englander* declared that Anglo-Saxon superiority rested in the race's "hiding power" of chastity and in that deeply felt "reverance for women" which enabled Saxons and barbarians to conquer England and Rome. America's position as a leader of the superior race was now seriously threatened by six thousand New York prostitutes, by Washington society where "the reputation of a harlot scarcely impairs the standing of a wife and a mother," and by the fact that adultery was not punished as a state offense.

In reaction to this tension, literature, Davis stated, "provided an outlet for both social and personal conflicts, and attempted to reassure the discontented." Reassurance would take the form of a restoration of "order and balance," which would be maintained "by a sentimental allegiance to motherhood, by a deification of respectable women, and by an unrestrained assault on seduction, lechery, prostitution, and adultery." Davis goes on noting that it was unlikely that "licentiousness constituted a greater problem in America in 1930 than it had in 1730." The concern, therefore, was the outgrowth of an especial American preoccupation with the possible social effects of democracy. Americans needed to prove that "liberty was not an excuse for profligacy," and that popular government would not lead inexorably "to anarchy and thus to unrestrained sexual indulgence." The peculiar and "excessive prudishness of Americans was partly a manifestation of this self-mistrust. In fiction, the identification of sex and death was the psychological result of the tension between fear and freedom." This developing notion that sex was un-American quickly eventuated in the proposition that sex outside of marriage "brought a rotting, a decomposition of human virtue and dignity." This was closely followed by the idea that even one "sexual experience" would render any girl "capable of any crime": a single lapse brought total ruin and damnation. "There was no room for a partial or temporary corruption; only death could atone for a ruin so total and absolute."

8. See the *New York Times* report of 26 August 1940, p. 17.

9. See the remarkable study by G.J. Barker-Benfield (1976).

REFERENCES

Amen, J.H. (1942) Report of the Kings County Investigation, 1938–1942.

Asbury, H.(1933) The Barbary Coast: An Informal History of The San Francisco Underworld. New York: Alfred A. Knopf.

——— (1940) The Chicago Underworld. New York: Alfred A. Knopf.

——— (1927) The Gangs of New York: An Informal History of the Underworld. New York: Alfred A. Knopf.

Barker-Benfield, G.J. (1976) The Horrors of the Half-Known Life: Male Attitudes Towards Women and Sexuality in Nineteenth-Century America. New York: Harper & Row.

Benjamin, H. and R.E.L. Masters (1964) Prostitution and Morality: A Definitive Report on the Prostitute in Contemporary Society and an Analysis of the Causes and Effects of the Suppression of Prostitution. New York: The Julian Press.

Block, A.A. (1977) "Aw—Your Mother's in the Mafia: Women Criminals in Progressive New York." Contemporary Crises 1 (January).

Chandler, D.L. (1975) Brothers in Blood: The Rise of the Criminal Brotherhoods. New York: E.P. Dutton.

Chesney, K. (1972) The Victorian Underworld. New York: Schocken Books.

Davis, D.B. (1957) Homicide in American Fiction, 1798–1860: A Study in Social Values. Ithaca, New York: Cornell University Press.

Feldman, E. (1967) "Prostitution, The Alien Woman and the Progressive Imagination, 1910–1915," American Quarterly 11 (Summer).

Goren, A.A. (1970) New York Jews and the Quest For Community: The Kehilah Experiment, 1908–1922. New York: Columbia University Press.

Harlow, A.F. (1931) Old Bowery Days: The Chronicles of a Famous Street. New York: D. Appleton.

Kaplow, J. (1972) The Names of Kings: The Parisian Laboring Poor in the Eighteenth Century. New York: Basic Books.

King, H.F. (1956) "The Banishment of Prudery: A Study of the Issue of Prostitution in the Progressive Era." Unpublished Ph. D. dissertation, Columbia University.

Kneeland, G.J. (1913) Commercialized Prostitution in New York City. New York: The Centruy Co.

Light, I. (1974) "From Vice District to Tourist Attraction: The Moral Career of American Chinatowns, 1880–1940." *Pacific Historical Review* XLIII (August).

Logan, A. (1972) Against the Evidence: The Becker-Rosenthal Affair. New York: Avon Books.

Lubove, R. (1963) The Progressives and the Slums: Tenement House Reform in New York City, 1890–1917. Pittsburgh: University of Pittsburgh Press.

McClure, S.S. (1909) "The Tammanyizing of a Civilization." McClure's Magazine 34 (November).

New York City. Department of Investigation and Accounts (1937) Investigating City Government in the La Guardia Administration: A Report of the Activities of the Department of Investigation and Accounts, 1934–1937.

New York State Court of Appeals. The People of the State of New York against Charles Luciano et al. Record on Appeal.

New York State Court of Appeals. The People of the State of New York against James J. Hines. Case on Appeal.

New York State Senate Committee to Investigate the Police Department of the City of New York (1895) Report and Proceedings. Albany: J.B. Lyon Co.

New York State Supreme Court, Appelate Division—First Judicial Department (1932) Final Report of Samuel Seabury, Referee. New York: Lawyers Press.

Pivar, D.J. (1973) Purity Crusade: Sexual Morality and Social Control, 1868–1900. Westport, Conn.: Greenwood Press.

Sann, P. (1971) Kill the Dutchman: The Story of Dutch Schultz. New Rochelle: Arlington House.

Seligman, E.R.A. (ed.) (1912) The Social Evil: With Special Reference to Conditions Existing in the City of New York. New York: G.P. Putnam's Sons.

Smith, D.C., Jr. (1975) The Mafia Mystique. New York: Basic Books.

Sutherland, E.H. and D.R. Cressey (1974) Criminology. Philadelphia: J.B. Lippincott Co.

Teresa, V. (1973) My Life in the Mafia. Greenwich, Conn.: Fawcett Publications.

Tobias, J.J. (1967) Urban Crime in Victorian England. New York: Schocken Books.

Turkus, B.B. and S. Feder (1951) Murder Inc.: The Story of the Syndicate. New York: Farrar, Straus and Young.

Turner, G.K. (1909) "The Daughters of the Poor." McClure's Magazine 34 (November).

Waterman, W.C. (1932) Prostitution and its Repression in New York City. New York: Columbia University Press.

Woolston, H.B. (1969) Prostitution in the United States: Prior to the Entrance of the United States into the World War. Montclair, New Jersey: Patterson Smith.

Women, Heroin, and Property Crime

James A. Inciardi

An overview of both the popular and professional literature on narcotic addiction suggests that stereotyping has been a persistent phenomenon in characterizations of the addict. Some four decades ago, sociologist Alfred R. Lindesmith reflected on this situation in his discussions of "dope fiend mythology," noting that in contrast to the contemporary available evidence, descriptions of heroin addiction typically focused on alleged maddening effects" of the drug and the "degenerate" nature of the users.[1] During the years since Lindesmith's initial reflections, many of the early myths and stereotypes have managed to endure, while at the same time a variety of new and even more colorful images have emerged.[2] Curiously, however, while any number of divergent portrayals of the addict have come to pass, perhaps the most persistent theme in the literature has been the characterization of the "woman addict as prostitute." And while there is considerable empirical evidence documenting some relationship between addiction and prostitution, the monolithic image of the woman addict as a prostitute should be called into question.

This article written for this volume.

The conception of the woman addict as typically being a member of the "oldest profession" is not without some basis in the historical literature. More than a century ago, prostitution had been cited as a major cause of morphine addiction, and in the decades that followed this early observation, discussions of the etiology of addiction among women were repeatedly studied within the framework of prostitution.[3] For example, as noted by Bingham Dai in his investigation of drug addiction in Chicago during the 1930s:

> That the pimp in his attempt to entice a girl to his service not seldom "dopes" her and makes her an addict so that she will have to depend on him for her drug and thereby becomes his woman is a matter of common knowledge.[4]

Alternatively, it has been a common hypothesis that due to high prices of heroin on the illicit drug marketplace, the addict is forced into a life of crime in order to support his/her habit.[5]

> Logically, criminality is bound to begin in a case of morphanism the moment the economic margin above living expenses is not sufficient to cover the purchase of the habitual amount of the drug . . . prostitution in women, stealing in one form or another in men, are the rule.[6]

Within a more contemporary perspective, there are extensive data that document a high incidence of prostitution among women addicts, suggesting that it may indeed be a primary means of support for their drug-taking. Of 168 women admitted for treatment at Lexington Hospital from June through December of 1965, for example, 47 percent had histories of prostitution and 79 percent of these relied on this form of criminality as their main source of support;[7] and other studies have demonstrated that as high as 71 percent of sampled cases utilized prostitution for drug support.[8] Such high incidences of prostitution among women heroin addicts have led a number of researchers to further examine the relationship between prostitution and addiction, questioning, specifically, the direction of the involvement—does prostitution lead to addiction or do they occur in a reverse order?[9]

That prostitution and addiction are related among numerous populations cannot be argued, for the data are manifest in this respect. What can be argued, however, is that there has been an overemphasis on the study of the causal nexus of the two phenomena to the neglect of other forms of criminality among women addicts, resulting in the single frame of reference typification of the "women addict as prostitute." And it is within this context that the current analysis has been structured.

In an effort to more fully understand the complexity and variety of drug-related crime among women, a sample of 149 women heroin users were interviewed at length in Miami, Florida, during 1978.[10] Of the 149 cases, some 79 percent (n = 117) were active addicts drawn from the street community while the balance were sampled from a local drug treatment program. These women were primarily whites (51 percent) and the rest either black (34 percent) or Hispanic (15 percent), with the total at a median age of 25.9 years. Most of these women were either unemployed or not in the labor force (67 percent), and few had current marital ties (15 percent).

All of these women had long histories of drug use, and all were addicted to heroin. Each respondent had used some ten different types of illicit substances and were using a median of 5.4 different kinds of drugs at the time of interview (or during the 90-day period prior to treatment entry for those in the local drug program). Furthermore, an analysis of their drug histories demonstrated a clear progression into drug use beginning at an early age.[11]

First use of drug	Median Age
alcohol	14.2
alcohol high	14.4
illicit drug (any drug, excluding alcohol)	15.5
marijuana	15.6
barbiturate	17.6
heroin	18.3
cocaine	19.3

All of these women addicts reported having criminal histories, yet only 87 percent had ever been arrested and only 68 percent had ever been incarcerated. The median age of their first crime was 15.8 years, with their *first criminal offenses typically being crimes against property*.

First criminal offense	Percent
robbery	4
assault	2
burglary	5
vehicle theft	1
shoplifting	40
other thefts	9
prostitution	15
drug sales	3
all other/no data	21

As such, for some 55 percent of the sample, a property crime was their first offense (burglary, shoplifting, or theft), followed by prostitution (15 percent), and the more personal crimes of robbery or assault (6 percent).

In an effort to obtain further insight regarding the intensity of the criminal involvement of these 149 women heroin addicts, each was questioned at length in terms of the number of offenses committed during the 12-month period prior to interview (or the 12 months prior to treatment entry). As indicated in Table 1, the absolute number of criminal offenses was 58,708, averaging some 394 crimes per case. Virtually *all* of these women had engaged in property crimes, while drug sales ranked second (74 percent of the sample), prostitution third (67 percent), and robbery fourth (21 percent). Furthermore, of the 58,708 criminal offenses, there were more instances of property offenses than any other crime, including prostitution. By including burglary, shoplifting, pick-pocketing, forgery and counterfeiting, dealing in stolen goods, confidence games, arson, vandalism, fraud, and all types of theft under the general category of "crimes against property," such criminality totals 20,309 offenses or 35 percent of all offenses.

TABLE 1. Criminal Activity During 12 Months, 149 Women Heroin Addicts, Miami, Florida, 1978.

Crime	Total Offenses	Percent of Total Offenses	Percent of Sample Involved	Percent of Offenses Resulting in Arrest
TOTAL	58,708	100.0	100.0	0.4 (n=215)
Robbery	1,180	2.0	20.8	0.8 (n=9)
Assault	125	0.2	8.7	7.2 (n=9)
Burglary	321	0.5	20.8	0.6 (n=2)
Vehicle Theft	64	0.1	5.4	0.0
Theft from Vehicle	431	0.7	18.3	0.2 (n=1)
Shoplifting	8,713	14.8	67.1	0.5 (n=47)
Pickpocketing	1,316	2.2	6.7	0.0
Prostitute Theft	2,941	5.0	47.7	0.1 (n=3)
Other Theft	1,681	2.9	22.1	0.5 (n=9)

Forgery/Counterfeiting	1,991	3.4	34.9	1.1 (n=21)
Con Games	259	0.4	15.4	0.0
Stolen Goods	2,258	3.8	37.6	0.3 (n=7)
Prostitution	19,246	32.7	67.1	0.3 (n=66)
Procuring	1,153	2.0	11.4	0.0
Drug Sales	15,990	27.2	73.8	0.2 (n=26)
Arson	89	0.2	3.4	0.0
Vandalism	26	<0.1	3.4	7.7 (n=2)
Fraud	219	0.4	8.7	0.9 (n=2)
Gambling	621	1.1	19.5	0.0
Extortion	42	0.1	4.0	0.0
Loan-sharking	1	<0.1	0.7	0.0
Alcohol Offenses	38	0.1	6.0	21.1 (n=8)
All other	3	<0.1	6.7	100.0 (n=3)

Mean Number of
Offenses per Subject   394

Prostitution ranked second at 33 percent, and drug sales third at 27 percent.

With prostitution accounting for only one-third of all criminal offenses, these data suggest that the stereotypical image of "women addict as prostitute" warrants some reconsideration. Not only do the data indicate that women addicts are more often property offenders, but they also call attention to the wide variety of criminal activities that women may indeed engage in. Some 21 percent of the sample participated in 1,180 robberies and the typically "male" offenses of auto theft and procuring were indeed apparent within this population. It might be added here that 20 percent of these women used handguns during the commission of their offenses, primarily in robberies. And finally, the data also testify that women heroin addicts, as defined by this population, are rarely arrested. Of the 58,708 offenses, less than one percent (n = 215) resulted in an arrest. As such, during the 12-month study period, there was an average of only one arrest for every 273 crimes committed, and an arrest/crime ratio of 1:73 for crimes against the person (robbery and assault), 1:216 for crimes against property, 1:291 for prostitution, and 1:615 for drug sales.

In summary, the data in this analysis call into question the traditional characterization of the "woman heroin addict as prostitute." The data clearly document that women addicts engage in a wide variety of crimes, suggesting that prostitution plays a considerably lesser role in their drug support activities than has been generally assumed. Furthermore, this analysis offers some evidence that women addicts' initiation into crime is rarely through prostitution and most often through a property offense, and that women addicted to narcotics are engaging in forms of criminality that have been generally considered male offenses.

One can only speculate as to the reasons for such findings that run counter to traditionally held conceptions. On the one hand, it could be argued that the nature and extent of crime among women addicts has always been as such, and that the overemphasis on prostitution resulted from the majority of previous studies that were biased towards samples of "officially known" cases—which were typically prostitutes. More logically, however, it is likely that up until a decade ago, women addicts who resorted to criminal activity as a mechanism of drug support confined their activities to prostitution and drug sales, with prostitution being the more expected and visible offense. Alternatively, however, there have been several changes in the nature of drug use since the late 1960s. As was argued in an earlier publication, heroin addicts of one and two decades ago concentrated primarily on narcotic drugs and limited their criminal activities to nonviolent activities—property crimes and drug sales among men and victimless crimes among women. With the revolution in the technology drugs during the 1950s and 1960s, a wider variety of substances became available, resulting in the emergence of the new "poly" or "multiple" drug user of the 1970s.[12] These new users, both men and women, began their drug careers at a younger age, used a wider variety of drugs than previously, and engaged in more diverse forms of criminal behavior in order to support their multiple addictions. The women targeted in this analysis are clearly of this newer drug using type, having initiated their drugs and criminal careers no later than their midteens, and using a median of more than five different substances at the time of interview. This reasoning, of course, is only speculation at this point, and would require confirmation through studies of other populations of women addicts. What also remains for further study in this behalf is some observation of the extent to which women addicts partake in crime in conjunction with men, in mixed groups, with other women, or as lone operatives.

NOTES

1. Alfred R. Lindesmith, " 'Dope Fiend' Mythology," *Journal of Criminal Law and Criminology*, 31 (July–August 1940), pp. 199–208.

2. See, for example, James A. Inciardi, "Drugs, Drug-Taking and Drug-Seeking: Notations on the Dynamics of Myth, Change, and Reality," in James A. Inciardi and Carl D. Chambers (eds.), *Drugs and the Criminal Justice System* (Beverly Hills: Sage, 1974), pp. 203–220.

3. F.E. Oliver, *The Use and Abuse of Opium*, Third Annual Report of the State Board of Health of Massachusetts, January 1871; L.L. Stanley, "Morphanism," *Journal of the American Institute of Criminal Law and Criminology*, 6 (1915–16), p. 586; Charles E. Terry and Mildred Pellens, *The Opium Problem* (New York: Bureau of Social Hygiene, 1928) pp. 119–122; see also, H. Wayne Morgan (ed.), *Yesterday's Addicts: American Society and Drug Abuse, 1865–1920* (Norman: University of Oklahoma Press, 19740.

4. Bingham Dai, *Opium Addiction in Chicago* (Shanghai: Commercial Press, 1937), p. 136.

5. Edwin M. Schur, *Narcotic Addiction in Britain and America* (Bloomington: Indiana University Press, 1962); Alfred R. Lindesmith, *The Addict and the Law* (Bloomington: Indiana University Press, 1965).

6. E.W. Adams, *Drug Addiction* (London: Oxford University Press, 1937), p. 37.

7. Carl D. Chambers, R. Kent Hinesley, and Mary Moldestad, "The Female Opiate Addict," in John C. Ball and Carl D. Chambers (eds.), *The Epedemiology of Opiate Addiction in the United States* (Springfield, Il.: Charles C Thomas, 1970) pp. 222–239.

8. Peter Cushman, "Methadone Maintenance Treatment of Narcotic Addiction—Analysis of Police Records of Arrests Before and During Treatment," *N.Y. State Journal of Medicine*, 72 (1972), pp. 1752–69.

9. For a seminal analysis of this issue see Jennifer James, "Prostitution and Addiction: An Interdisciplinary Approach," *Addictive Diseases: An International Journal* 2 (1976), pp. 601–618.

10. These cases were drawn from a larger study, generated by DHEW grant #1-RO1-DA-0-1827-03, from the Division of Research, National Institution on Drug Abuse.

11. All medians are based on the proportion who reported having used each given substance: 97% used alcohol, 99% used marijuana, 85% used barbiturates, 93% used cocaine, and *all* used heroin.

12. James A. Inciardi, "The Poly-Drug User: A New Situational Offender," in Freda Adler and G.O.W. Mueller (eds.), *Politics, Crime and the International Scene: An Inter-American Focus* (San Juan: North-South Center for Technical and Cultural Interchange, 1972), pp. 60–68.

The Economics of Prostitution

Gail Sheehy

Jack, shekels, mazuma, simoleons, Mr. Green, filthy lucre—big profit is the big Why of prostitution. And profiteering in the world's "oldest profession" is now called "hustling." Surrounding the obvious streetwalker is an assorted multitude of major and minor hustlers, all of whom play their part and earn their pay directly or indirectly from prostitution. The case extends from pimps, madams, Murphy men, knobbers, call girls, play-girls, and courtesans to preying street hustlers and hotel operators, pornographers and prostitution lawyers, politicians, police "pussy posses," and prominent businessmen, and includes, always offstage of course, the Mafia.

The stakes are high. Secrecy is stringent. Using the most current figures available, there are an estimated 200,000 to 250,000 prostitutes in the United States today. Taking the lower estimate, at only six contacts a day and at the bottom price of $20 per "trick," the millions of clients of prostitution contribute to the support of the underworld the incredible sum of between $7 and $9 *billion* annually. All of it untaxed.

Gail Sheehy, "The Economics of Prostitution: Who Profits? Who Pays?" *Ms.* (1 June 1973), pp. 58ff. This article adapted from *Hustling,* © 1973 by Gail Sheehy. Reprinted by permission of the author and Delacorte Press.

The profit figure is 10 times the entire annual budget of the U.S. Department of Justice. That fact alone would seem reason enough for tax-weary Americans to look more closely, rather than snicker, at prostitution.

The class ladder of the vocation begins with the lowliest, jail-calloused street hooker and ends with the pseudo-aristocratic courtesan playing in the big league for the highest stakes: wealth and social position. But before taking a climb up the class ladder, let's focus briefly on one of the key questions Americans always ask of any booming business: Who profits?

WHO PROFITS?

Here is a profit-and-loss rundown of the specific and related interests:

PROSTITUTES:
It sounds unbelievably glamorous. Come to the big city and make a minimum of $200 a night doing what comes naturally. Work six nights a week while you're young and pretty. It's the fastest way to make money in the shortest time. How else can a girl earn $70,000 a year?

There are several critical facts the recruiter fails to mention. The average *net* income for a streetwalker is less than $100 a week. "To the pimp she's nothing but a piece of meat," as one police veteran of prostitution vans puts it. And she ages very quickly. Prostitution is a physically punishing business. Right from the start a working girl begins to worry about her age. This is one profession in which seniority is not rewarded.

When, in the last few years, massage parlors and peep shows broke out all over the playing field of midtown Manhattan, I began to see Puerto Rican faces for the first time. These were inexperienced girls of no more than 21, sitting on the benches of sex parlors like scared second-stringers waiting to be called into a rough game. I noticed they were all wearing baby-doll wigs and asked why. "The wig, it gives me less age," said one skinny girl. She giggled guiltily when I asked how old she really was. "Twenty, but the men, they like eighteen."

The bottom line of the prostitute's profit sheet is this: the vast majority find themselves old at 30, bitter, and broke. In 2,000 interviews conducted over 10 years for their excellent book, *The Lively Commerce* (1971: Quadrangle; 1972: New American Library paperback), Charles Winick and Paul Kinsie found no more than 100 older prostitutes who had any money left. Because prostitution is a criminal offense in many states including New York, its practitioners are generally saddled with a police record as well, which demolishes their credit rating and further diminishes their chances of finding another job. They face the future locked into a day-to-day, cash-and-carry existence. Few of them can imagine where all the money went. The lion's share, of course, went to the next profiteer.

PIMPS:

"He doesn't do *nothing*. But the way he does nothing is *beautiful*." That description, coming from a starry-eyed beginner in the stable of a Times Square pimp, hits the nail on the head. She sees it as a source of pride. It is her earning power that allows her "sweet man" to drive around town in glorified idleness.

For this and a few meager services, the street pimp demands his girls bring in from $200 to $250 a night. The girls rarely see more than 5 percent. The pimp pockets all and doles out "walking-around money," $5 at a time. Because of his neurotic need to prove total control, the pimp makes no allowances for a girl who can't meet her quota. One night in a driving rainstorm, I accompanied a miserable streetwalker to a pay phone while she pleaded with her man: "I can't make but a bill [$100] tonight, the rain's sent everybody home." She got one word from the pimp: "Drown."

In New York City, for example, the prostitution boom began six years ago when the state penal code was revised. In the fall of 1967, the maximum penalty for prostitution was reduced from one year to 15 days or a $50 fine. That was also the end of the Women's Court Clinic, where a doctor routinely checked arrested girls and gave prophylactic treatments of penicillin.

A hue and cry went up from midtown businessmen and the hotel lobby in anticipation of the new law. They warned, quite correctly, that New York was about to be saturated with prostitutes from other, stricter states. And, as usual, this deeply complicated social problem became a superficial political football. By the fall of 1969, a conservative legislator sponsored a bill that upped the maximum penalty to 91 days or $500—when this bill became law, prostitution was elevated from a violation to a misdemeanor, and for the first time in New York State it became a "crime."

Apart from burdening prostitutes with criminal records, the amended legislation was beside the point. Judges barely catch the names as several dozen street girls glide past the bench — "I'm a seamstress"—and taxi back to their territories to finish the night's work. Ninety percent of the loitering (for the purposes of prostitution) cases are dismissed. Only the arresting officers are held up in court, filling out reports.

Even girls who are found guilty on the more serious "pross collars" (an arrest for actual prostitution), involving a specific proposal for a specific price made to a plainclothesman, are rarely jailed. Most judges let them go for a $25 to $50 fine—and a week to pay. Any girl can work that off in an hour or so. It amounts to a license.

Word of this leniency spread with greater interest through the pimp grapevine around the country. New York was wide open. Midtown became the nation's largest outdoor flesh showroom.

Despite all subsequent "crackdowns," amateur pimps are still rolling into New York from Detroit, Chicago, and even California. When local pimps have recruitment problems, they often cruise up to Montreal. A black pimp can always magnetize white *naïfs* from La Province by flashing his blister-top Cadillac.

Where does all his money go? Into "invisible investments": $15,000 custom-made cars which serve as floating country clubs (with false registration), a gypsy cab business, a home out of state, fenced clothes and jewelry, gambling at the racetrack, and to other phantom profiteers above him.

At the highest levels of pimping, very little cash changes hands. Says one white penthouse pimp, "You can buy anything with beautiful women."

PREYING STREET HUSTLERS:
Prostitutes carry a lot of cash—temporarily. No one knows this better than addicts and muggers, desperate pimps, and other competitive prostitutes. Murphy men make a game of selling dummy keys, for cash in advance, to customers dumb enought to believe a girl will be waiting for them in an empty apartment. Knobbers are men dressed as females hookers, who have figured out their own ripoff on prostitution. They charge the same price but offer only stand-up service, pleading monthly indisposition.

"Prostitutes are pitiful creatures really," says a captain in New York's Public Morals Division. "The trouble is, they attract all the vermin—the muggers and robbers."

HOTEL OPERATORS:
Fleabag prostitution hotels are run by a diehard little band of hirelings. They have no compunction about saying, "I come with the building." The standard rate quoted by New York street girls when they nuzzle up to negotiate with potential customers is "twenty and ten." The extra $10 is for the room. This goes directly to the hotel operator when the John signs the register, no bargaining about it. No allowances for personalized service either; 10 minutes to a trick is standard operating procedure. That means the hotel operator turns over each room four times an hour on a good night, and since the smallest fleabags operate five rooms for prostitution, the smallest operator piles up his little hills of green at about the rate of $200 an hour.

That is not to mention the take in watches, rings, credit cards, and traveling cash customarily lifted from Johns once they are inside the hotel room. Depending on the speciality hustles of the house—from mugging to the Murphy game where a clerk or pimp bursts in pretending to be the jealous husband—the customer is lucky to leave with his clothes. It is not unusual to see a customer flying into one of the midtown police precincts naked as a plucked chicken.

PORNOGRAPHERS:

The link between pornography and the infiltration of a new area by prostitutes is firmly established. One promises, the other delivers.

In May of 1971, the Peep Show Man was up to his ankles in sawdust on Lexington Avenue, hammering in stalls like make-do cattle pens. He looked like a hayseed Kentucky veterinarian. One couldn't have guessed he owned a string of 12 Times Square peep shows. But competition had saturated Times Square, he said, and so he followed his sixth sense to Manhattan's East Side.

"Only had three folks come by wantin' to know why I was puttin' such a thing in here," drawled the Peep Show Man that May. "Prob'ly be the first ones in to see it." And a week later there they were, one hip poking out of every stall, dropping quarters into the box to devour sexual images that have the approximate substance of shower-curtain decals.

Within a week prostitutes had followed. And what follows prostitutes is crime.

PROSTITUTION AND PORNOGRAPHY LAWYERS:

Lawyers who make their living by defending prostitutes form a small, closed, cynical fraternity. They charge what the traffic will bear. Theirs is a captive clientele. On the proceeds of prostitution they live very well, in the manner of legal pimps.

For all sorts of profiteers, 1967 was the year of the double bonanza. While New York was relaxing its prostitution law, the Supreme Court handed down a series of decisions lowering the restrictions on obscenity. Within three months organized crime had entered the midtown pornography business. Right behind them appeared another middleman, an old breed of lawyer with a lucrative new specialty—obscenity law.

What these lawyers are really defending is not the public's right to experience imaginative forms of sexual expression, but the rights of property owners and mob-connected operators to extract maximum profits from the weaknesses of ordinary mortals. It is not uncommon for obscenity lawyers to have their own financial interests in the sex industry. Another habit they have is writing "public-spirited" letters to major newspapers upholding the virtues of civil libertarianism, letters as transparent as a call girl's negligee.

And so, while further Supreme Court clarification of obscenity laws is awaited, sharpie lawyers do daily battle in lower courts over the delicacy of police busts and the incoherent distinctions between hard- and soft-core pornography. In the jargon of the stock market, they are "going to the moon."

POLITICIANS AND PUSSY POSSES:

For nearly a hundred years in New York, prostitution has been used as the whipping girl for political challengers to flog political incumbents. One thing has remained constant: New York's courts levy punishment exclusively on the real victims—prostitutes—while politicians ignore the structure of commercialized vice which sustains them.

It is fashionable to blame the whole mess on the police. Politicians respond to the immediate public outcry. City Hall simply enlarges the expensive, demoralizing game of round robin played by cops and prostitutes. Their "street sweeps" last only until the courts are choked with insubstantial cases and a louder cry comes back from the district attorney's office to the police commissioner's office: cut the arrests. Meanwhile, the girls evicted from one territory simply move to another, wait for calm, and return. And then the public cries "corruption" when an investigatory commission reports that a few houses of call girls are sustained on payments to the police.

Why should a frustrated police force take the blame for a social problem that both the courts and the cream of city officialdom refuse to face squarely?

PROMINENT BUSINESSMEN:

Landlords are the one aspect of prostitution that has been up to now almost totally ignored. It took me six months of research and roughly fifty pounds of documentation to put the names of landlords together with the properties in midtown Manhattan which housed prostitution hotels, peep shows, massage parlors, pornographic bookstores, and blue movies. And then I interviewed them.

The results were all very embarrassing. The names behind the booming sex industry belonged to a relative-by-marriage of President Nixon, several of the largest tax-paying property owners in the City of New York, respectable East Side WASPs, members of the Mayor's Times Square Development Council, Park Avenue banks . . . and at the outset of each interview, they had all lied.

Every city has these money-insulated real estate moguls. And every city to a greater or lesser degree guards them. It is hardly *comme il faut* for city officials to tattle on their peers, especially since they control much of the private capital and influence the political winds which keep a particular mayor aloft.

THE MAFIA:

No comment on the profiteers of prostitution can overlook the shadowy but certain presence of organized crime. Who knows better the weaknesses of men and who has had more experience in harnessing them?

Prostitution was selected as a profitable racket back in 1933, when the repeal of Prohibition forced Lucky Luciano to find new employments for the Mafia. The mob has had its ups and downs in the sex industry, but 1967 was a great year. Ever since the Supreme Court eased up on sexual expression, organized criminal exploiters have been creating an almost insatiable demand for paid sex, both live and simulated. The demand still grows; it seems by now unfillable. Who are the mob's patrons? Everybody.

Prostitution, then, is many things to many people, from the street corner to the penthouse to the hidden realms of profit beyond. The one thing prostitution is not is a "victimless crime." It attracts a wide species of preying criminals and generates a long line of victims, beginning with the most obvious and least understood—the prostitute herself.

UP THE CASTE LADDER

There is probably no vocation which operates with such a fierce system of social distinctions.

The streetwalker has nothing but slurs for "those lazy flat-backers," meaning call girls. The call girl expresses contempt for the ignorant "street hooker." The madam wouldn't be caught dead with a "diseased" street girl. The independent call girl has washed her hands of the "bloodsucking" madam or pimp. And so on.

The street hooker is at the bottom of the blue-collar end of the ladder. She far outnumbers anyone else in the business.

Separate and distinct is the whore-addict who turns to prostitution for support of her own or her boyfriend's habit rather than as a vocation in itself. A persistent myth about prostitution is that most girls are addicts. This is not only untrue, but it is impossible; because a girl working at the competitive speed—running five miles a night, six nights a week, and turning six to twelve tricks daily *despite* routine rotations through jail cells and courts—couldn't keep up the pace demanded by the pimp and keep up a habit as well. If and when she begins to require enough drugs to interfere with her work, the pimp will lower her to bottom woman in the stable or drop her.

In New York, the quality and price of street girls diminish as they move westward on the city map. On the more prosperous East Side, the merchandise is sharply divided into three subclasses.

In one class are the daytimers who pull a steady blue-chip business among Grand Central commuters, which accounts for their swelling ranks. They work the office buildings like a super-hospitality coffee wagon. Score the flustered account executive in the elevator, simple! Make a date for a "noonsie" in the office while the secretary is out to lunch. Discreet accommodations of all kinds are offered for the busy executive.

Daytimers can afford to be choosy. Haughty, white, and businesslike, these are your ex-models and jobless actresses who turn a trick for no less than $60. Their ranks also include bored suburban housewives who work primarily for kicks. With a few bills in the tote bag, they'll be home to slip the frozen scampi in the wall oven before husband plotzes off the 7:02. Enterprising!

Police estimate that 10 percent of those prostitutes working the Times Square area on weekends are housewives from Long Island and New Jersey. Their husbands are mailmen or clerks on fixed salaries that don't pay the taxes on suburban homes. Since prostitutes are not fingerprinted, even with frequent arrests the married streetwalker, operating under an assumed name, can be home by 10 with a foolproof alibi (at least on the police blotter) about her weekend activities.

"Got no pimps, these daytime dames," I heard a pimp complain. "They're no dope fiends out to support a habit. These girls make big money."

The early evening girls, class two among street hookers, scuffle in and out of the grand hotels until 11 and may go home with $300, even $400 on a good night. They are still new enough, plump-fleshed and pretty enough, to pass for wives on the arms of coventioneers. Many of them also manage to work independently. By ducking home early, they avoid the pimps and escape the midnight street sweeps by police.

After midnight the frenzy begins. The tough, the old, and the desperate inhabit this third, aberrant class of street prostitutes. Pimps also send out their rambunctious new girls to prove themselves at this hour. Everyone has a gimmick. Or a habit. Or a car.

Next rung up on the prostitution ladder are rent whores, girls who turn a few tricks to buy clothes or pay the rent. They are independent but considered by colleagues lazy and unprofessional.

Massage parlors, since their export from California to every major city, offer free-lance employment that appeals to a wide range of full- or part-time prostitutes. Young, unskilled girls from Puerto Rico, Canada, and the Caribbean are drawn in for lack of alternatives; groupies pick up money to finance their star-trailing trips; runaways and college girls are attracted to the tonier parlors operated by hippie capitalists. Massage parlors offer the advantages of an indoor job on a daily contract basis. Girls pay the manager in order to work and pocket what they can in tips. But when the police pressure is on and the total earnings are in, the indoor employee of a massage parlor makes considerably less than the streetwalker. This often puts her back on the street after closing time. (A recently passed New York City law aims to regulate massage parlors by licensing them. And, for the first time, the landlord of the building and the operator of the parlor are to be penalized as well as the practitioner.)

The white-collar end of the business begins with call girls. Those managed by a madam or pimp may turn over as much as 70 percent of their income in exchange for Johns' names and an apartment in which to entertain them.

The independent call girl clears an average of $1,000 a week. She may have worked her way up, but it is not uncommon now to find young call girls from wealthy families. Many seem to have substituted for old game-playing in drugs or revolutionary politics, playing at being prostitutes—as an antipathy device. The element of risk is injected into a tediously comfortable existence. Topping off this level is the playgirl. She is a traveling parasite. Floating from country to country, executive junket to political convention, she relies on tips from the grapevine of jumbo jet hustling.

Four common factors link most of the foregoing women. Absent or inoperative parents; an early and brutal sexual experience—often with a seductive father; an early pregnancy; and their resulting attitudes toward men: fear, dependence, rage. The rage of course must be repressed. To some degree it is sublimated in the process of exerting sexual power over men who must pay. Some rage leaks out, and it fuels the violent new breed.

HAUTE CLASSE HUSTLING

Women who are in the *business* of marrying wealthy men qualify as cash-and-marry contractors. A woman who prefers to retain some freedom by moving as a mistress from man to man could be called an incorrigible courtesan. Euphemisms are very important to women who operate in the elevated circles of hustling. Although dictionary definitions of "courtesan" always include the blunt synonym "a prostitute" ("or paramour, especially one associating with men of wealth"), at least the word has the elevation of a European history.

Certainly all marriage is not prostitution, and all live-in love affairs are not courtesanships. But most of us know or read about women belonging to that exotic breed who *plan* romance only with and for men of substance.

The thread of continuity connecting both kinds of behavior is that these women do not see themselves, nor do they require that other people see them, as people. They are willing commodities. They live their personal and professional lives by openly seeking or by cleverly insinuating themselves into a man's wallet. To the men in their lives, both are possessions. The prostitute is a temporary purchase, to be enjoyed like a bottle of wine and thrown away. The courtesan is a possession to keep (at least until he becomes bored), a sculpture to admire behind closed doors or to display as a prestige item.

It is not enough to be pretty, charming, graceful, impeccably dressed, and talented in the arts of hostessing and listening, as are all the celebrated courtesans of our day. To collect millionaires and gather from them convertible assets, these women use most imaginative devices:

Pump priming:
A femme fatale well known to TV audiences often uses this technique the morning after she first allows a man to spend the night. She heads straight for Tiffany's to buy him a gold cigarette case. She has it inscribed with a sentiment both flattering and tastefully torrid, such as: "Thank you, darling, for one of the most memorable evenings of love in my life." The man receives this wildly expensive gift for doing nothing more than taking her to bed. If her pump priming works, he responds with a $25,000 necklace from Harry Winston's.

Jewelry converting:
An executive salesman for one of New York's most exclusive diamond emporiums always advised cash-and-marry contractors: "Get these men to give you jewelry. If you ever fall on hard times, we'll be glad to buy the pieces back." The biggest coup was carried off by the wife of a stock market swindler. She knew, a few days before the market did, that the bottom was about to fall out of her husband's company. While he was staging a last fight to save the stock, she bounced into the diamond store and charged a half million or so worth of jewels. Her husband did go broke and fled to Brazil. She sold the baubles back to the store.

But this time the trick was too blatant. The executive salesman was caught and charged with fraud, along with the acquisitive wife whose trouble was being in too much of a hurry.

Collecting tangibles:

With an eye toward providing her own security in advancing age, the incorrigible courtesan taps her men for tangible, convertible gifts. Rented living quarters, no matter how sumptuous, are considered wholly undesirable. "They ask for a small *pied-à-terre,* and then shop for priceless antiques to fill it," says a Manhattan real estate agent accustomed to finding accommodations for the mistresses of her luxury clientele. "The antiques belong to them; they're salable!" Other convertible gifts are paintings, objets d'art, a co-op apartment, a piece of land, a country house.

In the process of collecting all these things on her breathtaking passage through the lives of affluent European lovers and American husbands, one envied courtesan became skilled at selling the right assets at the most propitious time. She had learned that with any less business acumen, the courtesan who is between lovers may find herself in a "sensitive cash flow position." This is not only embarrassing, but it's unattractive *and* suspicious. On reaching her mid-forties, she had consolidated all the gifts into her own estate—an exquisitely appointed home and many accumulated acres to go with it. When a super-millionaire suddenly appeared, he saw her as a member of his own rarefied circle. He offered a marriage contract setting on her a sum appropriate to her position—$10 million.

Inventing occasions:

"What kind of party shall we have for my birthday?" or, "Look at the calendar, darling, we'll be married a month on Saturday!" or, "It's almost a year since our first evening together, and I'm so sentimental—how shall we celebrate?" After the marriage, a frequent visitor in the home of a former courtesan was baffled by hearing her constantly float such ideas in the presence of guests. Another wealthy woman explained. It's a way of inventing occasions for which her husband will feel obliged to buy her a present.

Name-saving

After the divorce, a lady who carried the name of an aristocratic American family revered almost as royalty, never remarried. Bystanders were baffled. She took one famous lover in the domestic film industry and drove another lover to drink himself out of the British cabinet. But she would not marry. She was not about to erase the one asset on which she could always trade— her former husband's name.

We Americans are famous for institutionalizing our social and moral hypocrisies. The polite unemployed, spongers on the rich, are called playboys; the culture-bound poor, applying for public relief, are called welfare loafers. We often acknowledge such riddles in politics, law, and ordinary business life. But we generally miss the similar deceptions when they veil the activities of people in a less familiar world—the baffling, secretive, conniving netherworld.

Excepting China, there is not a civilized country in the world without prostitution. But only in America is the prostitute punished for prostitution per se—the barter of sex for money— and she is often punished by the same men who after hours seek her favors. Very little thought has been applied to tackling, or even taxing, the real profiteers. Even less thought has been given to creative experiments in rehabilitating the prostitute.

My point is that when applied to the multibillion-dollar business of hustling, our great moral hypocrisies again break down according to class lines. Prostitutes are not laughable social deviants. They are women operating at every level of a consumer society who too often begin as a baby-sitting problem and end as throw-away human beings.

The Molls

You've seen the corner gang girls on the streets of the inner city, talking tough, showing off, looking more menacing than "nice young girls" should. In association with "brother gangs" or by themselves, many of these gangs girls (some as young as 12- or 13-years-old) hang out at night, use obscene language, insult and play pranks on passersby, drink alcoholic beverages in public, mock social workers and "good kids."

As part of our reasearch on the gangs of Midcity (an inner-city district of an eastern seaport), we studied the Molls, one group of corner gang girls. Although girls' gangs have received little attention during the current wave of concern over gangs and gang violence, the Molls have their counterparts in most major American cities—for example, the Ghetto Sisters and female Savage Nomads of New York. A female field worker maintained continuing contact with the Molls for 30 months. At the start of the contact period the average Moll was 13.5 years old, and at the end, 16 years old. Although the size of the group

Walter B. Miller, "The Molls," *Society* 11 (November/December, 1973), pp. 32–35. Published by permission of Transaction, Inc., from *Society*, Vol. 11, November/December, 1973. Copyright © 1973 by Transaction, Inc.

varied according to the season and changing individual circumstances, the Molls could say of about 11 girls, "She hangs with us."

The molls were white and Catholic—mostly Irish, with one set of sisters of Irish-German background. Fathers who were known and employed worked at jobs as signhanger, plate glass cutter, and factory laborer. Most of the girls' mothers were employed outside the home, holding low-skilled jobs such as housemaid, laundry-press operator, machine operator in a shoe factory and kitchen worker in a hospital. All eight of the Molls' families were known to have received some form of assistance from public welfare agencies. All of their families had been on welfare.

As 14 year olds, the Molls were known in the neighborhood as "bad girls," and in one sense the girls shared this appraisal. The principal leader of the Molls once said of herself, "I'm a real gang girl!" In another sense, they felt this reputation to be unfair. To most neighborhood adults, it was axiomatic that girls who were "bad" after the fashion of the Molls must also be sexually "bad." The Molls resented the lumping together of sexual immorality and what they regarded as conventional illegal behavior. The same girl who boasted of being a real gang girl, fondly reminiscing at 16 of her gang's misbehavior at 14, said, "But we never was really *bad*—not in *that* [sexual] way. . . ."

CRIMINAL BEHAVIOR

What, in fact, was the character of the Molls' criminal behavior? By the time they were 17, all 11 of the Molls were known to have engaged in some form of illegal behavior. Five of the girls had been arrested, four had appeared in court, and two had been confined to correctional institutions. The Molls thus equalled the record of the Midicity boys' gang with the highest percentage of members known to have been arrested. Involvement in illegal acts ranked them well above two male gangs from the same city. Contrast their arrest rate of 45 percent with an 8 percent figure for the other female gang, a group of upwardly mobile black girls, the Queens. The Molls' six most frequent offenses were: truancy (15 involvements per ten girls per ten-month period); theft (4.7); drinking violations (3.3); property damage (2.8); sex offenses (1.3); assault (0.7).

PLAYING HOOKEY

Truancy, failure to attend school for a day, several days or extended periods, was the Molls' most frequent offense: Seven of the 11 girls were known to have truanted, with 44 instances of truancy having been recorded during the contact period. One girl deliberately stayed out of school for three weeks in hopes of being expelled from one school so she could enter another. While out of school the girls often stayed home, sometimes to perform household duties, sometimes to play records and gossip. Mothers' reactions to truancy varied, both among mothers and by the same mother at different times. In some instances daughters stayed home to care for younger siblings or do other household chores at the request of their mothers (especially those who worked during the day). In such cases mothers would write fraudulent excuse notes for the girls. Other mothers were opposed to truancy and punished theirs daughters for skipping school. The girls themselves gave a variety of reasons for truancy ranging from home obligations to boredom with studies. Whatever their reasons, the Molls' pattern of irregular school attendance between the ages of 14 and 16 represented an advance manifestation of their ultimate permanent discontinuation of schooling.

In accordance with compulsory education laws, all 11 girls were attending school (some irregularly) at age 14, but as the girls approached the age when leaving school was permitted, they truanted with increasing frequency. Once past age 16, all but two dropped out; none entered college. The Moll's drop-out rate was about 80 percent.

STEALING

Theft was the Molls' second most frequent offense, and as many girls were known to have stolen as to have truanted. Moll theft was generally quite minor in comparison with some of the boy's gangs. Girls stole postcards, magazines, popcorn, and fountain pens from local stores. Three of the girls engaged in shoplifting from downtown stores, and one was put on probation when caught. In one instance three girls stole $31 from the aunt of one of them and bought clothes with the money. The Molls themselves considered this theft their most serious, and they later made some attempts at restitution.

DRINKING

Illegal drinking was the third most frequent offense, with six girls known to have been involved. The girls drank beer, wine, and liquor at home, on the corner, at school, by themselves, and with their brother gang, the Hoods. Most Moll drinking was relatively light, resulting primarily in boisterous behavior. One girl who had been drinking quite heavily made a game of darting into the street to see how closely she could avoid being hit by cars. Several times the Molls were caught in illegal possession of liquor. Once two girls brought a bottle of whiskey to school and in another instance police caught the Molls and Hoods drinking beer in the park. None of these apprehensions resulted in official action. In the school incident the girls told authorities they had mistaken the bottle of liquor for a bottle of perfume.

VANDALISM

Property damage or vandalism, the Molls' fourth most frequent offense, ranked high in its capacity to disturb neighborhood residents. Two rough categories of property damage could be distinguished: acts undertaken primarily for excitement and amusement, and those undertaken primarily out of hostility. Some destructive acts appeared to be motivated primarily by a desire for "fun"—such as burning rubbish barrels in the Molls' hanging alley, burning the name "Molls" on the ceiling of the housing project recreation room and breaking windows in abandoned houses. The Molls also directed destructive acts against persons who had aroused their anger. They broke housing project windows after the project manager denied the girls permission to use the recreation room they had marked, and they smashed windows at the house of a neighborhood woman whom the Molls believed to be spreading untrue stories about them. The clearest instance of hostility-motivated vandalism occurred when the Molls' principal leader was committed to a correctional institution on the complaint of her mother. The mother told authorities that the girls had attacked her brand-new automobile with nails and glass and scratched it so extensively that it had to be completely repainted.

SEX OFFENSES

While much of the Molls' sexual behavior violated the moral standards of many middle-class adults, their involvement in sexual activities which violated legal statutes was low relative to other offenses. While indirect evidence (pregnancy) indicated that three of the Molls had engaged in sexual intercourse by age 16, the girls were very discreet about nonmarital sexual activity. This contrasts with their involvement in offenses such as truancy and vandalism, which they talked about quite freely and even boasted about, under appropriate circumstances.

ASSAULT

Direct involvement by the Molls in assaultive offenses was rare. Only one clearly illegal incident was recorded during the contact period; from their perch on the roof of the housing project Molls threw rocks at a customer leaving the delicatessen below. The rarity of assaultive offenses cannot be attributed simply to the fact that the Molls were female, since the other female gang, the Queens, showed 18 involvements in assaultive acts during the observation period, besting one of the male gangs in this respect.

The Molls also engaged in a number of offenses during the observation period which do not fall readily under the above categories. One summer they spent their time killing neighborhood cats. Several times they provided hideouts for prison escapees. At other times they carried knives and other weapons for Hoods who were involved in gang fighting.

The Molls' major offenses, then, were truancy, theft, alcohol violations and vandalism. (Truancy was no longer illegal after the age of 16, at which point many of the Molls dropped out of school, anyway.) The remaining three major violations approximate the crimes characteristic of lower-class adolescent males; the patterns differ only in that "property damage" appears in place of "assault." Much of the Molls' vandalism represented direct expressions of hostility against particular persons; the Molls attempted to hurt a person by hurting something he owned. Vandalism apparently served the Molls as a vehicle for expressing hostility, in much the same way as did assault for other groups.

FOLLOWING THE BOYS

One reason that the Molls' pattern of criminal involvement so closely resembled that of the males was that they had engaged in a serious attempt, particularly between the ages of 13 and 15, to find favor in the eyes of the Hoods, and to become recognized as *their* girls. Since the Hoods were among the most criminal of the male gangs whose court experience was exmamined, the Molls' campaign to gain their trust and affection involved showing that they shared a general orientation to law violation. One way of doing this was to approve, support and abet their criminal activities; another was to themselves commit, if only in attenuated form, the same kinds of offenses. The Molls themselves, while recognizing their desire to emulate the boys as only one of several motives, were aware that the wish to gain acceptance by the Hoods was an important reason for committing crimes. One used these words: "Ya know, if ya been hangin' with them *every night,* ya wanna do the same things as they do. Ya don't wanna be an *outcast!* When the boys hooked pickles, we hooked pickles. . . ." During this period failure to engage in male-type criminality invoked male-type sanctions. A Moll who refused to go along on a property-destruction venture was taunted with the words, "Fairy! fairy!" This accusation of non-masculinity was deserved, one of the girls explained, "because she won't do vandalism with us no more."

The Molls' attempt to emulate and be accepted by the boys also influenced their sexual behavior. Although one popular image of girls in gangs pictures them as freely available concubines, and much writing on female delinquency stresses the centrality of sexual offenses, the behavior of the Molls, particularly during early adolescence, appeared to be predicated on the assumption that the way to get boys to like you was to be *like* them rather than accessible to them. As already noted, the Molls did not flaunt their sexual exploits in order to win esteem, as they did in the case of other offenses; on the contrary, they were quite secretive about the sexual misbehavior they did engage in.

HOW BAD IS BAD?

A further aspect of the Molls' pattern of illegal behavior concerns their reputation as "bad girls." It has frequently been observed that standards applied to female behavior are stricter than those applied to male comportment, and that a degree of criminal involvement which might appear rather modest for boys is seen as quite serious for girls. How "bad" the Molls are judged to be depends a great deal on the basis of comparison one uses. Compared with male gangs of the same social status the Molls were not very criminal. Their rate of involvement in all forms of illegal behavior, including truancy, was approximately 25 offenses for each ten girls per ten-month period—less than one-tenth the rate of the male gangs of the same socioeconomic status. On the other hand, their rate was approximately the same as that of one of the higher status boys' gangs and, compared to middle-class girls, or even with the Queens, whose comparable rate was 6.8, the Molls appear quite criminal. Acts such as nightly public drinking by 13-year-olds, carrying knives for gang fighters, chronic and parent-abetted truancy—while scarcely unheard of among higher-status girls—are generally infrequent.

LEADERSHIP HIERARCHY

The leadership and clique situation among the Molls reflected the fact that their gang was small relative to those of the boys, that they were female rather than male, and that criminal involvement was an important aspect of gang activities. Moll members fell into two categories—more active and less active. The more active clique was comprised of six girls who hung out frequently and participated regularly in gang activities. The less active clique was made up of five girls who hung out less frequently and participated less often in gang activities. The more active clique was clearly dominant; it set the tone for the gang and provided its leadership.

There were two leaders—a principal leader, whose authority was clearly recognized, and a secondary leader. Both girls were members of the more active clique. The secondary leader served as a standby who assumed leadership when the principal leader was institutionalized, and relinquished it when she returned.

The more active clique was unequivocally the more criminal. Although all the girls were known to have engaged in illegal activity, the rate of involvement in illegal acts for the active clique was 23.7 involvements for each ten girls per ten-month period, compared to a rate of only 1.3 for the less active girls. Active members accounted for 43 of the gang's 44 recorded truancies; all had been arrested at least once; two had been sentenced in court. None of the less active girls had gone to court; and only one was known to have truanted. The two girls who finished high school both belonged to the less active clique.

It is clear that the more criminal clique represented the dominant orientation of the gang as a whole. Further, the principal leader showed the highest rate of illegal involvement of all 11 girls, and the secondary leader the second highest. There was little direct conflict between the two leaders. Instead, like parallel leaders of some of the boys' gangs, they competed for prestige by striving to excel in illegal accomplishments.

BEST FRIENDS

Aside from associational patterns which resembled those of the boys' gangs, there were other patterns which reflected the fact that the Molls were female. Prominent was a "best friend" pattern which cross-cut the two major cliques. Two girls would develop crushes on one another and spend much of their time together. They were then known as "best friends," and shared secrets and confidences until some violation of trust or competition over a boyfriend dissolved their special intimacy into the ordinary ties between gang members. Best-friend pairings were generally of limited duration, with different pairings and re-pairings succeeding each other during the contact period. The relative instability of the best-friend sets served to protect the solidarity of the larger group. The best-friend pattern, generally involving two girls but sometimes three, was more prevalent during the summer months, when jobs, visits, and other pursuits reduced the size and stability of the hanging group, and during the later part of the contact period, as an increase in the tempo of mating and a divergence of life paths weakened ties to the larger gang.

FEMINISM AND THE MOLLS

The Molls' life-style is a product of the subcultures to which these girls belong—particularly those of females, adolescents, urban dwellers, and lower status persons. Of particular interest in a day of expanding female consciousness is the question of the degree to which the Molls' way of life reflects the interests, concerns, and customary behavior patterns of other women.

Two objectives of contemporary American feminism are particularly relevant to the life-ways of the Molls: first, that females should have free and equal opportunities to participate in the full range of life enterprises to which they may aspire, including those occupations and pursuits traditionally seen as male; and second, that women should be characterized and judged as individuals in their own right rather than being seen simply as reflecting the status achieved by those males with whom they may be affiliated.

The Molls and similar young girls' gangs appear to have ample opportunity to follow the same adolescent pursuits as the boys in their peer group—nightly street-corner congregation, public outdoor drinking, extensive use of profanity and, in particular, a classic set of offenses traditionally associated with male juvenile delinquency—stealing, vandalism, drunkenness and, to a lesser degree, fighting. Equal opportunity may not be available in adult activities, although the Molls will be called upon, at least as often as their male peers, to be breadwinners and heads of households.

Despite their freedom to act like the boys, the Molls do not seek to be judged for themselves. The evidence is clear that the Molls and other young women like them not only did not resent the fact that their status was directly dependent on that of the boys, but actively sought this condition and gloried in it. The Molls accepted without question a declaration by one of the Hoods that "they ain't nuthin' without us, and they know it." Jackets of female gang members in New York bear the legend, "Property of the Savage Nomads."

The Molls and many of their sisters are either not yet aware of or attracted to the tenets of Women's Liberation. The set of objectives espoused by the adult, middle-class mainstream of contemporary feminism has, so far, passed them by. Gang girls may, as they grow older, develop different perceptions of themselves and may no longer be satisfied with reflected status. Or, they may find that their present life-style and assumptions prepare them adequately for the reality of their ultimate social position.

IV

Women in the Criminal Justice System

The articles in this part deal with sexism in the criminal justice system. In recent years, much of the research on female offenders has focused on this area, so that a considerable amount of evidence has accumulated. Most of the evidence indicates that male and female offenders are often treated differently, beginning with the criminal law and culminating with their treatment in correctional institutions. As we shall see, female offenders are treated more leniently than males in some cases, but more harshly in others. In either case, the end result is the same—to perpetuate traditonal sex role stereotypes. The passage of the Equal Rights Amendment will go far toward eliminating sex discrimination in the criminal law and the criminal justice system. While legal change is not sufficient to ensure the equal treatment of male and female offenders, it is certainly necessary. It is also necessary to devote more attention to the problems of the criminal justice system which affect both male and female offenders, such as the failure to rehabilitate and the oppressive nature of many correctional institutions.

Sex-based differences are often written into the criminal law itself. They appear in double standard definitions of delinquency, in age differentials in juvenile court jurisdiction, and in disparate sentencing statutes. Within the past decade, a number of sex discriminatory statutes have been challenged in the courts. For example, a New York delinquency statute (the PINS law) permitting juvenile court jurisdiction over females who were "persons in need of supervision" for two years longer than males was held unconstitutional by the New York Court of Appeals.[1] In another case, the U.S. Court of Appeals for the Tenth Circuit declared unconstitutional an Oklahoma statute that denied juvenile court proceedings to 16- and 17-year-old males who committed a crime but allowed such proceedings for females of like age.[2] These disparate provisions probably reflect the fear of sexual promiscuity and pregnancy in juvenile females and the belief that juvenile females are less serious and less dangerous offenders than juvenile males. Juvenile and adult women have also been subject to statutory inequalities in sentencing. These statutes were apparently enacted on the legislative rationale that females are more pliable and "more amenable to the rehabilitative process" than males and that, therefore, longer periods of confinement may actually be beneficial to them.[3] The first successful challenges to sentencing statutes of this type were made in the cases of *United States ex rel. Robinson v. York* and *Commonwealth v. Daniel,* both decided in 1968. The *Daniel* case is discussed in detail by Carolyn Temin in "Discriminatory Sentencing of Women Offenders: The Argument for ERA in a Nutshell."

Even when statutes are sex neutral, their enforcement may be sex discriminatory. It is commonly believed that the criminal justice system reacts less severely to women who have offended than men. The preferential treatment accorded female offenders by the male-dominated criminal justice system is most often attributed to chivalry. In "Chivalry and Paternalism: Disparities of Treatment in the Criminal Justice System," Elizabeth Moulds examines the concepts of chivalry and paternalism and their presence in the criminal justice system. She concludes that less harsh handling of female than male defendants does in fact occur and that this treatment can accurately be described as a form of paternalism. The more lenient treatment of women in the criminal justice system may be influenced by stereotypical beliefs that women are more emotional and less responsible than men, less culpable for their criminal acts, less dangerous, less set in their criminal ways, more easily deterred and rehabilitated, and more likely to suffer from formal criminal processing and particularly incarceration.

Unlike adult females, juvenile females are often dealt with more severely than males in the juvenile justice system. While self-report studies show that the pattern of female delinquency closely parallels that of males but at a much lower rate, females are disproportionately processed through the juvenile justice system for status offenses such as incorrigibility, running away, and promiscuity.[4] Juvenile females are more strictly supervised than males and more often subjected to official intervention for noncriminal behavior tolerated in males, ostensibly "for their own protection." Despite the fact that a much larger proportion of males than females are referred to the juvenile court for criminal acts, females are more often detained pending juvenile court proceedings and for longer periods of time.[5] Juvenile females referred for status offenses are also held in pretrial detention more often than those referred for criminal offenses.[6] Similarly, the juvenile court gives more harsh dispositions to females than males when they are involved in a status offense, but less severe dispositions when the offense is criminal, as Susan Datesman and Frank Scarpitti show in "Unequal Protection for Males and Females in the Juvenile Court." Finally, even though females are institutionalized for less serious delinquencies than males, they are confined for longer periods of time, perhaps to prevent them from becoming pregnant.[7]

Kitsi Burkhart, a journalist who has investigated prison conditions for women, has commented that "the only advantage women have over men in America's penal system is that fewer of them are exposed to it."[8] At present, only about four percent of the entire inmate population in federal and state correctional institutions are women. Marilyn Haft discusses some of the special problems faced by incarcerated women in "Women in Prison: Discriminatory Practices and Some Legal Solutions." Among other things, she notes that the range of educational and vocational programs available to female inmates is much narrower than those for males, and concentrate on domestic work or jobs considered suitable for women, such as hairdressing, typing, and sewing. Another study found that the average number of vocational programs for males in prison was 10 compared with only 2.7 for females. Similarly, an average of 3.2 industries existed in men's prisons but only 1.2 in women's prisons.[9] In addition, furlough and work release programs are less frequently available to female than male inmates. A national study of women's correctional programs found that work release programs for women were extremely rare, involving only 2 percent of the prison population and 1 percent of the jail inmates.[10] Another study in Washington, D.C., found that 29 percent of the eligible males but only 4 percent of the females received furloughs and that 30 percent of the males compared with only 9 percent of the females were given work releases. The reasons given by prison officials include the small number of women in prison as compared with men and the consequently higher cost per prisoner of administering the programs, and that rehabilitation programs are less important to women than men because they do not have to support dependents.[11] This belief is contradicted by the finding that 56 percent of incarcerated women have dependent children living at home.[12]

The loss of parental rights for women prisoners is discussed by Kathleen Haley in the final article, "Mothers Behind Bars: A Look at the Parental Rights of Incarcerated Women." There are no provisions for pregnant women or for women with children in most correctional institutions. Women prisoners who enter prison pregnant are encouraged to have the child and to give it up for adoption. All women, including women in prison, should have the right not to have a child and to keep a child that is born to them. Most correctional institutions do not permit children to visit and even when visits are allowed, mothers must see their children through glass or metal barriers that prevent any physical contact. Although no American prisons have long-term child care facilities, such a program does exist in West Germany. The Kinderheim program allows women prisoners to live with their children in prison and to "vacation" at home with their children every six months. Another program at the Purdy Treatment Center near Tacoma, Washington, permits female inmates to serve as teaching aides in a nursery school attended by neighborhood children. Haley suggests that the Kinderheim and Purdy programs could serve as models to construct a truly rehabilitative atmosphere for incarcerated mothers.

The evidence examined in this part of the book indicates that women are treated differently at least by some portions of the criminal justice system. By and large, the differential treatment has put women offenders at a disadvantage, even punishing them more severely because of their sex. Although a number of changes have taken place to equalize the treatment of both men and women, much remains to be done before our criminal justice system will be truly without sex bias.

NOTES

1. *Patricia A. v. City of New York,* 335 N.Y.S. 2d 33 (1972).

2. *Lamb v. Brown,* 456 F. 2d 18 (1972).

3. *State v. Costello,* 282 A. 2d 748 (1971).

4. For a discussion of these self-report delinquency studies, see Part I of this volume.

5. See, for example, Meda Chesney-Lind, "Judicial Enforcement of the Female Sex Role: The Family Court and the Female Delinquent," *Issues in Criminology,* 8 (Fall 1973), pp. 56–57; 62–63.

6. Margery L. Velimesis, *Report on the Survey of 41 Pennsylvania County Court and Correctional Services for Women and Girl Offenders,* Section Three, Girls and the Juvenile Court, Pennsylvania Division of the American Association of University Women (April 1969), pp. 26–27.

7. Kristine Olson Rogers, " 'For Her Own Protection . . . ': Conditions of Incarceration for Female Juvenile Offenders in the State of Connecticut," *Law and Society Review,* 7 (Winter 1972), pp. 226–227.

8. Kitsi Burkhart, "Women in Prison," *Ramparts,* 9 (June 1971), pp. 21–22.

9. Ralph R. Arditi, Frederick Goldber, Jr., M. Martha Hartle, John H. Peters, and William R. Phelps, "The Sexual Segregation of American Prisons," *Yale law Journal,* 82 (May 1973), pp. 1269–1273.

10. Ruth M. Glick and Virginia V. Neto, *National Study of Women's Correctional Programs,* U.S. Department of Justice (Washington, D.C.: U.S. Government Printing Office, June 1977), p. 84.

11. Barbara A. Brown, Ann E. Freedman, Harriet N. Katz, and Alice M. Price, *Women's Rights and the Law: The Impact of the ERA on State Laws* (New York: Praeger Publishers, 1977), pp. 86–87.

12. Ruth M. Glick and Virginia V. Neto, op cit., p. 116.

Discriminatory Sentencing of Women Offenders: The Argument for ERA in a Nutshell

INTRODUCTION

In 1963, the President's Commission on The Status of Women published the following statement in its report, *American Women:*

> Since the Commission is convinced that the U.S. Constitution now embodies equality of rights for men and women, we conclude that a constitutional amendment need not now be sought in order to establish this principle. But judicial clarification is imperative in order that remaining ambiguities with respect to constitutional protection of women's rights be eliminated.[1]

This statement is now familiar to all those who are active in the fight against legally sanctioned sex-based discrimination. It provided a theme with which to unite all the painstaking case-by-case legal battles of the sixties. It encouraged lawyers, regardless of their area of expertise, to seek out discriminatory legislation and bring it into the courts so that the hoped-for constitutional standards could be applied to forever nullify statutory inequalities.

"Discriminatory Sentencing of Women Offenders," by Carolyn Engel Temin, in *American Criminal Law Review* (ACLR), Vol. 11, No. 2, 1973, pp. 355–372. Reprinted with the permission of the American Bar Association's Criminal Justice Section, and available through the ABA.

It was against this background that the attack on statues prescribing longer sentences for women offenders than for male offenders convicted of the same criminal conduct was launched. Although earlier decisions militated against success,[2] the issue seemed to be the perfect one for achieving the desired constitutional construction. The issue embodies the deprivation of personal liberty—a right that came to the forefront in the sixties; and the statutes being attacked discriminated solely on the basis of sex. To uphold them, a court would have to find that something in the very nature of being a women justifies a legislature in maintaining that a woman be incarcerated for a longer period than a man. It was hoped that the shock value of raising the equal protection issue in this context would produce the desired judicial reaction—the application of the "overriding legislative purpose" doctrine to sex-based discrimination. The precedents thus established could then be applied to other areas (such as employment discrimination) where the issues were not always so finely chiselled.

Suits were brought challenging the sentencing statutes of Pennsylvania[3] and Connecticut.[4] In both cases, *Commonwealth v. Daniel*,[5] and *United States ex rel. Robinson v. York*,[6] the courts held that there could be no rational basis for statutory classifications which impose longer sentences on women than on men convicted of the same offense. The statutes were found to invidiously discriminate against women in violation of equal protection clause of the fourteenth amendment.[7] While the immediate objective of overturning these statutes was achieved, the battle for the ultimate goal, judicial recognition that classification by sex alone violates the fourteenth amendment, was lost. Both courts agreed that sex-based discrimination in sentencing statutes was unreasonable, but neither would hold that *all* sex-based discrimination was unreasonable.[8]

Daniel and *Robinson* were a great disappointment to those involved in the "fourteenth amendment approach" to equality under the law since they had very little applicability to situations not involving criminal sanctions. Nevertheless these opinions did achieve an important and much desired end which raised hopes of future successes. They discredited the earlier cases[9] which had blindly approved discriminatory sentencing statutes without conscientiously examining the state's purported justification for the classification. Even more encouraging was the suggestion by the *Robinson* court that discrimination on the basis of sex is no less inherently suspect than racial classification.[10] The adoption of this reasoning would have subjected other statutes which draw lines on the basis of sex to exacting judicial scrutiny and required the states to justify them by a compelling state interest.[11]

The hopes raised by the modest achievements of *Daniel* and *Robinson* were short-lived. On October 27, 1971, the Supreme Court of New Jersey handed down its appalling decision in *State v. Costello*,[12] refusing to hold that a sentencing statute similar to the Pennsylvania and Connecticut laws violated the equal protection clause on its face. Disinguishing *Robinson*, it criticized and discarded the precedent of *Daniel* and resurrected the decaying corpses of *Heitman, Platt, Brady* and *Gosselin*.[13] What had been so slowly and painstakingly accomplished was undone. The lesson is explicit and unavoidable. Freedom from sex-based discrimination will not come through judicial expansion of existing constitutional guarantees. The history of the fight against sex-based discrimination in criminal sentencing statutes presents a strong example of the absolute necessity for the Equal Rights Amendment.

EARLY HISTORY

It is one of the often encountered ironies of history that statutes imposing longer sentences on women than on men convicted of the same offense grew out of an effort to improve the lot of the female prisoner. The movement dedicated to this purpose had its origins somewhere around 1869 when Indiana became the first state to establish a separate reformatory for women. Prior to this, women prisoners had been incarcerated in the same county jails and penitentiaries housing male convicts.[14] By 1917, fourteen states had established similar institutions.[15] They were usually referred to as "reformatories" or "industrial homes" to distinguish them from penitentiaries.[16]

The reformatory ideal embodied much more than a physical plant. It embraced the notion—then revolutionary—that women criminals should be "rehabilitated" rather than "punished." It therefore followed, according to the correctional thinking of that period, that women should be detained in the institution for as long a time as necessary to achieve the desired level of "rehabilitation." In order to accomplish this, the statutes which established these "rehabilitative homes" also contained special sentencing provisions which applied only to the women sentenced to the particular institution.[17] Since most of these statutes required the courts to sentence to the "reformatories" all women over sixteen years of age who had been convicted of any crime,[18] the practical result was sex-based differential sentencing.

PENNSYLVANIA'S MUNCY ACT

If the sentencing statutes had merely been different they might not have been such a problem. The difficulty arose from the fact that either on their faces or in practical application, they resulted in women getting longer sentences than men. In fact, in the early twentieth century it was thought that the ideal sentence to a women's reformatory should be "indeterminate" with no limits at all on the minimum and maximum terms that an inmate could be forced to serve. Fortunately, most states put some limit on the maximum sentence—usually the maximum term prescribed by law for the particular offense.[19]

Pennsylvania created the State Industrial Home for Women by the Act of July 25, 1913, P.L. 1311,[20] known colloquially as the "Muncy Act" (after the geographical location of the institution). The sentencing provision of this Act is an excellent example of the type of statute being discussed here.[21] It required that all women over the age of sixteen years who had been convicted of an offense punishable by more than one year imprisonment be given a general sentence to Muncy. If the offense was punishable by a term of three years or less, they could be confined for three years. If the crime called for a term longer than three years, then the maximum punishment prescribed by law for the offense was the maximum sentence.[22] The judge possessed neither the discretion to impose a shorter maximum sentence than the maximum provided by law nor the power to fix a minimum sentence at which the woman would be eligible for parole.

By contrast, the Pennsylvania statute for sentencing male offenders to a penitentiary permits the judge in his discretion to impose a shorter maximum sentence than the maximum prescribed by law. In addition the judge is required to set a minimum sentence which can be no longer than one-half of the maximum sentence actually imposed.[23] Where the statute prescribes "simple imprisonment," the judge may impose a flat sentence (stating the maximum term only), but may not exceed the maximum term provided by law for the offense.[24]

The sentencing laws of Pennsylvania discriminated against women in five ways:

1. They permitted a court to send a woman to Muncy for three years even if the maximum for the offense was less than three years, whereas a man could not be sentenced to more than the maximum punishment prescribed by law.
2. They mandated that women receive the maximum legal penalty if convicted of a crime punishable by more than three years, whereas a man could be sentenced to less than the maximum prescribed by law.
3. A woman was not to receive any minimum sentence, whereas a man was to have a minimum sentence not to exceed one-half of the maximum sentence imposed except in those cases where the judge in his discretion could impose a flat sentence stating a maximum only.[25]
4. Under Pennsylvania law, where a sentence is imposed for less than two years, the jurisdiction to parole is in the sentencing

judge; whereas, if the sentence imposed is two years or more, jurisdiction to parole lies exclusively with the parole board.[26] Since all sentences to Muncy were for more than two years, they came under the jurisdiction of the parole board. A person sentenced to less than two years may engage a lawyer to present and argue a petition for parole on his behalf. The prisoner may also present witnesses and enjoy the full panoply of due process rights. The Pennsylvania Board of Probation and Parole, on the other hand, makes its decisions in closed sessions and does not permit representation by counsel at its hearings.[27]

5. Under Pennsylvania law, where a statute prescribes "simple imprisonment," the sentence must be served in the county jail rather than in a state correctional institution.[28] Under the Muncy Act only women sentenced for offenses punishable by one year or less were eligible to serve their sentences in the county jail. There are very few such offenses in the Pennyslvania criminal code. Therefore, many women ended up in a penitentiary (i.e., Muncy) for offenses which would have merely sent a man to the county jail.[29]

Statutes similar to the Muncy Act are still in effect in Massachusetts,[30] New Jersey[31] and Connecticut.[32] Iowa law permits women to be confined up to five years for a misdemeanor,[33] whereas men can only be imprisoned for a maximum of one year unless otherwise stated in the statute defining the offense.[34] In Maine, women between the ages of 17 and 40 can be sentenced to reformatories for up to three years even if the maximum punishment for the offense is less.[35] Men, on the other hand, can only receive such treatment between the ages of 17 and 26.[36] Maryland permits judges to sentence women convicted of crimes punishable by three months imprisonment to the state women's reformatory for an indeterminate period not to exceed the maximum term of imprisonment provided by law.[37] Men are subject to such sentences only between the ages of 16 and 25.[38] Men over the age of 25 who are sentenced to the penitentiary receive a term stating both minimum and maximum limits.[39]

Some state legislatures have seen fit to change previously discriminatory sentencing provisions. Arkansas orginally permitted women misdemeanants to be sentenced to confinement in the women's penitentiary,[40] whereas only male felons could be so confined. This was changed in 1971 specifically because it discriminated against women.[41] The discriminatory statutes which were upheld in *Dunkerton*,[42] *Heitman*,[43] and *Brady*[44] have been repealed by the legislatures of Kansas and Ohio respectively and replaced by non-discriminatory measures.[45]

THE CASE OF *COMMONWEALTH v. DANIEL*

On May 3, 1966, Jane Daniel was convicted of simple robbery[46]—an offense carrying a maximum penalty of ten years under Pennsylvania law.[47] The trial judge sentenced her to serve one to four years in the County Prison. Thirty-one days later[48] her sentence was vacated on the grounds that it was illegal and she was given the required ten-year sentence to Muncy. The opinion of the trial court makes it clear that there were no other reasons for the change in sentence.[49] An appeal was taken to the Superior Court of Pennsylvania on the sole ground that the Muncy Act constituted a denial of equal protection of the laws under the fourteenth amendment of the United States Constitution by arbitrarily discriminating against women as a class.

This case was the first attack ever launched against the Muncy Act. The facts of the case were particularly helpful since they presented a situation where the defendant would clearly have received a much shorter sentence if she had been eligible for sentencing under the statute for men. If the judge had been permitted to exercise his discretion, Ms. Daniel would have served a minimum of one and a maximum of four years, but under the Muncy Act she was required to serve a minimum of three and one-half and a maximum of ten years.[50]

The main obstacle to the appeal was the fact that all previous attacks on similar sentencing statutes in other jurisdictions had failed,[51] for the courts which had faced this question had uniformly held that differential sentencing was constitutional on the ground that women constituted a reasonable class for discriminatory treatment in sentencing statutes. The following language illustrates the "legal" reasoning which produced this doctrine:

> It required no anatomist or physiologist or psychologist or psychiatrist to tell the Legislature that women are different from men. In structure and function human beings are still as they were in the beginning "Male and female created He them." It is a patent and deep-lying fact that these fundamental anatomical and physiological differences affect the whole psychic organization. They create the differences in personality between men and women and personality is the predominating factor in delinquent careers. . . .

> *   *   *

> . . . [T]he female offender not merely requires, but deserves, on account of matters touching the perpetuation and virility of the species, correctional treatment different from the male offender, both in kind and degree; . . . Let it be conceded that the industrial farm for women may fail to accomplish the results hoped for; the statute represents a serious effort on the part of Legislature to deal justly with a subject of great public concern, . . . and this Court is not authorized to declare that the classification . . . is either arbitrary or unreasonable."[52]

The Superior Court of Pennsylvania denied the relief requested and adopted the reasoning of the earlier cases. It held that the legislative distinction which imposed longer sentences on women than men was reasonable in view of the state's purpose of providing more effective rehabilitation for women. The opinion relied on the same factors which the prior decisions had found persuasive; the inherent physical and psychological differences between men and women.[53] The decision was particularly disappointing because of its complete disregard of any of the legal reasoning presented by the appellant's brief and oral argument. The case presented one of the earliest opportunities for a practical application of the arguments outlined in the seminal article, *Jane Crow and the Law* by Pauli Murray and Mary Eastwood.[54] It was a dismal failure.

The only ray of hope was the opinion of Judge J. Sydney Hoffman, the lone dissenter.[55] He argued that the majority was wrong in merely applying the traditional rational basis equal protection test to legislation which impinged on the fundamental right to personal liberty.[56] He contended that where basic civil rights are involved, it should be incumbent upon the state to show a compelling state interest which justifies the legislative classification. Judge Hoffman recognized that there could be no overriding justification for a statute which, "under the guise of special rehabilitative treatment for women, . . . accomplishes little more than the imposition of a harsher punishment for women offenders."[57]

DAISY DOUGLAS

Although this opinion could not become the law of the commonwealth, it was extremely helpful in convincing the Supreme Court of Pennsylvania to allow an appeal from the decision of the superior court. While the appeal was pending, a second attack on the Muncy Act was begun in the case of Daisy Douglas.

Daisy Douglas and her paramour, Richard Johnson, were tried together and convicted of robbery. Ms. Douglas, whose past record consisted of a number of arrests for prostitution, was duly sentenced to Muncy for the maximum term allowed by law for the offense of aggravated robbery—twenty years. Her co-defendant, whose past record consisted of six prior convictions for burglary, received a sentence of not less than three nor more than ten years in the men's penitentiary. A petition under Pennsylvania's Post-Conviction Hearing Act was filed on behalf of Ms. Douglas on the ground that her sentence constituted a denial of her fourteenth amendment rights. Her petition was dismissed on the sole ground that the judge was "constrained" to follow the decision of the superior court in the *Daniel* case.[58] An appeal was taken and the case was consolidated with the *Daniel* case for argument before the Supreme Court of Pennsylvania.[59]

For some reason, the *Douglas* case is never mentioned in articles which discuss *Daniel,* but it played an extremely important role in obtaining the successful result in the supreme court. The superior court in *Daniel* had said that a major flaw in the appellant's attack on the Muncy Act was her failure to substantiate the claim that if she were a man she would have received a maximum sentence of four years. Actually the court misunderstood the appellant's claim. Her argument was that if Jane Daniel could have been sentenced under the statute which applied to male offenders, she would have received a lesser sentence. Nevertheless the appellant's failure to produce data which supported this assertion prevented the court from overturning the Muncy Act on the basis that it discriminated against women.[60]

The facts of *Douglas* presented the unequivocal proof of the discriminatory effect of the Muncy Act which had been found lacking in the superior court. Male and female co-defendants were jointly tried and convicted of the same offense. The male, with a serious past criminal record, was sentenced to ten years. The female was required by statute to be sentenced to twenty years even though her past criminal involvement was extremely minimal. The male was eligible for parole after three years; the female was technically eligible for parole at any time but in practice was not considered eligible for three and one-half years.[61] Further proof of sex-based disparity in sentencing was provided by statistics kept by the Pennsylvania Board of Probation and Parole.[62] These showed that men on parole, convicted of a second similar offense, were rarely, even under these circumstances, sentenced to the maximum punishment permitted by law for the offense.

The consolidated appeals were argued on January 5, 1968, and on July 1, 1968, the supreme court reversed the judgments below and remanded the cases for resentencing. The court held that, while legislative classification on the basis of sex alone did not violate the equal protection clause, it could find no reasonable justification for a statute which imposed longer sentences on women than men convicted of the same crime. Acknowledging that

> . . . there are undoubtedly significant biological, natural and practical differences between men and women which would justify, under certain circumstances, the establishment of different employment qualification standards,[63]

the court specifically found that

> . . . the considerations and factors which would justify a difference between men and women in matters of employment, as well as in a number of other matters, *do not govern* or justify the imposition of a longer or greater sentence on women than is imposed upon men for the commission of the same crime.[64]

With these words, the Supreme Court of Pennsylvania emphatically stated that the Constitution of the United States does not embody equal rights for women, although it does prevent the imposition of longer sentences on women than on men convicted of the same offense. A similar result was reached by the United States District Court for Connecticut in the case of *United States ex rel. Robinson v. York*[65] decided on February 28, 1968. That case struck down a Connecticut statute relating to the sentencing of women misdemeanants which was exactly the same as the Muncy Act Provision.[66] Since both courts reached the same conclusion independent of each other, it appeared, at the time, that the issue of the constitutionality of disparate sentencing statutes had been layed to rest forever. In the works of Leo Kanowitz, the *Robinson* and *Daniel* decisions appeared to be the "early heralds of a new day."[67]

MUNCY ACT AMENDMENT

But then came the backlash. On July 16, 1968, just a little more than two weeks after the Supreme Court of Pennsylvania handed down the decision in *Daniel*, the legislature passed a new version of the Muncy Act. The amendment provided that in sentencing a woman for a crime punishable by more than one year, the court "shall not fix a minimum sentence, but shall fix such maximum sentence as the court shall deem appropriate, so long as such maximum sentence does not exceed the maximum term specified by law for the crime for which the prisoner is being sentenced."[68] Thus the small victory achieved by *Daniel* was narrowed still further. Although women would not have to receive a longer maximum sentence than men, they were still to be denied the right to have their minimum sentence set by a judge. By retaining this type of so-called "indeterminate" sentence at Muncy, women were still being denied equal treatment.[69]

The 1968 amendment to the Muncy Act has been challenged in Pennsylvania courts on two occasions. Immediately after its passage, in the case of *Commonwealth v. Blum*,[70] the superior court was asked to find than the new statute discriminated merely because it was different that the statute which applied to men and because it had been shown in the *Daniel* case that women serving indeterminate sentences were held in prison for longer periods of time before being released on parole than men who had been given minimum sentences.[71] The superior court affirmed the judgment of the trial court per curiam.[72] Subsequently the Supreme Court of Pennsylvania denied allocatur[73] and the Supreme Court of the United States denied certiorari.[74] Actually this issue would appear to have been disposed of in the *Daniel* case where as part of its discussion the court indicated that the only part of a sentence which has any legal validity is the maximum sentence and that the minimum sentence is only an administrative notice that the person is eligible for parole consideration.[75]

In the more recent case of *Commonwealth v. Piper*,[76] the superior court once again avoided facing the issue by rendering a per curiam opinion. Judge Hoffman, however, wrote a dissenting opinion in which he stated that the 1968 Muncy Act is unconstitutional because the minimum sentence significantly affects parole eligibility and therefore the act results in discrimination between men and women in terms of consideration for parole.[77] The case is now pending on appeal to the Supreme Court of Pennsylvania.

It should also be noted that due process constitutes another basis for arguing that the 1968 Muncy Act is discriminatory. In Pennsylvania a man is entitled by law to have his minimum sentence set by a judge, at a hearing where representation by counsel is constitutionally mandated,[78] in open court and with the full panoply of due process rights; whereas a woman's minimum sentence is decided by the parole board, at a closed session, where she has no representation, or any other procedural rights.[79] Arguably, this constitutes as much a denial of equal protection as the imposition of mandatory maximum sentences.

NEW JERSEY AND *STATE v. COSTELLO*

An even more devastating blow to the *Daniel* doctrine was dealt by the Supreme Court of New Jersey in the recent case of *State v. Costello*.[80] This case, the first since *Daniel* and *Robinson* to treat the issue of differential sentencing, involved a constitutional attack on a New Jersey statute similar to the Muncy Act.[81] The law requires that women convicted of crimes punishable by five years or less be sentenced to the Women's Correctional Institution for the maximum prescribed by law. If the offense is punishable by more than five years, then the judge may either sentence them to five years imprisonment, or to anything over five years but not to exceed the maximum prescribed by law. Men, on the other hand, receive a sentence stating a minimum and maximum within the limits prescribed by law.[82]

The court dismissed the *Robinson* case as inapplicable to this situation because it involved a statute which sentenced women to a longer maximum term than a man *could* have been sentenced for. Technically, this distinction is correct, since the New Jersey statute, unlike the Connecticut law, does not actually increase the maximum provided by law for the offense. It does, however, force judges to impose the maximum in all cases where they are sentencing a woman for an offense punishable by five years or less, and the result, as it was in *Daniel*, is that women receive longer sentences than men convicted of the same offense. *Robinson,* like *Daniel,* dealt with the issue of the constitutionality of the result of such statutes (i.e., longer sentences for women) and not with the method by which this result was obtained. The New Jersey court's reading of *Robinson* appears far too narrow.

The court refused to follow the ruling in *Daniel* that there could be no rational basis for a legislative classification which imposed longer sentences on women than on men for the same criminal conduct. Instead it remanded the case to the Appellate Division to give the state the opportunity to show a substantial justification for the sentencing scheme.[83] The opinion relied to a large extent on the reasoning of a recent case comment in the *Harvard Law Review.*[84] This article criticized the *Daniel* court's holding that statutory provisions like the Muncy Act would be arbitrary under all circumstances and suggested that such statutes could be sustained upon a showing of a "substantial empirical basis" for the classification. The author argued that social and psychological differences between men and women which rendered the latter more susceptible to rehabilitation might be a substantial justification for differential sentencing.[85]

If this reasoning sounds familiar, then it should come as no surprise that the court dredged up *Heitman, Platt, Brady,* and *Gosselin*[86] as precedent for the propostiton that sex-based discriminatory sentencing is not constitutionally prohibited.[87] The fact that most of the statutes vindicated in those cases are no longer on the books either never came to the court's attention or was not deemed significant.

A fifth case cited by the court in favor of the proposition was *Wark v. State.*[88] This 1970 decision from the Supreme Judicial Court of Maine upheld a statutory scheme whereby men could receive an unlimited sentence for jail break, whereas women could receive no more than eleven months for the same offense.[89] The Maine Court indicated that even if its previous decision in *Gosselin*[90] would have to be reexamined in the light of *Daniel* and *Robinson,* these cases were not controlling.[91]

The court held that the legislature could reasonably have concluded that since men are stronger, more aggressive and more disposed toward violent action than women, they constituted a greater risk of harm upon their escape and required a longer sentence to deter them from such conduct. The Supreme Court of the United States denied certiorari.[92]

The *Costello* case was remanded and the defendant was given a chance to have her sentence reconsidered.[93] Ultimately, the defendant received a sentence which did not involve the issues raised here and the case was not appealed further.[94] [Ed. Note: Two years later the same court was presented the issue again in *State v. Chambers*, 63 N.J. 287, 307, A.2d 78 (1973) in which women defendants had received indeterminate sentences to the New Jersey Correctional Institution for Women for gambling offenses. At the postconviction hearing in one of the cases, *Vacca*, the state had been unable to give convincing data to support its discrimination. Consequently, the Supreme Court of New Jersey held that indeterminate sentences for women offenders violated the equal protection clause of the Fourteenth Amendment where men offenders convicted of the same offenses would have received a minimum-maximum state prison term. The decision gave women already serving indeterminate sentences at the Correctional Institution the choice of applying to be resentenced for a minimum-maximum term or retaining the indeterminate sentence originally imposed. In the future, the court declared, men and women offenders must be accorded equal treatment when being sentenced.]

Slightly less than a month after the *Costello* decision, the United States Supreme Court decided in *Reed v. Reed*[95] that the states may classify on the basis of sex if the criteria for the classification bear a reasonable relation to the objective of the statute whose constitutionality is in question. Nothing in that decision is helpful in predicting the outcome of an appeal on the *Daniel-Costello* issue. It merely reaffirms the standard used by both the Pennsylvania and New Jersey courts to reach their disparate conclusions.

CONCLUSION

The inconsistent positions taken by the courts on the issue of differential sentencing deomonstrate the need for the equal rights amendment. As one commentator put it:

> . . . one cannot say that the possibility of achieving substantial equality of rights for women under the Fourteenth and Fifth Amendments is permanently foreclosed. But the present trend of judicial decisions . . . indicates that any present hope for large-scale change can hardly be deemed realistic.[96]

Any case by case attack is subject to the same pitfalls as the one described here. A favorable decision in one jurisdiction is not binding on any other. Courts may interpret precedents too narrowly, thus diminishing the effect of an important decision. And a victory in the courts can be undone by the legislature. The fight must then begin again for territory already won.[97]

Only by ratification of the Equal Rights Amendment can we assure that statutory schemes such as discriminatory sentencing acts will cease to exist. The question remains as to the effect that the ERA will have on such statutes. It has been suggested that under ERA, special sentencing statutes relating to women would fall, leaving them subject to the "standard laws."[98] Another analyst states that where there are no conflicting laws, one for men and one for women, the one containing the most beneficial provisions will survive.[99] The question will then be which type of sentencing scheme is preferable.[100]

Regardless of the result, the Equal Rights Amendment will bury for all time, the useless, chauvinistic discussions in the cases concerning the "unique" physiological, psychological and sociological aspects of women. These learned, intellectual acrobatics which have been used for so long to justify the demeaning, condescending and crass treatment of humans who are female by humans who are male have no place in a society seeking equality of treatment for all its members.

REFERENCES

1. Established by Exec. Order No. 10,980, 3 C.F.R. 138 (Supp. 1961).

2. *See*, e.g., State v. Heitman, 105 Kan. 139, 181 P. 630 (1919); *Ex parte* Dunkerton, 104 Kan. 481, 179 P. 347 (1919); Platt v. Commonwealth, 256 Mass. 539, 152 N.E. 914 (1926); *Ex parte* Gosselin, 141 Me. 412, 44 A.2d 882 (1945), *cert. denied sub nom.* Gosselin v. Kelley, 328 U.S. 817 (1946): *Ex parte* Brady, 116 Ohio St. 512, 157 N.E. 69 (1927). These cases upheld discriminatory sentencing acts against constitutional challenges.

3. Pa. Stat. Ann. tit. 61, § 566 (1964).

4. Conn. Gen. Stat. Ann. § 17–360 (1958). (Now Conn. Gen. Stat. Ann. § 18–65 (Supp. 1972).)

5. 430 Pa. 642, 243 A.2d 400 (1968).

6. 281 F. Supp. 8 (D. Conn. 1968).

7. 430 Pa. at 648, 243 A.2d at 403; 281 F. Supp. at 17.

8. 430 Pa. at 649–50, 243 A.2d at 403–04; 281 F. Supp. at 13.

9. *See* cases cited note 2 supra.

10. 281 F. Supp. at 14. The court said:

> This statute, which singles out adult women convicted of misdemeanors for imposition of punishment by imprisonment for longer terms than may be inposed on men, must be supported by a full measure of justification to overcome the equal protection which is guaranteed to them by the fourteenth amendment. In Loving v. Virginia, 388 U.S. 1, 87 S.Ct. 1817, 18 L.Ed. 2d 1010 (1967), where penalties were imposed on the basis of racial classification, the Supreme Court enunciated a strict standard for testing equal protection:
>
> . . . .
>
> While the Supreme Court has not explicitly determined whether equal protection rights of women should be tested by this rigid standard, it is difficult to find any reason why adult women, as one of the specific groups that compose humanity, should have a lesser measure of protection than a racial group.

11. Leo Kanowitz summarized the importance of *Daniel* and *Robinson* in this manner:

> The various opinions in the *Daniels* [sic] and *Robinson* cases are of extreme importance for a number of reasons. For one thing, they undermine earlier cases in other jurisdictions upholding sex-based discrimination in sentencing rules and practices. They also represent a significant breakthrough . . . in the undifferentiated "sex is a reasonable basis for classification" approach that has held sway for so long in this area. What is more important is that their analytical approach—emphasizing the greater burden of justification to sustain an unequal deprivation of a "basic" civil right or analogizing a female group to a racial group—creates the possibility of successfully attacking, on constitutional grounds, a variety of other sex-based discriminatory rules and practices. In their own way, this handful of decisions may be the early heralds of a new day in the general treament of men and women in American law and life.

L. Kanowitz, *Women and the Law* 172 (1969).

12. 59 N.J. 334, 282 A.2d 748 (1971).

13. 59 N.J. at 343–44, 282 A.2d at 753–54. *See* cases cited 2 supra.

14. Rogers, *A Digest of Laws Establishing Reformatories for Women in the United States,* 8 J. Crim. L.C. & P.S. 518 (1917).

15. Idem. at 520. In addition to Indiana these included Massachusetts (1874), New York (1881), Iowa (1900), New Jersey (1910), Ohio (1911), Pennsylvania (1913), Wisconsin (1913), Maine (1915), Minnesota (1915), Connecticut (1917), Kansas (1917), Michigan (1917), and Rhode Island (1917).

16. Idem. It is interesting to note that in most cases the names of these institutions have been changed and today most of them bear the designation "state correctional institution for women." In these cases the name change reflects the true state of affairs. These are no more nor less than penitentiaries for women. *See* Commonwealth v. Stauffer, 214 Pa. Super. 113. 117, 251 A.2d 718, 722 (1969).

17. *Compare* Conn. Gen. Stat. Ann. § 18–65 (Supp. 1972) *with* § 53a–35 (Supp. 1972). *Compare* Mass. Gen. Laws. Ann. ch. 279, § 18 (Supp. 1972) *with* ch. 279, § 24 (Supp. 1972).

18. *See,* e.g., Conn. Gen. Stat. Ann. § 18–65 (Supp. 1972).

19. Rogers, supra note 14, at 526, 535. But Minnesota law originally provided that women could be sentenced to the reformatory for a term which would be "without limit as to time." Minn. Laws 1915, ch. 324, § 1, *as amended* Minn. Stat. Ann. § 243.90 (1972).

20. Pa. Stat. Ann. tit. 61, ch. 7 (1964). A 1959 amendment changed the name of the institution to the State Correctional Institution of Muncy. Act of October 22, 1959, P.L. 1356.

21. Pa. Stat. Ann. tit. 61 § 566 (1964). *See also* Conn. Gen. Stat. Ann. § 18–65 (Supp. 1972); Mass. Gen. Laws Ann. ch. 270, § 18 (1972); N.J. Stat. Ann. § 30:4–155 (1964).

22. These were the sentencing provisions in force at the time the *Daniel* case was brought in 1966. They were later changed by case law and statutory amendment as will be discussed *infra*.

23. The statutory language refers to this as an "indefinite" sentence. In this article I have refrained from describing sentences as indefinite, indeterminate, definite, or otherwise since these terms are not used uniformly throughout the states.

24. Pa. Stat. Ann. tit. 19, § 1057 (1964). Note that although the statutory language states "any person," prior to the *Daniel* case it only applied to men.

25. Under Pennsylvania law a minimum sentence is the time a person must serve before becoming eligible for parole. Flat sentences are only available for a small number of minor crimes. Since the repeal of the "good time" statute in Pennsylvania on July 22, 1965, flat sentences have fallen into disuse. (Before its repeal, Pennsylvania's good time statute only applied to flat sentences and enhanced their appeal in the eyes of criminal defendants who often requested them at the time of sentencing.) Since women have no minimum sentence under the Muncy Act they are theoretically eligible for parole at any time after sentencing. On its face this appears to discriminate in favor of women. The actual effect of this provision will be discussed *infra*.

26. *See* Pa. Stat. Ann. tit. 61, § 331.1 *et seq.* (1964).

27. The hearings referred to here are those where the decision to parole from a sentence is made. Pennsylvania does permit representation of counsel at hearings which consider technical violations of parole. *See* Commonwealth v. Tinson, 433 Pa. 328, 249 A.2d 549 (1969).

28. Pa. Stat. Ann. tit. 19, § 891 (1964).

29. This effect of the Muncy Act was declared unconstitutional at Commonwealth v. Stauffer, 214 Pa. Super. 113, 251 A.2d 718 (1969). In Pennsylvania the county jail is preferable to Muncy because of its location and other less tangible reasons which make "county time" less onerous to serve. A person incarcerated at Muncy is almost always cut off from her relatives and friends.

30. Mass. Gen. Laws Ann. ch. 125, § 16 (1958).

31. N.J. Stat. Ann § 30:4-155 (1964).

32. Conn. Gen. Stat. Ann. § 18-65 (Supp. 1972). Although the *Robinson* case declared the provision relating to misdemeanants to be unconstitutional, the felony sentencing provision has never been attacked. It is exactly the same as that provided under Pennyslvania's Muncy Act.

33. Iowa Code Ann. § 245.7 (1969).

34. Idem at § 687.7 (1950).

35. Me. Rev. Stat. Ann. tit. 34, § 853–54 (Supp. 1972).

36. Idem § 802. This provision is similar to the provision complained of as being discriminatory in *Ex parte* Gosselin, 141 Me. 412, 44 A.2d 882 (1945), but discrimination still exists based on the different age eligibility limits for the sexes.

37. Md. Ann. Code art. 27, § 689(e) (1957).

38. Idem § 689(d).

39. Idem § 690.

40. Ark. Acts 1939, No. 117, § 1, at 270.

41. Ark. Stat. Ann. § 46-804 (Supp. 1971).

42. *See* note 2 supra.

43. Idem.

44. Idem.

45. Kan. Stat. Ann. § 21-4601 *et seq.* (Supp. 1970); Ohio Rev. Code Ann. §§ 5145.01, 5143.23 (Anderson 1970).

46. Brief for Appellant, Commonwealth v. Daniel, 430 Pa. 642, 243 A.2d 400 (1968) [hereinafter cited as Brief for Appellant].

47. Pa. Stat. Ann. tit. 18, § 4704 (1963).

48. If the sentence had not been illegal, it would have become final after 30 days. Pa. Stat. Ann. tit. 12, § 1032 (Supp. 1972); Commonwealth *ex rel.* Perotta v. Myers, 203 Pa. Super. 287, 201 A.2d 292 (1966).

49. Brief for Appellant, supra note 46, at apps. 1, 2.

50. Although theoretically a woman sentenced under the Muncy Act was eligible for parole at any time, in actuality the authorities at Muncy required that a certain amount of time be served before parole was considered depending on the offense for which the woman was convicted. *See* Commonwealth v.

Daniel, 210 Pa. Super. 156, 167, 232 A.2d 247, 253 (1967) (Hoffman, J., dissenting).

51. *See* cases cited supra note 2.

52. State v. Heitman, 105 Kan. 139, 146–48, 181 P. 630, 633-34 (1919).

53. This court is of the opinion that the legislature reasonably could have concluded that indeterminate sentences should be imposed on women as a class, allowing the time of incarceration to be matched to the necessary treatment in order to provide more effective rehabilitation. Such a conclusion could be based on the physiological and psychological make-up of women, the type of crime committed by women, their relation to the criminal world, their role in society, their unique vocational skills and pursuits, and their reaction as a class to imprisonment, as well as the number and type of women who are sentenced to imprisonment rather than given suspended sentences.

Commonwealth v. Daniel, 210 Pa. Super. 156, 164, 232 A.2d 247, 251-52 (1967). It should be noted that the defendant's name was Jane Daniel. The superior court opinion incorrectly spelled her name as Daniels. It appears correctly in the opinion of the supreme court.

54. Although blacks have successfully invoked the protection of the Constitution, women have been unable to do so. The difficulty in asserting women's rights lies not in the limited reach of the fourteenth amendment, but in the failure of the courts to isolate and analyze the discriminatory aspect of differential treatment based on sex. Laws discriminate by defining crimes to the acts of one sex but not the other and by differentiating in the punishment of criminals of different sexes. The Civil Rights Act of 1964, Title VII, prohibits employment discrimination based on sex, however the Act does not totally preempt state laws which discriminate by sex (e.g., laws prohibiting women from working at night in certain industries, weight lifting limitations for women, and maximum hour laws). The recent increase in activity concerning the status of women indicates a gradual trend in the law not to protect women by restriction and confinement, but to protect both sexes from discrimination. Murray & Eastwood, *Jane Crow and the Law: Sex Discrimination and Title VII,* 34 Geo. Wash. L. Rev. 232 (1965).

55. 210 Pa. Super. at 167, 232 A.2d at 253.

56. In my view, the "any rational basis" formula is inadequate to test the validity of the Muncy Act against the present challenge. That doctrine derives from a number of cases upholding economic regulatory measures or statutes not directly impinging on personal liberties or fundamental rights. . . . Surely, the proper inquiry here . . . is whether there clearly appears in the relevant materials some "overriding statutory purpose" requiring the imposition of more severe penalties on women than on men and requiring the delegation of the sentencing power to a nonjudicial agency in whose hands it is manifestly susceptible to abuse.

210 Pa. Super. at 169–70, 232 A.2d at 254 (Hoffman, J., dissenting).

57. . . . [U]nder the guise of special rehabilitative treatment for women, the legislature, in the Muncy statute, has adopted a system which accomplishes little more than the imposition of a harsher punishment for women offenders. As such it denies them the equal protection of the laws guaranteed by the Constitution of the United States.

210 Pa. Super. at 172, 232 A.2d at 255 (Hoffman, J., dissenting).

58. Brief for Appellants at app. 8, Commonwealth v. Daniel and Douglas, 430 Pa. 642, 243 A.2d 400 (1968).

59. Since Daniel was already pending before the supreme court it was possible for Douglas to skip the usual necessary stop at the superior court and proceed directly to the supreme court.

60. . . . [A]ppellant argues that because she is a woman she has received a maximum sentence of ten years; . . . that if she were a man she would have received a maximum term of four years. . . . This argument rests on an invalid assumption, viz., that a man committing this crime would have received a maximum term of four years. Judge Stern's prior sentence of one to four years was imposed upon Jane Daniels, a female, and we cannot speculate as to what the sentence would have been had the person robbing the bar in question been a male.

210 Pa. Super. at 165, 232 A.2d at 252.

61. See Brief for Appellants, supra note 58.

62. Idem. at app. C.

63. 430 Pa. at 649, 243 A.2d at 403.

64. 430 Pa. at 650, 243 A.2d at 404.

65. 281 F. Supp. 8 (D. Conn. 1968). Apparently this decision had no influence on the ruling of the Pennsylvania Supreme Court as it was not cited in its opinion.

66. Conn. Gen. Stat. Ann. § 17-360 (1958).

67. L. Kanowitz, supra note 11, at 172.

68. Pa. Stat. Ann. tit. 71, § 566 (Supp. 1972).

69. For a general discussion of the effect of the indeterminate sentence at Muncy see Temin, The Indeterminate Sentence: The Muncy Experience, Prison Journal (1972). In Commonwealth v. Stauffer, 214 Pa. Super. 113, 251 A.2d 718 (1969), the court, relying on Daniel, held that women could not be sentenced to Muncy for crime that was punishable by simple imprisonment since a man in that case could only be sent to the county jail. See Commonwealth ex rel. Monaghan v. Burke, 169 Pa. Super. 256, 82 A.2d 337 (1951). The effect of Stauffer is that women can get a minimum-maximum sentence for crimes punishable by "simple imprisonment" since the indeterminate sentence is only for sentences served at Muncy.

70. 220 Pa. Super. 703, ——A.2d——(1972).

71. See Commonwealth v. Blum, Brief for Appellant, Superior Court of Pennsylvania, October Term, 1969 Nos. 208, 209.

72. 220 Pa. Super. 703,——A.2d——(1972).

73. 221 Pa. 691,——A.2d——(1972).

74. 408 U.S. 516 (1972).

75. 430 Pa. at 647–48, 243 A.2d at 403.

76. 221 Pa. Super. 187, 289 A.2d 193 (1972).

77. 221 Pa. Super. at 290, 289 A.2d at 196–97.

78. Mempa v. Rhay, 389 U.S. 128 (1967); Gideon v. Wainwright, 372 U.S. 335 (1963).

79. See Temin, supra note 69.

80. 59 N.J. 334, 282 A.2d 748 (1971).

81. N.J. Stat. Ann. § 30:4-155 (1964).

82. Idem.

83. 59 N.J. at 345, 282 A.2d at 755. The equal protection challenge was first raised on appeal in the Supreme Court and thus there was no record on this issue.

84. Harv. L. Rev. 921 (1969).

85. Under the regimen of a "substantial empirical basis" test, the state would be required to show affirmatively that there are significant social and psychological differences between male and female offenders such that the latter are particularly susceptible to rehabilitative treatment under the "flexible" indeterminate sentence. The Daniels [sic] court stated that there are no differences which would justify the penal effect of the legislature's classification. However, there is considerable evidence that women who perform criminal acts possess as a group a number of distinct qualities and characteristics and a plausible argument can be made that the rehabilitative possibilities are greater for a class which, for example, demonstrates a noticeably lower frequency of recidivism and parole violations than the class of male offenders.

82 Harv. L. Rev. at 923–24.

86. *See* cases cited supra note 2.

87. 59 N.J. at 344, 282 A.2d at 754.

88. 266 A.2d 62 (Me. 1970).

89. Idem at 64. Maine is not alone in prescribing longer sentences for men convicted of prison breach than for women. *See*, e.g., Conn. Gen. Stat. Ann. § 18–66 (Supp. 1972) and § 53a-169-70 (1958).

90. *See* note 2 supra.

91. 266 A.2d at 64.

92. 400 U.S. 952 (1970).

93. 59 N.J. at 347, 282 A.2d at 755.

94. Citizen's Advisory Council on the Status of Women, Item No. 24-N, February 1972.

95. 401 U.S. 71 (1971).

96. Brown, Emerson, Falk, & Freedman, *The Equal Rights Amendment: A Constitutional Basis for Equal Rights for Women,* 80 Yale L.J. 871, 882 (1971) [hereinafter cited as Brown].

97. As in the case of the "new" Muncy Act. *See* notes 71 & 72 supra and accompanying text.

98. Brown, supra note 96, at 966. The authors of that article were evidently not aware that the legislature passed a new Muncy Act that in Pennsylvania, at present, women are still given special sentences. (A new sentencing code presently pending in the legislature would apply equally to men and women and would give the sentencing judge the option of imposing a minimum-maximum sentence on a Muncy-type sentence. S.B. 440.)

99. Eastwood, *The Double Standard of Justice: Women's Rights Under the Constitution,* 5 Valparaiso L. Rev. 281, 298 (1971).

100. The author of this article has discussed her preference in Temin, *The Indeterminate Sentence: The Muncy Experience,* Prison Journal (Spring 1972).

Chivalry and Paternalism:
Disparities of Treatment
In the Criminal Justice System

Elizabeth F. Moulds

Equality of treatment by law, as symbolized by the image of a blindfolded woman balancing the scales of justice, is among the most fundamental principles of American democracy. Equality as a matter of practice, however, has fallen far short of the ideal for much of the criminal justice system in the United States. Differential treatment, based on race, sex, class, education, age, geographical region, or physical appearancy, has been accorded individuals and entire groups by the criminal justice system.

The two groups that seem to have been most studied as victims of potential and actual discriminatory treatment by the criminal justice system have been racial minorities and the poor. Dramatic inequities related to race and poverty have been especially troubling to the American public in recent years, and a substantial amount of research has been conducted as a result of these concerns.

Elizabeth Moulds, "Chivalry and Paternalism: Disparities of Treatment in the Criminal Justice System," *Western Political Quarterly*, Vol. 31, No. 3, pp. 416–30. Reprinted by permission of the University of Utah, Copyright Holder. Edited and adapted. Omitted data may be found in the original article and are available from the author.

In contrast, an examination of the literature indicates that other areas of unequal treatment have been given comparatively little attention by most scholars. This pattern is particularly evident in the case of women. This is ironic in view of the fact that females constitute over 50 percent of the population of the United States. A quick survey of the indexes of major textbooks dealing with criminology and the criminal justice system reveals that the terms "women," "girls," and "females," appear only sporadically. Until quite recently, when women have been considered in such works, the pattern has been to devote a few pages or, at most, a single chapter, to their unique characteristics and experiences in the criminal justice system. Prior to 1970 there was a very limited number of major works dealing specifically with women and the criminal justice system.[1] Since 1970 the attention given this topic has been on the rise. A few new major works and numerous journal articles have reversed the earlier trend of treating women in the criminal justice system as a tangential topic. Recent analysis has focused on women as a primary subject of interest, and much use is being made of the ideology of feminism in explaining women's involvement in and treatment by the criminal justice system.[2]

Those who have studied women in the criminal justice system report that women generally are treated more gently than men by officials at all levels of the system. The frequent and casual explanation for this unique and gentle treatment of women is that it is an example of American male chivalry at work.[3] This explanation merits careful examination, as the term chivalry implies basic forms of human interaction befitting a model of political paternalism. If the gentle treatment women are said to enjoy is based on this political inferiority, we should be aware of the high price paid for the so-called benefits of chivalry.[4]

This paper will be devoted to examining the notions of chivalry and paternalism as models for treatment of women in the United States and will specifically examine the differential treatment of women by the criminal justice system with respect to these notions. The central focus of this examination will be on data concerning sentencing patterns. An empirical analysis based on two nationwide studies from the 1960s will be compared to data collected in California 1970–74 in order to determine quantitatively the possible existence of a "chivalry factor."

It is hoped that this study will be beneficial in providing insight into the unequal treatment of women by the criminal justice system and into some of the reasons underlying that unequal treatment.

The explanation generally offered for preferential treatment of women in the criminal justice system is that it is a result of the practice of chivalry. The 1967 study done by Reckless and Kay for the President's Commission on Law Enforcement and Administration of Justice serves as an example:

> Perhaps the most important factor in determining reported and acted-upon violational behavior of women is the chivalry factor. Victims or observers of female violators are unwilling to take action against the offender, because she is a woman. Police are much less willing to make on-the-spot arrests of or to "book" and hold women for court action than men. Courts are also easy on women, because they are women.[5]

If chivalry is indeed the potential source of this vast amount of disparate treatment, as was asserted by Reckless and Kay, it is critical to establish the meaning of "chivalry" and the way in which it functions in our culture.

The term chivalry emerged in Europe during the Middle Ages. It described an institution of service rendered by the crusading orders to the feudal lords, to the divine sovereign, and to womankind. "Ladies" were special beneficiaries of the practice of chivalry—knights were sworn to protect their female weakness against dragons and devils. After the disappearance of chivalry as a formal institution, however, a number of chivalrous practices regarding women continued to exist in the world of social convention. A code of manners, elaborated upon by the French Courts, is the most obvious legacy of the era of chivalry.[6]

Insofar as manners define proper behavior for "ladies" and "gentlemen," the modern concept of chivalry has provided us with a set of behavior models which assist in defining the relationship of males and females. However, this concept of chivalry is helpful primarily in describing the superficial elements in male-female relationships, namely, the social amenities. This focus on the benefits women presumably derive from the practice of chivalry has diverted attention from the obvious accompanying power relationship of male domination. The power relationship is more accurately described by the term paternalism.

Paternalism is a far more complex concept than chivalry, and its practice is far more destructive in terms of psychological, social, and political implications. If paternalism in fact colors the perceptions of officials exercising discretion in the criminal justice system, such a practice threatens the basic tenets of a democratic society. As such, paternalism merits independent examination as a possible explanation for the behavior of criminal justice officials.

Paternalism has been defined as follows:

> The derivation of the term "paternalism" from a Latin-English Kinship term suggests its root meanings: a type of behavior by a superior toward an inferior resembling that of a male parent to his child. . . .
> Within different types of paternalistic systems, the following three basic ideas . . . can be found. First, since a "child" is defenseless and lacks property, he requires assistance and support. Second, since a "child" is not fully aware of his role and therefore not fully responsible, he requires guidance. . . . The third idea holds that since a "child" is ignorant, he can be deceived, or treated in such a way as to serve the interests of the "adult" without becoming aware of this.[7]

A cursory examination of the history of the legal status of women in the United States reveals the inferior position of women and their unique treatment by the legal system. The common law of the United States recognized and supported the subjugation of women. It assumed women to be defenseless and in need of support and guidance. It often denied to women the responsibility of political decision-making, the right to determine their residence, and the right to property.[8]

Other major historic examples of the subjugation of women in America have been extensively documented.[9] The lengthy denial of women's suffrage, the barring of women from numerous occupations, the passage of protective legislation for women in the labor market, the Supreme Court's approval of special treatment of women, the exclusion of women from political participation in such matters as jury duty, and the continued failure over a 55-year period of an Equal Rights Amendment (ERA) have all served to allot to women a special and less than equal position in the American political arena. The rationale for this treatment was expressed 100 years ago by the U.S. Supreme Court: "Man is, or should be, woman's protector and defender. The natural and proper timidity and delicacy which belongs to the female sex evidently unfits it for many of the occupations of civil life."[10] It was expressed more recently by Senator Sam J. Ervin, Jr. (D.-N.C.) speaking against the ERA: "I am trying to protect women and their fool friends from themselves."[11]

The long-term implications of this paternalism are most serious. The laws enacted by legislatures and the decisions of courts have set the tone for the inferior regard of women held by much of society. They have contributed to the institutionalization of the assumptions that are the bases of such laws. Kanowitz described the process:

> Though such rules may not result in less favorable or even in different treatment for females, the mere fact that they contain language . . . that emphasizes irrelevant differences between men and women cannot help influencing the content and the tone of the social, as well as the legal, relations between the sexes. . . . Not only do legal norms tend to mirror the social norms that govern male-female relationships; they also exert a profound influence upon the development and change of those social norms. Rules of law that treat of the sexes *per se* inevitably produce far-reaching effects upon social, psychological and economic aspects of male-female relationships beyond the limited confines of legislative chambers and courtrooms.[12]

> If a child is taught idleness by being amused all day long and never being led to study, or shown its usefulness, it will hardly be said, when he grows up, that he chose to be incapable and ignorant; yet this is how woman is brought up, without ever being impressed with the necessity of taking charge of her own existence. So she readily lets herself come to count on the protection . . . of others.[13]

The social and personal loss inherent in the resultant female productivity is incalculable.

It is important to be wary of a society which permits paternalism to color the perceptions of those who make and enforce the law. Those perceptions profoundly affect behavior of those in power and the behavior of those paternalized in a manner that is inconsistent with the operation of a democratic state. A basic denial of self-determination is what is taking place.

DISPARATE TREATMENT OF MALES AND FEMALES AND PATERNALISM: MYTH OR REALITY?

This analysis demonstrates the validity of the hypothesis that less harsh handling of female than male criminal defendants does in fact take place in the criminal justice system and that this differential treatment can be accurately described as a form of paternalism. A key indicator of paternalistic behavior is action taken to "protect" women (who are assumed to be weak, defenseless, and in need of guidance) either from themselves or from some identifiable evil (specifically prison for the purpose of this study). Language in judicial decisions is useful in this regard, as is the frequently expressed assumption that prison is a harsh and evil place—an environment unsuited to the tender needs of women. The primary focus of this analysis will be on sentencing as a measure of official treatment of males and females in the criminal justice system, but other discretionary acts will be reviewed briefly (arrest and conviction in particular).

Before examining the quantitative materials, it is important first to make note of two significant areas of treatment of females in the criminal justice system which superficially appear to deviate from the norm of gentleness shown later in this article. The first area is that of special indeterminate sentencing statutes for women in states which sentence men to determinate (and shorter) sentences for the same crimes. The legislatures and courts in these states make repeated references to the flexible female psyche which is "more amenable to the rehabilitative process" than that of males.[14] It is "for their own protection" that these states keep women incarcerated longer than men for the same crime.[15] It is no coincidence that these states have historically distinguished between prisons and penitentiaries (which have been for men) and "rehabilitative facilities," "reformatories," "industrial homes," and "state correctional institutions" (which are for women).[16] In the second area, the treatment of young women by the juvenile justice system, the same phrase, "for their own protection," is used to justify stricter supervision of young women than young men. Here, particularly with regard to status offenses (running away, incorrigibility, and promiscuity, for example), it has been repeatedly demonstrated that there is a substantially higher arrest and incarceration rate for young females than for young males.[17] This practice has been described as judicial enforcement of the sexual double standard.[18] The role of the juvenile court has been consistently seen as paternal since the stated function of the court is to act *in loco parentis*. Young females are treated paternally both for their youth and for their femaleness. The "protection" offered by the courts is that of a closely supervised living environment. So, although the harshness apparent in these two patterns of treatment deviates from the norm of gentleness for females in the criminal justice system, it is consistent with the more general pattern of paternalism.

DISPARATE TREATMENT: AN EMPIRICAL ANALYSIS

The appropriate place to begin a quantitative examination of possible disparities in the treatment of men and women is with two studies from the early 1960s which analyzed criminal justice treatments using sex as a variable, those of Edward Green and Stuart Nagel.[19] Green's study of judicial attitudes in criminal sentencing is the more limited of the two in that it focused only on the city of Philadelphia and examined only sentencing. Nagel's study was much more comprehensive in that he obtained a nationwide sample of state cases for the year 1962 from an American Bar Foundation study and data for all federal criminal cases decided in 1963.

Green analyzes the 1,437 recorded cases tried in Philadelphia's non-jury court in 1956-57. He suggests that "the fact that females constitute only 91, or 6.3 percent, of the cases may reflect that there is a favorable bias toward women that results in proportionately fewer females' cases eventually going on to trial; or it may indicate that for cultural and biological reasons women are not as criminally inclined as men.[20] A recomputation of Green's data on sentencing patterns into categories of incarceration and nonincarceration shows that of the women in the sample 51, or 61.5 percent, were incarcerated and 35, or 38.5 percent, were not incarcerated (probation, fine, or suspended sentence were the options here). Of the men, 1,071, or 79.6 percent, were incarcerated and 275, or 20.4 percent, were not incarcerated. Green's interpretation of these figures is that they "would seem to support the view that chivalric attitudes, or at least a tendency to react more in the spirit of rehabilitation rather than punitively toward women, enter into the administration of criminal justice."[21] However, when Green measured for sentencing differences where no prior felony conviction existed and with the grade of crime controlled, he found no statistically significant difference between the handling of males and females convicted of felonies and only a very slight significance favoring women's nonincarceration in misdemeanor convictions. This last set of findings is not consistent with the findings of Nagel or with the California data presented in this study. Sentencing patterns favored women in both other data sets. Although each of the three studies approached the data in a slightly different manner, all three did control for crime and both the Green data and the California data were controlled for prior record. The fact that Green's study was of a single city might help explain its different findings.

Nagel's findings, much more than Green's, seem to support the contention that women receive more lenient treatment by persons exercising discretion in the law enforcement process. In his examination of criminal treatment (safeguards for the innocent and type of sentencing) Nagel found both juveniles and women (whom he placed together in a classification of "paternalized persons") enjoyed more favorable sentencing treatment than others. He expanded on his analysis of the American Bar Foundation data in a later article with Lenore Weitzman[22] and in a more recent book.[23] The Nagel-Weitzman article described the paternalism pattern as follows:

> In criminal proceedings, it involves unfavorable treatment with regard to such safeguards for the innocent as having an attorney or having a jury trial. It involves favorable treatment, however, with regard to being kept out of jail pending trial, not being convicted, and not being sentenced to jail if convicted.[24]

Since Nagel's analysis of the ABF state data and the 1963 federal data was limited to a sample of two offenses and the numbers of women involved were quite small, a more thorough assessment of the original data seemed appropriate. In order to analyze further the possible impact of paternalism on officials of the criminal justice system, all of Nagel's federal and state data on sentencing were recomputed with regard to the hypothesis presented in this paper.[25] A cross-tabulation of both data sets was conducted in which the sentencing patterns for males and females were compared. The findings of the cross-tabulation analysis of the federal data are presented in Table 1.

It is clear from Table 1 that the disposition patterns for males and females are different in every category of sentencing. Harsh

TABLE 1. Comparison of Type and Length of Male and Female Sentences in Federal Courts in 1963, Showing Women Received Lighter Sentences

					Sentence					
	% 5 or more years	% 3-5 years	% 1-3 years	% 6 mos.-1 year	% less than 6 mos.	% fine	% prob. after another sentence	% probation	% unsupervised prob.	% Total
Male	8.0	11.9	14.6	8.6	10.3	7.9	1.4	36.1	1.2	100 (N=27927)
Female	4.7	6.3	10.2	4.5	5.6	2.8	.7	63.9	1.3	100 (N=2417)

sentences, specifically those involving incarceration in federal prison, were given proportionately more often to males than to females. For example, the harshest sentence noted in Table 1, a sentence to five or more years in prison, was given to 8 percent of males sentenced and to 4.7 percent of females sentenced. The lightest sentences (probation with and without supervision) were given to women twice as often as to men (65.2 and 37.3 percent respectively). In short, almost two out of three females convicted of federal felonies in 1963 were granted probation. The significance of these percentage differences is clear from the cross-tabulation analysis which reveals a very strong statistical correlation between severity of sentence and sex.[26]

In addition to a recomputation of Nagel's federal data, the sample data on sentences at the state level were also subjected to a cross-tabulation analysis to examine any possible differences in sentencing in state courts related to sex. The results are in Table 2.

Table 2 shows a pattern similar to that of the federal data, although the differences between the sentences accorded males and females were not as substantial. Nevertheless, the differences were significant.[27] Thus Nagel's state sentencing data also support the conclusion presented previously that males and females are treated differently at the sentencing phase of the criminal justice system and that the direction of the difference clearly is in terms of less harsh treatment for females.

In view of the fact that the data used in the analysis just discussed were collected over ten years ago, and because of the many political developments related to women which have taken place during that period, more recent data for the state of California were obtained from the California Bureau of Criminal Statistics and analyzed.[28] In this case, aggregate data concerning the treatment of all adults arrested for felony matters in California for the years 1970–74 were examined to determine whether the patterns of differential treatment indicated by the recomputation of the Nagel data were also evident in the California data.

TABLE 2. Comparison of Male and Female Sentencing by Selected State Courts* in 1962, Showing Women Received Lighter Sentences

	% Death	% Prison	% Fine	% Suspended Sentence	% Probation	% Other	% None	% Total
Male	0	43.1	5.9	3.3	22.9	.5	24.3	100 (N=9479)
Female	0	25.8	7.9	5.1	31.9	.6	28.7	100 (N=681)

* A sample of 194 counties located in all 50 states

Although California sentencing data offer the best basis for comparison with the Nagel data, it is useful also to examine data indicating the use of discretion by officials of the criminal justice system other than judges.[29] Arrest data and data concerning disposition of cases in Superior Court broaden the scope of the study in that they permit some analysis of decisions of more officials than judges: police officers, prosecutors, and juries.

Table 3 shows the proportional outcome of California's handling of male and female felony arrests in 1974. For both males and females there is a reduction in the number of cases at each step in processing through the courts. A very large number of felony arrests each year are subsequently charged as misdemeanors or dropped altogether from the courts. These cases never reach Superior Court. Table 3 shows the percent of male felony arrests reaching Superior Court in California in 1974 (16.6 percent) and the percent of female felony arrests reaching Superior Court (13.5 percent). Once a case reaches Superior Court in California it is resolved by (a) conviction; (b) acquittal; or (c) dismissal. Table 3 shows the percent of male and female cases disposed of [by conviction] in California Superior Courts in 1974 to be 14.4 and 10.9 percent of males and females arrested that year.[30] Persons found guilty face a variety of sentences, the most severe of these being the death sentence or a sentence to state prison. Table 3 offers a comparison of these two sentences for males and females in California in 1974 (shown as a percentage of those arrested). The pattern clearly shown in Table 3 (and also evident in the

TABLE 3. Superior Court Dispositions,* Convictions in Superior Courts, and Sentences to Death or Prison in California, by Sex, Shown as a Percentage of Felony Arrests in California in 1974

	Felony Arrests		Superior Court Dispositions*	Felony Convictions	Sentences to Death or Prison
Male	100%	(232,289)	16.6%	14.4%	2.3%
Female	100%	(35,615)	13.5%	10.9%	0.7%

*Disposed of in Superior Court by dismissal, acquittal, or conviction.

1970–73 data, but not presented here) is that at each measured step in the criminal justice process where discretion is exercised, females were more frequently favored by the system than were males.

. . . Data for the period 1970–73 . . . indicate that females received comparatively gentle sentences in every year even though substantial changes occurred in the conviction and arrest figures over this period. There was a notable decline from 1970 through 1974 in the number of persons convicted of felonies (a drop from 49,679 in 1970 to 37,367 in 1974). At the same time there was a clear trend toward increasing proportions of sentences to incarceration (prison, jail, and civil institutions) for males and females convicted of felonies. Accompanying the higher proportions of incarcerations was a decrease in the proportion of fines and probation grants for both sexes.

It should be noted at this point that the bench responsible for the sentencing of persons convicted of felonies in California in 1974 was overwhelmingly male. Of the 478 Superior Court judges sitting that year, only five were women.[31] Any analysis of paternalism patterns, then, is made in the context of an almost exclusively male bench.

. . . the percentage of females granted probation (42.4) was more than double the percentage of males granted probation (20.1). In addition, the percentage of females receiving prison sentences (6.6) was less than half the percentage of males so sentenced (15.9). Death sentences were given only to males. In short, the patterns of disposition found in the California data were strikingly similar to those revealed by analysis of Nagel's federal and state data: the treatment afforded males and females convicted of felonies in California followed the same disparity patterns found nationwide and in a sample of states ten years earlier.

Although the preceding analysis indicated substantial differences in the treatment accorded males and females at the sentencing stage of the criminal justice process, it is possible that those differences, or part of those differences, could be accounted for by factors other than sex. For example, several studies have indicated that race was related to the severity of sentences given to a particular individual.[32] Others have found income or economic class to be related to patterns of sentencing defendants.[33] Severity of the crime committed and prior record of the defendant are also relevant. In order to isolate the impact of these factors, the male-female sentencing data for California were organized to permit comparison of sentences given to males and females by race, offense, and prior record.

. . . Examination of the percentage of individuals of the various races receiving a particular type of sentence indicates that females of all races received less harsh treatment than did their male counterparts. This pattern existed in highly similar form for the period 1970-73, although the data are not presented here. The data also indicated that nonwhite females received slightly harsher treatment than white females and that nonwhite males received harsher treatment than white males. Fifty-eight and two-tenths percent of nonwhite females convicted were sentenced to some type of incarceration, while 56 percent of white females convicted were sentenced to incarceration. The comparable percentages for males were 82.4 for nonwhites and 77.5 for whites.

. . . Although there is clearly a variation in the severity of sentencing from offense to offense, the pattern of comparatively gentle treatment of women is pervasive. The proportionately higher levels of probation granted women are substantial. . . . The only exception (forcible rape) is for a crime for which only one woman was convicted in 1974. The only crime for which proportionately more women were sent to prison than men was that of sex law violations (and here the total N for females sent to prison was only three). The crimes for which women receive substantially harsher than average sentences (high proportion of prison sentences especially) are also crimes for which men receive harsher than average sentences. As the crimes increase in severity, both males and females move in the direction of more severe sentences. Since males have harsher sentences even for the least severe crimes, however, the numbers of males sent to prison tend to accumulate quickly for the most severe crimes. Further analysis of the data . . . is difficult in the absence of knowledge of the degree of crime committed for each offense.[34]

Additional insight into sentencing patterns can be gained by comparing male and female sentencing while controlling for prior record. Prior records, along with probation officers' reports are presented to California judges in most felony sentencings. The influence of prior record as well as type of crime, therefore, can be quite substantial. . . . Persons with one or more prior prison commitments are far more likely to be sent to prison than persons with no prior record or a prior record resulting in less than a prison commitment. Probation is most frequently granted to persons with no prior record. These patterns of increasing sentencing severity with increasing prior record are present for both sexes. The pattern of gentler treatment for females dominates each category of prior record. Prison and probation sentences are important examples here. In each of the three categories of prior record men receive substantially more sentences to prison than women and women are granted probation more frequently than men. The pervasive pattern of gentler treatment for women remains clear even after controlling for prior record.

Both the Nagel data and the California data revealed a significant relationship between the female sex and gentle treatment in the criminal justice system. Sentencing patterns in both data sets worked to the advantage of women. Controlling for race, type of crime, and prior record has resulted in the same basic pattern: consistently less harsh treatment for women than for men.[35]

CONCLUSIONS

This article has examined the concepts of chivalry and paternalism and their presence in the decision-making process of the criminal justice system. It is clear from the data that the criminal justice system treats women substantially differently from the way in which it treats men. It is apparent that women receive gentler handling than do men. This handling is pervasive regardless of race, type of crime, or prior record. What the data do not show is why this differential treatment exists. The discussion of the manner in which chivalry and paternalism operate in American culture and American law offers the beginning of an explanation. The assumption that women are in need of protection has been a very common one both in legislatures and in the criminal justice system. Both the reasons given and the actions taken by officials in the criminal justice system have reflected the assumption that women are different from men in ways that justify for women softer, more caring, protective treatment. It can be reasonably concluded from these findings that the term "chivalry factor," or perhaps more accurately, "paternalism factor" is an appropriate one to describe the use of discretion by officials of the criminal justice system.

Several other matters should be reviewed in concluding a discussion of the chivalry factor. There is a real question concerning the impact of the women's movement of the last decade on female criminality and on the attitudes of officials in the criminal justice system regarding female crime. It has been suggested elsewhere that "the female crime rate shows some tendency to approach closest to the male in countries in which females have the greatest freedom and equality . . . and to vary most from the male rate in countries in which females are closely supervised. . . . "[36] It would follow from this that as women's social, economic, and political positions change in the United States (in the direction of equality with males), their criminal participation could be expected to increase and to assume more of the character of crime traditionally viewed as male. It seems reasonable to expect that attitudes of chivalry and paternalism also would decrease accordingly. The data presented here, though, do not reflect any dramatic change in that direction. Comparison of the Nagel data and the more recent

California data is difficult in this area because of the different geographical sources of the data and the different categorization of treatment. A review of the California data over the five-year period used for this study suggests only a slight trend toward the increased incarceration of both sexes with the increase in the percentage of females being incarcerated being slightly higher than the percentage of males. Although the women's movement may not have had a strong impact upon judges and other officials of the criminal justice system by 1974, the last date for which data are presently available, future data should be examined carefully in order to gain insight into possible changing behavior patterns on the part of these officials. Also, as we see increases in the number of women serving in official roles in the court room and criminal justice system, it will be important to examine the comparative use of discretion by male and female officials.

It is relatively easy to dismiss the findings presented in this article with regard to the gentler handling of females if one is only superficially concerned with either crime control or with women. It is true that women are excused more easily than men in criminal justice system and a frequent response to this phenomenon is that women should be grateful for this gracious treatment.

We should, however, consider possible long-term impacts on women. It is true that women do enjoy certain benefits of a chivalry factor. They are arrested, prosecuted, and sent to institutions less often than are men—the benefit to them is their freedom. A major cost to them, however, is the continuation of a state of public consciousness which holds that women are less able than men and are thus in need of special protective treatment. This results in extensive personal psychological, social, economic, and political damage to the democratic notions of self-determination and equality. Within the criminal justice system there will be public policy implications of these attitudes. To the extent that paternalistic views of women dominate the criminal justice system, programs designed for women within that system will be affected by those views. For example, if women are viewed to be naturally passive and dependent, prison "rehabilitation" may be geared to reestablish those norms in women through appropriate counseling and vocational training programs.[37] The existence of passivity and dependency in human beings, however, may make them of limited productivity in the society at large. It is strongly suggested here that the policies of the criminal justice system with regard to women be reevaluated in light of an acknowledged paternalistic bias present in that system and in light of changing views concerning innate characteristics of women.

Finally, the identification of a chivalry/paternalism factor in the criminal justice system poses basic questions for future directions of the system. If one regards the institutions of the present criminal justice system as functional, there may be a societal threat posed by the continued lack of institutionalization of women criminals whose actions have been excused by officials of the system. These women have gone unpunished or unrehabilitated far more often than their male counterparts. If, on the other hand, one does not regard the present criminal justice system as functional perhaps there are some valuable lessons to be learned from the gentler handling of women. Why has it been possible to control criminal behavior on the part of one-half of the adult population with one-twentieth the amount of incarceration? Why are women granted probation almost twice as often as men? Why have police seen gentleness in the arrest process as both desirable and possible for women but not for men? In a period of increasing pressure for forceful law and order, it is important to ask the question whether we are headed in precisely the wrong direction in our approach to criminality. Addressing ourselves more to the human needs of the people who become involved in criminal activity might evolve more productive policies than those policies which emphasize police hardware and tougher prison security.

REFERENCES

1. For reviews of the early literature see: Dorie Klein, "The Etiology of Female Crime: A Review of the Literature," *Issues in Criminology* 8 (Fall 1973): 3–30; and Christine E. Rasche, "The Female Offender as an Object of Criminological Research," *Criminal Justice and Behavior* 1 (December 1974): 301–19.

2. The more extensive recent works have been: Freda Adler, *Sisters in Crime: The Rise of the New Female Criminal* (New York: McGraw-Hill, 1975); Karen DeCrow, *Sexist Justice: How Legal Sexism Affects You* (New York: Random House, Vintage, 1974); Leo Kanowitz, *Women and the Law: The Unfinished Revolution* (Albuquerque: University of New Mexico Press, 1969); Rita J. Simon, *Women and Crime* (Lexington, Mass.: Heath, 1975); and Carol Smart, *Women, Crime and Criminology: A Feminist Critique* (London: Routledge and Kegan Paul, 1977). Collections of articles and special issue volumes also to be noted are: Annette M. Brodsky, ed., *The Female Offender* (Beverly Hills: Sage, 1975); "Women and the Criminal Law," *American Criminal law Review* 11 (Winter 1973); and "Women, Crime, and Criminology," *Issues in Criminology* 8 (Fall 1973).

3. See, for example, Stuart Nagel, *The Legal Process from a Behavioral Perspective* (Homewood, Ill.: Dorsey Press, 1969), p. 92.

4. The term "sexism" also has been used recently to describe the set of behaviors of criminal justice system officials examined here. See, for example, Dorie Klein and June Kress, "Any Woman's Blues: A Critical Overview of Women, Crime, and the Criminal Justice System," *Crime and Social Justice* 5 (Spring-Summer 1976): 34–49; and Ellen S. Cannon and Susette M. Talarico, "Women and Crime: A Study in Power," paper presented at Annual Meeting of the American Political Science Association, Chicago, September 1976.

5. Walter Reckless and Barbara Kay, *The Female Offender: Report to the U.S. President's Commission on Law Enforcement and the Administration of Justice* (Washington, D.C.: U.S. Government Printing Office, 1967), p. 16.

6. F.J.C. Hearnshaw, "Chivalry," in Edwin Seligman, ed., *Encyclopedia of the Social Sciences,* III (New York: Macmillan, 1935), 436–40.

7 ."Paternalism," in David L. Sills, ed., *International Encyclopedia of the Social Sciences,* II (New York: Macmillan, 1968), 472.

8. See Kanowitz, *Women and the Law,* for a discussion of women's legal status historically in the U.S.

9. See, for example, Kirsten Amundsen, *A New Look at the Silenced Majority: Women and American Democracy* (Englewood Cliffs: Prentice-Hall, 1977): DeCrow, *Sexist Justice;* Eleanor Flexner, *The Women's Rights Movement in the United States* (New York: Atheneum, 1972); Kanowitz, *Women and the Law;* and William L. O'Neill, *Everyone Was Brave: A History of Feminism in America* (Chicago: Quadrangle Books, 1971).

10. *Bradwell v. The State,* 83 U.S. 130 (December 1872) at 141.

11. DeCrow, *Sexist Justice,* p. 289, quoting from the Miami *Herald,* Oct. 16, 1970.

12. Kanowitz, *Women and the Law*, p. 4.

13. Simone de Beauvoir, *The Second Sex* (New York: Bantam, 1952), p. 679.

14. In New Jersey, for example, see, *State v. Costello,* 282 A. 2nd 748 (1971).

15. For a discussion of these indeterminate sentencing statutes, see, Carolyn E. Temin, "Discriminatory Sentencing for Women Offenders: The Argument for ERA in a Nutshell," *American Criminal Law Review* 11 (Winter 1973): 355–72.

16. Ibid., p. 358.

17. Meda Chesney-Lind, "Judicial Enforcement of the Female Sex Role: The Family Court and the Female Delinquent," *Issues in Criminology* 8 (Fall 1973): 51–70; Peter C. Kratcoski, "Differential Treatment of Boys and Girls by the Justice System," *Child Welfare* 53 (1974): 16–22; and Reckless and Kay, *The Female Offender,* p. 8–12.

18. Chesney-Lind, "Judicial Enforcement"; and Smart, *Women, Crime and Criminology,* pp. 131–36.

19. Edward Green, *Judicial Attitudes in Sentencing* (New York: St. Martin's Press, 1961); and Nagel, *The Legal Process,* Chapter 8.

20. Green, *Judicial Attitudes,* pp. 51–52.

21. Ibid., p. 52.

22. Stuart Nagel and Lenore Weitzman, "Women as Litigants," *Hastings Law Journal 23.* (November 1971): 171–98.

23. Stuart Nagel, *Improving the Legal Process: Effects of Alternatives* (Lexington, Mass.: Lexington Books, 1975), Chapter 7.

24. Nagel and Weitzman, "Women as Litigants," p. 173.

25. Data source for the federal data, Stuart Nagel, *Federal Court Cases,* ICPR 7245. Inter-University Consortium for Political Research, P.O. Box 1248, Ann Arbor, Michigan, 48106; Data source for the sample state data, American Bar Foundation, *State Criminal Court Cases,* Principal Investigators: Lee Silverstein and Stuart Nagel, ICPR 7272. Inter-University Consortium for Political Research.

26. An analysis of variance was conducted on the cross-tabulations in order to test further the significance of sex as a variable. For this analysis, the null hypothesis was that there were no significant differences in the sentencing of male and female defendants. The analysis of variance resulted in a computed F of 667.3120 for the federal data. This F level compares with an expected level at $\geq$ .05 of F = 1.85, and at $\geq$ .01, F = 2.35. As such the computed F levels are higher than the figures from the F Table, and the null hypothesis can be rejected. For a discussion of the analysis of variance see Samuel A. Kirkpatrick, *Quantitative Analysis of Political Data* (Columbus, Ohio: Merrill, 1974), pp. 53–57.

27. The computed F for the state data was 13.8551 with an expected level at $\geq$ .05, F = 2.10 and at $\geq$ .01, F = 3.74.

28. All California data contained in the article were provided by the California Department of Justice, Bureau of Criminal Statistics, P.O. Box 13427, Sacramento, California, 95813. Copies of machine tabulations were made available through the Bureau.

29. A study which helps to bridge the gap between the Nagel and Green studies and the 1970–74 California data is that done by Rita J. Simon, *Women and Crime.* Although Simon did not examine sentencing *per se,* her findings provide a useful supplement to the sentencing data offered here. Simon uses the F.B.I. Uniform Crime Reports to show changes in arrest patterns for men and women for the period 1953–72 (see pp. 19–47). She follows her analysis of arrest data with an analysis of male and female convictions: in 89 U.S. Federal District Courts 1963–71, in California Superior Courts 1960–72, and in Ohio 1969–71. Here she shows numbers of males and females convicted and the percent of females among convictions, by offense. Her conclusion is that "these data allow us to say only that women as recently as 1972 seem to be receiving some preferential treatment at the bar of justice" (see pp. 49–67).

30. "Disposition in Superior Court" includes all resolutions of matters which were arraigned in those courts, namely dismissals, acquittals, and convictions.

31. *Women in the Justice System,* Transcript of Hearing of the California Joint Committee on Legal Equality, February 22, 1974, p. 5. It was not possible to distinguish male from female judges in the data collected by the California Bureau of Criminal Statistics. Should this become possible in the future, it would provide the basis for additional research into patterns of judicial paternalism.

32. See, for example, Henry A. Bullock, "Significance of the Racial Factor in the Length of Prison Sentences," *Journal of Criminal Law, Criminology, and Police Science* 52 (November-December 1961): 411–17; Green, *Judicial Attitudes,* pp. 56–62 and Tables 27–35; and Nagel, *The Legal Process,* pp. 93–95 and Tables 8-1 through 8-8.

33. Indigence and sentencing is discussed by Nagel, *The Legal Process,* pp. 87–89 and Tables 8-1 through 8-8. See also, Dallin H. Oaks and Warren Lehman, *A Criminal Justice System and the Indigent* (Chicago: University of Chicago Press, 1968); and American Bar Foundation, *Defense of the Poor in Criminal Cases in American State Courts: A Field Study and Report* [by] Lee Silverstein [project director]. Chicago, 1965 (Vol. 1).

34. For an excellent parallel study of sentencing disparities in Kentucky, see, John R. Faine and Edward Bohlander, Jr., "Sentencing the Female Offender: The Impact of Legal and Extra-Legal Considerations," paper presented at Annual Meeting of American Society of Criminology, Tucson, Arizona, November 1976. This study concerned sentences of a sample of 1603 felons, convicted between July 1972 and January 1975 in Kentucky. The findings of this study are very similar to the findings presented in this article concerning California. After controlling for race, previous criminality, seriousness and type of offense, social status, and personal-demographic variables, the authors of the Kentucky study found that "1) Female offenders tend to be accorded favorable treatment in the criminal justice system; and 2) white women tend to enjoy more lenient dispositions than black female defendants" (p. 37).

35. The data made available through the California Bureau of Criminal Statistics were provided in tabular form. These data were adequate to validate the hypothesis of this paper. The present analysis of disparate treatment of

criminal defendants may well be expanded by use of the computer tapes prepared under the Bureau's new offender based tracking system.

36. Edwin H. Sutherland and Donald R. Cressey, *Criminology*, 8th ed. (Philadelphia: Lippincott, 1970), p. 127.

37. For a discussion of this problem see: Smart, *Women, Crime and Criminology*, pp. 140–45.

Unequal Protection for Males and Females in the Juvenile Court

Susan K. Datesman
Frank R. Scarpitti

Ostensibly, juvenile and family courts were established as specialized tribunals for the protection of child offenders.[1] Under the *parens patriae* doctrine, the juvenile court was to provide for the care, protection, and treatment of the child in place of the natural parents. In 1909, a leading juvenile court judge wrote that the doctrine of *parens patriae* allows the court "to take [the child] in hand and instead of first stigmatizing and then reforming it, to protect it from the stigma [of criminality]" (Mack, 1909:109). The proceedings and dispositions of the juvenile court were, therefore, not supposed to be either criminal or punitive in nature. The purpose of the juvenile court was not to adjudicate guilt and mete out punishment but instead to help the child see the error of his or her ways and to offer "treatment" and "rehabilitation" before more serious criminal pursuits were undertaken. Due process safeguards were considered

"Unequal Protection for Males and Females in the Juvenile Court" by Susan K. Datesman and Frank R. Scarpitti is reprinted from *Juvenile Delinquency: Little Brother Grows Up*, Vol. 2, Sage Research Progress Series in Criminology, Theodore N. Ferdinand, Editor, © 1977, pp. 59–77 by permission of the Publisher, Sage Publications, Inc. (Beverly Hills/London).

unimportant and juvenile court judges were granted wide discretion since it was assumed that the court was acting on behalf of the child and for the child's best interest. Consequently, not only children whose behavior contravened criminal statutes were eligible to "benefit" from the rehabilitative services offered by the juvenile court, but also children whose behavior gave evidence of delinquent tendencies.

Anthony Platt (1969) has demonstrated, however, that the motives of early reformers were less humanitarian than has often been supposed. In his important study, *The Child Savers,* Platt discusses the invention of delinquency as a legal category at the turn of the century. The imposition of normative restraints on children constituted the main thrust of the child-saving movement:

> Many of the child savers' reforms were aimed at imposing sanctions on conduct unbecoming youth and disqualifying youth from the benefit of adult privileges. . . . Their central interest was in the normative behavior of youth—their recreation, leisure, education, outlook on life, attitudes to authority, family relationships, and personal morality. (Platt, 1969:99)

Many acts of juveniles that had previously not been reacted to or had been handled informally now came under the auspices of the state. It is significant that the first law defining juvenile delinquency (in Illinois in 1899) specifically authorized penalties for predelinquent as well as delinquent behavior (Platt, 1969:138).

Acts which are predelinquent are termed juvenile status offenses, since only juveniles can commit them. Juvenile status offenses include such vague and broadly defined behavior as ungovernability, incorrigibility, and immorality. Typical of such broadly phrased delinquency statutes is Maine's, which says that the court may treat as an offender any juvenile "living in circumstances of manifest danger of falling into habits of vice and immorality." Similar delinquency statutes existed in 41 states in 1969.[2] Recently, several of these state statutes have been struck down as unconstitutionally vague, but others have withstood constitutional challenge.[3]

Unhappily, the reality of the juvenile court has fallen far short of the protective, rehabilitative rhetoric of the child savers. In practice, the legal processing of juveniles is highly stigmatizing and punitive. Despite the euphemistic terminology, the delinquent label "has come to involve only slightly less stigma than the term 'criminal' applied to adults" (*In re Gault*, 1967:27) and adjudication as a delinquent infringes on the rights of juveniles and curtails their freedom no less than a criminal conviction. In recognition of this reality, the United States Supreme Court extended minimum procedural safeguards to juvenile proceedings in the *Kent* (1966), *Gault* (1967), and *Winship* (1970) decisions. The right to trial by jury, however, is not available to juveniles (*McKeiver*, 1971). Also, recent studies concerned with the impact of *Gault* have shown that many juvenile courts have failed to fully comply with due process requirements (Lefstein et al., 1969; Langley, 1972), particularly in the case of status offenders (Finkelstein et al., 1973). Moreover, these decisions did not touch upon what rights a juvenile has in the preadjudication phase or the postadjudication or disposition stage.

There exists, therefore, a great potential for the unequal and discriminatory treatment of adolescents brought before the juvenile court. The Task Force Report on Juvenile Delinquency and Youth Crime noted that broadly written delinquency statutes, especially when administered with procedural informality, "establish the judge as arbiter not only of the behavior but also of the morals of every child. . . . The situation is ripe for overreaching, for imposition of the judge's own code of youthful conduct" (President's Commission on Law Enforcement and Administration of Justice, 1967:25). The considerable discretion granted juvenile court judges to make moral judgments would appear to pose a greater danger to female juveniles than males. Given that the limits of acceptable behavior are much narrower for females than males, judges may mete out more severe dispositions to female juveniles who appear before them than males. And indeed, what little data we have indicate that this is the case.

Gibbons and Griswold (1957), for example, found that males and females in the state of Washington were dismissed from juvenile court jurisdiction in about the same proportions, but that females were more likely to be institutionalized than males. A study by Terry (1967) in Wisconsin found that while females were placed under informal supervision by the probation department more often than males, females brought before the juvenile court were more often sent to an institution. Finally, Chesney-Lind (1973), in her study of the Honolulu juvenile court, found that female juveniles were less likely to be immediately released and more likely to be institutionalized than males.

These few available studies do not necessarily reveal a sex bias, however, since many considerations influence a judge's disposition. We might logically expect legal factors, such as type of offense and prior offense record, to influence the relationship between sex and disposition. Unfortunately, the studies of Gibbons and Griswold and Chesney-Lind did not use legal variables as controls in their analysis, and while Terry did control for legal factors, his analysis does not allow an examination of the contingent associations within subcategories of the legal variables. The present study attempts to overcome these handicaps by exploring the relationship between sex and disposition while accounting for the influence of instant offense type and previous record.[4]

FINDINGS

The data presented in this paper were obtained from the court records of 1,103 juveniles appearing before the family court of a medium-sized city in an eastern state during a 7-month period. The sample consists of 103 white females, 97 black females, 559 white males, and 344 black males. First, it may be noted that half of the females referred to the family court but only one-fifth of the males were charged with juvenile status offenses—running away, ungovernability, truancy, and curfew violation.[5] It may be noted further that 68 percent of the females as compared with 54 percent of the males were appearing before the court for the first time. Even so, females received somewhat harsher dispositions from the court than males (Table 1), although the relationship is of small magnitude (gamma = + .11).

When type of offense is introduced as a control on the original relationship between sex and disposition, some interesting findings emerge (Table 2). A negative relationship is found to exist between sex and disposition for felons (gamma = −.47) and misdemeanants (gamma = −.14) while a positive relationship obtains for status offenders (gamma = +.45). That is, in the case of felonies and misdemeanors female juveniles receive a more lenient disposition while in the case of status offenses males receive a more lenient disposition. Among juveniles referred for felonies, twice as many females (65%) as males (32%) were dismissed or warned. This difference is maintained, although the margin is not as great, for females

TABLE 1. Family Court Disposition by Sex

Disposition	Male	Female
Dismissed	9.2%	7.3%
	(78)	(13)
Warned	34.1%	33.3%
	(289)	(59)
Fined	10.0%	1.7%
	(85)	(3)
Unsupervised probation	6.6%	8.5%
	(56)	(15)
Probation officer	33.5%	41.8%
	(284)	(74)
Public institution	6.6%	7.3%
	(56)	(13)
Total percent	100%	100%
	(848)	(177)
Gamma	+.11	

TABLE 2. Family Court Disposition by Offense Type and Sex

Disposition	Felony		Misdemeanor		Status Offense	
	Male	Female	Male	Female	Male	Female
Dismissed	8.1%	14.7%	10.1%	13.6%	5.8%	0.0%
	(23)	(5)	(29)	(6)	(9)	(0)
Warned	23.9%	50.0%	44.8%	50.0%	35.3%	16.9%
	(68)	(17)	(128)	(22)	(55)	(14)
Fined	3.5%	0.0%	11.2%	2.3%	0.6%	0.0%
	(10)	(0)	(32)	(1)	(1)	(0)
Unsupervised probation	9.5%	17.6%	5.9%	13.6%	5.1%	2.4%
	(27)	(6)	(17)	(6)	(8)	(2)
Probation officer	46.0%	11.8%	23.8%	20.5%	44.9%	68.7%
	(131)	(4)	(68)	(9)	(70)	(57)
Public institution	9.1%	5.9%	4.2%	0.0%	8.3%	12.0%
	(26)	(2)	(12)	(0)	(13)	(10)
Total percent	100%	100%	100%	100%	100%	100%
	(285)	(34)	(286)	(44)	(156)	(83)
Gamma	−.47		−.14		+.45	

(64%) and males (55%) referred for misdemeanors. However, this pattern is reversed among status offenders: males were more than twice as likely (41%) as females (17%) to be dismissed or warned. It is interesting that in no case are the percentage differences between males and females sentenced to an institution greater than 4%, although the direction of these differences is consistent with the general pattern. Female juveniles brought before the court as status offenders were least likely to be dismissed or warned and most likely to be placed under supervision by a probation officer and institutionalized.

In Table 3, the dispositions handed out to first offenders, controlling for type of offense, are presented. Among felony offenders with no prior records of delinquent behavior, 71 percent of the females were dismissed or warned whereas only 34 percent of the males were so handled (gamma = −.52). A similar although weaker difference is shown for female (76%) and male (64%) misdemeanants with no records of previous offenses (gamma = −.21). Again, just the opposite obtains among status offenders with no records of prior delinquent behavior: the percentages dismissed or warned are 23 percent for females but 38 percent for males (gamma = +.37). The percentage differences between males and females sentenced to an institution are negligible for all three offense types.

Among status offenders who have a record of one or more previous offenses,[6] the harsher treatment of female juveniles is even more apparent (gamma = +.60). None of the female juveniles were dismissed as compared with 10 percent of the males; the percentages warned were 7 percent and 34 percent, respectively. In contrast, 71 percent of the females and 40 percent of the males were given supervision by a probation officer, and 21% of the females but only 13 percent of the males received institutionalization.

It appears, then, that males receive harsher dispositions than females for criminal offenses, but that females receive harsher dispositions than males for noncriminal status offenses, especially when they are repeat offenders. Research has indicated

TABLE 3. Family Court Disposition by Offense Type and Sex for First Offenders

Disposition	Felony		Misdemeanor		Status Offense	
	Male	Female	Male	Female	Male	Female
Dismissed	6.5%	16.7%	12.0%	16.2%	2.3%	0.0%
	(10)	(4)	(18)	(6)	(2)	(0)
Warned	27.5%	54.2%	52.0%	59.5%	36.0%	23.1%
	(42)	(13)	(78)	(22)	(31)	(12)
Fined	3.9%	0.0%	8.7%	0.0%	1.2%	0.0%
	(6)	(0)	(13)	(0)	(1)	(0)
Unsupervised probation	11.1%	12.5%	5.3%	13.5%	7.0%	1.9%
	(17)	(3)	(8)	(5)	(6)	(1)
Probation officer	49.0%	12.5%	21.3%	10.8%	48.8%	67.3%
	(75)	(3)	(32)	(4)	(42)	(35)
Public institution	2.0%	4.2%	0.7%	0.0%	4.7%	7.7%
	(3)	(1)	(1)	(0)	(4)	(4)
Total percent	100%	100%	100%	100%	100%	100%
	(153)	(24)	(150)	(37)	(86)	(52)
Gamma	−.52		−.21		+.37	

that stereotypes may influence the application of delinquent labels. Garrett and Short (1975), for example, found that social class and delinquency are strongly linked in the view of police. Police see lower-class boys as more likely to be involved in delinquent behavior than middle-class boys. Similarly, the disparate treatment which males and females are afforded by the juvenile court may reflect stereotypic notions about proper sex role behavior. Females are supposed to be delicate and frail and in need of male protection. Thus, it may be the case that relative to males, female juveniles are advantaged with respect to criminal offenses because chivalrous judges, who are mostly male, view them as weaker, less responsible, less dangerous, and more likely to be harmed by a harsh disposition.[7]

In the case of status offenses, however, stereotypic notions may work to the disadvantage of female juveniles. Running away, incorrigibility, truancy, and similar designations commonly constitute euphemisms for sexual offenses—"The underlying vein of many of these offenses is sexual misconduct by the girl delinquent" (Vedder and Somerville, 1970:147). Male juveniles are allowed a greater latitude of freedom in sexual behavior than are females. Through the socialization process, girls are taught that the female is inherently less sexual than the male, that sex cannot be enjoyed outside of a love (and preferably a marriage) context, and that it is incumbent upon them to impose sexual restraints, to be, as Margaret Mead has put it, "the conscience for two" (1949:280). Boys, on the other hand, are taught that they have strong sex drives, that sex per se is pleasurable, and that they should "go as far"with girls as possible. Therefore, censure is diverted away from the male and onto the female who is sexually active.[8] In view of this double standard of sexual morality, the more severe dispositions made by the juvenile court against female status offenders can perhaps be understood.

It is interesting to note a parallel between the disparate treatment male and female juveniles are afforded by the juvenile court for criminal and status offenses and sex-based discrimination in juvenile delinquency statutes. For example, in Oklahoma until 1972, females under 18 who committed crimes were allowed to be processed as juveniles, but juvenile proceedings were limited to males under 16. The Oklahoma Supreme Court upheld the constitutionality of the statute against an equal protection challenge on the grounds that it exemplified a legislative judgment "premised upon the demonstrated facts of life" (*Lamb* v. *State,* 1970). The United States Court of Appeals for the Tenth Circuit reversed, declaring that the statute violated the equal protection clause. The federal court did not find the unexplained "demonstrated facts" helpful in finding a rational justification for the unequal treatment accorded 16–18-year-old males and 16–18-year-old females (*Lamb* v. *Brown,* 1972).

By contrast, some states have determined that female juveniles require more "protection" from "immoral" but noncriminal conduct than males. Connecticut law until 1972 authorized the imprisonment of unmarried females between 16 and 21 if they were "in manifest danger of falling into habits of vice" or "leading a vicious life," but did not proscribe this type of behavior when engaged in by males of the same age group. In 1966, in *Connecticut* v. *Mattiello,* a Connecticut circuit court upheld the constitutionality of the statute against a claim of vagueness by reasoning that the safeguards of due process were inapplicable since the objective was to protect young females rather than to punish them.

Attention is directed next to Table 4, where the effects of offense type, race, and sex are simultaneously considered. These findings show the same general pattern as in Table 2. Relative to males in the same race category, females are accorded less severe treatment in the case of felonies and misdemeanors but more severe treatment in the case of status offenses. However, there are some interesting differences.

In general, the discrepancy between the dispositions given males and females brought before the court on felony and misdemeanor charges is less for blacks than whites. Among blacks referred for felonies and misdemeanors, the gamma coefficients are −.39 and −.08, respectively, while the compar-

TABLE 4. Family Court Disposition by Offense Type, Race, and Sex

| | Felony | | | | Misdemeanor | | | | Status Offense | | | |
| | Black | | White | | Black | | White | | Black | | White | |
Disposition	Male	Female	Male	Female	Male	Female	Male	Female	Male	Female	Male	Female
Dismissed	9.9%	13.0%	6.7%	18.2%	11.1%	11.1%	9.6%	15.4%	9.2%	0.0%	2.5%	0.0%
	(12)	(3)	(11)	(2)	(12)	(2)	(17)	(4)	(7)	(0)	(2)	(0)
Warned	26.4%	47.8%	22.0%	54.5%	42.6%	44.4%	46.1%	53.8%	50.0%	14.6%	21.3%	19.0%
	(32)	(11)	(36)	(6)	(46)	(8)	(82)	(14)	(38)	(6)	(17)	(8)
Fined	2.5%	0.0%	4.3%	0.0%	0.0%	5.6%	18.0%	0.0%	1.3%	0.0%	0.0%	0.0%
	(3)	(0)	(7)	(0)	(0)	(1)	(32)	(0)	(1)	(0)	(0)	(0)
Unsupervised probation	5.8%	21.7%	12.2%	9.1%	11.1%	5.6%	2.8%	19.2%	1.3%	4.9%	8.8%	0.0%
	(7)	(5)	(20)	(1)	(12)	(1)	(5)	(5)	(1)	(2)	(7)	(0)
Probation officer	41.3%	8.7%	49.4%	18.2%	25.9%	33.3%	22.5%	11.5%	23.7%	65.9%	65.0%	71.4%
	(50)	(2)	(81)	(2)	(28)	(6)	(40)	(3)	(18)	(27)	(52)	(30)
Public institution	14.0%	8.7%	5.5%	0.0%	9.3%	0.0%	1.1%	0.0%	14.5%	14.6%	2.5%	9.5%
	(17)	(2)	(9)	(0)	(10)	(0)	(2)	(0)	(11)	(6)	(2)	(4)
Total percent	100%	100%	100%	100%	100%	100%	100%	100%	100%	100%	100%	100%
	(121)	(23)	(164)	(11)	(108)	(18)	(178)	(26)	(76)	(41)	(80)	(42)
Gamma	−.39		−.61		−.08		−.20		+.54		+.34	

able coefficients for whites are −.61 and −.20. Among blacks, 61 percent of the female felons were dismissed or warned as compared with 36 percent of the male felons, giving a difference of 25 percentage points. Among whites, 55 percent of the female felons and 29 percent of the male felons were dismissed or warned, giving a difference of 44 percentage points. The percentage differences between male and female felons sentenced to an institution are about the same for both blacks (5%) and whites (6%).

Among misdemeanants, there can be observed a 2 percent difference between blacks males and females dismissed or warned as contrasted with a 13 percent difference between their white counterparts. The exception to this pattern is institutionalization, where females are treated more like males among whites (difference = 1%) than among blacks (difference = 9%). The overall pattern holds when considering only misdemeanants who are first offenders where the gamma coefficients are −.15 for blacks and −.25 for whites.

Additional computaticns on the data presented in Table 4 reveal that racial differences are weaker among males referred for felonies (gamma = +.02) and misdemeanors (gamma = +.13) than among their female counterparts (gamma = +.19 and +.27, respectively). That is, in the case of felonies and misdemeanors, black females relative to white females receive more severe dispositions than black males relative to white males.

The above findings may reflect the fact that male and female roles are less differentiated among lower-class blacks than among middle-class whites.[9] Rainwater (1970:164–166) states that lower-class black families are matrifocal in type and center around feminine authority, feminine equality, and male marginality whether the husband is absent or present in the family unit. Matrifocal means that "the continuing existence of the family is focused around the mother, that the father is regarded (to a greater or lesser degree) as marginal to the continuing family unit composed of mother and children" (Rainwater, 1970: 164). The matrifocal emphasis in family and kinship systems derives from the fact that many black females have been forced to share or assume the financial responsibilities for their families because of structural impediments which lessen the economic viability of black men (see Liebow, 1967).

Consequently, included in the socialization of black females is an attempt to prepare them for the contingency that black males might not be able to support their families entirely. Thus Rainwater points out that:

> The female role models available to girls emphasize an exaggerated self-sufficiency (from the point of view of the middle class) and the danger of allowing oneself to be dependent on men for anything that is crucial. (1966:199)

And Ladner observes that: "In sum, women were expected to be *strong* and parents socialized their daughters with this intention because they never knew what the odds were for them having to utilize this resourcefulness in later life" (1971:131). It appears that the traditional division of labor which assigns females the major role of housewife and excludes them from the labor market is less tenable among blacks than among whites. The passivity and dependency aspects of the female role are deemphasized in the socialization of black females since these traits would prove dysfunctional for enabling them to cope with the exigencies of marriage. Thus Axelson found a greater acceptance of working wives among black males than among white males and suggests that "the dominating white culture, more than the Negro subculture, has a well-defined set of normative sanctions supporting the role of wife and mother" (1970:459).

It appears that black females as a group are more likely to violate sterotypic notions of proper female behavior than whites. Therefore, we suggest that judges may deal more severely with black female juveniles who are charged with criminal acts than with their white counterparts because they view black females as less wedded to the female role and hence as less in need of protection.[10] At the same time, it appears that black females still receive some measure of consideration relative to black males when the offense is criminal because they are female.

Turning now to status offenses, gamma coefficients of +.54 for blacks and +.34 for whites indicate that black males and females are given less comparable dispositions than white males and females. Among blacks, a 44 percent difference to the disadvantage of females was found between males (59%) and females (15%) who were dismissed or warned for status offenses. Among whites, the comparable percentages are 24 percent and 19 percent, giving a difference of only 5 percentage points. About 15 percent of black males and females were institutionalized as compared with 3 percent of white males and 10 percent of white females. Further examination of the data reveal that racial differences in court dispositions are greater among male status offenders (gamma = +.10). That is, white males are accorded more severe dispositions than black males while black females are treated more severely than white females, although the differences for females were very small.

When prior delinquent involvement is held constant, the coefficients for blacks are +.56 for first offenders and +.55 for repeat offenders as compared with +.22 and +.89 for whites. Although the small N's caution against firm conclusions, it appears that, while status offenders with prior records are given more severe dispositions than first offenders for all sex-race groups, the disparity in treatment is particularly large for white female juveniles. Without exception, white female status offenders with prior records of delinquent behavior receive either supervision by a probation officer or institutionalization.

It is interesting to note that black males are given less harsh dispositions for juvenile status offenses than any other group. Such a finding is consistent with Reiss's observation that:*

> Upper- and particularly middle-status persons in American society are regarded as the guardians of morality; women are so regarded more than men. . . . Proscribed sexual relations between parties who have a low social status, such as Negroes,

criminals, or "low-class," are more readily accepted than proscribed sexual acts between whites, conformers, or middle-class
persons. (1960:319)

Thus, status offenders who are white and/or female may be
treated more harshly because the departure from normative
expectations is greater for them than for blacks and/or males. It
follows that white females should receive the harshest dispositions and black males the most lenient dispositions, which is the
case in our data, at least for repeat offenders.

SUMMARY AND DISCUSSION

The data of the present study indicate that the family court makes
less severe dispositions against female juveniles than against
males when they are involved in a criminal offense but more
severe dispositions against females than males when they are
involved in a noncriminal status offense, especially when they
have a prior offense record. This pattern holds for both blacks
and whites. However, the court tends to give more similar dispositions to black males and females than to white males and
females when the offense is criminal. Among status offenders,
black males receive the most lenient treatment while white
females who are repeat offenders receive the most severe treatment.

It appears that the differences in the dispositions handed out
to males and females by the family court may be explained in
part by the differences between the roles ascribed to females and
those ascribed to males. Females are supposed to be weaker, less
responsible, and less dangerous than males, and they are thought
to require greater protection. Because of these role differences,
judges, who are usually men, may regard the criminal acts
committed by female juveniles less seriously than those committed by their male counterparts, and may be more reluctant to
deal harshly with them. However, sex-role definitions may
work to the disadvantage of female juveniles referred to court

for status offenses, usually implying sexual delinquency. Since greater moral censure attaches to female juveniles involved in sex-related offenses than to males, judges may feel that greater legal censure is warranted as well.

These findings suggest that the juvenile court has utilized its discretionary power in the service of traditional sex roles. Thus, while particular female juveniles referred to the court for criminal offenses may benefit in the short term, the long-term effect is the same—to reinforce and perpetuate outmoded sex roles. In the final analysis, the juvenile court appears to be less concerned with the protection of female offenders than the protection of the sexual status quo. Double standard treatment in the juvenile court on the basis of sex cannot be tolerated in a society committed to achieving equality of rights for males and females.

The unequal treatment of male and female juveniles by the court is part of the more general problem of injustice in juvenile proceedings. It is evident that the juvenile court has failed to fulfill the high hopes of *parens patriae*. The Task Force Report states: "The great hopes originally held for the juvenile court have not been fulfilled. It has not succeeded significantly in rehabilitating delinquent youth, in reducing or even stemming the tide of juvenile criminality, or bringing justice and compassion to the child offender" (President's Commission, 1967:7).

Obviously, the juvenile court system is badly in need of reform. A major first step would be to remove status offenders from the jurisdiction of the juvenile court, as advocated by the President's Commission and the National Council on Crime and Delinquency. The harsh dispositions meted out to status offenders, particularly when they are female, are clearly disproportionate to their "crimes," which are perhaps better viewed as "problems of growing up" (Lerman, 1971:39). Problems of growing up may be more effectively handled outside the juvenile court. Along this line, the Juvenile Justice and Delinquency Prevention Act of 1974 has funded states to develop community-based alternatives to traditional forms of detention and institutionalization.

Removing status offenders from juvenile court jurisdiction would allow the court to focus its attention and resources on juveniles who have committed serious criminal acts. The constitutional protections accorded adults facing criminal prosecution should then be extended to juvenile court proceedings. The recent Supreme Court holding in *Breed v. Jones* (1975) is therefore encouraging. In *Breed,* the court held that a juvenile transferred to stand trial as an adult after adjudication for the same offense in juvenile court is subject to double jeopardy. Also, criminal procedural safeguards must be applied to all stages of the juvenile court process. Perhaps then equal protection and equal punishment for both sexes will be closer to realization in the juvenile court.

NOTES

1. Discussions of the juvenile court's history, philosophy, and operation may be found in, e.g., Dunham (1958), Caldwell (1961), President's Commission on Law Enforcement and Administration of Justice (1967), Kittrie (1971:102-168), Haskel and Yablonsky (1974:389-415).

2. See *Baylor Law Review* (1969:352, 358-359, 369-371). See also *Yale Law Journal* (1973:745).

3. In 1973, the Supreme Judicial Court of Maine upheld the Main statute in *S.S. v. State,* 229 A.2d 560 (1973), concluding that the statute was "sufficiently definite to withstand constitutional attack on grounds of vagueness" at 579. Similar cases are *United States v. Meyers,* 143 F. Supp. 1 (D. Alaska 1956); *People v. Deibert,* 117 Cal. App. 2d 410, 256 P. 2d 355 (2d Dist. 1953); *E.S.G. v. State,* 447 S.W. 2d 225 (1969), *cert. denied* 398 U.S. 956 (1970). However, several states have struck down such statutes as unconstitutionally vague, e.g., *Gonzalez v. Mailliard,* Civil No. 50424 (N.D. Calif., filed February 9, 1971); *Gesicki v. Oswald,* Civil No. 71-3276 (S.D.N.Y., filed December 22, 1971); *In re Brinkley,* J 1365-73 (D.C. Super. Ct., June 14, 1973).

4. In the analysis of our findings, gamma and partial gamma coefficients are used to assess the strength of the relationships. The legal variables are controlled by subdivision, and the relationship between sex and family court disposition is examined within these subcategories.

5. It is interesting to note that studies of self-reported delinquency show no such discrepancy between the types of delinquent behavior engaged in by males and females. Status offenses such as running away and ungovernability are frequently used as cover charges to avoid the stigma of a sexual offense (Reiss, 1960). Gold (1970) found that sex offenses, running away, and in-

corrigibility accounted for only 8% of the total delinquent acts reported by girls and 6% of the offenses reported by boys. Hindelang (1971) found that engaging in promiscuous sexual behavior contributed only 4% to the total delinquencies reported by girls and 8% to the offenses reported by boys. In general, self-reported studies of delinquency indicate that, while boys report a much higher proportion of delinquencies than girls, the pattern of female delinquent conduct closely parallels that of males. Why, then, are so many female juveniles referred to the juvenile court for status offenses? First, it is probable that a parental request for court intervention is far more likely to occur in the case of a daughter who is sexually active than in the case of a son (see Andrews and Cohn, 1974:1395, n.83, 88; 1397, n.95). Second, there is some evidence to suggest that police are less likely to arrest girls than boys involved in criminal offenses but more likely to arrest girls than boys involved in sexual offenses (Monahan, 1970).

6. The number of females in our sample was not large enough to allow a meaningful comparison with males in the case of felons and misdemeanants with prior offense records.

7. Unfortunately, we have no data on whether in fact judges do hold these stereotypical beliefs about females and, if so, to what extent they influence actual behavior. However, the sexist attitudes of judges are patently apparent in many statutes and court cases. See, for example, Johnston and Knapp (1971) and Frankel (1973).

8. The double standard of sexual morality has sometimes been formalized in juvenile delinquency statutes. See, for example, *Patricia A. v. City of New York* (1972).

9. Blacks were overwhelmingly concentrated in the lower half of the income distribution for the total sample while whites were concentrated in the upper half.

10. In addition, some of the harsher treatment given black females may reflect the fact that the larcenies and assaults they commit are of a more serious nature than those of white females; unfortunately, the data do not allow an assessment of this possibility.

CASES

Breed v. Jones, 421 U.S. 519 (1975).
[In re] Brinkley, J 1365-73 (D.C. Super. Ct., June 14, 1973).
Connecticut v. Mattiello, 4 Conn. Cir. Ct. 55 (1966), *cert. denied* 395 U.S. 202 (1969).
E.S.G. v. State, 447 S.W. 2d 255 (1969), *cert. denied* 398 U.S. 956 (1970).
[In re] Gault, 387 U.S. 1 (1967).
Gesicki v. Oswald, Civil No. 71-3276 (S.D.N.Y., filed December 22, 1971).
Gonzalez v. Mailliard, Civil No. 50424 (N.D. Calif., filed February 9, 1971).
Kent v. United States, 363 U.S. 541 (1966).
Lamb v. Brown, 456 F.2d 18 (1972).

Lamb v. State, 475 P.2d 829 (1970).
McKeiver v. Pennsylvania, 402 U.S. 528 (1971).
Patricia A. v. City of New York, 335 N.Y.S.2d 33 (1972).
People v. Deibert, 117 Cal. App. 2d 410, 256 P.2d 355 (2d Dist. 1953).
S.S. v. State, 299 A.2d 560 (1973).
United States v. Meyers, 143 F. Supp. 1 (D. Alaska 1956).
[In re] Winship, 397 U.S. 358 (1970).

REFERENCES

Andrews, R.H., Jr., and Cohn, A.H. (1974). "Ungovernability: The unjustifiable jurisdiction." Yale Law Journal, 83(June):1383–1409.

Axelson, L.J. (1970). "The working wife: Differences in perception among Negro and white males." Journal of Marriage and the Family, 32(August): 457–464.

Baylor Law Review (1969). Comment, " 'Delinquent child': A legal term without meaning." 21:352–371.

Caldwell, R.G. (1961). "The juvenile court: Its development and some major problems." Journal of Criminal Law, Criminology, and Police Science, 51(January/February):493–511.

Chesney-Lind, M. (1973). "Judicial enforcement of the female sex role: The family court and the female delinquent." Issues in Criminology, 8(Fall):51–59.

Dunham, H.W. (1958). "The juvenile court: Contradictory orientations in processing offenders." Law and Contemporary Problems, 23(Summer):508–527.

Finkelstein, M.M., Weiss, E., Cohen, S., Fisher, S.Z. (1973). Prosecution in the juvenile courts: Guidelines for the future. Washington, D.C.: U.S. Government Printing Office.

Frankel, L.J. (1973). "Sex discrimination in the criminal law: The effect of the Equal Rights Amendment." American Criminal Law Review, 11(Winter): 469–510.

Garett, M., and Short, J., Jr. (1975). "Social class delinquency: Predictions and outcomes of police-juvenile encounters." Social Problems, 22(February): 368–383.

Gibbons, D.C., and Griswold, M.J. (1957). "Sex differences among juvenile court referrals." Sociology and Social Research, 42(November/December): 106–110.

Gold, M. (1970). Delinquent behavior in an American city. Belmont, Calif.: Brooks/Cole.

Haskell, M.R., and Yablonsky, L. (1974). Crime and delinquency. Chicago: Rand McNally.

Hindelang, M.J. (1971). "Age, sex, and the versatility of delinquent involvements." Social Problems, 18(Spring):522–535.

Johnston, J.D., Jr., and Knapp, C.L. (1971). "Sex discrimination by law: A study in judicial perspective." New York University Law Review, 46(October): 675–747.

Kittrie, N.N. (1971). The right to be different. Baltimore: Johns Hopkins University Press.

Ladner, J. (1971). Tomorrow's tomorrow. Garden City, N.Y.: Doubleday.

Langley, M.H. (1972). "The juvenile court: The making of a delinquent." Law and Society Review, 7(Winter):273–298.

Lefstein, N., Stapleton, V., and Teitelbaum, L. (1969). "In search of juvenile justice—*Gault* and its implications." Law and Society Review, 3(May):491–562.

Lerman, P. (1971). "Child convicts." Transaction, 8(July/August):35–44, 72.

Liebow, E. (1967). Tally's Corner: A study of Negro streetcorner men. Boston: Little, Brown.

Mack, J.W. (1909). "The juvenile court." Harvard Law Review, 23:104–122.

Mead, M. (1949). Male and female. New York: Dell.

Monahan, T.P. (1970). "Police dispositions of juvenile offenders." Phylon, 21(Summer):129–141.

Piliavin, I., and Briar, S. (1964). "Police encounters with juveniles." American Journal of Sociology, 70(September):206–214.

Platt, A.M. (1969). The child savers. Chicago: University of Chicago Press.

President's Commission on Law Enforcement and Administration of Justice (1967). Task Force Report: Juvenile delinquency and youth crime. Washington, D.C.: U.S. Government Printing Office.

Rainwater, L. (1966). "Crucible of identity: The Negro lower-class family." Daedalus, 95(Winter):172–216.

——(1970). Behind ghetto walls. Chicago: Aldine.

Reiss, A.J. (1960). "Sex offenses: The marginal status of the adolescent." Law and Contemporary Problems, 25(Spring):309–333.

Terry, R.M. (1967). "Discrimination in the handling of juvenile offenders by social control agencies." Journal of Research in Crime and Delinquency, 4(July):218–230.

Vedder, C.B. and Somerviller, D.B. (1970). The delinquent girl. Springfield, Ill.: Charles C Thomas.

Yale Law Journal (1973). Note, *"Parens patriae* and statutory vagueness in the juvenile court." 82(March):745–771.

Women in Prison:
Discriminatory Practices
and Some Legal Solutions

Marilyn G. Haft

INTRODUCTION

Increasing concerns have recently developed in society for the problems of women and the problems of prisoners. Unfortunately, these concerns have rarely coalesced. As a group, women in prison suffer the mutually reinforcing problems of both women and prisoners. However, due perhaps to their relatively small number, their predominantly nonmilitant posture, and the apparent infrequency of overt brutality by their keepers, women prisoners have been neglected, even by the women's rights and the prisoners' rights movements.

This article will discuss some of the legal and social problems faced by women in the criminal justice system. The emphasis will be on the special problems of adult women incarcerated in institutions. Some attention, however, will be paid to the uneven manner in which adult and juvenile females are sentenced.

The criminal justice system has shown little interest in the problems peculiar to female offenders. There are considerably fewer statistics showing where women are incarcerated, what

This article originally appeared in *Prisoners' Rights Sourcebook* (1973) edited by Michele G. Hermann and Marilyn G. Haft, published by Clark Boardman Company, Ltd., 435 Hudson Street, New York, N. Y. 10014. Copyrighted by Clark Boardman Company, Ltd.

crimes they have committed, and what sentences they have incurred. Even the comprehensive study of crime published in 1967 by the President's Commission on Law Enforcement and Administration of Justice contains no statistics on women.[1]

Women derive one major benefit from being ignored by the system: proportionately fewer of them are arrested than men, and an even smaller proportion are convicted and incarcerated.[2] While it could be argued that this merely reflects the rarity of criminal activities by females, it seems likely that the reason fewer women are actually subject to the system is due in part to the fact that most law-enforcers, from the police to judges, are males, and as such are more lenient towards adult females.[3] They are merely reflecting the attitudes of men in the larger society who act out what is euphemistically known as the "chivalry factor."[4] They have a paternalistic protectiveness towards women and assume therefore that women need to be sheltered from manly experiences like jail and formal proceedings in criminal cases. They more often look the other way, excuse, forgive, and are thus unwilling to report and detain women.

DISCRIMINATION IN SENTENCING

Although it is believed that women generally serve shorter sentences than men, women may be sentenced to longer terms than men for the same crimes. In all but five states where participation in prostitution is illegal for both males and females, unequal enforcement of the laws results in prosecution of the women only. This phenomenon, although common, is blatant violation of the equal protection clause and is beginning to be challenged by those accused of prostitution. Certain jurisdictions have statutes dictating indeterminate sentencing for women only. Those sentenced under indeterminate sentences must receive the maximum punishment for that crime. For example, if burglary is punishable by statute by one-and-one-half to three years, the judge must sentence the prisoner coming under the indeterminate sentencing laws to zero to three years Therefore, in jurisdictions where inderterminate sentencing applies to women only, a woman's sentence may be potentially longer than the time a man can serve for the same violation.

It was originally believed that indeterminate sentencing was a progressive measure beneficial to women. This was based on the theory that women are more amenable to rehabilitation and therefore should be benefited with longer confinements and exposure to a rehabilitative atmosphere. These measures have been challenged with increasing success on grounds of unequal protection of the laws.[6] However, careful study is needed to determine just how many states have longer sentences for women than men through indeterminate sentencing schemes. In some states such as Connecticut, Maryland, Ohio, Massachusetts, and Kansas, it is clear than unequal sentencing still exists while the laws in other states are not as explicit. Some states have obscure provisions; for example, Maine has provisions for indeterminate sentencing for male and female alike, but the men can be sentenced under this law up to age twenty-six, while the women are subject to it until age forty.

DISCRIMINATION AGAINST FEMALE JUVENILES

The chivalry factor can be a double-edged sword. For instance, the male role of protecting women has worked to the detriment of female juveniles. The double sexual standard in society has caused the sexual and moral misbehavior of girls to be considered more serious than similar behavior by boys, and it is consequently more strictly repressed and punished. Girls are incarcerated for far less serious offenses than boys, and they are kept incarcerated for longer periods of time. According to the President's Commission on Law Enforcement and Administration of Justice, more than half of the girls before juvenile courts in 1965 were referred for conduct that would not be criminal if committed by adults, while only one-fifth of the boys were referred for such conduct.[7] Incarcerated girls are often "criminals without crimes," having been committed for such offenses as running away from home, being incorrigible, ungovernable and beyond the control of their parents, being promiscuous, engaging in sexual relations, and becoming pregnant.[8]

There is also some evidence that although girls are confined on less serious charges, they in fact spend longer periods of time in institutions.[9] Although there is no clear reason for this disparity, it may stem from fear that the young girls may become pregnant or morally depraved. Since they are seen to be weaker than males and less able to care for their moral beings, they are kept incarcerated for their own protection. Girls may also be kept on parole longer periods of time than is required of boys.

One successful legal challenge to the practice of committing to institutions juveniles who have not been convicted of crimes was brought in New York State. Here, the "wayward minor" statute permitted youths between ages sixteen and twenty-one to be confined in adult prisons if they were found to be *"wilfully disobedient to the reasonable and lawful commands of parent, guardian or other custodian and . . . morally depraved or . . . in danger of becoming morally depraved."*[10] In *Gesicki v. Oswald*,[11] a three-judge federal court ruled that the statute was unconstitutionally vague and that it impermissibly punished a status or condition rather than a criminal act.

A successful legal attack on the unequal treatment of female juveniles was mounted in the case of *Matter of Patricia A.*[12] There the New York statute which subjected females to the jurisdiction of juvenile courts for longer periods of time than males was declared unconstitutional. The language in that opinion deals directly with the double sexual standard applied to young girls and boys:

> The argument that discrimination against females on the basis of age is justified because of the obvious danger of pregnancy in an immature girl and because of out-of-wedlock births which add to the welfare relief burdens of the State and city is without merit. It is enough to say that the contention completely ignores

the fact that the statute covers far more than acts of sexual misconduct. But, beyond that, even if we were to assume that the legislation had been prompted by such considerations, there would have been no rational basis for exempting from the PINS definition, the 16- and 17-year-old boy responsible for the girl's pregnancy or the out-of-wedlock birth. As it is, the conclusion seems inescapable that lurking behind the discrimination is the imputation that females who engage in misconduct, sexual or otherwise, ought more to be censured, and their conduct subject to greater control than males.[13]

Statutes in other states which particularly victimize female juveniles have been vulnerable to litigation as a denial of equal protection.[14] In *Lamb v. Brown*[15] the Tenth Circuit held that the Oklahoma statute providing for different treatment of males and females between the ages of sixteen and eighteen was unconstitutional as a denial of equal protection. Several states have recently amended their juvenile acts to eliminate the distinction of treatment based on sex.[16]

LACK OF EQUAL FACILITIES FOR WOMEN IN PRISON

Because so many women are screened out in the earlier stages of the criminal justice system, it is widely believed that only hard-core offenders are finally incarcerated.[17] Many of the women are poor and often black. "Chivalry" does not seem to extend to these minority women.[18] Mounting evidence supports the conclusion that the criminal justice system as a whole screens out the middle-class offender, while leaving the poor and often racial minorities to be imprisoned.

There are approximately 16,000 adult women incarcerated in the United States. About 800 are in the three federal institutions for women. Seven thousand are in state institutions, and about 8,000 are in more than 3,500 local jails scattered throughout the country. Only twenty-six states, plus Puerto Rico and the District of Columbia, have separate institutions for women. Sixteen other states have women housed in facilities that are under control of wardens of male prisons,[19] and in eight states the women are transferred to sister states for incarceration.[20] This causes even greater separation between the women and their families than would normally be experienced in the isolation of prison.[21]

Since women are always housed separately from men, they may often be held in prisons within male prisons.[22] In small county jails, women may be virtually confined to solitary as a result of rules that forbid mixing with the opposite sex. In jails where some facilities are available, women are frequently denied their use in order to prevent any contact with the more numerous male population. For example, use of the law library, when there is one in a county jail, may be denied to the female detainees. Similarly, recreation, education, and vocational programs may not be available to women in the county jails. There are many such instances of blatant violation of the equal protection clause suffered by women in jails.

DISCRIMINATORY TRAINING PROGRAMS FOR WOMEN IN PRISON

Despite all indications that women in prison are poor, under-educated, and lack the vocational training necessary to become self-supporting, there are very few institutions offering organized educational or vocational opportunities. The reasons usually given for the lack of programs for women are the relatively small number of women prisoners, the consequent high cost of training per prisoner, and the feeling that women criminals are less of a threat to society than male criminals and therefore do not necessitate the same financial expenditures.[23]

In those institutions where vocational training programs have been established for female offenders, they are almost always limited to training women as domestics or other "women's" occupations, such as hairdressing, typing, and sewing. Although all prison vocational training must be severely criticized for not being related to job possibilities after release, men may receive training in such higher paying occupations as auto repair, electronics, radio and television repair, printing, baking, and carpentry.[24]

Many women's institutions pride themselves in turning out good housekeepers; the emphasis is on behaving like a "lady" or looking attractive and keeping things clean and neat.[25] It is little wonder that these women, poor, ill-trained and unskilled, may turn to prostitution upon their release and are prone to revolving-door recidivism.[26] All released exoffenders have enormous problems in finding jobs, but a female exoffender has two strikes against her. Her sex and record put her at the bottom of the list of the unemployed and unemployables in this country. There is no reason why women prisoners should not have the same vocational and educational opportunities as their male counterparts. If the legislatures and the departments of correction will not allocate the money to provide equal treatment, the courts should.

CHILDREN, ABORTIONS, CONTRACEPTIVES, AND FAMILY PLANNING EDUCATION

A large number of women in prison have children or are pregnant.[27] Most institutions make no provisions for pregnant women or for women with children. Most jails do not permit children to visit, or where they are permitted to visit, glass or metal barriers often prevent any physical contact. In states where abortions are legal, pregnant prisoners often find it difficult to have an abortion. When children are born in prison, the mothers are pressured to give them up for adoption.[28] Some prisons have nurseries where the babies can stay up to eighteen months after birth, but after that time the children must be sent away.[29] There are no reports of child care facilities in prison nor provisions for contraceptives or family planning education.

Women who have children prior to imprisonment often see them placed in foster homes, thus critically disrupting the family during the time of incarceration. Upon release these women face great difficulty in regaining custody of their children. Since most prisoners are released on parole, they are under the custody and supervision of their parole officers and are required to prove, in a series of informal steps, that they are willing and capable of caring for their children. Because of the lack of standards in determining parental fitness, determinations by the parole officers or the social agency caring for the child may be arbitrary. In cases where custody is denied, the parent is entitled to a family court hearing on the issue of fitness. Unfortunately, few exoffenders, male or female, know about the right to a hearing.

DISCRIMINATORY PAROLE STANDARDS

Another area where women prisoners may be subject to different treatment because of society's double standard towards the sexes is parole. Although there is still no established right to due process safeguards against arbitrary denial of parole, some attention should be given to different criteria which may be used in the decision to grant parole to men as opposed to women. Parole boards have been loathe to divulge the reasons for their decisions to grant or deny parole, and to date most courts have not forced them to do so.[30] However, such information can be gathered by interviewing prisoners to ascertain what questions they were asked when they met the parole board.

The results may indicate a pattern whereby women are required to meet higher standards to show the board that they will not live "in sin" upon release. While it is a common condition of parole that all prisoners, male and female, may not live with any member of the opposite sex to whom they are not related or married, this rule may well be unequally enforced. Society's view that extramarital sex is normal for men but depraved for women is likely to cause parole to be refused or revoked more easily for women than for men. Unfortunately, proof of this assertion would involve enormous efforts to gather information in an area still too shrouded in secrecy. Although women violate parole at almost precisely the same rate as males, no statistics exist explaining the reasons for these violations.[31] Perhaps a challenge that sexual conditions such as these violate all parolees' right to privacy will be a more successful route.

LEGAL SOLUTIONS TO THE PROBLEMS OF WOMEN IN PRISON

There has been a glaring absence of cases brought on behalf of women prisoners in the growing body of prisoners' rights law.[32] Because many of the class actions filed on behalf of male prisoners are brought on an institution-by-institution basis, the remedies that are won in those cases are not extended to women. The task of establishing the rights of women prisoners therefore is formidable. Not only must those rights generally afforded prisoners be extended to women, but special attacks must also be launched to solve those problems peculiar to women in prison.

Where women are excluded from training programs, work-release, halfway houses, furloughs, and other advantages available to male prisoners, a challenge should be made under the equal protection clause of the fourteenth amendment. According to a plurality of the Supreme Court in *Frontiero v. Richardson*,[33] the state must show a compelling state interest before it may afford different treatment to persons on the basis of sex. It is clear that the states and federal government have no compelling interest to justify discriminatory treatment of female prisoners.

Attempts to force the state to admit women to educational and training programs may be met with the argument that since the right to treatment has not yet been generally established for prisoners, women cannot complain of exclusion from the few programs that do exist.[34] However, this argument may be countered by showing that the constitutional distinction between "rights" and "privileges" is disappearing. Even where the state or federal government is not required to provide programs, once it does it cannot exclude whole classes of prisoners from participation on a discriminatory basis.

Only one case is known where female prisoners successfully challenged their exclusion from a correctional program as a denial of equal protection. In *Dawson v. Carberry*,[35] inmates of San Francisco's female jail sued in federal district court to gain participation in a work-furlough program from which they had been excluded. Jail officials claimed that it would be too expensive to provide this program for the few women prisoners. Although there was no final decision rendered in the case, the court adjourned for three months to give the correction officials an opportunity to formulate a program for the women.[36] The transcript of the hearing indicates that the judge considered the exclusion of the women from the program to be unconstitutional as a violation of the equal protection clause.

The question of whether the state can be made to spend money on separate facilities for women should be answered in the affirmative. In *Seidenberg v. McSorley's Old Ale House*,[37] a federal district court rejected the argument that a tavern could not accommodate women because it lacked the necessary restrooms, since only its past policy of discrimination had prevented it from making such an expenditure in the first place. In *Shapiro v. Thompson*,[38] the Supreme Court struck down a one-year residency requirement for the receipt of welfare payments, holding that although a state may limit its expenditures, it may not accomplish that limitation by invidious distinctions between classes of its citizens. Discrimination solely on the basis of sex is invidious. Both these cases point to the affirmative duty of the state to make equal expenditures on women's prison facilities. Lawsuits need to be instituted to ensure that the duty is fulfilled.

However, that duty can be a mixed blessing for women prisoners. Theoretically the routes are open for courts and legislatures to force the twenty-four states which do not have separate women's penitentiaries to expend untold sums of money to build "equal" prisons for women.[39] This would be a calamity. Society does not need more fortress-like schools for crime and human degradation. Instead, this set of circumstances should be viewed as an unusual opportunity for those states that have unequal facilities and programs for women to spend money on alternatives to prisons, such as community facilities, halfway houses where children can live with their mothers, vocational training programs, and extensive counseling services.

MODEL LEGAL EDUCATION AND COUNSELING PROGRAMS

Women's prisons may not be as overtly brutal as male penitentiaries, but they are often institutions where covert oppression is wholesale. The women are treated like children, and even elderly prisoners are referred to as "girls." They are made to feel even more helpless and childlike than other prisoners. The psychological oppression has worked to such an extent that few women in prison have the sense of political consciousness possessed by many of their male counterparts, nor do they have confidence in their ability to help themselves legally or socially. Their ghastly self-image is consciously reinforced by the condescending boarding-school atmosphere.

There are, of course, female institutions, whether county jails or state penitentiaries, where barbaric conditions exist that are comparable to those in the worst male institutions. Due perhaps to women's self-image as helpless creatures, jailhouse lawyers are almost nonexistent in women's prisons. Since there is generally very little contact with the outside community, these conditions remain unchallenged.

Women inmates in all prisons are vitally concerned with the legality of their convictions and are distressed about their often complicated family law problems. Aside from being so psychologically oppressed that most believe they cannot help themselves, they are handicapped by the lack of law libraries and training, which would help them solve their own legal problems.

In response to this problem, a legal education and counseling clinic has been set up at Bedford Hills Correctional Facility. (This is the only institution for women serving sentences above a year in New York State.)

In the past, two approaches have been used to assist prisoners with legal problems. One entails lawyers and law students making independent evaluations of legal problems and decisions about them, leaving the inmate passive and uninvolved, perplexed and often dissatisfied with the ultimate results. The other aims at teaching inmates enough about the law to understand their own legal problems, but it leaves inmates frustrated and confused because it fails to provide enough legal assistance actually to remedy those problems.

After a study of these alternatives, a program was organized at Bedford Hills Correctional Facility to offer a novel approach to the problems of women in prison. A clinical law program was established at New York University Law School utilizing law students and volunteer attorneys to provide both legal counseling and legal education to the inmates. The project was made available to all the women in the prison, including those with reformatory sentences and those on work-release. Any inmate participating in the program was helped to fill out a comprehensive questionnaire to ascertain what her legal problems were. The first six months of the program were devoted to instruction by the law students and lawyers on how to use the law library. These classes were conducted on an intensive, small group basis. Before each legal research class the students and lawyers provided counseling and legal services to remedy the women's most urgent legal problems, which were primarily in family law and criminal law. Periodically, general lectures were given on subjects of interest to all inmates, such as parole, court structure, jurisdiction, and civil disabilities. During these months the law students studied the law and procedure for postconviction remedies and family law at weekly seminars at the law school so that they could be well acquainted with both these areas in order to assist the inmates, and they prepared a legal manual for inmates' use covering many substantive areas. After they completed these legal studies and considered the inmates' needs and desires, the students each chose an area of expertise. The major areas of specialization were criminal appeals, postjudgment motions, federal habeas corpus, prisoners' rights, and family law. All this work was done with close guidance from two supervising attorneys.

In the second six months of the year the inmates, lawyers, and law students grouped into workshops where substantive law was discussed in the context of the inmates' individual cases. Each inmate elected the class that dealt with her most urgent legal problems. There were classes in criminal appeals, basic criminal law and procedure, habeas corpus, family law, and prisoners' rights. As the workshops progressed, the inmates and lawyers worked together on the preparation of individual cases.

The formation of the Women's Prison Project involved the complex process of bringing four separate groups together in mutual cooperation. First, the lawyers and law students had to meet to discuss and formulate the project. Next, the approval of the Department of Correction was needed, both from the administration at Bedford Hills and from the Commissioner of Correction in Albany. Third, it was necessary to consult with the inmates. To this end, several informal meetings were held between the project directors and inmates at the prison (both on an individual and group basis) to ascertain the desires, reactions, and suggestions of the women at the prison. Finally, it was arranged for the project to be offered as a clinical program at New York University Law School in order to facilitate the regular participation of law students in the program and to ensure the continuity of the project.

The program, which is in its second year, had and has a number of goals. The common thread that runs throughout may be summarized in one word: change. Fundamentally, the program aims at changing the inmates' level of legal knowledge. The legal services component of the project hopes to change the life situations of the women by helping them to alleviate their own problems—family, civil, criminal—in prison and out.

There are less tangible changes the program wishes to accomplish, the primary one being to change the self-perceptions of the inmates as prisoners and as women. More specifically, it is hoped that the prisoners can be aided to develop an increased sense of themselves and their rights and abilities, which will enable them to organize themselves and seek reforms within the prison. This is necessary because the political consciousness which is so prevalent in male institutions is totally lacking in women's prisons where submission and docility prevail. Additionally, since one of the goals of the clinic is to reduce the isolation of the women, the clinic functions as an informal mobilizer of other community groups and professions. For example, doctors and social agencies have been encouraged to tend to the women's problems.

Since in recent years it has become increasingly clear that the entire prison system has become bankrupt and should be replaced, the best thing one can hope to do for women prisoners is to work for their release. The clinical program seeks to do this not only by aiding women in their individual criminal cases with the hope of winning their release but by teaching the women preventive law, so that in the future they will know how to avoid being sent back to prison.

Needless to say, legal education programs are not the whole answer to keeping women out of prisons and jails. Although litigation may help to remedy the most egregious prison conditions, it cannot be seen as the solution to diverting women from prisons. Legislative and administrative remedies as well as litigation will be necessary to form alternatives to prison.

334   *Women in the Criminal Justice System*

REFERENCES

1. The most recent comprehensive survey of correctional facilities for women is J. Lekkerkerker, *Reformatories for Women in the United States* (1931). This work has been updated only by an unpublished dissertation, K. Strickland, *Correctional Institutions for Women in the United States,* June 1967 (Ph.D dissertation, Syracuse University, available through University Microfilms, Ann Arbor, Michigan). *See also* K. Burkhart, *Women in Prison* (1973). Other published works on women's prisons have been limited to sociological descriptions of a single institution. See, for example, R. Giallombardo, *Society of Women: A Study of a Women's Prison* (1966); D. Ward and G. Kassebum, *Women's Prison: Sex and Social Structure* (1965).

2. Uniform Crime Reports. These indicate that men and boys are arrested more often as compared to women on a 6-to-1 ratio and are convicted and admitted to federal and state institutions on a 20-to-1 ratio.

3. The Uniform Crime Reports indicate that female crime has doubled in the last decade. Over all, arrests of women for violent crimes increased 69 percent from 1960 to 1970, while the total crime rate for women rose 74.9 percent during that decade. The precentage increase for men was 25 percent. See Nagel and Weitzman, *Women as Litigants,* 23 Hastings L.J. 171 (1971).

4. *See* Reckless and Kay, *The Female Offender* (consultant report presented to the President's Commission on Enforcement and Administration of Justice (1967)).

5. *See* State v. Devall, No. 12-73-7806 (La. Dist. Ct., Feb. 8, 1974), Louisiana prostitution statute declared unconstitutional as a denial of equal protection; State v. Fields, No. 72-4788 (Alaska Dist. Ct., June 27, 1973); U.S. v. Moses, No. 17778-72 (Colo. Super. Ct., Nov. 3, 1972); Portland v. Sherill, No. M-47623 (Ore. Cir. Ct., Multnomah County, January 9, 1967), defining prostitution as an offense that can be committed only by women is a violation of the equal protection clause. For a discussion of prostitution and the equal protection clause, see generally, *The Equal Rights Amendment: A Constitutional Basis for Equal Rights for Women,* 80 Yale L.J. 871, 962-965. L. Kanowitz, *Women and the Law,* at 16-17 (1969); Rosenbleet and Pariente, *The Prostitution of the Criminal Law,* 11 Amer. Crim. L. Rev. 373 (1973); M. Haft, *Hustling for Rights,* The Civ. Lib. Rev. (Winter/Spring 1974).

6. *See* Harvin v. United States, 445 F. 2d 675 (D.C. Cir. 1971) (on rehearing en banc); United States ex rel. Sumrell v. York, 288 F. Supp. 955 (D. Conn. 1968); United States v. York, 281 F. Supp. 8 (D. Conn. 1968, where the court invalidated a statute requiring an indeterminate sentence for female offenders with a maximum of three years when male offenders convicted of the same offense would receive a maximum of twleve months—the state was required to but could not demonstrate that women required longer periods for incarceration; Liberti v. York, 28 Conn. Supp. 9, 246 A.2d 106 (1968), where the court invalidated a differential sentencing scheme because there was no basis factually and statistically for such differential treatment; State v. Costello,

59 N.J. 334, 282 A.2d 748 (1971), where the court required substantial empirically-grounded justification for the differential intermediate sentencing scheme, which the state could not provide on remand; Commonwealth v. Daniel, 430 Pa. 642, 243 A.2d 400 (Sup. Ct. Pa., 1968), where the court invalidated a statute which required the judge to fix an indeterminate sentence at the statutory maximum for female offenders only. But see Wark v. Robbins, No. 721377 (1st Cir. April 12, 1972), where the court upheld differential penalties for men and women who escape from prison, because men and women were housed by the state in separate facilities with different security characteristics, and therefore were not "similarly situated" in order to meet the threshhold requirement for an equal protection challenge.

7. *Report by the President's Commission on Law Enforcement and Administration of Justice: The Challenge of Crime in a Free Society,* at 56 (1967).

8. See Singer, *Women in the Criminal Justice System* (1972) (an unpublished paper presented to the N.Y.U. School of Law Conference on Women and the Law, October 1972, on file with the author).

9. U.S. Department of Health, Education and Welfare, Children's Bureau, *Statistics on Public Institutions for Delinquent Children*—1964 (1965).

10. N.Y. Code Crim. Proc. § 913-a(5) (b).

11. 366 F. Supp. 371 (S.D. N.Y. 1971).

12. 31 N.Y. 2d 83, 286 N.E. 2d 432,335 N.Y.S. 2d 33 (1972).

13. Idem, 31 N.Y. 2d at 88, 335 N.Y.S. 2d at 37.

14. Harringfield v. Dist. Ct. of Freemont Co., 95 Idaho 540, 511 P. 2d 822 (1973).

15. 456 F. 2d 18 (10th Cir. 1973).

16. Ill. Public Act 77-2096, effective Jan. 1, 1973; Idaho Code § 32-101, effective July 1, 1972; Texas Code § 51.02, effective Jan. 1, 1973.

17. A national survey by the Women's Prison Association, *A Study in Neglect: A Report on Women Prisoners* indicates that women convicted in thirty-seven states and sent to prison are sent there for violent crimes.

18. The few statistics that are available do support the conclusion. A survey of women prisoners at the three federal prisons (by the Labor Department) and Bedford Hills Correctional Facility, which is the only New York State women's institution for women serving more than a year sentence (by the Legal Education and Counseling Project) show that most of the women come from the city ghettos, from minority groups, and are very poor. Additionally, the very recent national survey by the Women's Prison Association in New York, supra note 17, indicates that in the thirty-seven states studied, minority women are represented in disproportionately large numbers in prisons.

19. Figures provided by the U.S. Department of Labor, Women's Bureau, Washington, D.C. The American Correctional Association Directory lists all state institutions and populations.

20. Montana, North Dakota, and Wyoming all send their female offenders to Nebraska. New Hampshire, Rhode Island, and Vermont send theirs to Massachusetts. Idaho sends theirs to Oregon, and Hawaii sends theirs to mainland federal prisons.

21. See Park v. Thompson, No. 72-3605 (D. Hawaii, 1972), a case where a woman inmate was transferred from Hawaii State Prison to the federal prison on Terminal Island in California because there was no facility to house her in Hawaii. The district court ordered the inmate back to Hawaii for a due process hearing on whether she was justifiably transferred and found her transfer illegal as a denial of equal protection. The state maintained that the inmate must be transferred back to a mainland institution because there were not sufficient vocational and educational programs and services for rehabilitation of women offenders in Hawaii. The inmate claimed that the lack of equal facilities and programs for women offenders was a denial of equal protection. On the issue of remoteness of women's institutions, see generally Note, *The Sexual Segregation of American Prisons*, 82 Yale L.J. 1229 (1973). For a discussion of transfer of prisoners from one institution to another as a denial of due process, *see* Milleman, *Due Process Behind the Walls*, in *Hermann and Haft, Prisoners' Rights Sourcebook: Theory, Litigation, Practice*, 79.

22. There are some sexually integrated state and federal prisons. The Federal Correctional Institution at Fort Worth, Texas, is the only truly sexually integrated adult facility in the country. The Pennsylvania women's institution at Muncy, and the Massachusetts women's institution at Framingham have begun to take male inmates, but thus far few have been admitted, *N.Y. Times*, April 12, 1973, at 51 Col. 1. In the other states where women prisoners are technically housed in the same state institution as male prisoners, they are held in separate units of those institutions, with little or no mixing of the populations. This is the case, for example, in Florida, Mississippi, and New Mexico, ACA Directory, supra note 19 at 55-56. For a discussion of the present and future sexual integration of prisons, see Note, *The Sexual Segregation of American Prisons*, supra note 17.

23. *A Study in Neglect: A Report on Women Prisoners*, supra note 17.

24. For descriptions of the difference in job training offered males and females in New York, Connecticut, and New Jersey, see Singer, *Women in the Criminal Justice System*, supra note 8 at 39-40; The District of Columbia Commission on the Status of Women, *Female Offenders in the District of Columbia*, at 16 (1962); and Goldman, *Women's Crime*, 22 Juvenile Court Judges J. 33-34 (1971); and Note, *The Sexual Segregation of Prisons*, supra note 21 at 1269-1273.

25. Katherine Perutz, *Beyond the Looking Glass* at 225-241.

26. C. Barros, J. McArthur and S. Adams, *A Study of Post-Release Performance of Women's Detention Center Releases, (1970)*. Of 116 releasees reported in 1969, 36% had been booked back in at the end of 18 months.

27. The Pennsylvania Division of the American Association of University Women found that 80% of women arrested on whom records were available had dependent children. Valemesis, *Criminal Justice for the Female Offender*, J. Amer. Ass'n Univ. Women (1969).

28. Konopka, *The Adolescent Girl in Conflict*, at 22-23 (1966); Goldman, supra note 19. Although abortions are offered, the women must pay for them, therefore no abortion is available if an inmate is indigent.

29. Burkhart, supra note 1 at 411.

30. Monks v. New Jersey, 58 N.J. 238, 277 A. 2d 193 (1971).

31. National Council on Crime and Delinquency, *Uniform Crime Report* (1970), reports that for individuals paroled by 55 agencies in 1968, 29% violated parole within one year of release. Men outnumbered women in appearances before the parole board by a ratio of 20-to-1.

32. See Garnes v. Taylor, No. 159-72 (D. D.C. filed January 25, 1972), an omnibus suit which raises many of the same issues as in class actions for men. This suit challenges the conditions in the District of Columbia Women's Detention Center. It also deals with problems peculiar to women, such as prostitution, and asks as part of the relief that day care centers be set up for women with children. See also Park v. Thompson, No. 72-3605 (D. Hawaii, 1972); Dawson v. Carberry, No. C-71-1916 (N.D. Calif., filed Sept. 1971); Barefield v. Leach, No. 10282 (C. N.M., 1973).

33. 411 U.S. 677 (1973). Four members of the Court held in that case that any classification based on sex was "inherently suspect" and subject to "strict judicial scrutiny." In practical terms, the plurality opinion equates the discriminatory treatment with the discriminatory treatment of blacks. This court would find no difficulty in outlawing racial segregation in prison, see Washington v. Lee, 263 F. Supp. 327, (M.D. Ala.), *affd per curiam*, 390 U.S. 333 (1968), and by analogy would be hard pressed to accept discrimination against women prisoners based on their sex.

34. See Koren, *The Right to Medical Treatment*, and Silbert and Sussman, *The Rights of Juveniles Confined in Training Schools*, in Hermann and Haft, *Prisoners' Rights Sourcebook: Theory, Litigation, Practice* at 165, 357; and Holt v. Sarver, 309 F. Supp. 362 (E.D. Ark. 1970).

35. No. C-71-1916 (N.D. Cal., filed September 1971).

36. Another instance where women prisoners successfully asserted their right to participate in a correctional program offered to men was in Mississippi, where female offenders won the right by threat of legal action to conjugal visits, which had been given to male offenders for many years.

37. 317 F. Supp. 593 (S.D. N.Y. 1970).

38. 394 U.S. 618 (1969).

39. See Note, *The Sexual Segregation of American Prisons*, supra note 21, in which the probabilities of having courts mandate large amounts of money for building women's facilities is deemed unlikely. However, the fourteenth amendment is viewed as a likely vehicle to equalize programs and services in instances where comparatively little expense is required. The adoption of the Equal Rights Amendment is seen as a panacea for women's prisons. If the Amendment is adopted it can be used as a justification for the sexual integration of prisons whereby each prisoner will be placed within the system according to his or her individual requirements. Geographical location, programs, and services to fit individual needs would be the sole legitimate basis for placement in an institution and in programs within the institutions. Sex would no longer be a basis for such placement. In passing the ERA, Congress clearly intended that benefits be extended whenever possible to those excluded previously, S. Rep. No. 92-689 92nd Cong. 1st Sess. 4-6 (1972). Therefore the

advantages women presently have in prisons as compared with men, such as more privacy and lower security measures, may be extended to men where appropriate. Those benefits men presently have over women in prisons, including more programs, more services, homogeneity in security and offender classification because their larger numbers permit such classification, and more favorable geographical location, may be extended to women prisoners.

Mothers Behind Bars:
A Look at the Parental Rights
of Incarcerated Women

INTRODUCTION

For women prisoners the loss of parental rights is almost as painful as their loss of freedom. Even the reform-minded see "women as prisoners [first] and not . . . prisoners as women."[1] The worst excesses are committed against prisoners who are also mothers.

Unfortunately, most correctional institutions do not have provisions for pregnant women nor for women with children.[2] Patty Wood, a member of the Prisoner's Union in San Francisco, a group of convicts and exoffenders working to help prisoners, was asked about her worst personal experience:

> I was six months pregnant when I was arrested. I got absolutely no medical attention for the next three months. I never saw a doctor at all. I had to really hustle to even get them to give me milk. It was my first baby so I didn't know anything about it. My water burst at 3 A.M. I told the matron but she told me I'd be alright. They wouldn't take me over specially. The regular bus for the hospital left the prison at eight in the morning, so I went on that. I think it was the loneliest I've ever been.[3]

Kathleen Haley, "Mothers Behind Bars: A Look at the Parental Rights of Incarcerated Women," *New England Journal on Prison Law*, 4 (Fall 1977), pp. 141–155. Reprinted by permission.

Most institutions make no provisions for visitation by the children; where they are permitted to visit, it is under the constraint of glass or metal barriers which prevent any physical contact.[4]

A statistical profile of women in prison shows that many are mothers and their double role burdens them with grave emotional problems.[5] It is incumbent upon society to address them. This article discusses the women who are mothers and the social and legal ramifications of the broad discretionary powers invested in the courts for making determinations as to the welfare of children of incarcerated mothers.

DISRUPTION OF THE MOTHER-CHILD RELATIONSHIP

Upon conviction for a crime, female offenders who are mothers face a two-pronged sentence. First, they must serve the prison term, and second, they must cope with the additional punishment of a temporary or permanent deprivation of parental rights. While male prisoners are also parents, the father has traditonally been relieved of the day-to-day responsibilities of child care. Furthermore, as study of California's women inmates contends:

> The role of the mother is more crucial for the mother herself than is the father's role to him, and . . . her separation from her children and the concomitant major change in her role more directly strike at her essential personal identity and her self-image as a woman.[6]

Though the imprisonment of men may raise a similar problem, it is not likely to be as frequent or as psychologically troubling as occurrence. In recent studies of how many children are affected by the imprisonment of a parent, nationwide averages of children per imprisoned parent indicate a great variance.

Men committed for felonies left behind an average of 1.3 children, compared to a figure of 2.43 for incarcerated women.[7] Moreover, when men go to prison they generally assume that their wives, or a female relative, will care for their children. Yet the women sentenced to prison can make no such assumption.[8]

It has been found that arrangements for child care, during the mother's incarceration, may vary according to ethnic factors.[9] According to the National Study of Women's Correctional Programs blacks were most likely to rely on their parents to care for their children rather than on husbands or nonrelatives; Indians and whites were more likely to have their children living with their husbands or placed with nonrelatives, including foster homes.[10]

Whether the children remain within the family or under the care of the state, there remains the task of explaining to the child what has happened to his or her incarcerated mother and why.[11] Such problems concerning communication must be addressed. The entire ongoing relationship between the incarcerated mother and her children must be evaluated.

THE DETERMINATION OF CHILD PLACEMENT

The determination of the placement of an unattended child is made by the courts which, in turn, are guided by standards established by the legislatures. Statutes authorizing the involuntary termination of parental rights deal, first, with the standards for a finding of unfitness or neglect and, second, with the disposition following such a finding.[12] The courts, depending on the statute and its application, then make a specific order which may range from a temporary denial of custody to a permanent termination of parental rights. In considering the moral, intellectual and material welfare of the child, the court will place the child in a foster home, with close relatives of the prisoner-mother or, as a final alternative, in an institution.[13]

PARENTAL RIGHTS

An adequate legal definition of a biological parent's rights in her child has yet to be formulated. During the nineteenth century, the courts characterized the parent's right as a property interest and later as a trust revocable by the state.[14] More recently, a parent's right in her child is viewed as a bundle of rights encompassed by the relationship.[15] Still another tack taken by the courts balances the parent's rights against a certain obligation owed to the child.[16]

While a clear definition of parental rights is elusive, one commentator identifies the following rights:[17] right to possession,[18] right to visit the child,[19] right to determine education,[20] right to determine religious upbringing,[21] right to discipline the child,[22] right to choose medical treatment,[23] right concerning the child's name,[24] right to consent to marriage,[25] right to services,[26] right to determine nationality and domicile,[27] and right to appoint guardians and consent to adoption.[28] Regardless of the exact nature of the right, society recognizes that a natural parent has a special interest in the care, custody, and nurture of her child.[29]

LEGISLATIVE STANDARDS

Only a limited number of legislatures have gone so far as to specifically designate the parent's incarceration as sufficient, in and of itself, to permit the total termination of parental rights.[30] However, the courts in many states have equated a parent's imprisonment with abandonment of parental responsibility and have implied the power to terminate parental rights upon incarceration.[31]

A termination of all parental rights by court order means severing all legal bonds between the biological parent and her child.[32] In the eyes of the law, a parent whose rights have been terminated becomes a stranger to the child, with no right to custody, visitation, or communication.[33] As one author has commented, "It is not unreasonable to require the courts, when making this determination [with regard to an incarcerated mother] to consider . . . the parental relationship prior to confinement, the attendant circumstances surrounding the conviction, and the possibility of placing the child in temporary custody."[34]

The court, depending on the jurisdiction, may use any of three methods to terminate the parental rights of a women prisoner:[35]

1. an adjudication that the child is neglected;[36]
2. a special hearing[37] which may be instituted under a remarkable variety of circumstances, for example: neglectful or abusive behavior by the parent;[38] depravity;[39] open and notorious fornication;[40] mental illness;[41] intoxication or habitual use of drugs;[42] failure to provide financial support;[43] divorce;[44] or
3. an adoption proceeding by permitting the court to waive the necessity of consent to the adoption by the natural parent.[45] These statutes authorize such waiver when: the child has been abandoned;[46] the consent is being withheld contrary to the best interests of the child;[47] or the parent has been declared unfit.[48]

A mother is considered fit if she is capable of performing her parental duties and does not subject her child to "substantial immoral or debasing" influences at home.[49] In *Chaffin v. Frye*,[50] a mother of two children was denied custody on the basis of a criminal record and involvement in an ongoing homosexual relationship. The primary factor militating against an award of custody to the appellant was her homosexual lifestyle. The court found that:

> She has lived with her female companion since 1968 and will continue to live with her in the same apartment that the children would live in. Although appellant denies she ever engaged in immoral conduct in front of the children or engaged in any immoral conduct with her companion during the past two years, the probation officer believes the possibility of homosexual conduct still exists. The children told him they know appellant is a homosexual, but they never saw her engage in immoral conduct.[51]

Although the appellant was capable of performing her parental duties, the fact that she openly lived in a homosexual household was sufficient to deny her child custody.

A mother's incarceration alone does not display the necessary elements of unfitness. Unfitness, in general, means "unsuitable, incompetent or not adapted for a particular use or service."[52] Confinement evidences only a present inability to perform her parental duties and thus necessitates a continuance of some custodial arrangement during the mother's imprisonment or for a reasonable period thereafter.[53] In *State v. Grady*[54] an incarcerated mother appealed from an order terminating her parental rights. The court in *Grady* stated that under the circumstances, to destroy the tie between the children and the mother who bore them would be a "species of unintended vindictive justice."[55] Using a "preponderance of the evidence test," the court held that the evidence was insufficient to establish that the mother was unfit to continue her parental relationship.

Although this is not a recent case, the humane approach indicates the possibilities for the—development of parental and children's rights. In making its decision the court examined the appellant's unfortunate circumstances and concluded

> It is no slight thing to permanently deprive a parent of the care, custody and society of a child, or a child of the protection, guidance and affection of a parent, notwithstanding that the parent has erred in the past, and especially when there is yet a possibility that the parent may later demonstrate a rehabilitation by sufficient conduct and character in accord with the accepted standards and duties of motherhood.[56]

Imprisonment is not abandonment per se, but rather a separation because of social circumstances and/or misconduct. The statutes in these instances are said to be designed to further the best interests of the child. Courts generally favor the natural parent, but the court must also consider the totality of the mother's circumstances and the depth of maternal regard,[57] before it can properly decide the mother's fitness to have custody of the child after her release.

While the courts may modify their procedure for resolving parental fitness, any modification remains subject to the guidelines established by the legislatures. It is necessary, therefore, that the legislatures seek to reevaluate the criteria. Most legislatures have been reluctant to alter their guidelines on parental fitness, maintaining that existing guidelines serve the child's best interest. Unfortunately, in using the "child's best interest" criterion to outline standards of parental unfitness, inequities have resulted in applying it to women.[58]

The significance of the present statutory scheme is the potential effect the classifications have upon the requirement that a parent consent to the adoption of her child.[59] It is important to note that, as indicated above, some jurisdictions do waive the necessity of consent if the child has been abandoned, the consent is being withheld contrary to the best interests of the child, or the parent has been declared unfit.[60] Thus, a child may be adopted, without the consent of the parent, if the parent's rights have been involuntarily terminated.

The statutes defining the measurements of the termination decision emphasize the conduct of the natural parent. It is often suggested that, "this can be disadvantageous to the parent, when the court is influenced by 'immoral conduct.'"[61] In fact, conduct such as depravity or promiscuity, which is sometimes cited as demonstrating that the parent is unfit, may have little to do with the parent-child relationship. Moreover, such undefined indicia can also be disadvantageous to the child, particularly when the court fails to adequately consider the child's physical and psychological well-being.

In *Alsager v. District Court of Polk County, Iowa*,[62] the court declared the Iowa termination statute unconstitutionally vague under the due process clause of the Fourteenth Amendment. The Iowa statute permits termination of parental rights where, *inter alia*, the court finds "conduct . . . likely to be detrimental to the physical or mental health and morals of the child,"[63] or that "the parents have substantially and continuously or repeatedly refused to give the child necessary parental care. . . ."[64]

In pronouncing the Iowa statute unconstitutional, the court considered the state's interest in protecting children, yet found in favor of a parent's interest in raising children in an environment free from governmental interference.

Under the concept of *parens patriae* it was reasoned that the state should intrude into private family life when necessary to insure the welfare of the child.[65] This concept was glorified in the juvenile courts from 1900 through 1950.[66]

Ketcham and Babcock[67] have proposed guidelines for drafting and applying statutes which would authorize involuntary termination of parental rights; they suggest that legislatures: 1) limit the circumstances to where the drastic step is genuinely warranted, 2) aid the court to focus on relevant questions, and 3) minimize the child's ordeal by reducing time for making and administering a decision.[68] Application of these legislative guidelines would make it necessary to delete the incarceration category of unfitness or, as with the other categories (adultery, drunkenness, cruelty, desertion, or nonsupport), take into account countervailing circumstances.

While redefinition of the qualifications for fitness is a necessary innovation, it alone is an incomplete remedy. The present system destroys the ongoing psychological parent-child relationship which approximates a "species of unintended vindictive justice."[69] Therefore, it is imperative that programs be implemented which eliminate this additional punishment and increase the possibilities for rehabilitation and positive postrelease behavior.

Means by which the legislatures can attain these desirable results and also achieve their goal of satisfying the child's best interests are: maintaining infants in prison with the mother, extending the state work release programs, extending the visitation privileges accorded the prisoner-mother, or a combination of all of these.[70] Programs designed to facilitate communication between the parent and child during the mother's incarceration should be an integral part of any correctional institution that houses women.

It is generally accepted that the first three years are the critical period in the formation of a child's basic personality character and intellectual development.[71] During the tender years the mother is the focal point of the child's existence. When the mother is imprisoned she is unable to play the pivotal role in her child's maturation that would otherwise be hers.

SUGGESTED REFORMS

Little is done within the prison or without to help women behind bars cope with motherhood. Women are encouraged to give up for adoption children that are born in prison.[72] In *Apgar v. Beauter,*[73] a woman detained in a county jail gave birth to a child and sought to care for the child in jail pending a trial. In overruling the sheriff's decision the court interpreted the New York statute to allow an inmate mother to return to prison with her child subject to the conditions that: 1) the mother is physically able to care for the child, and 2) it seems desirable for the welfare of the child.[74] After the first year the statute mandates that the child leave the correctional institution. The officer in charge (in this case the sheriff) is the one to determine if the situation is desirable for the child. Hence, this statute is inadequate in that it imposes a time limit on care for the child within New York correctional institutions. Likewise the statute places an inordinate amount of decisionmaking power in the hands of the "officer in charge." The statute is vague according to the interpretation in *Apgar.* The court in imposing the second condition shifted the responsibility for separation of mother and child to the local authorities.

A few prisons have nurseries where babies can stay for a short time after birth, but to date there are no long-term child care facilities in women's institutions in the United States. An enlightened penologist in West Germany has implemented her belief that if preschool children are allowed to remain with their incarcerated mothers, the children, the mothers and ultimately the nation will benefit.[75] Helga Einsile, the recently retired director of Preungesheim prison in West Germany, saw the completion of the Kinderheim (children's home). The Kinderheim can house twenty women prisoners—usually prostitutes, drug offenders, and shoplifters—and up to twenty-five of their children.[76]

California has a statute that allows a mother to keep her child in prison if the child is under two years of age, at the discretion of the welfare board.[77] If the situation is exceptional the two year limit may be extended for a longer period.

The Kinderheim program provides the mothers and their children with spacious, brightly lighted cells that contain modern furniture. Except for their forty-hour work week, mothers are free to spend time with their children. It has been established that this program has greatly reduced the rate of recidivism; of the fifty mothers who have lived in Kinderheim, only one has returned to prison.[78]

In a women's reformatory outside Tacoma, Washington, the inmates staff a nursery school funded by the Department of Health, Education and Welfare; the school's students are children from the neighborhood around the Purdy Treatment Center.[79] Any prisoner, regardless of her crime, may apply for a position as a teaching aide, although women whose pasts include crimes of violence are not likely to survive the rigorous screening process.[80]

With Kinderheim and the program at Purdy as models it would be possible to construct a truly rehabilitative atmosphere for incarcerated mothers. Healthy family associations could be maintained through group living quarters which would resemble an apartment complex with a separate apartment for each mother and her child. A nursery administered by the mothers on an assignment basis would allow the prisoner-mother to receive instruction in child care, nutrition, and other related subjects.[81]

Work-release is a program which provides inmates with an opportunity to be released into the free community for employment purposes.[82] An extension of this program would provide a means for the mother to be released in order to perform her parental duties. This system could be integrated with a work commitment. The Kinderheim program allows incarcerated mothers a "vacation" at home with their children every six months.[83] Increased family affiliations can only prompt rehabilitation and further the best interests of the child.

Obviously certain changes in the law are required in order to put into practice the aforementioned reforms. While it is recognized that most of those involved in the application and implementation of the law, from the judges to the prison directors, are males, feasible proposals such as Kinderheim and the Purdy Center can be used to establish similar facilities for incarcerated mothers.

Because imprisonment of a mother is likely to leave her children in a crisis, and because the situation is one over which society has some control, a recommended strategy of intervention should include the following considerations:

1. counseling to aid the mothers in their expectations of the circumstances to the affected children;
2. where feasible, have women live in a special community residence where they could receive emotional support, advice, and guidance within a stable and comforting environment;
3. allowing children to either remain with their mothers or permitting regular inside/outside visitation.

A program for incarcerated mothers such as this would allow the individual to remain within the social context and allow the problem-solving to develop in the realistic climate of the community, friends, and family.

NOTES

1. Note, *Female Offenders: A Challenge to the Courts and the Legislatures,* 51 N.D.L. Rev. 827, 829 (1975).

2. Haft, *Women In Prison: Discriminatory Practices and Some Legal Solutions,* 8 Clearinghouse Review 1, 4 (1974).

3. Price, *Life In Prison.* 3 Women: A Journal of Liberation 36 (No. 3, 1972).

4. Haft, *Women In Prison: Discriminatory Practices and Some Legal Solutions,* 8 Clearinghouse Review 1, 4 n.6 (1974).

5. A profile of incarcerated adult women, drawn by the Eighth National Women and the Law Conference, indicates that: two-thirds of women prisoners are under thirty years of age, the median age of felons being twenty-seven years; one-half of the imprisoned female population is black; less than one-fifth of prisoners are married at the time of incarceration; and fifty-six percent of incarcerated women had dependent children at home prior to incarceration. See generally *Focus,* University of Wisconsin, Madison, Wisconsin (March 1977).

6. Note, *Female Offenders: A Challenge to the Courts and the Legislatures,* 51 N.D.L. Rev. 827, 841 (1975), citing M. Buckley, *Breaking Into Prison* 97 (1974).

7. Sack, Seidler and Thomas, *The Children of Imprisoned Parents: A Psychosocial Exploration,* 46 American Journal of Orthopsychiatry 618 (Oct. 1974).

8. Note, *Female Offenders: A Challenge to the Courts and the Legislatures,* 51 N.D.L. Rev. 827, 841 (1975).

9. R. Glick and V. Neto, The National Study of Women's Correctional Programs 119 (1977).

10. The following chart, from R. Glick and V. Neto, *idem,* breaks down child care arrangements by ethnic group:

Source of Childcare in Percentage

Ethnic Group	Husband	Woman's Parents	Other Relations	Other Persons/ Agency*	Total (N)
Black	3.9	56.1	30.4	9.6	(2315)
White	16.6	28.0	34.1	21.3	(1480)
Hispanic	12.5	45.0	31.0	11.5	(468)
Indian	16.9	22.6	33.2	27.3	(138)
Other	7.9	46.1	19.7	26.3	(76)
Total	9.5	44.4	31.6	14.5	(4477)

*Includes friends and foster homes.

11. Weintraub, *The Delivery of Services to Families of Prisoners,* 40 Fed. Probation 29 (December, 1976).

12. Ketcham and Babcock, *Statutory Standards for the Involuntary Termination of Parental Rights,* 29 Rutgers L. Rev. 530, 531 (1976).

13. See, e.g., Mass. Gen. Laws ch. 119, § 26 (West Supp. 1977); N.Y. Soc. Serv. Law art. 6, § 383 (McKinney 1976); Minn. Stat. Ann. § 260.191 (West Supp. 1977).

14. *In re* W., 29 Cal. App. 3d 623, 629, 105 Cal. Rptr. 736, 740 (Ct. App. 1972); 3 J. Story, Commentaries on Equity Jurisprudence § 1760 (1918).

15. Nevelos v. Railston, 65 N. M. 250, 254, 335 P.2d 573, 576 (1959).

16. *In re* Lutheran Children and Family Service of Eastern Pennsylvania, 456 Pa. 429, 432, 321 A.2d 618, 621 (1974).

17. See generally Eekelaar, *What are Parental Rights?*, 89 L.Q. Rev. 210 (1973).

18. See, e.g., Hewer v. Bryant, [1970] 1 Q.B. 357, 372.

19. See, e.g., S. v. S., [1962] 2 All E.R. 1, 3; see also Cal. Civ. Code § 197.5 (West Supp. 1975).

20. See, e.g., Wakeham v. Wakeham, [1954] 1 All E.R. 434.

21. See, e.g., J. v. C., [1969] 1 All E.R. 788, 801.

22. See, e.g., R. v. Woods, [1921] 85 J.P. 272.

23. Children and Young Persons Act 1933, § § 1 (1) and (2) (a) (England).

24. See, e.g., *In re T.*, [1963] Ch. 238.

25. See, e.g., Marriage Act 1949, § 3 and Schedule 2 as amended by the Family Law Reform Act 1969, § 2 (England); see also Cal. Civ. Code § 4101 (West Supp. 1975).

26. See, e.g., Clarke, Hall and Morrison, Children at 519 (7th Ed. 1967).

27. See, e.g., British Nationality Act 1948, § 7(1); see also Cal. Civ. Code § 213 (West Supp. 1975).

28. Guardianship of Minors Act 1971, § § 4(1)–4(2) (England).

29. Stanley v. Illinois, 405 U.S. 645 (1972).

30. See, e.g., N.Y. Dom. Rel. Law § 111 (McKinney 1977).

    2. The consent shall not be required of a parent or of any other person having custody of the child:

    . . .

        (d) who has been deprived of civil rights pursuant to the civil rights law and whose civil rights have not been restored. . . .

See also *In Re* Anonymous, 79 Misc.2d 280, 359 N.Y.S.2d 738 (1974).

31. Logan v. Coup, 238 Md. 253, 208 A.2d 694 (1965); *In Re* Jacques, 48 N.J. Super. 523, 138 A.2d 581 (1958).

32. Ketcham and Babcock, *Statutory Standards for the Involuntary Termination of Parental Rights*, 29 Rutgers L. Rev. 530, 531 (1976).

33. Idem.

34. Comment, *The Prisoner-Mother and Her Child*, 1 Cap. U. L. Rev. 127, 133 (1972).

35. Areen, *Intervention Between Parent and Child: A Reappraisal of the State's Role in Child Neglect and Abuse Cases*, 63 Geo. L. J. 887 (1975).

36. See, e.g., Kan. Stat. Ann. § 38-824(c) (1973); Ohio Rev. Code Ann. § 2151.35.3(D) (Page Supp. 1975).

37. See, e.g., Ky. Rev. Stat. Ann. § 199.600 (Baldwin Supp. 1975).

38. See, e.g., Cal. Civ. Code § 232(a) (2) (West Supp. 1975); Hawaii Rev. Stat. § 571-61(b)(3) (Supp. 1974).

39. See, e.g., Ill. Ann. Stat. ch. 4, § § 9.1-1 D. (h), 9.1-8 (Smith-Hurd 1975).

40. See, e.g., Ill. Ann. Stat. ch. 4, § § 9.1-1 D (i), 9.1-8 (Smith-Hurd 1975).

41. See, e.g., Ill. Ann. Stat. ch. 4, § § 9.1-8 (e-f) (Smith-Hurd 1975).

42. See, e.g., Iowa Code Ann. § 232.41(2) (d) (West 1969).

43. See, e.g., Ind. Code Ann. § 31-3-1-6 (g) (1) (Burns Supp. 1975); *cf.* Minn. Stat. Ann. § 260.221 (b) (2) (West Supp. 1975).

44. See, e.g., N. J. Stat. Ann. § 9:2-19 (West 1976).

45. See Areen, *Intervention Between Parent and Child: A Reappraisal of the State's Role in Child Neglect and Abuse Cases,* 63 Geo. L. J. 887, 928 (1975); Mass. Gen. Laws ch. 210, § 3 (West Supp. 1977).

46. See, e.g., Mo. Ann. Stat. § 211.441.1 (2) (a) (Vernon 1962); Pa. Stat. Ann. tit. 1, § 1.2 (Supp. 1975); Ind. Code Ann. § 31-3-1-6 (g) (1) (Burns Supp. 1975).

47. See, e.g., D. C. Code Encycl. § 16-304 (e) (West 1977); Mass. Gen. Laws ch. 210, § 3 (a) (ii) (West Supp. 1977); Conn. Gen. Stat. Ann. § 17-38a (a) (1975).

48. See, e.g., Ill. Ann. Stat. ch. 4, § 9.1-8 (Smith-Hurd 1975).

49. McAllister v. McAllister, 455 S.W.2d 31 (Mo. Ct. App. 1970).

50. Chaffin v. Frye, 45 Cal. App.3d 39, 119 Cal. Rptr. 22 (1975).

51. Idem at 43, 119 Cal. Rptr. at 23.

52. Petition of Kauch, 358 Mass. 327, 329, 264 N.E.2d 371, 373 (1970); see also Petition of New England Home for Little Wanderers, 328 N.E.2d 854, 860 (Mass. 1975).

53. State v. Grady, 231 Or. 65, 371 P.2d 68 (1962).

54. Idem.

55. Idem at 68, 371 P.2d at 70.

56. Idem at 68, 371 P.2d at 69.

57. Foster and Freed, *Child Custody (Part 1),* 39 N.Y.U.L.R. 423, 436 (1964).

58. See Bennett v. Clemers, 230 Ga. 317, 196 S.E.2d 842 (1973); *In Re* Levi, 131 Ga. App. 348, 206 S.E.2d 82 (1974).

59. Comment, *The Prisoner-Mother and Her Child,* 1 Cap. U.L. Rev. 127 (1972).

60. Ketcham and Babcock, *Statutory Standards for the Involuntary Termination of Parental Rights,* 29 Rutgers L. Rev. 530, 546 (1976).

61. Note, *In the Child's Best Interests: Rights of the Natural Parents in Child Placement Proceedings,* 51 N.Y.U.L.R. 446, 449 (1976).

62. 406 F. Supp. 10 (S. D. Iowa 1975).

63. Iowa Code Ann. § 232.41 (2) (d) (West 1976).

64. Iowa Code Ann. § 232.41 (2) (b) (West 1976).

65. Ketcham and Babcock, *Statutory Standards for the Involuntary Termination of Parental Rights,* 29 Rutgers L. Rev. 530, 546 (1976).

66. Idem.

67. Idem.

68. Idem.

69. State v. Grady, 231 Or. 65, 67, 391 P.2d 68, 70 (1962).

70. Comment, *The Prisoner-Mother and Her Child,* 1 Cap. U. L. Rev. 127, 138 (1972).

71. Idem.

72. Haft, *Women In Prison: Discriminatory Practices and Some Legal Solutions,* 8 Clearinghouse Review 1, 4 (1974).

73. 75 Misc. 2d 439, 347 N.Y.S.2d 872 (Sup. Ct. 1973).

74. Idem.

75. Newsweek, January 12, 1976, at 71.

76. Idem.

77. Cal. Penal Code Ann. § 3401 (West 1975).

> Admission and retention of children of inmates; period of retention; subsequent placement and care; hospitalization for childbirth; expense; provision for care.

If any woman received by or committed to said institution has a child under two years of age, or gives birth to a child while an inmate of said institution, such child may be admitted to, and retained in, said institution until it reaches the age of two years, at which time said board may arrange for its care elsewhere; and provided further, that at its discretion in exceptional cases said board may retain such child for a longer period of time.

Any woman inmate who would give birth to a child during her term of imprisonment may be temporarily taken to a hospital outside the prison for the purposes of childbirth, and the charge for hospital and medical care shall be charged against the funds allocated to the institution. The board shall provide for the care of any children so born and shall pay for their care until suitably placed.

(Added by Stats.1941, c. 106, p. 1116, § 15.)

Derivation: Stats.1929, c. 248, p. 492, § 9; Stats.1941, c. 53, p. 697, § 1.

78. Newsweek, January 12, 1976, at 71.

79. Newsweek, November 24, 1975, at 133.

80. Idem.

81. Comment, *The Prisoner-Mother and Her Child*, 1 Cap. U. L. Rev. 127, 140 (1972).

82. Idem.

83. Newsweek, January 12, 1976, at 71.

V

Women's Crime and Women's Emancipation

Changes in the rate and patterns of female criminality have been linked to equality between the sexes, the "emancipation" of women, and even the women's liberation movement itself. The supposed link between changes in women's roles and female criminality is not new. Otto Pollak noted in *The Criminality of Women* that criminologists since the 1870s had been predicting that

> the progressing social equalization between the sexes and particularly the entrance of women into ever wider fields of economic pursuits would lead to an increase in the volume of female crime and thereby to a decrease, if not a disappearance, of the sex differential apparent in criminal statistics.[1]

In the same vein, a staff report to the National Commission on the Causes and Prevention of Violence stated that "the 'emancipation' of females in our society over recent decades has decreased the differences in delinquency and criminality between boys and girls, men and women, as cultural differences between them have narrowed."[2]

At a recent national conference on women and crime, there was a good deal of heated discussion about the relationship

between female criminality and the women's movement, sometimes dubbed "the shady side of liberation."[3] Freda Adler, author
of *Sisters in Crime* and the keynote speaker, hypothesized that
"woman's progress in the male-dominated world is largely to
blame for a higher female crime rate than during the days when
women were 'weak and meek'."[4] She asked, "Might it be that,
just like their sisters in legitimate fields, female offenders are
striving for higher positions in the criminal hierarchy?"[5] Others,
such as Karen DeCrow, then president of the National Organization for Women, were "horrified and outraged about the so-
called correlation between the Women's Liberation Movement
and the increase of female crime."[6]

It would seem that the first priority would be to consider
whether, in fact, changes in the rate and patterns of female
criminality have occurred. Our examination of arrest and self-
report data on female criminality in the introduction to this
volume showed the following: Female crime is increasing and
females are accounting for a larger share of total arrests, although
not dramatically so. Female arrests have gradually increased from
10.7 percent of total arrests in 1960 to 16 percent in 1977, a rise
of about 5 percent. The female percent of arrests for violent index
crimes has remained fairly constant for adult women. While
there is some evidence in the UCR data that the juvenile female
percent of arrests has increased for aggravated and other assault,
this appears to have leveled off in recent years. Moreover, self-
report studies of delinquency do not show a decrease in sex
differences for such violent acts as fistfighting, gangfighting,
and strong-arm theft.

The female percent of arrests has increased most dramatically
for larceny and fraud and to a lesser extent for forgery and
counterfeiting and embezzlement, although the latter two offenses represent only a small percentage of total female arrests.
Among adult women, the female percent of arrests also increased
for vagrancy; arrests for this offense show an erratic pattern of
change over the years, however, which is difficult to interpret.
Vagrancy statutes are sometimes used to arrest (female) prosti-

tutes. Juvenile females are also responsible for a larger share of arrests for liquor law violations and running away. The largest increases in the female percent of arrests were thus not for traditional male crimes but rather for traditional female crimes.

Consideration should also be given to the question of whether the roles played by females in crime are changing. One piece of evidence comes from Ward et al. who studied two groups of women incarcerated in the California Institution for Women during 1962-1964 and in 1968.[7] Some of the data indicate that women's roles in crime are becoming more active. For example, guns were used in almost half of the murders and robberies committed by the 1968 group, but only about one-quarter of those committed by the 1962-1964 group. Also, the number of women acting alone in robbery almost doubled from 10 percent to 19 percent. Moreover, when others were involved, women in the 1968 group tended to take more active roles, particularly in robberies. Other data, however, do not suggest that women are playing more active criminal roles. For example, the use of guns in assaults declined, as did the use of knives and other household implements. Further, women in the 1962-1964 group were involved in murders and assaults as the sole perpetrator in about three-quarters of the cases, as were the women in the 1968 group. Thus, it is difficult to reach a conclusion on the basis of these contradictory findings.

Some evidence is also available, though, concerning the roles of juvenile females in crime. Walter Miller, for example, recently conducted the first nationwide study ever undertaken of the nature and extent of gang violence.[8] Miller estimates that gang members are 90 percent or more male. Females are involved now, as in the past, primarily as "auxiliaries" or "branches" of male gangs. In New York, police estimated that half of the gangs had female branches but that females acounted for only about 6 percent of the total known gang population. Miller did not find much support for the claim that female criminality, either in general or in connection with gang activity, is both more prevalent and violent than in the past. For example, less than 10 percent of the 4,400 arrests of gang members recorded by Chicago police in 1974 involved females. In Philadelphia, the municipal gang control agency did not classify a single girls' group as posing a "serious threat." Similarly, Miller reports that "stories told about the nature of female participation in gang activities (weapons carriers, decoys for ambush killings, participants in individual or gang fighting) did not differ significantly from those told in the past."[9] He further reports that the status of gang girls is directly dependent on that of male gangs.

> The evidence is clear that the Molls and other young women like them not only did not resent the fact that their status was directly dependent on that of the boys, but actively sought this condition and gloried in it. The Molls accepted without question a declaration by one of the Hoods that "they ain't nuthin' without us, and they know it." Jackets of female gang members in New York bear the legend "Property of the Savage Nomads."[10]

Most respondents felt that females were not a particularly serious element of current gang problems.

In another study, Gold and Reimer examined the self-reported delinquent involvement of comparable and representative national samples of boys and girls in 1967 and 1972.[11] They found that delinquency had declined among boys but increased among girls due to their greater use of alcohol and especially marijuana. Apparently, girls were dating more frequently in 1972 and their greater use of drugs was linked with their association with boys. About three-quarters of the girls but only one-quarter of the boys used marijuana with others of the opposite sex. The authors conclude that "more frequent drug use among girls was in part caused by what the boys they went with were doing more often. The girls went along."[12] There was little evidence that girls were acting more independently, at least when using marijuana.

On the basis of this evidence, it is impossible for us to conclude that female crime has increased dramatically or that females are much more involved in traditional male crimes. While there is some evidence that females are playing more active roles in crime, there is also evidence that they are not doing so. One possibility is that changes in female sex roles have not been extensive enough or in a direction that would lead to changes in female criminality. Norland and Shover have correctly pointed out that there is conceptual ambiguity regarding gender roles and that "this makes it very difficult to understand what it is that is related to criminal involvement."[13] For example, is it that women's definition of self is more "liberated" or that their employment opportunities have expanded to allow more legitimate opportunities for crime or that they are becoming more "masculine?"

The perspective that female crime is due to the "masculinization" of female behavior can be traced back to Lombroso. According to Lombroso, the female offender often has a "virile cranium," considerable body hair, and constitutional anomalies and brain capacity that are more similar to a man than a noncriminal woman.[14] Lombroso's influence can be seen in contemporary works such as Cowie, Cowie, and Slater's *Delinquency in Girls*.[15] These authors state:

> Is there any evidence that masculinity or femininity of bodily constitution plays any part in predisposing to delinquency and in determining the form it takes? . . . Markedly masculine traits in girl delinquents have been commented on. . . . Energy, aggressiveness, enterprise and the rebelliousness that drives the individual to break through conformist habits are thought of as being masculine more than feminine traits. . . . We can be sure that they have some physical basis.[16]

Cowie et al. confuse maleness and femaleness, which are biological terms, with masculinity and femininity, which are social and psychological terms. In addition, Dorie Klein points out that Cowie et al. have "an ahistorical sexist view of women, stressing the *universality* of femininity in the Freudian tradition, and of women's inferior role in the nuclear family."[17] Historical and cross-cultural data indicate that femaleness and femininity can be related in a number of different ways. It is even possible that in a nonsexist society " 'masculinity' and 'femininity' would disappear, and that the sexes would differ only biologically, specifically by their sex organs."[18]

The current version of the masculinization perspective has been linked by some to women's emancipation. For example, it has been proposed that "the emancipation of women appears to be having a twofold influence on female juvenile crimes. Girls are involved in more drinking, stealing, gang activity, and fighting—behavior in keeping with their adoption of male roles."[19] Further, it has been suggested that female delinquents appear to be developing "a certain level of imitative male machismo competitiveness" that makes them "almost indistinguishable from male inmates."[20] Norland and Shover have pointed out that the masculinization perspective is too often employed in a tautological way in that no systematic evidence has been presented to show that women who commit so-called masculine crimes are themselves more "masculine" than those who do not commit such crimes.[21] Perhaps most importantly, this perspective represents a misunderstanding of the goals of the women's movement which does not aim to make women "more like men," but rather to increase the flexibility of roles for both sexes.

To some extent, the women's movement has been successful in this regard. Research generally indicates that role definitions have become more egalitarian in recent years.[22] Nevertheless, the traditional division of labor within the family continues to receive more support than inequalities in pay and opportunities in the workplace. The roles of wife and mother continue to be of primary importance to many women. Over half of the women in a recent national survey agreed that "it is much better for everyone involved if the man is the achiever outside the home and the woman takes care of the home and family."[23] According to another national poll, over three-quarters of the women regarded being married with children as the ideal fulfillment of life and only 32 percent would combine this with a full-time job.[24] Although somewhat better, the sex-typing of occupations persists in the workplace as well. For example, a recent study found that certain academic disciplines were viewed as "masculine" or as "feminine" by college students and that this was strongly related to the percentage of female participants within these disciplines.[25] In addition, most people still prefer to work for a man and only in predominately female fields such as nursing and hairdressing do people prefer to deal with a woman.[26]

There is no evidence that women who break the law are less likely to support such traditional sex roles than other women. Eve and Edmonds, for example, found that female college students who reported a lower number of nonviolent offenses were slightly more likely to subscribe to feminist ideology than those who reported a higher number of such offenses.[27] They also found that self-perceived "masculinity" was moderately related to "fun crime" offenses (joyriding, shoplifting, and drug use) but negatively related to feminism. In another study, Gloria Leventhal found that incarcerated women were more likely than female college students to support traditional female roles and less likely to respond positively to unstructured questions about the women's movement.[28] Female inmates, however, perceived themselves as being more "masculine" than the college students.

A national study of women's correctional programs conducted by Ruth Glick and Virginia Neto also queried incarcerated women about traditional male and female roles.[29] Only 42 percent felt that men could take good enough care of children while 62 percent felt that having children was important. About half agreed that men have the right to insist that women stay at home rather than work and that men should support women. Incarcerated women were most likely to accept women in jobs that are high status or predominately female and least likely to accept women in skilled trades such as plumbing. The study directors concluded that the majority of incarcerated women "were still traditional in their concepts of the importance of motherhood and women's continuing dependence on men. There was little evidence of militant feminism."[30]

Even if criminal and delinquent women do not seem very

supportive of the women's movement or its principles, it is possible that the push for equal employment rights may have had an impact on female criminality. Women cannot embezzle, for example, unless they are in a position which affords them that opportunity. Whether women have these kinds of jobs is thus an important consideration. Government statistics indicate a steady gain in women's labor force participation. They accounted for 28.1 percent of all civilian employees in 1947, 33.4 percent in 1960 and 41 percent in 1977.[31] The expansion in female employment has been attributed to the growth in predominately female occupations, to the emergence of occupations defined as female from the start, and to females taking over previously male occupations.[32]

The majority of women are employed in white-collar positions according to the classification system used by the Bureau of Labor Statistics. White-collar workers include professionals, managers, sales workers, and clerical workers. Between 1962 and 1974, the largest employment gains for women occurred in the clerical category which was already 68.8 percent female in 1962; by 1974, women constituted 77.6 percent of the employees in this category.[33] During the same period, the employment of women professionals rose from 35.9 percent to 40.5 percent of all such workers, of managers from 15.3 percent to 18.5 percent, and of sales workers from 39.2 percent to 41.8 percent.

Despite these gains, women have not moved rapidly into positions of power, prestige, and high economic rewards. In 1960, only 22.3 percent and 9.1 percent, respectively, of women employed in white-collar positions were at the top status levels— professional and managerial workers.[34] In 1972, 23.8 percent were in professional positions and 7.5 percent were in managerial positions. In 1977, these percentages were 25.3 percent and 9 percent, respectively. Among men, the distribution of white-collar positions is quite different. Twenty-nine percent were in the professional category in 1960, 34.5 percent in 1972, and 36.1 percent in 1977. In the managerial category, the corresponding percentages were 36.3 percent, 32.8 percent, and 33.3 percent.

The use of broad occupational categories has also been criticized for underestimating the actual amount of occupational differentiation by sex.[35] The use of the category Professional, Technical, and Kindred, for example, obscures the fact that professions such as lawyers, physicians, and chemists are predominately male, while professions such as registered nurses, elementary school teachers, and librarians are predominately female. Between 1962 and 1974, the female percent of employees increased slightly in the three predominately male occupations and decreased slightly in the three predominately female occupations.[36] In either case, however, females tend not to be in the highest status positions. For example, women physicians are disproportionately represented in less prestigious and relatively lower paying specialties such as psychiatry and pediatrics and underrepresented in the more prestigious, higher paying specialties such as surgery.[37] Similarly, males employed in the female semiprofessions (nursing, school teaching, librarianship, and social work) are disproportionately represented in the higher status and administrative components.[38]

Thus, it does not appear that the proportion of women employed in higher status occupations is much greater now than in the past. If women do not occupy positions of high status, they cannot commit those kinds of crimes defined by Edwin Sutherland as white-collar crimes. Not surprisingly, women who are involved in employee theft generally occupy lower status positions and commit thefts which are relatively petty.[39] Those in lower status positions are more closely supervised, less sophisticated in financial manipulations, and less able to offer restitution, making their crimes more likely to be detected and prosecuted. It is thus possible that some of the increase in embezzlement among women may be due to greater numbers of women bank tellers, cashiers, payroll clerks, and the like in lower status clerical and sales positions. It should be pointed out, however, that even if women were in positions of high status, it is unlikely that many of their crimes would show up in official criminal statistics. Those in higher status positions are less subject to supervision and more skilled in financial manipulations, so that their crimes are more easily concealed. If they are caught, they are more likely to be able to replace the money, and restitution is often more important to the employer than prosecution. In fact, it has been estimated that only one percent of embezzlement cases are prosecuted in the criminal courts.[40]

It seems clear, however, that the bulk of the increases in larceny, fraud, and forgery among women cannot be accounted for solely by expanded occupational opportunities. For the most part, these offenses do not appear to be occupationally related, making it necessary to consider other possible explanations. For one, increases may be related to changes in market consumption patterns over the past two decades. A greater reliance on self-service marketing and credit card purchasing has increased the opportunities for primary consumers, many of whom are women, to engage in larceny, fraud, and forgery.[41] Similarly, there is more opportunity to commit welfare fraud due to an expanded welfare system. Women are disproportionately represented as welfare fraud plaintiffs since about 90 percent of all suspected cases involve Aid-to-Dependent Children grants and 75 percent of the recipients are women.[42] Also, technological developments have increased the computerization of record-keeping and the possibility that welfare fraud and other types of fraud such as passing bad checks or credit cards will be detected.

In addition, since a large percentage of the increase in larceny arrests among women is due to increases in the arrests of women for shoplifting, changes in store policies regarding shoplifters may have had an effect.[43] It has been estimated that for every shoplifter that is apprehended, thirty-five others get away, and that between $2 and $5 billion worth of goods are stolen annually.[44] Faced with this situation, retail merchants are taking more aggressive action against shoplifters, and are increasing their use of contract guard services or hiring their own in-house guards. Most major department stores also belong to retail protective associations. In New York, for example, several stores belong to the Stores Mutual Protective Association which is reputed to have over half a million files on shoppers or store employees allegedly guilty of theft.

Another possible reason for increases in the female percent of arrests for larceny, fraud, forgery, and embezzlement is related to the economy, the labor market and unemployment. Joseph Weis has suggested

> that the increase in certain categories of property offenses reflects a depressed economy and concomitant widespread unemployment, particularly among women who are entering or returning to the job market or who may have greater demands placed upon them than in the past to support their households.[45]

The evidence suggests that economic pressures upon women are considerable. For example, the median income of women is well below that of men and their unemployment rate is higher. In 1976, the median income for year-round, full-time workers was $8,312 for women, and $13,859 for men.[46] For women over the age of 20 the unemployment rate was 7.7 percent, while for men over 20 years old it was 5.8 percent. During the 1970s, there was a large increase in the number of families in which women had the primary economic responsibilities. In March 1977, 7.7 million families were headed by women, the highest level ever recorded.[47] One of every 3 black families was headed by a women compared with 1 of 5 Hispanic families and 1 of 9 white families. Families headed by women were more likely than husband-wife families to have children to support and to have very low incomes. About 56 percent of these women were in the labor force, mostly in low-skill, low-paying jobs. The unemployment rate was twice as high for black women who headed families (16.4 percent) as for white women (8.1 percent), and the median income of black families headed by women was only $5,069 compared with $8,226 for white families. In 1976, 1 of every 3 of these families had incomes below the officially defined poverty level compared with 1 of 9 families headed by a man without a wife and 1 of 18 husband-wife families. Families headed by women accounted for all of the increase between 1969 and 1976 in the number of families below the poverty level.

These are the women who are most often in prison. For example, a survey of women in 41 county jails and prisons in Pennsylvania found that about 80 percent had to support themselves.[48] Over half of the women were unemployed at the time of arrest and most had previously held jobs as domestics, restaurant workers, or low-skilled industrial workers. Black women were overrepresented in jail populations. In Philadelphia, where the black female population was about 30 percent, over three-quarters of the women in jail were black.

Similarly, a national survey of incarcerated female offenders found that half of the women were black, although blacks comprised only 10 percent of the adult female population in the study states.[49] About a fifth of the female inmates were married compared with three-fifths of all adult women in the general population, and 44 percent of these were not living with their husbands prior to incarceration. About 56 percent of the incarcerated females had dependent children living at home and over half had received welfare. Finally, these women, particularly the minority women were overrepresented in low-paying jobs compared with women in the general population.

A more direct examination of the relationship between the "emancipation" of women and women's crimes can be found in a recent study by Widom and Stewart.[50] They examined the effects of various status-of-women variables on female crime rates across nations as well as across the fifty states. In the cross-national data, high levels of equality (such as years women have had the full vote and female education) were generally unrelated to the female murder rate, positively related to female arrest rates for minor larceny, fraud, and drugs, and negatively related to prostitution. Industrialization and technological advance were found to be associated with female arrest rates in a similar fashion. Widom and Stewart caution that it is difficult to separate the effects of equality from the overall effects of "moderni-zation."

The findings were even more complex for the cross-state data. Several of the status-of-women variables were unrelated to female arrest rates, including females in state offices, equality to enter contracts, and equality in suits for consort loss. Fraud and forgery and counterfeiting were related to fewer of the status-of-women variables than the other offenses. In general, higher female arrest rates were associated with lower levels of economic differentiation by sex, equal pay laws, community property laws, and laws making each partner eligible for alimony. On the other hand, lower female arrest rates were associated with female involvement in the labor force, female college education, female legislators, and female mayors. The authors suggest that "it is possible that equality without *actual* equality is related to high female crime rates, while the combination of legal and actual equality is related to lower female crime rates."[51] In addition, nonstatus-of-women variables accounted for more of the variation in crime rates than did the status-of-women variables.

In conclusion, the authors state that:

> Only the foolhardy would attempt to draw simple and clear-cut conclusions from data as complex as these. However, one simple, clear-cut conclusion we may draw is that the problem of female criminality is *not* unidimensional and simple. Female crime rates can be shown even with these concurrent data to be influenced by many of the same factors that influence male crime . . . as well as by variations in the legal and actual status of women.[52]

It is clear, therefore, that the relationship between women's "emancipation" and women's crime is neither simple nor direct, but very complex. At the present time, however, the evidence seems to indicate the following. First, the female percent of total arrests has increased primarily for certain property offenses—larceny, fraud, forgery and counterfeiting, and embezzlement—and other nonviolent offenses, including vagrancy for adult women and liquor law violations and running away for juvenile women. For the most part, these are offenses which are very much in keeping with traditional female roles. While employee theft and embezzlement among women may have increased slightly due to their greater participation in lower level clerical and sales occupations, the majority of female larceny, fraud, and forgery do not appear to be occupationally related. Female arrests for these offenses have more likely increased as a result of greater opportunities for shoplifting and certain kinds of fraud such as welfare fraud and passing bad checks, more aggressive action taken by retail merchants against shoplifting and employee theft, and especially the current economic crisis and greater economic pressures placed on women.

Further, while there is some evidence that women with more "masculine" personality traits are more involved in crime, this is not related to women's "emancipation" or the women's movement. The women's movement does not represent an attempt to emulate the male sex, but to integrate both sex roles and to explore possibilities beyond the stereotypes. Carol Smart has pointed out that "if some women seem to be emulating men, it is not because of the philosophy of the Women's Movement; it is primarily because there are at present only two socially acceptable identities available to individuals, the stereotypical and polarized masculine and feminine models."[53]

There is also little evidence that women who are committing crimes and being incarcerated support the women's movement. The majority of women in prison are poor and minority women. However, in the sense that many women in prison are responsible for their own support and often the support of their children, and to the extent that their crimes are linked to this traditionally male responsibility, a link between the adoption of male roles and female criminality could conceivably be made. Such forced "emanicipation," however, stems from economic necessity more than from demands for equality between the sexes. A similar situation exists during periods of war. In war years, as women take over male occupations and assume other typically male responsibilities necessitated by war, the female crime rate rises.[54] Again, this situation results from factors other than a demand for equality, in this case a demand for extra labor. It is important, therefore, that the effects of opportunity be distinguished from those of equality.

While the women's movement itself has had little impact, if any, on the rise in female criminality or changes in the nature of female criminality, its influence has been felt in other ways. First, it is possible that the women's movement may have contributed to changes in the handling of females in the criminal justice system. Los Angeles police captain Rudy DeLeon was quoted in *Newsweek* as saying, "In the past, police were reluctant to search women on the streets. Now they can get frisked like everybody else—we can't afford to take chances any more."[55] Even though women are not generally committing more violent crimes, it is possible that the criminal justice system may react more severely to females now than in the past to the extent that female offenders are perceived as more violent or more nearly equal with males. Unfortunately, no systematic studies have been done on whether such perceptions are held by police, attorneys, jurors, and judges, or the impact such perceptions have on the apprehension and adjudication of female offenders.

There is some evidence that the preferential treatment of female offenders by the judicial system is diminishing. Elizabeth Moulds's review of California sentencing data between 1970 and 1974 revealed a slight trend toward the increased incarceration of both sexes with a slightly higher increase in the percentage of females than males being incarcerated.[56] In another study, Rasche and Foley examined the length of sentences received by inmates of the Missouri State Correctional Center for Women between 1959 and 1974.[57] They found an overall decrease in sentence length during the first twelve years of the period studied but an increase between 1971 and 1974. They also found that the percentage of black female inmates decreased for crimes against persons but increased for property offenses during this period, while the percentage of whites imprisoned for these crimes showed no significant change. They suggest that the increase in sentence length may in part be due to the ideology of judges that "could well be a backlash response to the changing roles of women in society, but this cannot be determined from the present data."[58]

Additional evidence is provided by Steffensmeier et al. who investigated the handling of male and female defendants in the Pennsylvania Courts of Common Pleas for the years 1970 and 1975.[59] In both 1970 and 1975, females were generally dismissed more often than males; however, this preferential treatment of females diminished for murder, simple assault, robbery, weapons, and burglary but increased for liquor violations. In 1970, slightly more females than males were found not guilty, while there were no overall differences between the sexes in 1975; females received less preferential treatment (not guilty decisions) in 1975 than in 1970 for simple assault, burglary, and worthless checks. Females were also given lighter sentences in both 1970 and 1975, although the differences were generally somewhat smaller in 1970; however, this preferential treatment of females decreased for murder, aggravated assault, and robbery. The authors suggest that these changes in handling may be due to changing definitions of women and sex roles or, alternatively, to an increasing concern with the rights of all defendants and a reluctance to base decisions on extra-legal factors.

At the same time, the percentage of females in the total inmate population has not changed greatly. Using data from the Bureau of Prisons, Rita Simon reports that the proportion of female commitments to all state penal institutions was 5.1 percent in 1950 and 4.7 percent in 1970.[60] She also found that the proportion of female commitments to New York State correctional institutions declined between 1963 and 1971, while the proportion of female inmates in California correctional institutions was about the same in 1972 as in the 1950s. As was the case with arrests, however, the increase in the number of female inmates has been greater than that of males. For example, data collected by the Bureau of the Census show that the growth in the female inmate population in federal and state correctional institutions between 1975 and 1976 was 15.1 percent compared with a 9.2 percent increase among male prisoners.[61] Despite their faster rate of increase, females were still so few that their percentage of the entire inmate population was virtually unchanged, 3.6 percent compared with 3.8 percent. This compares with a figure of 3.2 percent in 1971.

It appears that the preferential treatment accorded females may have diminished at certain decision-making points in the criminal justice system in recent years, although further studies would be necessary to substantiate this claim. In any case, the women's movement has at least called public attention to the disparate treatment of males and females in the criminal justice process. In some instances, women's rights groups have actively supported women accused of crimes, such as Inez Garcia and Joan Little, both accused of murdering the men involved in raping them. In addition, support groups for rape victims have formed in many cities, often taking the name Women Organized Against Rape (WAR). Women's rights groups, with other groups and organizations, have also endorsed the decriminalization of prostitution. Several prostitutes' rights groups have even organized, including COYOTE in San Francisco, PONY in New York, and ASP in Seattle.

Attention has also been focused on sex-based disparities in the criminal law itself as well as in the treatment of males and females in prison. A number of court cases have challenged sex discrimination in such areas of the criminal law as jurisdictional age for juveniles, definitions of delinquency, sentencing, rape, and prostitution. Cases challenging prison conditions for women have included discriminatory booking procedures, lack of access to legal research material, denial of equal access to vocational education and work release programs, and lack of adequate medical care.[62] While these challenges have not always been successful (although many have), they have at least highlighted inequalities in the definition and application of the criminal law and in prison procedures and conditions for male and female inmates.

In addition to court challenges, changes have occurred through legislation. For example, since 1970, 18 states have enacted amendments making their definition of prostitution sex-neutral and 11 have criminalized the activities of clients.[63] Also, several states have recently passed legislation to correct sex discrimination in the sentencing process. With respect to juveniles, a number of states have removed status offenses, under which female juveniles are often charged with sexual or related offenses, from the jurisdiction of the juvenile court. While these changes are certainly in the right direction, the passage of the Equal Rights Amendment (ERA) would greatly hasten the elimination of sex-based disparities in the criminal law.[64] The amendment provides that the United States Congress and the state legislatures would have two years after ratification to bring all statutes into compliance with the ERA. Under the ERA, criminal laws that distinguish between males and females in a way that is improper will have to be rewritten to apply equally to both sexes, or else eliminated. It is hoped that the passage of the ERA is not too far in the future.

In a related area, the push for equal employment opportunities has enhanced opportunities for females in the criminal justice system. In 1968, Indianapolis was the first American city to put policewomen in patrol cars.[65] In 1974, excluding New York, there were 350 to 400 women on patrol duty compared with only 7 women on patrol duty in the whole country two years earlier. At present, females make up almost 5 percent of the New York City police force and almost 8 percent of the Washington, D.C., police force.[66] While women still constitute only a small proportion of police, attorneys, and judges, it will be interesting to examine the impact of increases in the number of women in these positions on the policies of the criminal justice system with regard to both males and females.

Do all of these changes forecast an inevitable increase in female criminality? Will sex equality mean similar crime rates as well? If, as some argue, there are no differences between the sexes except for those imposed by sex role socialization, we should expect male and female crime rates to be exactly the same in a nonsexist society. Although that may be theoretically true, for the foreseeable future, it is extremely unlikely that males and females will be equally involved in crime. For example, both historical and cross-cultural studies lead us to conclude that female involvement in violent crime is not likely to increase very much. On the other hand, the proportion of females involved in property crimes is likely to continue to rise, expecially for those typically female property crimes. As in the past, women's crimes of the future will have less to do with their equality than with their economic and social opportunity. If, indeed, we ever achieve a truly nonsexist society, this picture may change. At the moment however, we can conclude with some certainty that the women's emancipation movement which we have experienced in the United States since the late 1960s has had an insignificant impact on the crimes of women.

NOTES

1. Otto Pollak, *The Criminality of Women* (New York: A.S. Barnes and Company, 1961), p. 58. Orginally published in 1950.

2. Donald J. Mulvihill, Melvin M. Tumin, and Lynn A. Curtis (eds.), *Crimes of Violence*, 12, A Staff Report Submitted to the National Commission on the Causes and Prevention of Violence (Washington, D.C.: U.S. Government Printing Office, 1969), p. 425.

3. Nancy Loving and Lynn Olson, *Proceedings: National Conference on Women & Crime*, February 26–27, 1976, Washington, D.C., National League of Cities and U.S. Conference of Mayors (1976).

4. Ibid., p. 6.

5. Ibid., p. 5.

6. Ibid., p. 72.

7. David A. Ward, Maurice Jackson, and Renee E. Ward, "Crimes of Violence by Women," in Donald J. Mulvihill, Melvin M. Tumin, and Lynn A. Curtis (eds.), *Crimes of Violence*, 13, A Staff Report Submitted to the National Commission on the Causes and Prevention of Violence (Washington, D.C.: U.S. Government Printing Office, 1969), pp. 901–902. Excerpted in Part III of this volume.

8. Walter B. Miller, *Violence By Youth Gangs and Youth Groups as a Crime Problem in Major American Cities*, U.S. Department of Justice (Washington, D.C.: U.S. Government Printing Office, December 1975).

9. Ibid., p. 24.

10. Walter B. Miller, "The Molls," *Society*, 11 (November/December 1973), p. 35. Reprinted in Part III of this volume.

11. Martin Gold and David J. Reimer, "Changing Patterns of Delinquent Behavior Among Americans 13 Through 16 Years Old: 1967–72," *Crime and Delinquency Literature*, (December 1975), pp. 483–517.

12. Ibid., p. 509.

13. Stephen Norland and Neal Shover, "Gender Roles and Female Criminality: Some Critical Comments," *Criminology*, 15 (May 1977), p. 98.

14. Dorie Klein, "The Etiology of Female Crime: A Review of the Literature," *Issues in Criminology*, 8 (Fall 1973), p. 10. Reprinted in Part II of this volume.

15. John Cowie, Valerie Cowie, and Eliot Slater, *Delinquency in Girls* (London: Heineman, 1968).

16. Ibid., pp. 171–172.

17. Dorie Klein, op. cit., p. 27.

18. Ibid.

19. Freda Adler, *Sisters in Crime* (New York: McGraw-Hill, 1975), p. 95.

20. Ibid., p. 98.

21. Stephen Norland and Neal Shover, op. cit., p. 99.

22. See, for example, Ann P. Parelius, "Emerging Sex-Role Attitudes, Expectations, and Strains Among College Women," *Journal of Marriage and the Family*, 37 (February 1975), pp. 146–153; Alan E. Bayer, Sexist Students in American Colleges: A Descriptive Note," *Journal of Marriage and the Family*, 37 (May 1975), pp. 391–397; and Karen Oppenheim Mason, John L Czajka, and Sara Arber, "Changes in U.S. Women's Sex-Role Attitudes, 1964–1974," *American Sociological Review*, 41 (August 1976), pp. 573–596. Another study, however, found that early adolescent girls demonstrated few changes in attitude toward themselves and toward their sex role between 1968 and 1975. See Diane E. Bush, Roberta G. Simmons, Bruce Hutchinson, and Dale A. Blyth, "Adolescent Perception of Sex-Roles in 1968 and 1975," *Public Opinion Quarterly*, 41 (Winter 1977–1978), pp. 459–474.

23. Barbara Everitt Bryant, *American Women Today and Tomorrow*, National Commission on the Observance of International Women's Year (Washington, D.C.: U.S. Government Printing Office, March 1977), p. 25.

24. Connie de Boer, "The Polls: Women at Work," *Public Opinion Quarterly*, 41 (Summer 1977), p. 275.

25. Saul D. Feldman, *Escape From the Doll's House* (New York: McGraw-Hill, 1974), pp. 37–75.

26. Connie de Boer, op. cit., pp. 273–274. Women who enter predominately male fields may be viewed as unfeminine or incompetent, although this is not always the case. Men who enter predominately female fields may also be perceived in negative terms. For example, one study found that male nurses were rated by high school students as unattractive, unrealistic, and unambitious. See Susan Hesselbart, "Women Doctors Win and Male Nurses Lose," *Sociology of Work and Occupations*, 4 (February 1977), pp. 49–62.

27. Raymond A. Eve and Kreelene R. Edmonds, "Women's Liberation and Female Criminality: or "Sister, Will You Give Me Back My Dime?" Paper presented at the National Society of Social Problems meeting, San Francisco, California (September 1978).

28. Gloria Leventhal, "Female Criminality: Is 'Women's Lib' To Blame?" *Psychological Reports*, 41 (December 1977), pp. 1179–1182.

29. Ruth M. Glick and Virginia V. Neto, *National Study of Women's Correctional Programs*, U.S. Department of Justice (Washington, D.C.: U.S. Government Printing Office, June 1977).

30. Ibid., p. 172.

31. U.S. Bureau of the Census, *Statistical Abstract of the United States— 1977*, 98th edition (Washington, D.C.: U.S. Government Printing Office, 1977), p. 387.

32. Edward Gross, "Plus Ca Change. . . ? The Sexual Structure of Occupations Over Time," pp. 39–51 in Athena Theodore (ed.), *The Professional Woman* (Cambridge, Massachusetts: Schenkman, 1971), p. 43.

33. Stuart H. Garfinkle, "Occupations of Women and Black Workers, 1962– 1974," *Monthly Labor Review*, 98 (November 1975), pp. 25–35. See also Elizabeth Waldman and Beverly J. McEaddy, "Where Women Work—An Analysis by Industry and Occupation," *Monthly Labor Review*, 97 (May 1974), pp. 3–13; and Rudolph C. Blitz, "Women in the Professions, 1870–1970," *Monthly Labor Review*, 97 (May 1974), pp. 34–39.

34. *Statistical Abstract of the United States—1977*, p. 406.

35. Edward Gross, op. cit., p. 42.

36. Stuart H. Garfinkle, op. cit., p. 28.

37. Jill Quadagno, "Occupational Sex-Typing and Internal Labor Market Distributions: An Assessment of Medical Specialties," *Social Problems*, 23 (April 1976), pp. 442–453.

38. James W. Grimm and Robert N. Stern, "Sex Roles and Internal Labor Market Structures: The 'Female' Semi-Professions," *Social Problems*, 21 (June 1974), pp. 690–705.

39. Alice Franklin in Freda Adler and Rita James Simon (eds.), *The Criminology of Deviant Women* (Boston: Houghton Mifflin, 1979), pp. 167–170.

40. James T. Carey, *An Introduction to Criminology* (Englewood Cliffs, New Jersey: Prentice-Hall, 1978), p. 466.

41. Joseph G. Weis, "Liberation and Crime: The Invention of the New Female Criminal," *Crime and Social Justice*, (Fall-Winter 1976), p. 25.

42. Nancy Loving and Lynn Olson, op. cit., pp. 39–40.

43. Ira J. Silverman, Manuel Vega, and A. Leo Gray, "Female Criminality in a Southern City: A Comparison Over the Decade 1962–1972." Paper presented at the annual meeting of the American Society of Criminology, Tucson, Arizona (November 1976), p. 10.

44. George O'Toole, *The Private Sector* (New York: W.W. Norton, 1978), pp. 4–5; 9; 153.

45. Joseph G. Weis, op. cit., p. 25.

46. *Statistical Abstract of the United States—1977*, pp. 393, 452.

47. Beverly L. Johnson, "Women Who Head Families, 1970-77: Their Numbers Rose, Income Lagged," *Monthly Labor Review*, 101 (February 1978), pp. 32–37. See also Allyson Sherman Grossman, "The Labor Force Patterns of Divorced and Separated Women," *Monthly Labor Review*, 100 (January 1977), pp. 46–53.

48. Margery L. Velimesis, *Report of the Survey of 41 Pennsylvania County Court and Correctional Services for Women and Girl Offenders,* Section One, The Women, the Jails, and Probation, Pennsylvania Division of the American Association of University Women (April 1969), pp. 15–22; and Margery L. Velimesis, "Women in County Jails and Prisons," mimeographed paper (April 20, 1972).

49. Ruth M. Glick and Virgina V. Neto, op. cit., pp. 104–140.

50. Cathy Spatz Widom and Abigail J. Stewart, "Female Criminality and the Changing Status of Women." Paper presented at the annual meeting of the American Society of Criminology, Atlanta, Georgia (November 1977).

51. Ibid., p. 21.

52. Ibid., p. 23.

53. Carol Smart, *Women, Crime and Criminology* (London: Routledge and Kegan Paul, 1976), p. 74.

54. Edwin H. Sutherland and Donald R. Cressey, *Criminology* (Philadelphia: J.B. Lippincott, 1974), p. 243.

55. "The Woman's Touch," *Newsweek* (January 6, 1975), p. 35.

56. Elizabeth F. Moulds, "Chivalry and Paternalism: Disparities of Treatment in the Criminal Justice System," *Western Political Quarterly,* XXXI (September 1978), p. 429. Reprinted in Part IV of this volume.

57. Christine E. Rasche and Linda A. Foley, "A Longitudinal Study of Sentencing Patterns for Female Offenders." Paper presented at the annual meeting of the American Society of Criminology, Tucson, Arizona (November 1976).

58. Ibid., p. 12.

59. Darrell Steffensmeier, John H. Kramer, and Cynthia Kempinen, "Erosion of Chivalry?: Changes in the Handling of Male and Female Defendants from 1970 to 1975." Unpublished paper (no date).

60. Rita James Simon, Women and Crime (Lexington, Massachusetts: D.C. Heath, 1975), pp. 70–74.

61. U.S. Department of Justice, *Prisoners in State and Federal Institutions on December 31, 1976* (Washington, D.C.: U.S. Government Printing Office, February 1978), pp. 19, 21.

62. Barbara A. Brown, Ann E. Freedman, Harriet N. Katz, and Alice M. Price, *Women's Rights and the Law: The Impact of the ERA on State Laws* (New York: Praeger, 1977), p. 87.

63. Ibid., pp. 80–81, 85.

64. Ibid., pp. 45–96; and Lois J. Frankel, "Sex Discrimination in the Criminal Law: The Effect of the Equal Rights Amendment," *American Criminal Law Review,* 11 (Winter 1973), pp. 469–510.

65. "'Patrolwomen' Show They Can Handle the Heavies," *The New York Times* (January 27, 1974), p. 38.

66. "Philadelphia Loses Case on Police Sex Bias," *The Philadelphia Inquirer* (February 14, 1979), p. 2.